CULTURAL
POLITICS
IN
GREATER
ROMANIA

Alba Iulia Coronation poster, Coronation Album. October 15, 1922
(see page iv for balance of caption)

Cultural Politics

IN

Greater Romania

REGIONALISM, NATION BUILDING,
& ETHNIC STRUGGLE, 1918–1930

Irina Livezeanu

Cornell University Press

ITHACA AND LONDON

First published 1995 by Cornell University Press
First printing, Cornell Paperbacks, 2000

Printed in the United States of America

Library of Congress Cataloging-in-Publication Data

Livezeanu, Irina.
  Cultural politics in Greater Romania : regionalism, nation
building, and ethnic struggle, 1918–1930 / Irina Livezeanu.
    p. cm.
  Includes bibliographical references and index.
  ISBN 0-8014-2445-3 (hardcover)
  ISBN 0-8014-8688-2 (pbk.: alk. paper)
    1. Romania—Politics and government—1914–1944.   2. Nationalism—Romania.
3. Romania—Intellectual life—20th century.   4. Romania—Ethnic relations.   I. Title.
DR264.L58   1995
949.8'02—dc 20   94-32401

Cornell University Press strives to use environmentally responsible suppliers and materials
to the fullest extent possible in the publishing of its books. Such materials include vegetable-
based, low-VOC inks and acid-free papers that are recycled, totally chlorine-free, or partly
composed of nonood fibers. Books that bear the logo of the FSC (Forest Stewardship Council) use paper taken from forests that have been inspected and certified as meeting the highest
standards for environmental and social responsibility. For further information, visit our
website at www.cornellpress.cornell.edu.

1 3 5 7 9 Cloth printing 10 8 6 4 2
1 3 5 7 9 Paperback printing 10 8 6 4 2

Allegorical female figure symbolizing Greater Romania. She is dressed in native folk costume
and holds the crown, about to place it on her own head. Above flies the Byzantine eagle
with the Orthodox cross in its beak. In the background stand rulers from Romania's past,
including Vasile Lupu, Emperor Trajan, Alexandru the Good, Stephen the Great, Carol I,
Mircea the Old, Michael the Brave, and Vlad the Impaler. Below this group are medallions
with the portraits of King Ferdinand and Queen Maria, the protagonists of the ceremony in
which they were to be crowned monarchs of Greater Romania. The medallions are flanked
by compositions made up of the coats of arms of the medieval principalities and vojevodships
constituting the various parts of Greater Romania: (*left*) Wallachia, Dobrudja, Oltenia, Banat;
(*right*) Moldavia and Transylvania. On either side, a soldier and a peasant, the pillars of the
state, hold up its structure, here symbolized by an ornamental folk motif reminiscent of peasant
doorways in Maramureş Romanian villages. This framing of the composition represents the
contribution of the army and the peasantry to the Great Union and the connection between
the state and the populist nation. Courtesy of Cabinetul de Stampe, Biblioteca Academiei,
Bucharest

To the memory of Allan Wildman

Contents

Maps

Preface

In the mid-1980s, when I began the research on which this book is based, Romania's 1920s seemed a distant, completely closed historical period, a golden age of cultural flowering and freedom which shimmered all the brighter for the "darkness" that had enveloped the country after 1947, and especially in the second half of the Ceauşescu regime. Dissident intellectuals from Poland, Hungary, and Czechoslovakia were popularizing nostalgic notions of their Western precommunist past, Milan Kundera reviving the immediately successful label "Central Europe" for those Eastern European countries that were more western than others. Romanians joined the scramble to fit their realm into Kundera's European Center, implicitly about to break off from the rest of the bloc and rejoin Europe, that is, Western Europe. The whole area west of the Soviet Union which became the Soviet bloc has been described by western historians as "independent Eastern Europe" in the years between the two world wars. This idealized aura of democracy, independence, opportunity, and creativity first attracted me to the study of interwar Eastern Europe. My historical curiosity was further aroused by the demise of democracy in interwar East Central Europe long before the area's Sovietization. In the debates during the 1970s and 1980s over Central Europe's tragic fate under communism, this topic was largely ignored. The dissidents argued their cultural and political case for disengagement from the Soviet Big Brother without reference to the political and ethnic problems that had marked the history of East Central Europe before communism. Perhaps not accidentally, the pre–World War I multinational Habsburg Empire featured prominently in their writings. But no conscientious student of history could help noticing the crisis-ridden transition from multinational empires to national independence, or the ethnic nationalism endemic in Eastern Europe in the interwar period. Accounts that pointed only to the international causes of dictatorship, authoritarianism, and collectivism—invoked explicitly by communist ideologues, but also by dissidents, through their silences—seemed suspect in their simplicity.

Since 1989, the interwar period has lost that sense of absolute closure and inaccessibility it had when it could only be idealized. The interwar years have once again assumed contemporary relevance, and the debates over national identity and appropriate course of development have been reignited. Nation building, nation splitting, and ethnic cleansing now dominate the European agenda. In the wake of the German reunification, the breakup of the Soviet Union and Czechoslovakia, and the ethnic wars in Bosnia, Croatia, and Transcaucasia, no one can ignore the potency of nationalism in Eastern and Central Europe. The difficult unification of West and East Germany clearly demonstrates the predicaments of nation building, even when ethnic kinship between the two kinds of Germans is not at issue. In Germany the process of unification and its hardships has engendered a nationalist revival under, in some cases, neo-Nazi banners. Although the Germans mobilized by extremist ideology constitute a small minority, elements of their program are validated by government policy and support from broader constituencies. Xenophobia is, moreover, not just a German affair but a European one. Problems of transition and identity have proven intractable as well throughout the Commonwealth of Independent States; the effort to assemble ethnically pure nations in the ruins of multinational states has taken its most tragic form in former Yugoslavia.

In some Eastern European countries, new generations of indigenists and Europeanists have rejoined debates dating to the interwar years. The political ghosts of that period—Piłsudski, Dmowski, Horthy, Pavelić—and several available monarchs are again making headlines. In Romania, the works of the 1920s "new generation" writers, censored under communism, are being reissued and read with fresh interest. Nationalist thinkers and politicians from Nae Ionescu, Mircea Eliade, and Emil Cioran to Nichifor Crainic and Ion Antonescu have reentered the contemporary scene largely as heroes of a pre- and anticommunist past. The cultural politics of Greater Romania is therefore even more topical now. I hope that my investigation of the dynamics of that politics will establish a more realistic, less idealized context, for both the interwar political and literary debates and those of the 1990s.

In Romania, as in the rest of East Central Europe, nationalism is a charged subject. I have striven for objectivity, though I undoubtedly have a point of view. Born in Romania, I was schooled mostly in the United States, and on one very abstract level this book has been a journey from the New World to the universe of my grandparents. While reworking the manuscript, I encountered the polarities one can expect on this subject. Some readers objected to a pro-Romanian tone in my work; others found my assessment of Romanian nationalism too negative. Although either criticism by itself might have worried me, both together did so much less, for they suggested that I was standing on a middle ground that neither "side" found congenial. Most important, the final product benefited from all these views, which focused my efforts on grounding the analysis of Romanian nationalism in evidence about the process of nation building and cultural politics.

I thank the many people who have contributed to the making of this book. Roman Szporluk first sparked my interest in the twin subjects of nation building and nationalism, and helped me frame the original conceptualization of my study at the University of Michigan. Geoff Eley's assistance at the drafting stage was enormous and much appreciated. Bill Rosenberg, John Fine, and Amy Saldinger read the work in progress and offered excellent advice and warm encouragement. I am also indebted to friends and colleagues at other institutions for their thoughts and suggestions later on. I thank Gale Stokes, Victor Eskenasy, Daniel Chirot, Sorin Antohi, Tony Judt, and Matei Călinescu for evaluating the book at different stages.

The History Department at Ohio State University provided a good environment for finishing this book. I thank Carole Fink and Eve Levin, in particular, for their friendship and mentoring, and specifically for the time they took with my writing. Les Benedict, Michael Berkowitz, and Margaret Newell among others also offered valuable insights on some chapters. Dagmar Herzog contributed support and suggestions at critical moments. Two readers for Cornell University Press deserve thanks as well. They stimulated my thinking not least through their diverging views of my work. John Ackerman, my editor at Cornell, stood by me with utmost conviction and saw the project through in several invaluable ways. I thank him for his solid judgment.

On a more technical level, Sarah Weisberger helped edit the manuscript at an unwieldy point in its transformation. Barbara Dinneen and Carol Betsch completed that process masterfully. Diana Constantinescu acted as my proxy in Bucharest to check last details from afar. She was helped in turn by Iulian Voicu and Emanuel Bădescu at Cabinetul de Stampe, Biblioteca Academiei. I also thank Jeff Otto and Jared Ingersoll for last-minute research assistance and Jim Fields for cartographic work.

Finally, I am grateful for the financial and scholarly resources I have received from a number of organizations. Research for this book was supported in part by a 1982–84 grant from the International Research and Exchanges Board (IREX) with funds provided by the National Endowment for the Humanities, the United States Information Agency, and the U.S. Department of State, which administers the Soviet and East European Training Act of 1983 (Title VIII). A second IREX grant in 1990, though destined for another project, allowed me to collect, in my spare time, additional data and pictures for this book. My research in New York, Israel, and France was funded by the Memorial Foundation for Jewish Culture and the Rackham School of Graduate Studies at the University of Michigan. Fellowships from the University of Michigan and the American Council of Learned Societies financed the writing of my doctoral dissertation. A Social Science Research grant from Colby College and a generous leave from the Ohio State University gave me the time necessary to complete the research and revise the manuscript. A grant from the University of Pittsburgh's Russian and East European Center defrayed final publication expenses. The Center for European Studies at Harvard offered me access to Widener Library and a congenial community in 1989–90. I thank Abby Collins for her hand in this. The Center for Studies of Social Change at the New School for Social Research provided an intellectual home in 1991 thanks to Louise and Charles Tilly. My parents' financial assistance was extremely welcome, not to mention indispensable on a few occasions.

I received essential research help from the staff of the Romanian State Archives. I especially thank Varvara Aioanei, who kept me company in the often unheated and lonely room reserved for foreign researchers in the 1980s. The staffs of the Central University Library (in particular Ion Stoica), the Central State Library, and the Romanian Academy Library in Bucharest; the Yad Vashem Archives and the Central Archives for the History of the Jewish People in Jerusalem; in France, the Alliance Israélite Universelle archives, the French Army archives at Vincennes and the Diplomatic Archives at the Quai d'Orsay; and the YIVO Institute Archives in New York all made this work possible through their expertise. Adolph Armbruster of the Bukowina-Institut in Augsburg was most efficient and generous with materials on Bukovina. Dan Berindei, Ion Stanciu, and Şerban Papacostea hosted me at the Iorga History Institute in Bucharest. Octavian Ghibu welcomed me into his private archives and library, and he engaged me in numerous stimulating conversations. The staff of the Cultural Section of the American Embassy in Bucharest also helped ease my research in Romania. Friends and relatives, too many to name, made a tremendous difference to my state of mind during research trips to Romania, Israel, and France. In Bucharest, particularly, I received physical and spiritual nourishment when goods, spirit, and humanity were in short supply.

IRINA LIVEZEANU

Columbus, Ohio

Preface to the
Cornell Paperbacks Edition

This book has enjoyed mostly positive reactions in its hardback (Cornell, 1995) and Romanian (Humanitas, 1998) editions, and I have made only slight, technical revisions for the paperback. I would like then to use this preface to respond in turn to some of the most substantial responses to the book, in the hope of advancing the scholarly project that we are all, readers and writers, involved in.[1]

For their help with revisions I thank Michael Shafir, Bozenna Goscilo, David Commins, Svetlana Schreiber, and, of course, John Ackerman. I am grateful for the careful critiques of Ernest Latham, Jr., Marcel Cornis-Pope, Catherine Durandin, Wim van Meurs, Dennis Deletant, Richard Frucht, John Cole, James Niessen, Constantin Iordachi, Mary Ellen Fischer, Claude Karnoouh, Andrei Markovitz, Cathie Carmichael, Z. Ornea, Tamas Stark, Raphael Vago, and Sandra Dungaciu, among others.

[1] While this is not an exhaustive list, see the reviews of Ernest Latham, Jr., "România interbelică şi minorităţile," 22 7, no. 7 (February 1996): 14; Richard Frucht, *Slavic Review* 55, no. 1 (Spring 1996): 179–180; Dennis Deletant, *Slavonic and East European Review* 74, no. 4 (October 1996); Marcel Cornis-Pope, *European Studies Journal* 13, no. 1 (1996): 101–107; Wim van Meurs, *Zeitschrift für Siebenbürgische Landeskunde* 19, no. 1 (1996): 98–101; John Cole, *Contemporary Sociology* 25, no. 6 (November 1996): 740–741; Harald Heppner, *Südost-Forschungen* 56 (1997): 448–449; Claude Karnoouh, *Revue des études slaves* 69, part 3 (1997): 473–476; Mary Ellen Fischer, *American Historical Review* 101 (October 1996): 1244; Cathie Carmichael, *Europe-Asia Studies* 48, no. 5 (July 1996): 861–862; Constantin Iordachi, *Sfera Politicii* 6, no. 64 (1998): 57–60; Z. Ornea, "Chestiunea naţională în anii '20," *România literară*, September 22, 1998, p. 9; Raphael Vago, *Jewish History* 12, no. 1 (Spring 1998): 143–146; Tamas Stark, *Szazadok* 132, no. 5 (1998): 1192–1197; Botond Zákonyi, "A román múlt egy metszete," *Régió: Kisebbségi Szemle* 9, no. 1 (1998): 230–239; Thomas Hegarty, *Etnos-Nation: Eine Europäische Zeitschrift* 6 (1998): 167–168; and Sandra Dungaciu, "O Analiză occidentală a naţionalismului românesc," *Revista de Teorie Socială* 2, no. 4 (1998): 69–74.

Sorin Alexandrescu has borrowed the ideas I developed on the rural/urban and class divisions between ethnic Romanians and minorities in the newly joined territories in his *Paradoxul român* (Bucharest: Editura Univers, 1998), ch. 1, "Construcţia României Mari," esp. pp. 46–70.

While no one has contested the book's factual substance, several reviewers have suggested alternative interpretations or a more inclusive scope for the phenomena I explore. I have generally welcomed these critiques as friendly amendments to my discussion of Romania's cultural and national politics in the 1920s.

Ernest Latham observed that I had written little about the population that may now be the most hated minority group in Romania: the Gypsies or Roma. He also suggested including a section on Southern Dobrudja, alongside the chapters on Bessarabia, Bukovina, and Transylvania. I have not filled these lacunae, but his comments set a research agenda. Romanian Gypsies are just beginning to be studied by a new generation of social scientists.[2] In any case, during the interwar years, Gypsies represented a type of minority very different from the Hungarians, Germans, Jews, Ukrainians, and Russians I focused on in my book, having neither the elite urban character of some nor the compact rural character of others. As for the *Cadrilater* or southern slice of Dobrudja with its ethnic and religious mix of Romanians, Turks, Tatars, Bulgarians, and Old Believers—the integration of this area, annexed before World War I, might better be studied as part of the history of the Romanization of all Dobrudja.[3]

Marcel Cornis-Pope was critical of my not considering the " 'post-colonial' conditions that enabled the emergence of nationalistic ideologies in the aftermath of World War I and their reappearance after the collapse of the Soviet Empire."[4] While I have not used this precise vocabulary, the post-imperial framework of interwar Romanian history is undeniable, and I believe my study documents its presence. Cornis-Pope further objected to the chronological parameters of the book, which ends with 1930, the starting point for most histories of interwar Romania. I chose 1930 as a terminus because I had discovered during my research that it was precisely in the relatively unknown and politically less eventful decade of the 1920s that I could best examine the social and institutional effects of territorial expansion and thus the conditions for radical nationalist mobilization. The much-invoked decade of the 1930s can benefit, in my judgment, from a close reading of its predecessor. On this subject I would cite Claude Karnoouh's statement that "one can no longer count the political and cultural history books published about the Romanian interwar period." Despite this "efflorescence of publications from and about the [Romanian] interwar period," he notes that they are all "always about the

[2] See *Rromathan: Studii despre rromi* 1, no. 1 (1997), edited by Vasile Ionescu, Liviu Chelcea, and Puiu Lățea.

[3] Constantin Iordachi, one of the new generation of Romanian historians, is at work on such a project.

[4] Cornis-Pope, p. 102.

1930s."[5] The 1920s deserve attention both in their own right, and as a prelude to the 1930s, about which much is known and little is understood.

Cornis-Pope also argued that I over-emphasized the causal effect of Romania's efforts to nationalize its enlarged lands and population on the emergence of the radical nationalist movement. I stand by this "strong narrative" not in the abstract, but in the Romanian case, and do so based on extensive archival research. I thank him, however, for pointing out the need for a sharper "focus on . . . counter-trends which attempted to slow down the process of integration and centralization, promoting regionalist values or [alternatively] cosmopolitan (anti-nationalistic) concepts of culture."[6] While I certainly focused on regionalism, I mentioned only in passing those groups or individuals favoring cosmopolitan concepts of culture, though I explained their marginalization in interwar Romania. They constitute substantial food for thought and fodder for another book.

In his review, Constantin Iordachi too has differed with aspects of my interpretation, challenging the notion of a wide nationalist consensus in interwar Romania, one which, I have argued, included both mainstream politicians and the extreme right. Iordachi sees interwar Romanian society as "the terrain of acute ideological confrontation between differing views of development," and calls "the homogenizing *Kulturkampf* of the nation state and the radical nationalism of the Legionary Movement" "distinct socio-political projects."[7] While I do not disagree, I continue to insist on the overlapping goals of the two kinds of nationalists, which stemmed from their facing the same ethno-demographic problems, and from the fact that the older nationalists had brought up the younger ones and attempted to instill in them a certain type of ethnic patriotism. The fathers did not replicate themselves exactly in the sons, but their efforts did bear fruit, if not the precisely desired one.

In closing, I can do no better than to cite a remark made in a footnote by Sorin Antohi, since many readers, certainly those who do not read Romanian, will have missed it. It is an eloquent invitation from the side of Romanian historiography to an open debate of the wider implications of my book. "Irina Livezeanu's analysis," he writes:

suggests that the nationalist turn of part of Romanian society in the 1930s [a turn that has been itself] much better studied [than the 1920s], was prepared by the very policies of the [Romanian] state between 1918 and 1930. The Legionnaires were not the exalted mutants of a benign historical evolution; rather they appeared precisely because of the cultural policies of the

[5] Karnoouh, pp. 473–474.
[6] Cornis-Pope, p. 104.
[7] Iordachi, p. 59.

Romanian state after the formation of Greater Romania. The question is: did an alternative exist? In my opinion, Irina Livezeanu's argument could inspire here [in Romania] a similar debate, *mutatis mutandis*, to the famous "Fischer controversy" which agitated German historiography in the 1960s.[8]

Antohi goes on to explain to Romanian readers, who more than likely have never heard of the well-known German controversy, the implications of Fritz Fischer's book for German society, and, by analogy, of *Cultural Politics* for contemporary Romanian historiography and society:

> In his 1961 book *Der Griff nach der Weltmacht* [*Germany's Aims in the First World War* in English translation][9] Fischer demonstrated on the basis of documents that Wilhelmine Germany's war aims were radical from the start, and not limited to demands for the redistribution of colonial posses-sions; thus an important myth of German historiography which subtextually implied that . . . Hitlerism had been a mutation, was brought down, with all the inevitable consequences for the legitimation of West German democ-racy.[10]

As far as I know, this invitation has gone largely unheeded in Romania to date.

---

[8] Sorin Antohi, *Exercițiul distanței: Discursuri, societăți, metode,* 2d ed. (Bucharest: Nem-ira, 1998), p. 316 n. 14.

[9] Fritz Fischer, *Germany's Aims in the First World War*, with an introduction by Hajo Holborn and James Joll (New York : W. W. Norton, 1967).

[10] Antohi, *Exercițiul distanței*, p. 316 n. 14.

A Note on Place Names
and Spelling

Many of the places that this book is about have had several different names depending on who is talking about them, in what language, and in the context of what national and political program. Since much of the narrative unfolds in multiethnic settings, it would have been cumbersome to append parentheses to each place name acknowledging one, two, or three alternative appelations. I have used the Romanian geographic names, except when quoting sources that did otherwise. In doing so, I am following the official usage of the Romanian state during the interwar period. When referring to these same places during their pre-Romanian existence, I have generally followed that other official usage. I have made exceptions, however, for Romania's capital, Bucureşti, the only city I have called by its consecrated English name, Bucharest, and for rivers, regions, and mountains similarly having English names that are in common usage.

Unless citing postwar Romanian secondary sources, I have maintained the prewar spelling conventions used in my sources. Where more than one version of a personal or geographic name existed, I have made an effort to standardize them.

CULTURAL
POLITICS
IN
GREATER
ROMANIA

Introduction

Our country, in which we [Romanians] hold both the historic rights, and the rights of the State-constitutive and State-making people, as well as [being] the absolute majority, our Country whose unity is based on the very unity of the Romanian people between the Dniester and the Tisa, this country has facing its overwhelmingly Romanian rural population an urban population that, for the most part, belongs to other peoples; its trade and industry and a large share of banking, thus the main sources of wealth, are in the hands of these non-Romanian inhabitants. [Our country] thus exhibits the phenomenon of a mismatch between town and countryside. This is an abnormal, unnatural situation, because between the Romanian rulers and the Romanian rural population is interposed a bourgeoisie [that is] for the most part non-Romanian.

—Traian Bratu, 1923

Nationalism and the Politics of Unification

In 1939, at the Romanian pavilion of the New York World's Fair, the following inscription—written in large block letters on a marble pillar in the main hall—greeted visitors: "ROMANIA HAS OVER 20 MILLION PEOPLE COMPLETELY UNITED IN LANGUAGE, TRADITION, AND CULTURE."[1] In 1940, soon after the fair, large sections of Greater Romania (in Romanian, România Mare) were annexed by the Soviet Union and Hungary respectively, in accordance with the terms of the Molotov-Ribbentrop Pact and the Second Vienna Award. Besides bearing a certain note of tragic irony, the World's Fair inscription is an interesting historical artifact in other ways too, since even before Romania's dismemberment, the image of perfect unity invoked there belied the ethnic and regional diversity and conflicts troubling Romania after

[1] *Enciclopedia României*, vol. 4 (Bucharest: Imprimeria națională, 1943), p. 314. Translations of foreign-language sources are my own, unless otherwise noted.

1

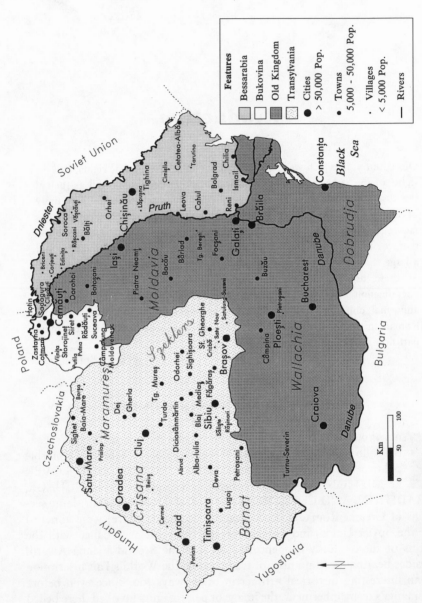

Greater Romania, Provinces

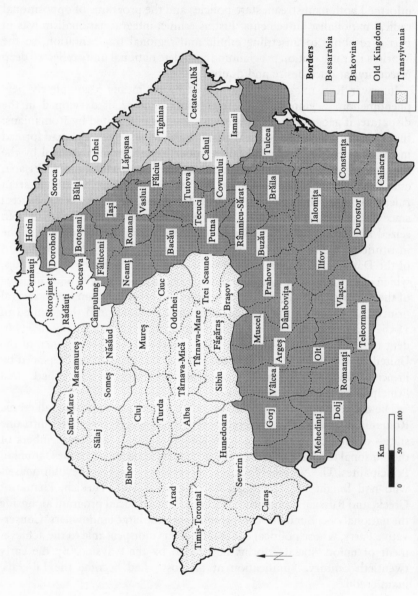

Borders

Bessarabia	Old Kingdom
Bukovina	Transylvania

Greater Romania, Counties and Regions

1918. The motto of the Romanian pavilion, however, articulated perfectly the national idea that had come to dominate Romanian politics and society during the interwar period. The ideal of a unitary, ethnically pure polity informed both mainstream state policies and the programs of oppositional radical nationalist movements. Just as ethnic, integral nationalism was in part a response to unsettling ethnic and regional fragmentation, so the World's Fair inscription proclaiming complete national unity reflected deep insecurity: at once desire and doubt.

Interwar Romanian nationalism was by no means a completely new phenomenon. Beginning in the eighteenth century, it developed in the disparate, if geographically contiguous, settings inhabited by Romanians: the Danubian Principalities of Wallachia and Moldavia, which had formed in the thirteenth century and fallen under loose Ottoman control by the fifteenth; Transylvania and the adjoining districts of Maramureş, Crişana, and Banat, at various times under Habsburg, Ottoman, and Hungarian rule; Bukovina, the northern part of Moldavia, under Austrian control since 1775; and Bessarabia, the eastern part of Moldavia, which had been seized and incorporated by Russia in 1812. From the standpoint of the institutional expression of an emerging national identity, the Romanians of the Danubian Principalities were the most fortunate. These two states, which since the Middle Ages had shared not only the ethnicity and language of the majority population, but also political institutions, and even several princes, nevertheless maintained separate statehood until they united in 1859–61. The United Principalities were recognized as formally independent by the European powers in 1878. In 1866, the native prince of the United Principalities, Alexandru Ioan Cuza, was deposed and replaced by Prince Carol I of the German Hohenzollern dynasty. In 1881, the United Principalities became a kingdom.

The concept of Greater Romania—that is, the idea of uniting all ethnic Romanians and all the contiguous territories where they lived into one state—originated in the Romanian Kingdom chiefly among members of the National Liberal Party, the main architects of the union of the Danubian Principalites. The National Liberals, successors to the 1848 revolutionaries who had fought for Romanian independence from Turkish, Phanariot Greek, and Russian domination, had developed a social program alongside the national one. But in the compromise with the large landowners' Conservative Party, whose political cooperation was indispensable to the achievement of union, social reforms had fallen by the wayside. By the early twentieth century, "unification at all cost" had become the Liberals' main credo.[2]

[2] Stephen Fischer-Galati, "Romanian Nationalism," in Peter Sugar and Ivo Lederer, eds., *Nationalism in Eastern Europe* (Seattle: University of Washington Press, 1969), p. 389. On

The Greater Romania idea emerged victorious with the collapse of the empires in 1917–18. Fittingly, the Romanian delegation to the Paris Peace negotiations was led by Premier Ion Brătianu, a scion of a leading Liberal Wallachian family—although in fact the Romanian patriots who made possible the Great Union of 1918 came from all the provinces. This book is the story of their creation, and thus one of achievement. It concentrates, however, not on the politics and diplomacy leading up to Romania's great union but rather on aspects of nation building which followed Greater Romania's actual birth. Thus this book also tells a story of unanticipated hardships and of nationalist solutions to the substantial problems posed by Romanian nationalism's very success—the 1918 unification of the Old Kingdom (or Regat) with Transylvania, Bukovina, and Bessarabia.

I might here point out that Greater Romania is not exceptional in its nation-building efforts, and that every account of nation building relates unpredictable challenges and struggles. For no matter how much shared background and how many dramatic, myth-generating, historical events bring members of a nation together, bearers of local identities tend to resist total substitution of the greater, national, more abstract identity for the smaller, more familiar, more "authentic" one tied to age-old traditions. The particular forms that nation building and nationalism took in Romania in the interwar period, however, are of course historically unique. Much of the newer literature—as against earlier discussions of nationalism which were variously steeped in the foundation and survival myths of the nations investigated—recognizes that rigorous ideological and political labor is essential to turn segmented populations, even if ethnically related, into politically and culturally coherent nations.[3] Even Western European nations that had previously been considered solid "natural" units by comparison with the younger, ethnically defined Eastern European nations, appear as new and vulnerable constructions under close historical scrutiny. France, for example, whose national cohesiveness since the French Revolution is so often assumed in the older historiography, was definitively "deconstructed" some years ago by Eugen Weber's investigation of late nineteenth and early twentieth century French nation building.[4]

Liah Greenfeld has also examined France, as well as England, Russia, Germany, and the United States, in her work on nationalism. She argues persuasively that in Europe all but the first, English, national identities

---

the aspirations of different groups of Romanian nationalists and reformers, see pp. 373–390; Daniel Chirot, *Social Change in a Peripheral Society: The Creation of a Balkan Colony* (New York: Academic Press, 1976), pp. 109–117; and Paul Michelson, *Conflict and Crisis: Romanian Political Development, 1861–1871* (New York: Garland, 1987).

[3] Geoff Eley, "Nationalism and Social History," *Social History* 6 (January 1981): 90, 92.

[4] Eugen Weber, *Peasants into Frenchmen: The Modernization of Rural France, 1870–1914* (Stanford, Calif.: Stanford University Press, 1977).

were in significant ways collectively forged reactions to other national precedents.[5] If then *ressentiment* against more powerful, more Western, nations played a part in the building of the German, Russian (and even French) identities, it is quite possible that such factors also shaped the less fortunate and powerful, and, in most cases, later-developing nations of Eastern Europe. Greenfeld also argues that nations are not necessarily the product of modernization and industrialization, as others have suggested, but can anticipate "the development of every significant component of modernization." She maintains that the only precondition of nationalism is the idea of the nation. In contrast, Ernest Gellner holds that nationalism is the fairly recent product of "the organization of human beings into large, centrally educated, culturally homogeneous units," and that "the roots of nationalism [are] in the distinctive structural requirements of industrial society."[6]

Here we have, then, two distinct ways of conceiving of nationalism. Both approaches can help us understand Eastern Europe, the traditionally less industrialized, less "modern" part of the continent, where nationalism has been and continues to be a phenomenon of overwhelming importance. In interwar Eastern Europe nationalism seems to have followed a Greenfeldian recipe; that is, it was more directly linked to the imperatives of national unification—as states and elites attempted to consolidate their gains (or compensate for their losses) and to adjust to novel political circumstances—than to the exigencies of industrialization. To state it very simply, interwar Eastern European nationalism was motivated more by politics than by economics.

Yet one must also concede that a two-way relationship exists between industry/modernity and nationalism, though perhaps less in the initial emergence of nationalist ideas than in their spread. It is only under conditions of advancing urbanization and literacy that national identity can take root and influence mass politics beyond the narrow circles of nationalist vanguards. Here one can usefully adapt Alexander Gerschenkron's concept of the flexibility of prerequisites for industrialization to countries that are latecomers to nation building even as they are to industrialization.[7] Just as the state in industrially backward societies can substitute budgetary policies for the organic accumulation of capital to generate the sums needed for industrialization, so the state can presumably substitute cultural policies

[5] Liah Greenfeld, *Nationalism: Five Roads to Modernity* (Cambridge, Mass.: Harvard University Press, 1992).

[6] Ibid., pp. 21 and 3–4, and Ernest Gellner, *Nations and Nationalism* (Ithaca: Cornell University Press, 1983), p. 35.

[7] Alexander Gerschenkron, "Reflections on the Concept of Prerequisites of Modern Industrialization," in his *Economic Backwardness in Historical Perspective* (Cambridge, Mass.: Belknap Press, 1962).

for the structures of industrial society which Gellner stipulates as prerequisites for the development of nationalism. The role of the Romanian state in designing and executing such policies is one of the themes of this book.

The creation, recreation, enlargement (and even diminution) of East European states after World War I according to Wilsonian principles of self-determination provided the occasion for shaping national identities. Some identities, such as the Czechoslovak and Yugoslav, had to be invented almost from scratch, but others, such as the Polish, Hungarian, and Romanian, had "merely" to be reconstituted to suit the radically changed circumstances of postwar arrangements—no small feat in a world dominated by highly industrialized and powerful nations and by newly radicalized and polarized ideologies. I argue in this book that in Romania, among other places in interwar Eastern Europe, the reconstitution of the nation within its newly enlarged boundaries brought opportunities for national redefinition as well as profound social and cultural crises, and that these two aspects were intricately linked to each other. The unification of the Romanian lands in 1918 constituted a national revolution—despite the unquestionable linguistic, historical, and cultural ties existing among the Romanians from the old and new territories—and this revolution initiated the turbulent nation building and civil strife that characterized the decades between the two wars. This picture of discontinuous, disruptive, and painful development differs significantly from the mainstream of contemporary, as well as older, Romanian historiography, which stresses themes of uninterrupted unity and continuity in Romania's national development from the time of the ancient Dacians until the Greater Romanian period and beyond. The Great Union of 1918, and the Greater Romanian era as its result, has generally been portrayed in exclusively positive, apotheotic terms as a moment of unquestioned national triumph.[8]

I suggest that the "embarrassment of riches" Romania faced with the postwar settlement was an ambiguous and difficult gift. Like the "Trojan horse," it brought apparent and momentary glory but concealed untold social, demographic, political, and cultural challenges. The very means to national fulfillment was also the source of potential, and in time actual, tensions, for unification also meant the incorporation of large minority populations that were more urban, more schooled, and more modern than

---

[8] For an analysis and partial bibliography of this extensive historiography, see Paul E. Michelson, "Unity and Continuity in Romanian History," *Canadian Review of Studies in Nationalism* 8 (1981), and Michelson, "Romania," in *Nationalism in the Balkans: An Annotated Bibliography*, ed. Gale Stokes (New York: Garland, 1984). Just two examples among many of this type of historiography are Mircea Muşat and Ion Ardeleanu, *De la statul getodac la statul român unitar* (Bucharest: Editura ştiinţifică şi enciclopedică, 1983), translated as *From Ancient Dacia to Modern Romania* (Bucharest: Editura ştiinţifică şi enciclopedică, 1985), and Ştefan Pascu, *The Making of the Romanian Unitary National State: 1918* (Bucharest: Editura Academiei R. S. R., 1989).

the Romanians; the imposition of Western democratic processes, such as the equal rights of minorities, which were widely perceived as illegitimate, alien grafts; and clear demonstrations of disunity within the ethnic Romanian community itself, which was affected as well as the minorities by regionally differentiated traditions, cultures, and allegiances.

Problems of nation building in Greater Romania constitute one focus of this book; a second, closely related concern is the emergence of extreme nationalism among university youth and the acceptance and backing of this ideology by mainstream politicians and a broad spectrum of public opinion. The populist nationalism that dominated much of Romania's political, social, and cultural discourse in the interwar period was both a by-product and an agent of the energetic nation-building activity of those years. Given the overwhelmingly rural character of the Romanians, the foreignness of the towns in the new provinces, the need to expand Romanian elites to the size of the new territories, and the priority of establishing a Romanian presence in the crucial cultural and urban spheres, the process of nation building was accompanied by the rise of a generalized anti-urban, populist, xenophobic, and anti-Semitic discourse. This nationalistic climate favored the growth of fascism. In Romania, the origins of fascism are to be found in the movement of nationalist students—the "generation of 1922."

The Demographics of National Expansion

Romania more than doubled its territory and population after World War I. This expansion was accomplished by the annexation of the provinces of Bessarabia from Russia, Bukovina from Austria, and Transylvania from Hungary. Although by world standards Romania was still a small country, with fourteen and a half million people in 1919 it became, after Poland, the second most populous country in East Central Europe.[9] In 1914 the Old Kingdom, including Southern Dobrudja, which Romania had annexed from Bulgaria after the Second Balkan War, had 137,903 square kilometers. The territory of Greater Romania in 1919 was 295,049 square kilometers. In the same period, Romania's population increased from 7,771,341 to 14,669,841. According to the 1930 census, Romania's population was 18,057,028. The country was predominantly rural, with only 20.2 percent

[9] Institutul central de statistică, *Anuarul statistic al României 1937 şi 1938* (Bucharest: M. O., Imprimeria naţională, 1939) (hereafter ICS), p. 41.

Table 1. The population of Greater Romania,
by province and rural-urban distribution, 1930

	Total	Rural (%)	Urban (%)
Greater Romania	18,057,028	79.8	20.2
Old Kingdom	8,791,254	76.2	23.8
Transylvania	5,548,363	82.6	17.4
Bukovina	853,009	73.3	26.7
Bessarabia	2,864,402	87.0	13.0

Source: Institutul central de statistică, *Anuarul statistic al României 1937 și 1938*, pp. 44–45.

of the population living in urban areas (table 1). Close to three-quarters (72.3 percent) of Romania's general population worked the land. Industry was even less developed than urbanization: only 9.5 percent of Romania's population (including dependents) made a living in industry and mining. A higher proportion—18.2 percent—was involved in tertiary sectors: commerce, banking, transportation, communication, public services, the free professions, and so forth.[10] Thus the nonagricultural population in Greater Romania was more bureaucratically than industrially oriented.

Greater Romania was ethnically and religiously quite diverse, but the bulk of the minorities lived in the new provinces. Whereas fewer than 8 percent of old Romania's population had been members of minority groups, the largest of these being the Jews,[11] new Romania had a non-Romanian population of close to 30 percent (table 2).

Romanians constituted a little over two-thirds of the country's population, with a large Hungarian (or Magyar) minority in Transylvania, and smaller but sizable German, Ukrainian, and Russian minorities in the new provinces. The Jews were also a significant group, particularly in urban areas, in both the old and the new territories.[12]

Not only were the Romanians ethnically "diminished" with the addition of the new provinces, but the urban-rural balance shifted against them. Ethnic Romanians formed 71.9 percent of the general population in 1930, but they composed only 58.6 percent of the urban population.[13] In the Old Kingdom three-quarters of the urban population was Romanian, but

[10] ICS, pp. 41, 44, and Joseph Rothschild, *East Central Europe between the Two World Wars* (Seattle: University of Washington Press, 1977), pp. 283, 285.

[11] Rothschild, *East Central Europe*, p. 284.

[12] Barbara Jelavich, *History of the Balkans: Twentieth Century*, vol. 2 (Cambridge: Cambridge University Press, 1983), p. 26.

[13] See Dumitru Șandru, *Populația rurală a României între cele două războaie mondiale* (Jassy: Editura Academiei R. S. R., 1980), p. 51.

Table 2. The population of Greater Romania, by ethnicity, 1930

	Number	Percentage of total
Romanians	12,981,324	71.9
Hungarians	1,425,507	7.9
Germans	745,421	4.1
Jews	728,115	4.0
Ukrainians[a]	594,571	3.3
Russians	409,150	2.3
Bulgarians	366,384	2.0
Gypsies	262,501	1.5
Others[b]	544,055	3.0
	18,057,028	100.0

Source: Institutul central de statistică, Anuarul statistic al României 1937 și 1938, pp. 58–61.

[a] This group includes the Hutsuls.

[b] Nationalities that each constituted less than 1 percent of the population, i.e., Turks, Tatars, Gagauzi, Greeks, Armenians, Albanians, Poles, Czechs, Slovaks, Serbs, Croats, Slovenes.

in the various new provinces Romanians made up one-third of the townspeople (table 3).

In general, then, the Romanians were the bulk of the peasants in the new provinces and in large measure in the old ones too, since Romania was 80 percent rural. In Bessarabia, Bukovina, and Transylvania the small urban population tended to be non-Romanian. The nationalization of the towns, urban elites, and cultural institutions—three elements closely interlinked in the underdeveloped world of newly united Romania—frequently provoked ethnic confrontation between Romanian peasants and non-Romanian townspeople. The Romanian peasant was the nation's common denominator throughout all of the provinces, old and new. The peas-

Table 3. Percentage of Romanians in general and
urban populations, by province, 1930

	General Population (%)	Urban population (%)
Greater Romania	71.9	58.6
Old Kingdom	88.5	74.3
Transylvania	57.8	34.7
Bukovina	44.5	33.0
Bessarabia	56.2	31.0

Source: Calculated from Dumitru Şandru, Populaţia rurală a României între cele două războaie mondiale, p. 52, and Institutul central de statistică, Anuarul statistic al României 1937 și 1938, pp. 58–60.

ant became the symbol of the nation and the ally of the state and was invited to become educated, to enter the middle class, to move to town, to join the bureaucracy, or to take an industrial, or more often, a commercial job. By accepting these invitations, the peasantry could raise not only its own status but also that of the nation. But clearly such moves were no easy task, for a villager with little or no urban experience, limited previous education, and no business or friendship networks outside of the village, for they placed him or, less often, her in competition with the members of much more experienced "foreign" elites.[14] Thus the national revolution could potentially erupt into interethnic warfare, as the state and Romanian individuals and groups attempted to displace the "foreign" minorities from their long-held positions. These "foreigners," moreover, were not easily dislodged from their traditional places in the professions, cities, and schools. Their social networks were not to be erased as swiftly as the international boundaries that were redrawn by armies and diplomats at the conclusion of the war. A protracted, bitter struggle between peasant and urbanite, between village and town, between Romanian and foreigner ensued. Many Romanians viewed this as a battle over the very survival of their rightfully enlarged state. The minorities did not speak with one voice, for they were divided by ethnic group, religion, maternal language, politics, and province, but most of them came to regret the reversal of fate which relegated them to subordinate status.

The Reforms and the "Jewish Question"

Romania undertook three other revolutionary initiatives at the time of its unification: universal male suffrage, a sweeping land reform, and the emancipation of the Jews. These measures, in themselves democratic, were potentially destabilizing. They brought both peasants and Jews into the electoral arena, to which they had previously been denied access.[15] Since in Romanian social, ethnic, and cultural symbolism the Jew was the antipode of the peasant, the reforms set the scene for conflict between the two

[14] On the use of the term "foreign" to refer to national minorities in the Balkans and Eastern Europe, see Jelavich, *History of the Balkans*, pp. 135–136. She compares the new regimes unfavorably with the older, imperial ones: "The new national regimes were to adopt a much more unconciliatory view. The position of a member of a minority could be much worse under their rule than under the old empires. . . . The national leaderships throughout the peninsula acquired the habit of applying the word "foreign' to minority citizens, even when the families might have lived in the region for centuries."

[15] Both Jews and peasants had been important actors in Romania's economy and politics even before their emancipation, as witnessed by the Great Peasant Revolt of 1907, which Moldavian peasants began by attacking local Jewish lease holders. See Chirot, *Social Change*, p. 150, and Philip Eidelberg, *The Great Romanian Peasant Revolt of 1907: Origins of a Modern Jacquerie* (Leiden: Brill, 1974).

newly enfranchised groups: in fact, however, the peasants proved less the protagonists in this contest than the self-appointed but widely recognized spokespeople of the peasantry and the nation—that is, the nationalist youth. Furthermore, by partially satisfying peasant demand for land, the land reform made it possible for the national question to displace the social question—that of the peasantry and its land-hunger—as the chief issue of Romanian society. In Greater Romania, then, territorial expansion and postwar reforms contributed to the recrudescence of a nationalism, tinged, as in the 19th century, with anti-Semitism, but now flourishing in a newly radicalized context of a stronger Romanian state and relatively weaker ethnic Romanian elites.

Already in the prewar period most Romanian nationalist opinion makers had reviled the Jews as an abnormal, detrimental presence in the Romanian nation. According to William Oldson, between 1859 and 1914 anti-Semitism became "an integral part of the intellectual life" of Romania to such a pervasive extent that "to be Romanian became synonymous with being an anti-Semite." Anti-Semitism "was espoused by some of the most important [Romanian] literary and historical writers" and by "the most gifted members of the intelligentsia."[16] Before the war the Jews had been excluded from citizenship and from acquiring rural property, and the character of the Jewish communities had been predominantly urban, commercial, and industrial.[17] But the concomitant Jewish emancipation and the nation-building policies carried out in Romania after the union of 1918 extended the "Jewish question" at the very moment of its apparent resolution. Despite, or perhaps because of, the Jewish enfranchisement (which many nationalists had direly opposed), public opinion singled out the Jews as the internal enemy par excellence.

The renewed importance of Jews in Romanian nationalist symbolism and the rise of anti-Semitism in the interwar period owed to several factors. Like some other national minorities, they were relatively more urban and educated, and they constituted more of an economic and professional elite than the "state-owning" Romanians. Unlike the other minorities, however, which were mostly confined to one particular region, the Jews lived in towns and cities throughout the country, thus establishing a kind of elite-urban common denominator for all the new and old provinces at a time when the Romanians were adopting a populist, peasant definition for

[16] William Oldson, *A Providential Anti-Semitism: Nationalism and Polity in Nineteenth-Century Romania* (Philadelphia: American Philosophical Society, [1991]), pp. 9–10. See also Leon Volovici, *Nationalist Ideology and Antisemitism: The Case of Romanian Intellectuals in the 1930s* (Oxford: Pergamon, 1991), pp. 6–16.

[17] Andrew Janos, "Modernization and Decay in Historical Perspective: The Case of Romania," in *Social Change in Romania, 1860–1940: A Debate on Development in a European Nation*, ed. Kenneth Jowitt (Berkeley: Institute of International Studies, 1978), p. 91; see also Jelavich, *History of the Balkans*, p. 26.

their nation. As Eastern Orthodoxy became an important marker of the Romanian nation for some nationalist intellectuals, such as the Orthodoxists led by Nichifor Crainic and joined by Nae Ionescu, the mentor of the new generation,[18] the Jews became unacceptable on religious grounds as well. (The Hungarians and Germans were not Eastern Orthodox either, but they at least were Christian.) The Jews thus were not the very things Romanians in their search for a unique national identity were defining themselves to be in their essence. Although not all Romanians agreed with this ruralist and religious self-definition, the bulk of intellectual opinion aligned itself with a "traditionalist" interpretation of Romanianness.[19] The image of the Jews was further implicated in and affected by the endless interwar debates about the national essence, in themselves a telling symptom of the deeply felt Romanian identity crisis. In these debates, both indigenists and Westernizers were comparing Romania with "the West." For the indigenists, who steadily gained ground from their opponents, the Jews—the minority most defended by Western governments and international institutions, and the most urban and most overrepresented minority on Romanian university rolls—took the place of the "West" as the implied term of comparison in the Romanian imagination. Applied anti-Semitism thus became a way to triumph over the West, at least in this symbolic form.[20] Furthermore, the Jews had been practically the only minority in the Old Kingdom, which became the state-making metropolis of Greater Romania and from where nation-building policies and nationalist slogans were launched. Thus to those from the Old Kingdom any discussion of minority issues tended to elicit echoes of the Jewish question.

The Nationalist Consensus

For Greater Romania the formal unification of territories at the conclusion of World War I was only the beginning of a long process of unification "on the ground." Whereas prewar nationalism had been rooted in irredentist aspirations for the Romanian provinces under foreign rule, the nearly

[18] Katherine Verdery, *National Ideology under Socialism: Identity and Cultural Politics in Ceauşescu's Romania* (Berkeley: University of California Press, 1991), pp. 47–48; Keith Hitchins, "*Gîndirea*: Nationalism in a Spiritual Guise," in Jowitt, ed., *Social Change in Romania*, pp. 146–156, 168–172.

[19] Keith Hitchins writes of the "*short* list of representative "Europeans' " (my emphasis) in "*Gîndirea*," p. 142, while Alexandru George describes the Lovinescu-led Europeanist literary circle "Sburătorul" as becoming "more and more an *oasis* of freedom" (my emphasis) in "Studiu introductiv," in Eugen Lovinescu, *Opere*, vol. 1 (Bucharest: Editura Minerva, 1982), p. 32.

[20] In this formulation I borrow from Liah Greenfeld's suggestive conceptualization of anti-Semitism in the German context. See Greenfeld, *Nationalism*, pp. 378–386.

all-pervasive character of Greater Romania's nationalist discourse was driven by the desire for rapid national consolidation and the social and political mechanisms involved in realizing that goal. As in other East Central European countries during the interwar period, in Romania integral nationalism became widely accepted as the ideological framework for politics at large. In order to assimilate the new provinces with their substantial minority populations and regionalized Romanian-speaking populations, the Romanian government initiated cultural and educational policies that resulted in intense national mobilization. These policies in turn fueled the existing populist, nationalist discourse that gradually came to dominate political, social, and cultural life after 1918.[21] The spheres of organized culture and student politics analyzed here clearly reflect this developing nationalist consensus.

Certainly, the consensus was not absolute. Communists and socialists for one were not part of it, but their opposition to nationalism only reinforced this nativist construction, especially as the communists fell into step with the Comintern's anti-Romanian stance, which aimed at Soviet expansion into Bessarabia and Northern Bukovina.[22] Some Romanians who were not part of the organized left also favored an open, "melting pot" policy toward Romania's ethnic minorities which would respect their equal rights as citizens and keep them loyal to the state. One such individual was Traian Bratu, a native of Transylvania, member of the National Peasant Party, professor of German and rector at Iaşi University during its time of troubles in the 1920s, a Senator representing Iaşi University, and President of the Senate in 1928–31. Bratu paid dearly for his generous prominority stance; it brought him into open conflict with A. C. Cuza and the latter's disciples, and in 1937 he lost an ear in an attack by nationalist youths.[23]

A nationalist consensus—once again with important exceptions—also characterized the intellectual history of interwar Romania, for which this book has implications. In examining the nationalist ideology prevalent in Greater Romania, I use a fairly inclusive definition of ideology, "where it means something more than what happens inside a few literati's heads . . . not just ideas and attitudes, but also types of behaviour, institutions, and

---

[21] In her discussion of nationalist discourse in 20th-century Romania, Katherine Verdery writes that "the interwar years became a concerted period for making national ideology hegemonic, the basis for a broad consent. . . . Only 20 percent of the population failed to find this ideology attractive." *National Ideology,* pp. 45–46.

[22] Michael Shafir, *Romania: Politics, Economics, and Society* (Boulder, Colo.: Lynne Rienner, 1985), pp. 18–20.

[23] See Traian Bratu, *Politica naţională faţă de minorităţi: Note şi observaţiuni* ([Bucharest]: Cultura naţională, [1923]), pp. 61–63.

social relations."[24] This book is therefore, among other things, an intellectual history of sorts, albeit one that intellectual historians of single, towering cultural figures or philosophical schools may not immediately recognize. Interwar Romania's rich intellectual and cultural activity is a source of justifiable pride for Romania's subsequent generations, and it has been the subject of much historical, sociological, and critical writing. Two of the most useful ways to dissect the cultural and intellectual trends of the period have been to focus on the debate over Romanian national identity between indigenists or traditionalists and Europeanists or Westernizers, and to look through the prism of "generations." Both views reveal a panorama of artistic, literary, critical, and philosophical activity impressive in quality and amount. The range of opinions, trends, and ideological positions on the Romanian cultural scene in the 1920s and 1930s is well-documented.[25]

Within the plurality of this output, the indigenists, representing a spectrum of intellectual nationalism, became increasingly dominant, pushing the "Europeans" to the edges of the literary establishment as the interwar decades advanced. Similarly, the "new generation" became the appelation of the right-wing nationalists of the postwar intellectual generation that in fact included Europeanists as well, though these were ever fewer over the course of the period under discussion. The career of literary critic Eugen Lovinescu, distinguished dean of the Europeanist orientation, is instructive. Lovinescu, who insisted in his writings on the interdependence of all European cultures, was and remains highly reputed for his works of literary history and criticism as well as for the "Sburătorul" literary circle that he sponsored and the talented young writers whom he nurtured. In the interwar period, however, Lovinescu was marginalized by the Romanian establishment in favor of his autochthonist adversaries, some of whom were his intellectual peers, but others of whom were undoubtedly his inferiors. Intellectual nationalists of right and center defeated Lovinescu's nomination for membership in the Romanian Academy in 1936, the very same time that the foremost Romanian anti-Semite, A. C. Cuza, Professor of Law at Iaşi University and mentor of right-wing student nationalists, was elected. Lovinescu's election was opposed not only by the preeminent leader of Orthodoxism and eventual Iron Guard ideologue Nichifor Crainic, but also by the respected historian and politician Nicolae Iorga, a far

---

[24] Geoff Eley, "What Produces Fascism: Preindustrial Traditions or a Crisis of a Capitalist State," *Politics and Society* 12, no. 2 (1983): 75–76.

[25] Hitchins, "*Gîndirea*"; Verdery, *National Ideology*, pp. 48–54; Z. Ornea, *Tradiţionalism şi modernitate în deceniul al treilea* (Bucharest: Editura eminescu, 1980); D. Micu, *Gîndirea şi gîndirismul* (Bucharest: Editura Minerva, 1975); and Ileana Vrancea, *Confruntări în critica deceniilor IV–VII (E. Lovinescu şi posteritatea lui critică)* (Bucharest: Editura Cartea românească, 1975), chap. 2.

more moderate and mainstream leader of Romanian national thought, and himself later a victim of the Iron Guard. A similar coalition of forces prevented Lovinescu from being honored with the Romanian Academy's prize in 1940 and from ever obtaining a university chair.[26] The point I wish to emphasize is that in the Greater Romanian literary and intellectual spheres—as in those of the cultural and educational policies which I examine at length in this book—there was a plurality of opinions, but that extreme and mainstream nationalism coalesced to exclude someone like Lovinescu from the Academy while ensuring the inclusion of extreme nationalists and anti-Semites like Cuza and Crainic in Romania's highest intellectual forum.

A related point applies to the ideological profile of "the new generation." Although the generation included leftists and rightists, indigenists and Europeanists, scholars reserve the term between quotation marks for the extreme nationalist, right-wing exponents of the youthful post–World War I Romanian intelligentsia, reflecting the preponderance of the latter in that generation.[27] Similarly, it is the autochthonist Nae Ionescu who is widely considered the "mentor of the 'new generation,' " and not the modernist Eugen Lovinescu, who also nurtured young literati. I accord little space here to intellectual currents per se; nevertheless, the ideological balance of these currents should be kept in mind, since literate Romanian culture was one of the most basic means of national integration available to nationalist educators and institutions, and since nationalist intellectual trends above all others were represented in a rich literary and journalistic production read by young and old, teachers and students, indeed by educated Romanians everywhere. Moreover, the vital context for these ideas and literary debates was the formation of Greater Romania and the campaigns to nationalize the country's elites and cultural institutions. These elements of "background" were part of interwar Romanians' daily reality and undoubtedly loomed large in the consciousness of Romanian intellectuals. Greater Romania's cultural and intellectual politics both bear the marks of the enormous nation building project the country embarked on after 1918.

Education and Culture as Instruments of Nation Building

To consolidate its territorial gains, the Romanian state expanded its ethnic Romanian elites so as to be able to oust those of the Hungarian, Austrian, and Russian regimes that had previously ruled these lands. The

---

[26] George, "Studiu introductiv," p. xxxi; Vrancea, *Confruntări,* pp. 69–71; George Călinescu, *Istoria literaturii române dela origini pînă în prezent,* 2d ed. rev. and enl. (Bucharest: Editura Minerva, 1982), p. 807; and Verdery, *National Ideology,* p. 53.

[27] See, for example, Vrancea, *Confruntări,* pp. 94, 101, 103, 110.

educational system was instrumental in this strategy. The Romanian government also supported the Romanization of urban areas where ethnic Romanians were in a minority and where their *felt* presence was even smaller than their numbers—for before 1918 Romanians did not constitute the urban elites of Bessarabia, Bukovina, and Transylvania. Even though the cities and towns of Romania's new provinces were about one-third Romanian in the 1920s, they did not generally exhibit even in that proportion a visible, Romanian character. Another, related, cause of this state of affairs was that ethnic Romanians did not initially control the crucial cultural strongholds of provincial society. Cultural institutions produce and project the public images of a society to itself and to the outside world. They also generate the society's elites most obviously by means of schools, but through the press and other media as well. These elites then staff the cultural institutions of which they are a product. For example, before World War I the Bukovinian capital of Cernăuți (Czernowitz) was 15 percent Romanian,[28] but the university, the theatre, most high schools, and daily newspapers were German; the Romanian presence in the city could thus hardly be felt outside of the Romanian community itself. After 1918, therefore, it was of paramount importance to acquire the means of production of culture which would produce Romanian elites and project the Romanian cultural presence broadly and publicly.

In this book, I document and analyze the acquisition of cultural and educational institutions by the Romanian state and local elites in order to elucidate the problems of unification, nation building, and nationalism. The centrality of education and literacy to the formation of modern nations and nationalism has been cogently argued by the "modernist" school of students of nationalism, perhaps most eloquently by Benedict Anderson and Ernest Gellner. But even those scholars who are skeptical of the wholesale modernity of these phenomena and who stress the premodern ethnic foundations of modern nations, notably Anthony Smith, fully acknowledge the essential role of educational systems in the transition from traditional *ethnies* to modern nations.

In the case of Greater Romania, national unification came late. It brought together disparate populations that were the historical product of diverse linguistic, ethnic, religious, cultural, and political experiences; throughout the country literacy was uneven and in some parts, particularly among ethnic Romanians, at an extremely low level. The Romanian elites felt their country to be "backward" by general European standards and by

---

[28] Calculated from Österreichische Statistik Herausgegeben v. der K. K. Statistischen Zentralkommission, *Bewegung der Bevölkerung der im Reichsrate Vertretenen Königreiche und Länder im Jahre 1910*, vol. 8, pt. 1 (Vienna: K. K. Hof- und Staatsdruckerei, 1912), p. 11; and Rudolf Wagner, *Von Moldauwappen zum Doppeladler: Ausgewählte Beiträge zur Geschichte der Bukowina* (Augsburg: Hofmann-Verlag, 1991), p. 263.

contrast with the more educated non-Romanian populations of their own country. Therefore, the use of educational institutions as a powerful instrument of homogenization, one potentially capable of accelerating the process of nation building, was extremely appealing and fully exploited by state makers and nationalists.[29] A cultural and educational explosion occurred in Romania after World War I, and a considerably larger proportion of the state budget was devoted to education than before the war. Andrew Janos has argued that the cultural revolution in interwar Romania was due in part to the state's efforts to raise literacy levels to more closely match the more educated national minorities, and thus to promote their assimilation.[30] An even more pressing goal was to replace minorities in elite positions with ethnic Romanians.

Ernest Gellner's arguments on the importance of culture once the "intimate structures of traditional society" have been eroded[31] are relevant to the Romanian case, even though the state here claimed merely to have returned the national community to a "state of grace" by reuniting the separated ethnic Romanian communities. The union of 1918 was no simple restoration of former national boundaries and cohesiveness. This event inaugurated ground-breaking cultural transformations, policies, and politics rather than the return, envisaged by Romanian nationalists, to an idyllic, natural, primordial state of the Romanian community. I strive here to ground the renewed debate on the extent to which nationality is best understood as primarily perennial, or as socially and historically constructed and therefore discontinuous. This book clearly illustrates that both the Romanian state and the Romanian nation needed considerable construction work of a cultural sort, despite undeniable ethnic continuities, in order to become politically viable.

Referring to the acceptance of the concept of "nation-building" by recent social scientists, William Bloom notes that "inherent in its usage is the fact that a *state* has already been created, and that the nation or community of solidarity, is to be built within it."[32] This seems to be what the nineteenth-century Italian revolutionary Massimo d'Azeglio had in mind *avant la lettre*, when he commented in 1860, in the wake of Italy's unification,

---

[29] Ernest Gellner, *Thought and Change* (Chicago: University of Chicago Press, 1965), and *Nations and Nationalism;* Benedict Anderson, *Imagined Communities* (London: Verso, 1983); Anthony D. Smith, *The Ethnic Origins of Nations* (Oxford: Blackwell, 1986), esp. pp. 136, 160.

[30] Janos, "Modernization," pp. 98, 107–108; see also Verdery, *National Ideology,* p. 44.

[31] Gellner, *Thought and Change,* p. 157.

[32] William Bloom, *Personal Identity, National Identity, and International Relations* (Cambridge: Cambridge University Press, 1993), p. 55.

"We have made Italy; now we must make the Italians."[33] One might usefully paraphrase him in regard to interwar Romania: once (Greater) Romania had been made, there remained the formidable task of making the Romanians. The new Romanian state faced a plethora of problems resulting from its newness and territorial good fortune. Institutional and legal homogenization, the replacement of foreign elites, the recruitment and expansion of national elites, the fight against regionalism, and the implantation or nurturing of national consciousness among uneducated and educated strata that had lived for as long as anyone could remember under foreign rule—remaining either illiterate or having been socialized into foreign cultures—all had to be accomplished before Greater Romania could become more than a fleeting embodiment of romantic nationalists' imaginations. Cultural work had to accompany the creation of a full range of political institutions, of a national elite, and of a versatile high culture and standardized written language acceptable and comprehensible to all.

The language and culture that can accommodate a complex society of an internationally recognized state in twentieth century Europe are aptly described by Ernest Gellner as those of "clerking." He contrasts industrialized, modern, literate societies where everyone has to have clerical skills in order to function efficiently with premodern societies in which the clerks form a thin stratum apart and discharge clerical tasks for the whole society.[34] The widespread adoption of clerking skills, usually in a new, urbanized, foreign-seeming environment, by previously unschooled, newly mobilized peasants can be arduous. John Plamenatz depicts the migration of villagers to towns belonging to an alien "clerking" culture with which they have to grapple, and he details the complex and paradoxical process to which it gives rise. The forging of the new migrants' culture involves both rejection and imitation of the urban, alien culture:

> As the social revolution gathers speed, as the number of people wanting to take the opportunities it creates grows rapidly, competition becomes fiercer, and the competitors less well placed to achieve success are keen to be as well placed as the others. If they are at a disadvantage because the language and culture of their ancestors are not well suited to the new opportunities, and if they are less well placed than others are to acquire the alien culture better suited to them, or if having acquired it their ancestry still counts against them, it becomes their interest to acquire a culture of their own as well suited to

---

[33] Quoted in Eric J. Hobsbawm, *The Age of Capital, 1848–1875* (New York: New American Library, 1979), p. 95.
[34] See Gellner's use of the term in *Thought and Change,* chap. 7 ("Nationalism"), and in *Nations and Nationalism,* pp. 31–33.

these opportunities as the alien culture. But this new culture cannot help but be in many ways an imitation of the alien one.[35]

If one aspect of this kind of cultural change is how individuals adjust to new and culturally different environments, another is the state's involvement with national culture in the era of nationalism, when national educational structures alone are big enough for the project of universal literacy and clerking skills. "But at the same time," Gellner argues,

> only the state is also strong enough to control so important and crucial a function. Culture . . . is now the necessary shared medium, the life-blood or perhaps rather minimal shared atmosphere, within which alone the members of the society can breathe and survive and produce. For a given society, it must be one in which they can *all* breathe and speak and produce; so it must be the *same* culture. Moreover, it must now be a great or high (literate, training-sustained) culture, and it can no longer be a diversified, locally-tied, illiterate little culture or tradition.[36]

Gellner's portrayal of the state's central and centralizing role as educator of modern nations applies, as we see in Chapter 1, to the educational policies of the Greater Romanian state. The crucial role of the state as educator and the importance of education in general in the building of modern nations are recognized by others as well. Anthony Smith, in some ways a sharp critic of "modernists" like Gellner, nonetheless concurs that the nation is "a mass educational enterprise" in modern times. Indeed, Smith argues that the "cultural revolution of the educator-state," that is, a revolution imparting national identity to all citizens, is third in a triptych, preceded by the economic or industrial revolution and the bureaucratic-military one.[37] Although Romania and other Eastern European states experienced belated and attenuated forms of the first two of these modernizing revolutions, they had all the more reason for a particularly vigorous version of the cultural revolution. It was this cultural-educational revolution that Romanian nation builders and educators hoped would facilitate the "digesting" of the human and territorial gains of 1918 and the solidifying of the Greater Romanian nation-state.

Finally, the focus on cultural work in an investigation of state and nation building is warranted by the salience of culture in the worldview of most nationalists.[38] The historian's need to empathize with her subject in order

[35] John Plamenatz, "Two Types of Nationalism," in *Nationalism: The Nature and Evolution of an Idea,* ed. Eugene Kamenka (London: Edward Arnold, 1976), pp. 32–33.
[36] Gellner, *Nations and Nationalism,* p. 37.
[37] Smith, *Ethnic Origins,* chap. 6 ("The Formation of Nations"), esp. pp. 133–137.
[38] According to Roman Szporluk, in the interwar period the *Weltanschauung* of the late 18th century proposing "a special linkage between the sphere of politics on the one hand

to understand it suggests the strategy of granting the nationalists their assumptions, all the while attempting to test them. This book thus follows the "homecoming" of the Romanian provinces to their cultural hearth as it investigates the arduousness and the politics of the process.

Politics in the 1920s:
From Parliamentarism toward the Abyss

Not only did Romania emerge from World War I demographically, socially, and territorially transformed, but the sphere of high politics was naturally also deeply affected by the events of the decade—the war, the reforms, and the country's tremendous expansion. Paul Shapiro has studied the difficulties of Romanian political parties in becoming truly national after the unification. He observes that "each of the political parties claiming to be 'national' after the war remained regional in outlook, organizational apparatus, and support base for some time. . . . In short, *the achievement of national territorial unity in the absence of national parties destabilized rather than stabilized Romania's political system.*"[39]

To put the account of Romania's cultural politics which follows in context, a brief overview of Romanian politics in the years 1918–1930 is necessary. Most striking about the chronicle of events is the unstable landscape, demonstrated by the frequent changes of government, the factionalism of the parties, and the leapfrog of political personalities from party to party. The power of the monarch to appoint governments that then organized parliamentary elections must be factored into the regularity with which those called to form cabinets succeeded in gaining legislative majorities. This feature of the political mechanism was heightened in 1926 when the Liberal Party passed legislation giving the party that won at least a 40 percent plurality—usually the party organizing the election—a "premium" of 50 percent of the seats plus a weighted proportion of the remaining seats. Although the opposition parties denounced the law as self-serving for the Liberals, they did not challenge it when they were in a position of power and thus benefiting from the premium themselves.

---

and that of culture—read: ethnicity—on the other" and . . . [holding] that "politics was an epiphenomenon of and therefore subordinate to culture" was dominant. Szporluk, "War by Other Means," *Slavic Review* 44 (Spring 1985): 20.

[39] Paul A. Shapiro, "Romania's Past as Challenge for the Future: A Developmental Approach to Interwar Politics," in *Romania in the 1980s,* ed. Daniel N. Nelson (Boulder, Colo.: Westview, 1981), p. 21. Shapiro concludes that Romania made impressive achievements in the interwar years toward greater political sophistication, and he claims also that increasing support for extremist right-wing parties was part of the progress. I consider this conclusion problematic.

Clearly, despite the sudden advent of universal male suffrage, inter-war Romania experienced at best a form of "managed" parliamentary democracy.

The immediate postwar years saw the demise of the Conservative Party, one of the two erstwhile "government" parties. Already weakened before 1914, the Conservatives fell as a result of their wartime pro-German sympathies and of the land and electoral reform that effectively wiped out the class of large landowners the party had traditionally represented. It was the Conservative Alexandru Marghiloman who had formed a pro-German government in the spring of 1918 and who had sued for peace with the Central Powers, measures that culminated in the imposition of harsh conditions and a several-months-long occupation of Romania. The one redeeming feature of this humiliating episode was the unexpected return to Romania of the province of Bessarabia in March 1918. In November, when the military balance once more shifted to the Allies, Marghiloman fell and Romania again fought with the Allies, but Bessarabia remained a part of Greater Romania. Marghiloman's government was followed by the month-long government of generals, headed by Constantin Coandă, which mobilized troops for the struggle for Transylvania.

The National Liberals also drew support from the landowning class, but theirs was the party of state-led industrialization, and, for those with long memories, of the ideals of 1848. As the sole surviving prewar government party, and as the party that had negotiated the return of Bukovina, Banat, and Transylvania both before entering the war and at the Paris Peace Conference at its conclusion, the Liberals became the oldest, strongest, and most prestigious interwar party. They shared in the nationalist consensus that dominated Romanian politics in the post–World War I era, though their nationalism was more moderate and conservative than the radical version championed by extremists of the new generation. The National Liberals' motto "through ourselves alone" advertised a Listian economic program from which Liberal-affiliated industrialists and financiers stood to profit. Until King Ferdinand's death in 1927, the monarch turned repeatedly to the Liberals as to a trusted ally.

The Liberals' first chance to govern came in December 1918, when they held power for almost a year. The Liberal premier Ion Brătianu spent much of the time in negotiations in Paris, but he resigned over the Allies' insistence that Romania strictly observe the terms of the Minorities Treaty, including the emancipation of Jews, long resisted by Romania since the nineteenth century. Brătianu was followed by a two-month long cabinet under General Văitoianu, who himself resigned before signing the treaty. The bloc of the National Party of Transylvania and the Peasantists under Alexandru Vaida-Voevod finally signed the treaty on December 29, 1919. The king dismissed this government in March 1920.

General Averescu, a war hero who had capitalized on wartime populist and anticorruption sentiment to form a People's League, later transformed into the People's Party, was then called to form a government. Averescu formed alliances with splinters of the Conservative Party and the National Party of Transylvania (the latter led by poet and journalist Octavian Goga). He also had the tacit support of the Liberals. In the elections organized in May 1920 the People's Party won 209 and the Liberals 17 out of 369 seats. Although a relatively minor political figure, Averescu passed a number of key measures. He unified the currencies of the new territories; he accomplished the administrative centralization of the new provinces, eliminating—to the displeasure of the provincials—the autonomous governing organs of Bukovina, Bessarabia, and Transylvania; he passed the land reform legislation that had been debated at length; and he severely repressed a left-wing labor upsurge. At least in some of these actions the general seemed to be the proxy of the Liberals. Averescu's popularity melted away within the year, and with the withdrawal of Liberal support, his government fell in December 1921.

In January 1922, the Liberals, headed by Ion Brătianu, assumed leadership of the country and retained control for much of the rest of the decade. This party was largely unpopular outside of the Old Kingdom, especially in Transylvania where the National Party was still hegemonic. In the elections of March 1922, Liberals received 260 seats while the People's Party dropped to 11. Thanks to their political machine and the disarray of the opposition, the most formidable of which were the National and the Peasant parties, the Liberals kept themselves in power. In October 1922, the Liberals staged the coronation of King Ferdinand as monarch of Greater Romania in the Transylvanian town of Alba Iulia, an event that the National Party boycotted despite its location and symbolism. The Liberals framed the Constitution of 1923, Article 1 of which stated that the Romanian Kingdom was unitary and indivisible, and they passed much more unificatory, centralizing, and nationalizing legislation, not the least of which concerned the system of educational institutions. The Liberals' 1920s program met with criticism particularly from the new provinces, the minorities, and the opposition parties. According to one historian, "the acts of unification and centralization were to the advantage of the Old Kingdom as against the provinces, of the Rumanians as against the minorities, and of the Liberal party as against all comers."[40]

The Liberal government served its full four-year term until 1926. It was succeeded briefly by another government headed by Averescu and an impartial cabinet headed by Prince Barbu Ştirbei, a relative of the Brătianu

---

[40] Henry Roberts, *Rumania: Political Problems of an Agrarian State* (New Haven, Conn.: Yale University Press, 1951), p. 118.

clan. Many Romanians felt that these regimes were nothing more than Liberal governments in disguise. The Liberals then returned to power "in person" in 1927, only to witness the deaths of King Ferdinand and of their own leader Ion I. C. Brătianu in the summer and fall of 1927, respectively. Vintilă Brătianu, who assumed the helm of the party, lacked his brother's prestige or political skill. His failure to get a much-needed foreign loan for Romania clinched the (temporary) demise of the Liberals.

In December 1928, in the first truly free elections of the interwar years, the National Peasant Party—formed through the 1926 union of the National Party of Transylvania and the Peasant Party of the Old Kingdom—won an overwhelming electoral victory. This party, much more democratic in its ethos and power base than its Liberal adversary, nevertheless failed to find effective and popular solutions to the country's intractable problems. Their failure, coming at the end of a decade of relative prosperity and the beginning of the worldwide economic crisis, marked "the beginning of the long descent into the abyss of 1940 and 1941"[41]—the abyss of fascist and authoritarian dictatorship.

Coupled with the National Peasant Party's failure was the return of King Carol to the throne on June 6, 1930. The National Peasants supported his restoration at the nadir of their popularity, hoping to be themselves strengthened by "having their own king" the way the Liberals had had Ferdinand until the latter's death in 1927. But the estranged monarch's restoration was also hailed by the youth faction of the Liberals led by Gheorghe Brătianu and by the spokesmen of the "new generation." The latter increasingly viewed the monarchy as a legitimate, native, political form, in contrast to the parliament and the parties deemed to be inappropriate grafts from the corrupt and decaying West. In this climate in the 1930s King Carol had a gradually widening mandate to manipulate the major parties, and, in 1938, to invest himself with dictatorial powers. He himself was then succeeded by an openly fascist government in 1940.

This book is organized into two parts. Both parts address the immense problems faced by nationalist elites of integrating the nation, but they highlight different settings and, to a large extent, different generations of actors.

Part I is a survey of the cultural work undertaken after the formation of Greater Romania. Here I focus on the theme of centralization and resistance to centralization, that is, on the regionalism manifested both by ethnic Romanians and non-Romanians, and on the efforts to Romanize towns, elites, and cultural institutions in Romania's new territories. In the first chapter I explore the educational policies of expansion and unification

[41] Ibid., p. 130.

originating in the post–World War I Romanian state, which was based disproportionately on the traditions and institutions of the Old Kingdom. The next three chapters delve into the cultural struggles in the new provinces annexed after World War I: Bukovina, Bessarabia, and Transylvania, each with its particular character. I wish to stress that the difficulties of state and nation building in Romania (and elsewhere) did not result solely from the presence of the ethnic minorities but also from the diverse identities and aspirations of the Romanians themselves. Chapter 5 is an investigation of the effects of the cultural, political, and social processes accompanying expansion and unification on politics and ideology at the "center," in the Old Kingdom, the original Romanian state. The Regat's reactions to the exigencies of expansion were crucial to the way the Greater Romanian state was shaped and to the emerging nationalist ideology of which anti-Semitism was an integral part.

In Part II I look at the same type of cultural struggles, this time in Romania's universities and in the hearts and minds of the "new generation." In Chapter 6 I examine the universities as institutions that were crucial both to the state, whose policies are analyzed in Part I, and to the socially, politically, and ideologically important "new generation." The universities were expected to generate a Romanian elite large enough to attend to the bureaucratic tasks of the expanded state; and yet, paradoxically, because of the explosive expansion of higher education, the question of an "intellectual proletariat" also arose. In the final chapter I examine the extreme nationalist ideology of protofascist nationalist students. Although far to the right of mainstream nationalism, the ideology and politics of the "generation of 1922" were legitimated by the mobilization and discourse that the state itself had engendered in its nation-building activities. In the 1930s this generation gave rise to a full-fledged fascist movement, best known as the Iron Guard.

I

CULTURAL STRUGGLES:

UNIFICATION, ROMANIZATION,

AND REGIONALISM

1

The State on the
Cultural Offensive

The integration of our kin [*neamului*] demands, in the first place, the unification of the educational establishment into a unique type of unitary school. In Romania's boundaries there are today four types of school organization that have developed under different circumstances and influences, and that have cut out for themselves particular life traditions. . . . The school must everywhere provoke a freshening of the spirit; to awaken the national consciousness to Romanian life and culture and to solidify the spiritual unity of all Romanians. Only by enlightening and strengthening the national consciousness can we boost the kin's vital powers and [power to] resist all the assaults from without and within, and ensure the endurance of our dominion in the Kingdom's new boundaries.

—Constantin Angelescu, 1924

Both "old" and "new" Romanians fought for the union of the new lands and the Old Kingdom; nevertheless, the unification was accomplished largely under the aegis and on the terms of the Old Kingdom whose institutions played a disproportionate role in the expanded state. Transylvanians, Bukovinians, and Bessarabians participated alongside the Regăţeni in the ongoing changes and institutional mergers, but the power structure of Greater Romania favored the Regat's reactions to the growing pains of the country and its solutions to the problems caused by the assimilation of new, diverse territories and populations. In short, institutionally and politically the Old Kingdom was the cornerstone of the Greater Romanian state.

Festive inauguration of the primary school "Priest Simeon Moruzov" in Zebil, Tulcea County, November 8, 1937. Courtesy of Cabinetul de Stampe, Biblioteca Academiei, Bucharest

Old Kingdom Educational Traditions

The educational structures in the Regat at the time of the Great Union were the product of nineteenth-century reforms. By introducing free and compulsory education before many other European countries, the reform law of 1864 marked for Romania "the beginning of a new school order." It was deemed exceptionally advanced for its time and among the most progressive in the world.[1] But compulsory education existed only on paper. The lack of buildings and qualified teachers, and the population's indigence and inertia kept over 50 percent of school–age children unschooled before World War I.[2] Illiteracy prevailed accordingly: 78 percent overall, and in

[1] See Onisifor Ghibu, "Probleme de organizare a învăţământului românesc, Cursuri ţinute la Seminarul Pedagogic universitar din Cluj, parte din *Cursurile de directori al învăţământului secundar şi din Cursurile pentru revizorii şcolari din Transilvania*" (1929), p. 12 [notes taken by an auditor], Ms., Arhiva O. Ghibu; and Ministerul învăţământului, *Istoria învăţământului din România* (Bucharest: Editura didactică şi pedagogică, 1971), p. 118.

[2] Ministerul învăţământului, *Istoria învăţământului*, p. 122, and Constantin Kiriţescu, "Haret, pedagog şi reformator şcolar," in *Comemorarea lui Spiru Haret de către Academia de Ştiinţe din România în şedinţa din 19 ianuarie 1943*, Publicaţiile Academiei de Ştiinţe din România, 3d ser.: Memorii şi monografii, no. 1, pp. 23–24. In 1904, only 41 percent of school-age children attended school.

the countryside as many as 85 percent of Romanians could not read and write in 1899.[3]

These conditions inspired Spiru Haret's school reforms. Haret's career in the Ministry of Education began in 1885, when he became secretary general to the Liberal minister Dumitru Sturdza.[4] Later Haret himself served as minister of education three times under Liberal administrations: 1897–1899, 1901–1904, and 1907–1910.[5] In a related endeavor, Haret wrote *Chestia țărănească* (The peasant question) in 1905, a work treating the subject from a stance of "enlightened populism."[6] Searching for ways to relieve the distress of the peasantry and resolve the "peasant question," Haret diagnosed the problem as one of culture.[7] His reforms were supposed to render the schools an effective means of "struggle against life's hardships" for peasants.[8] Having learned arithmetic, for example, the peasants could keep their books properly and avoid getting swindled by banks, moneylenders, landlords, and lease holders.[9]

In order to turn the schools to the peasants' advantage, and the peasant into "an educated producer," Haret broke with educational tradition in placing rural priorities over urban ones and practical matters over theoretical.[10] Haret's emphasis on agricultural education increasingly resembled "a militant campaign," as he called upon teachers and priests to mobilize their classrooms and congregations to change the face of the countryside.[11] He also urged teachers to help with rural banks and leasing cooperatives, and to lead such extracurricular cultural activities as reading circles, adult literacy classes, and conferences.[12] Based on the understanding that much more than a few years in school was necessary to truly raise the cultural level

---

[3] See Ministerul instrucțiunii, *Lege pentru învățământul primar al statului (școale de copii mici, școale primare, școale și cursuri de adulți, școalele și clasele speciale pentru copii debili și anormali educabili) și învățământul normal-primar* (Bucharest: Editura Cartea românească, 1925), pp. 77–78.

[4] Gheorghe Adamescu, "Biografia lui Spiru Haret," in Spiru C. Haret, *Operele,* vol. 1 (Bucharest: Editura Cartea românească, [1912?]), p. xxix.

[5] Emil Bâldescu, *Spiru Haret în știință, filozofie, politică, pedagogie, învățămînt* (Bucharest: Editura didactică și pedagogică, 1972), p. 187.

[6] Titu Georgescu and Ion Ilincioiu, "Intelectualitatea și răscoala țăranilor," in *Marea răscoală a țăranilor din 1907,* ed. Andrei Oțetea and Ion Popescu-Puțuri (Bucharest: Editura Academiei R. S. R., 1967), pp. 656–657. A second edition of the pamphlet was published in 1907.

[7] See Adamescu, "Biografia," p. xxxvii.

[8] Catherine Durandin, "Une Image de l'idéologie nationale roumaine: La voie de l'état nation paysan," CNRS, Paris, December 9–12, 1981, p. 12.

[9] Wilhelm Filderman, "My Life," Ms., Yad Vashem Archives, Jerusalem (hereafter YV), P 6 2-I, p. 31.

[10] Bâldescu, *Spiru Haret,* p. 249, and Durandin, "Image de l'idéologie," pp. 12–14.

[11] Durandin, "Image de l'idéologie," p. 14.

[12] Bâldescu, *Spiru Haret,* p. 248, and Damian Hurezeanu and Mircea Iosa, "Situația socio-economică și politică a țărănimii la începutul secolului al xx-lea," in Oțetea and Popescu-Puțuri, eds., *1907,* pp. 117–118.

Rural primary school building of the "Spiru Haret" type built at the turn of the century. This "generic" school was erected according to standard blueprints drawn by the Architectural Service of the Ministry of Cults and Public Instruction. The word over the door is "SCHOOL." Courtesy of Arhivele Statului, Bucharest

of the masses, Haret's innovations broadened the concept of schooling. Although his success was at best partial, his intention of making the schools and the teachers accessible and useful to the peasantry remained one of the great ideas in Romanian social and pedagogical thought for much of the twentieth century.[13]

Haret's broadly defined educational effort belongs squarely in the context of the Liberal Party's industrialization program for the Romanian economy during a period of declining world grain prices.[14] The Popular Banks Law of 1903 and the Village Cooperatives (obştii săteşti) Law of 1904 were intended to establish a viable village economy and a complementary domestic market for native industry. The Sunday cultural circles in which Haret encouraged teachers and priests to participate fostered popular banks and the village cooperatives.[15] Beginning in 1898, extracurricular cultural institutions became the nuclei of an alternative rural social struc-

---

[13] Bâldescu, Spiru Haret, p. 248. Nicolae Iorga's criticism was that "the rural school . . . was not even after Spiru Haret's reforms a means of elevating the peasant in his own place, but rather one to uproot him from his environment and to make him desert to town." Cited in Andrei Oţetea, "Istoriografia răscoalei," in Oţetea and Popescu-Puţuri, eds., 1907, p. 22.

[14] Philip Gabriel Eidelberg, The Great Romanian Peasant Revolt of 1907: Origins of a Modern Jacquerie (Leiden: Brill, 1974), pp. 71–72.

[15] Gheorghe Taşcă, "Haret ca economist social," in Comemorarea lui Spiru Haret, p. 15.

ture.[16] They challenged the power of landlords, *arendaşi* (leaseholders), and moneylenders, to whom the peasantry was economically, if not legally, enserfed.[17] Although existing rural power structures were never really dislodged before World War I, the networks of schools, popular banks, and cooperatives, together with the populist and Liberal propaganda among the peasantry, combined in 1907 to mobilize the peasants to violent rebellion after a new corn tax was imposed.

Haret became minister of education again in the Liberal government that came to power after the 1907 jacquerie. In this capacity he wrote a report to King Carol I on the activities of teachers and priests in the countryside on the eve of the revolt. This work attempted to minimize the role of rural intellectuals in the radicalization of the peasantry while simultaneously pleading with the priests and teachers to use their influence to pacify the peasantry.[18] The report leaves the impression that village intellectuals were in fact an important link in the class struggles of the countryside. As Georgescu and Ilincioiu have written about Haret:

> [Although] far from being a standard bearer of the peasants' uprising, the accusations brought by the conservatives against Spiru Haret as instigator of the villages' revolt are not completely baseless. He did not urge [any] uprisings, he did not approve of them, he even condemned them, but the complex of his actions was corroborated by factors fostering a spirit of dissatisfaction . . . [in] the Romanian village at the end of the nineteenth and the beginning of the twentieth century.[19]

More important perhaps is that the Romanian establishment under the influence of the Conservative Party viewed the activity of village intellectuals as dangerous to the fragile social stability of the village. Haret had himself set out to coopt radical socialists and channel their energies into a legal, Liberal Party–led movement. But this attempt at cooptation and moderation was itself radicalized by the forces in the countryside. In the aftermath of the 1907 uprising, administrative, judicial, and military authorities assigned responsibility for the revolt to teachers and priests who, they claimed, had transgressed and misinterpreted the Haret-instigated general program of extracurricular cultural activities.[20]

---

[16] Vladimir Ghidionescu, "Spiru Haret: Resumatul unei conferinţe ţinută la Cluj în Decembrie 1932," *Cuget clar* 6 (January–February 1933): 119–120.

[17] For the concept of "neoserfdom," see Constantin Dobrogeanu-Gherea, *Neoiobăgia,* 2d ed. (Bucharest: Viaţa românească, n.d.).

[18] Eidelberg, *Great Revolt,* pp. 190, 227, and Georgescu and Ilincioiu, "Intelectualitatea," pp. 664–665, 669.

[19] Georgescu and Ilincioiu, "Intelectualitatea," p. 657.

[20] Ibid., pp. 649–650.

Haret's Legacy

Romania's territorial expansion in 1918 provoked educational crises and stimulated school reforms. The interwar period saw a flurry of ministerial and legislative activity in the sphere of education. Between 1918 and 1924 alone, the Ministry of Education changed hands eleven times.[21] But the National Liberal Party, which held power the longest, had the greatest impact. Constantin Angelescu served as minister of education under National Liberal governments in 1919, 1922–1927, and 1933–1937. Symbolic of the National Liberals' aggressive cultural policies was their use of the term "cultural offensive" to describe their program of national unification by means of the school.[22] The two-pronged offensive consisted of expanding the educational network and unifying the four systems and traditions extant in Greater Romania.

During the interwar period, Haret's achievements inspired his successors. The most influential of these was Constantin Angelescu, who greatly admired Haret's ability to increase the number of schools, teachers, and pupils, and to raise literacy levels. According to Angelescu, Haret had built almost two thousand new primary schools and had opened 1,700 new teaching posts, doubling the number of pupils in primary schools to 600,000 and raising literacy from 22 to 39 percent of the population between 1897 and 1911.[23] This success notwithstanding, the highly charged nature of Haret's reforms and the potentially explosive effects of this type of cultural expansion could not have escaped his heirs and admirers. Yet in the interwar context, Haret's legacy resonated less ominously to reformers than one might expect for several reasons: first, by 1921 a very extensive land reform was implemented which answered some of the peasants' needs; second, the condition of the peasantry may have improved as a direct consequence of Haret's own efforts;[24] and third, Haret's nationalism made his social radicalism more palatable.

Instead of restaging Haret's work with its original social emphasis, interwar leaders undertook to exploit Haret's heritage for different ends,

[21] See Onisifor Ghibu, "Alte măşti, aceiaşi piesă. Cu prilejul discuţiei proiectului de lege a învăţământului primar în Parlamentul României întregite," in his *Prolegomena la o pedagogie românească* (Bucharest: Editura Cultura românească, 1941), p. 368, and Arhiva O. Ghibu, "Consideraţii generale cu privire la reforma învăţământului," Ms., pp. 4, 7, 10.

[22] As late as 1927 teacher conferences discussed the need to continue the cultural offensive. See Arhivele statului, Bucureşti, Fond Ministerul instrucţiunii şi cultelor (hereafter MIC), 1928/32/79.

[23] Constantin Angelescu, "Treizeci de ani dela moartea lui Spiru Haret," in *Comemorarea lui Spiru Haret*, p. 2. Haret's achievements are also cited in Bâldescu, *Spiru Haret*, pp. 303–304, 313–314, and in Ghidionescu, "Spiru Haret," p. 118.

[24] Henry L. Roberts, *Rumania: Political Problems of an Agrarian State* (New Haven, Conn.: Yale University Press, 1951), p. 31. Gheorghe Taşcă has suggested that Haret had only brought the Romanian peasantry from hopeless misery to ordinary poverty, in itself an enormous accomplishment. Taşcă, "Haret ca economist social," pp. 18–19.

namely to erase regional boundaries (rather than social ones) and to fight against the difficulties of the Romanian nation as a whole (rather than against the specific hardships of peasant life). While the danger of Haret's formula, as evidenced by the events of 1907, could not have been forgotten, such potency may have had a certain positive appeal, now that the goal of the state—nation building—coincided with the aspirations of an ethnically defined Romanian society. The cultural expansion project thus shed its destabilizing connotations, and interwar leaders saw it as a positive and powerful prospect: cultural mobilization could make the state secure and the nation united. Although Haret's successors once again directed education policy mainly at the peasantry, this class was now considered the reservoir from which the enlarged nation could draw force and form the elites that would extend the state into the new provinces.

Expansion

By "spreading and democratizing public education" Constantin Angelescu was "continuing [the work of Spiru] Haret forcefully and conscientiously."[25] Like Haret, Angelescu began with the observation that despite "compulsory" primary education, illiteracy was extremely high and vast numbers of children did not attend school, in both the old and the new territories (table 4).

Much of the underschooling of these children resulted from the inadequate number and condition of schools and classrooms, partly due to wartime destruction.[26] The cultural offensive sought to accommodate more children through a vigorous campaign of construction and renovation of school buildings. In four years, from 1922 to 1926, 4,007 new primary schools were built, 268 were bought, and 889 underwent radical repairs; 660 were still under construction in 1926. In addition, 1,511 new houses were built to serve as school directors' homes. Altogether, these constituted an impressive 7,335 new buildings in the service of elementary education.[27] By 1928 close to 7,800 new schools had been built. Almost 4,000 primary schools were built during Angelescu's second long term in office, 1933–1937. The number of primary schools increased from 7,915 before union, to 8,081 in 1918–1919, reaching 17,385 in 1937–1938.[28] The expansion

[25] Heinz Brandsch, *Pedagogi români contemporani*, Biblioteca învățătorilor, no. 8, trans. [from German] V. Beneş (Cluj: Editura revistei Satul şi şcoala, 1937), p. 33.

[26] A French observer blamed the low levels of primary education in Romania on the scarcity of buildings. Marcel Gillard, *La Roumanie nouvelle* (Paris: Alcon, 1922), p. 16. See also Constantin Angelesco, *Activité du Ministère de l'instruction, 1922–1926* (Bucharest: Editura Cartea românească, 1928), p. 10.

[27] Ibid., p. 17.

[28] Constantin Angelescu, *Evoluţia învăţământului primar şi secundar în ultimii 20 de ani* (Bucharest: Imprimeriile curentul, n.d.), pp. 12, 19.

Table 4. Literacy rates, by province, pre– and post–World War I

	Prewar (1897–1912) (%)	1930 (%)
Greater Romania		57.0
Old Kingdom	39.3[a]	55.8
Transylvania	51.1[b]	67.0
Bukovina	45.2[b]	65.7
Bessarabia	19.4[c]	38.1

Source: Enciclopedia României, vol. 1, pp. 142–143.
[a] 1912
[b] 1910
[c] 1897

of elementary schooling can also be judged by the increase in the number of elementary school teachers. Before the Great Union, Romania had 7,915 primary schools and 12,118 elementary school teachers. Both schools and teachers multiplied over the next two decades. By 1938 there were 47,914 teachers staffing Greater Romania's 17,385 state primary schools.[29]

Many teacher-training schools, known as "normal schools," were necessary to prepare instructors. The construction of 43 new normal schools began, although not all were finished, in 1923–1937. The construction of many other buildings was undertaken to move existing schools from rental to state-owned property.[30] Academic secondary schools also increased; from 1919 to 1928, their number grew from 67 to 356.[31] Already in 1919 many had been opened in the Old Kingdom in an attempt to catch up with the new provinces. A decree passed on September 9, 1919, to encourage the establishment of gymnasia and girls' schools and the transformation of gymnasia into lycées declared: "The comparison of our secondary education [in the Old Kingdom] with that of the new Romanian provinces is totally to our disadvantage: we have not only proportionally, but even in absolute numbers, fewer schools than in Transylvania, Bukovina, and Bessarabia."[32] Despite the element of competition with the new provinces, school construction also proceeded in the new provinces, where secondary schools, though more numerous, were also insufficient.[33] Angelescu justified the overall effort on the grounds of the peasantry's changed situation: "The great war that produced the profound democratization of peoples has certainly created for our rural population a different situation from

[29] Ibid., p. 19.
[30] Ibid., pp. 14–16, and Angelesco, Activité, pp. 17–18.
[31] Angelescu, Evoluția, p. 26.
[32] Angelesco, Activité, p. 24.
[33] Ibid., pp. 25–27, 36–37.

that which preceded 1916. Universal suffrage and the land allotment for the peasants have also transformed the material and moral state of this population. This situation therefore imperiously demanded that the popular masses be cultivated and enlightened . . . in the shortest possible time and in the most profound way."[34]

School Committees

As Romania's interwar state budgets could not by themselves sustain such a rapid expansion of the school system, much of the financial and labor costs incurred were paid with private monies garnered through school committees,[35] a network of which came into being with Decree No. 3138 in July 1919.[36] Though the school committees are generally associated with the name of Constantin Angelescu, they had a precedent in the short-lived *eforii* that Simion Mehedinți established in 1918 during his term as minister of education in the Marghiloman government.[37] In the Regat Casa școalelor had fulfilled a limited version of these committees' functions since 1896.[38] Angelescu traced his idea of school committees to his 1917 mission to the United States. He explained his vision of the new committees, in the spring of 1919: "Through the new organization of the School Committees each commune will have, from now on, the school its citizens desire. Our hope is that the care of citizens for their children's school of learning will hereafter be as great as it was in the past for their village or town church. They will be the founders of the school's construction with their money, their labor, [and] their hearts."[39]

In 1924, these school committees came under scrutiny on the occasion of the Primary School Reform Bill parliamentary debates. The Transylvanian-born Liberal senator Ştefan Pop defended them as worthy instruments of national consolidation:

When you request of the citizen that he come and contribute with his labor for his school, you will no longer have citizens estranged from the State's interests. When you enter a village and you see a magnificent building, if you ask a child, an old man, or a woman: "What is this building?" you will get the answer: "Sir, this is our school, this is our church," and not as before: "this is the State's school or church." Let everyone become aware that the

---

[34] Angelesco, *Activité*, p. 4.
[35] Angelescu, *Evoluția*, pp. 12, 15, 16.
[36] Constantin Hamangiu, *Codul general al României: Legi uzuale*, vol. 9–10 (Bucharest: Alcalay, 1919–1922), pp. 127–144.
[37] See Simion Mehedinți, "Numerus clausus," *Ideea europeană*, August 17, 1919, p. 203, and Angelescu, *Evoluția*, p. 16.
[38] See Arhivele statului, București, Fond Casa școalelor (hereafter CS), 1919/4/1.
[39] Ibid.

school is theirs. This is the way it should be. . . . The citizen will know . . .
that his duty is not only to feed his wife and children and take care of his
assets, but that besides this there is something else, namely that the best part
of his work should be for the State.[40]

Collectively, the school committees became, as planned, the principal
builder of new schools. Angelescu was satisfied that the "appeal . . .
addressed to the peasantry had had an unexpected response, and given
admirable results." He said that, "Everywhere the rural population had
risen with unforeseen élan, and with its own donations and labor had built
in all the corners of the country new seats of national culture."[41] In their
enthusiasm, the peasants had had guidance. The teachers who, like "true
apostles of the people's enlightenment," had urged the peasantry to make
any sacrifice for the building of schools, were joined by county prefects,
county administrators, mayors, priests, and school inspectors.[42] In effect,
all types of local notables, along with the peasants and school alumni,
made up the school committees.

People who could afford to contribute land, money, and produce did
so, while the poorer folk gave their labor, their time, and their cattle-
drawn carts. The state contributed wood and some cash. The number of
schools built in this way was most impressive at the primary school level
because of the mass participation and number of buildings involved, but the
construction of normal and academic secondary schools was also largely
financed by school committees. Even more than primary schools, secondary
schools were left to their own material devices. The Ministry of Education
supplied little more than control, curriculum, and staff. Here, everything
from physical maintenance, to teaching aids, libraries, cafeterias, and even
the staffing of extrabudgetary classes was the responsibility of school committees.[43] Besides mobilizing resources for school construction, the school
committees, at their best, provided a way of "harmonizing the sometimes
radically different points of view of the school, on the one hand, and of
the parents, on the other, [a way of] "capturing both series of forces."[44]
Moreover, the committees enforced attendance by applying fines for absen-
teeism.[45]

[40] Ministerul instrucţiunii, *Lege pentru învăţământul primar al statului* (Bucharest: Editura
Cartea românească, 1925), p. 190.
[41] Angelescu, *Evoluţia*, p. 12.
[42] Ibid., pp. 12, 13.
[43] Ibid., pp. 13, 16, 17.
[44] Ion Zamfirescu, "Contribuţiuni documentare şi interpretative pentru istoricul liceului
'Gh. Lazăr,' 1860–1935," in *Monografia Liceului "Gh. Lazăr" din Bucureşti, 1860–1935,
cu prilejul împlinirii a 75 de ani dela înfiinţarea lui*, ed. Ion Zamfirescu (Bucharest: Luceafărul,
1935), p. 101.
[45] Dimitrie Gusti, ed., *Un an de activitate la Ministerul instrucţiei cultelor şi artelor,
1932–1933* (Bucharest: Tip. Bucovina, 1934), p. 710.

The school committees themselves must have played a role in generating enthusiasm for the schools, especially among the rural population. They harnessed popular energy and financial resources toward the project of school expansion. They also communicated to the Ministry of Education the aspirations of their communities, legitimated by the work and money contributed locally. Educational expansion thus became a stake in the negotiations between local and national centers of power, within an increasingly nationalist discourse.

Expansion or Dilution?

The "cultural offensive" suffered only temporary and minor reversals, for the Liberals returned to power time and again to pick up where they had left off; however, Angelescu's ambitious program of school expansion did not altogether escape criticism from other educational and political leaders. In fact, the number of schools at all levels shrank after 1928 because of the economic crisis and perhaps also because the National Peasant and Averescu's People's Parties considered Angelescu's Liberal program of school expansion frenetic and unsound. New growth in the number of schools, teachers, and pupils occurred during Angelescu's second long term as Minister of Education, although it did not reach quite its former pace.[46] People criticized Angelescu precisely for his most obvious accomplishment, that of opening up large numbers of new schools. P. P. Negulescu, former minister of education under the Averescan government of 1920–1921, referred to the "excessive dilution" of teaching since the war, aggravated by the "dizzying multiplication . . . of normal schools, lycées, and gymnasia."[47] Commenting on the rapid rise in normal schools in particular, Negulescu wrote:

> It is not difficult to imagine in what conditions the number of these schools could have *tripled* in such a short time—during which the number of regular secondary schools also doubled, and that of the secondary vocational schools also grew, true, to a lesser degree, but grew nevertheless. . . . Of what quality could the quickly improvised teaching staff of all of these schools established *en masse* have been? It is a question that it is better not to answer.[48]

Rather than applaud Angelescu's feat of rapid school expansion, Negulescu complained that Romanian schools would be plagued by the graduates of the many new poor-quality schools for the following thirty-five

[46] Angelescu, *Evoluția*, pp. 19–20, 26–27.
[47] Petre P. Negulescu, *Reforma învățământului*, 2d ed. (Bucharest: Editura Casei Școalelor, 1927), pp. xcviii–xcix.
[48] Ibid., p. cxi.

years.[49] He also criticized the mobilization of private initiative through the school committees to raise funds for school construction, charging that a resulting lack of direction had "led to chaos in the construction campaign," and even to "a new type of ruin"—unfinished brick buildings, "waiting for years at a time to be at least covered [by a roof], slowly but surely worn down by intemperate weather."[50] Wilhelm Filderman, the president of the Union of Romanian Jews, was also distressed by the low quality of teachers, who under the Angelescu ministry included too many substitutes,[51] and by a general lack of solidity. He reproached Angelescu that, "without buildings, without a teaching staff worthy of the name, you continued to spread yourself on the surface, spreading thinner and thinner that which you pretended to consolidate."[52]

Dimitrie Gusti, Romania's foremost interwar sociologist and minister of education under the National Peasant government in 1932–1933, viewed Angelescu's school expansion work as hyperbolic and unrealistic. Gusti and his associates identified it with the exuberance prevailing after the war, intimating that a partly illusory optimism had enveloped everything at that time, including financial dealings. An apparent prosperity and the availability of easy credit fuelled such excesses as the establishment of too many schools. Once the mood passed, the inappropriateness of this exaggerated growth was quite obvious. According to Vasile Băncilă:

> After the war, we had . . . an almost general optimism. Greater Romania, with its need for cadre, with an opportunity for convenient financial foreign loans, and with a seductive agricultural prosperity, although it lasted only a few years, filled out the state apparatus and the number of schools to excess. At the basis of this process was a [certain] mentality. But today we are witnessing the bankruptcy of this mentality, and . . . the very crisis of the artificial bourgeois state which we created. We need a state with fewer cadre, [one] more suited to the structure of a people of peasants.[53]

Angelescu was of course furious at the undoing of his work by Averescan and National Peasant regimes. These governments were guilty, in Angelescu's eyes, of closing schools he had managed to open in such spectacular numbers, of "annihilating the energies" he had aroused during the cultural offensive, of "dissolving school committees and prohibiting that activity only in order to frustrate that work as if it did not belong to

---

[49] Ibid.
[50] Ibid., p. clxxxv.
[51] Filderman, "My Life," pp. 465–466.
[52] Ibid., pp. 474–509.
[53] Vasile Băncilă, "Învățământul secundar (Considerații generale)," in Gusti, *Un an*, p. 888.

the [whole] country."[54] Even when schools were suppressed as a result of the economic crisis Angelescu was indignant. In a speech made in December 1931, he applauded the handling of the economic crisis in France, Yugoslavia, and Czechoslovakia, where, despite the hardships, nobody had dared to touch the schools. Of Czechoslovakia Angelescu observed: "There is a crisis in all spheres, in commerce, in industry, and in the other branches of activity, but conscious of its mission, the Czechoslovak people assumes all the sacrifices, just in order that its schools and culture may remain strong."[55]

Unification and Regionalism

Angelescu's program was as much about expanding and democratizing the educational process as it was about unifying the four school systems inherited from prewar political structures. In fact, in Angelescu's writings about educational policies, school expansion is subordinated to the goal of unification, which generally receives first priority. In an overview of interwar educational developments, Angelescu wrote:

One of the first cultural problems posed immediately after the war was the spiritual unification of all the citizens of this country through [the institution of] the school; for we must not forget that until the union our school system, four distinct organizations in the four annexed provinces, had been subjected to different cultural influences that left profound marks on our spiritual structure, marks which, of course, weakened our national consciousness.[56]

The four educational systems unified in a gradual process that allowed for transitional stages of regional institutional autonomy. Following a "single directive," transitional institutions in each province were supposed to facilitate the supreme goals: a harmonious state life and the achievement of full national consciousness. In practice, Angelescu found the transitional autonomous educational administrations treacherous and counterproductive, and he put an early end to them. "The organs of transition" he wrote, "were supposed from the beginning to strive to follow this single directive; [but] hesitations and even attempts to remove this directive from the beginning made it necessary [to introduce] measures . . . to reduce their prerogatives more and more."[57]

[54] Biblioteca Academiei R. S. R. (this is the pre-1989 name for the Biblioteca Academiei române), Bucureşti, Colecţia de manuscrise, Arhiva Constantin Angelescu (hereafter AA), xv/ Varia 2.
[55] Ibid.
[56] Angelescu, *Evoluţia,* p. 10.
[57] AA xv/ Varia 1, [n.d.], 1922.

As the next three chapters reveal in more detail, some Romanians in the new provinces, and certainly many non-Romanians, resented the policies of centralization, considering them insensitive and premature. Onisifor Ghibu was a prominent Romanian Transylvanian nationalist educator who maintained an intense interest in educational policy even after the dissolution of Transylvania's Directing Council, in which he had served as Secretary General of Education. In a paper on the education reform projects, he argued that the educational unification policies were unnatural, or "formal," since they did not allow the desired fusion to happen gradually. As a result, the individual regions, all with their own particular defects, were not able to resolve these problems prior to centralization and ended up bringing them along into the Greater Romanian state.[58] Bessarabia, which was more backward than the other Romanian provinces, offers a case in point. Ghibu wrote in 1925: "The unification of education *now* is an absurdity. How can you put Bessarabia *all at once* on the same level with the other provinces? It needs a period of *revival* of at least ten years [to allow] the cultural values of the other provinces to seep into the blood of the [Bessarabian] population, which is still under the mirage of Russian culture, or ignorance."[59] Meanwhile, to Ghibu, this rapid unification meant that the rich cultural "dowries" of the new territories could not be recognized or incorporated into the new order either.[60]

Transitional Institutions

The transition to a school system unified throughout the entire Greater Romanian territory was administered by several sets of institutions. Transylvania had a semi-autonomous transitional government called Consiliul Dirigent (the Directing Council), Bessarabia had Sfatul Țării, which dissolved itself in 1918 to be followed by Consiliul de Directori (the Directors' Council), and Bukovina had a number of Secretariate de Serviciu (Department Secretariats).[61] The three provisional administrations, including their educational departments, were dismantled in April 1920, and various ministries in Bucharest took over their powers, supposedly continuing to apply, for the time being, existing provincial legislation (three sets of it). This willful and rather sudden attempt at centralization did not succeed in imposing perfect uniformity. The three disparate legislative systems of the

[58] Ibid.
[59] Arhiva O. Ghibu, Onisifor Ghibu, "Reforma învățământului? Document în formă de note," 1925, Ms. p. 2.
[60] Ghibu, "Considerații," p. 4. Transylvania's "dowry" was especially rich and valuable, according to Ghibu, since the province had given all the other Romanian provinces cultural "reawakeners." See "Expunere de motive și proectul de lege a organizării Ministerului instrucți-unii (primul proect) (1929)," AA I/ Ms. 1.
[61] AA I/ Ms. 1, and AA XV/ Varia 1, [n.d.], 1922.

new provinces required a new set of decentralized institutions, the General Secretariats of Cluj, Chişinău, and Cernăuţi. These organizations were to work closely with the appropriate central government branches during the period of liquidation of provincial rule.[62] But even the General Secretariats (and their successors from March 24, 1921, the General Directorates), which officially had no local initiative but were strictly limited to acting as provincial offices of the Bucharest ministries, were from Bucharest's perspective guilty of "vague regionalist" sentiments and insubordination.[63]

To Bucharest bureaucrats, subtle or not so subtle acts of sabotage of the unification process seemed to occur everywhere. The Bukovinian Education Secretariat, for example, resisted giving up its autonomy by refusing to honor Old Kingdom tenure lists and refusing to recall minority inspectors. It made appointments without ministerial approval, it did not welcome transfers of Old Kingdom schools to Bukovina, and it opposed the unification of the lycée program of study with that of the Old Kingdom. It was humiliating to Regat pride that a pupil from the Old Kingdom enrolled in a lycée in Bukovina was "in danger of being left back" because the curricula differed.[64]

Similarly, Regat officials viewed the Bessarabian Education Directorate with suspicion. The first director, Pantelimon Erhan, described in a ministry document as "the protector of all the foreigners in Bessarabia," was accused of abuses against the Romanians sent to Bessarabia from the Old Kingdom, while a successor was described as lacking the energy to protect the Directorate from foreign influences. The ministry was particularly frustrated with the Chişinău Directorate because it replaced Regat teachers with Bessarabian ones who did not know Romanian very well. Moreover, it made these appointments on the basis of Russian legislation, a codification of which the ministry was unable to obtain despite repeated requests.[65] Regăţeni teaching in Bessarabia complained of attempts to push them aside in favor of Bessarabians and claimed that when the local directorate wanted "to get rid of a candidate from the Old Kingdom, he is made to compete with a substitute teacher who has tenure under the previous Russian laws, and in this way the Romanian candidate is turned down."[66]

In 1922, Angelescu abolished the General Directorates of Education. In their place Romania was divided into sixteen school districts, or regional inspectorates. At the time this measure was officially described as a "decen-

---

[62] AA xv/ Varia 1, n.d.

[63] AA i/ Ms. 1, n.d., and AA xv/ Varia 1, [n.d.], 1922. See also D. Tomescu, "Administraţia în Ardeal, după desfiinţarea Consiliului Dirigent," in *Transilvania, Banatul, Crişana, Maramureşul,* vol. 1 (Bucharest: Cultura naţională, 1929), p. 751.

[64] AA xv/ Varia 1, [n.d.], 1922.

[65] Ibid.

[66] AA ix/ Varia 11, n.d.

tralization," sometimes even a "broad decentralization."[67] But the sixteen districts were perhaps more appropriately characterized in 1929 as the "simple executive organs" of the central ministerial administration.[68]

Educational Reform

Reforms in 1924, 1925, and 1928 affecting primary, secondary, and private education followed the administrative centralization. The main goal of this legislation was the legal unification of the separately evolved educational institutions of the new and old provinces and the creation of a single, uniform, centralized school system. Angelescu drafted all three reform bills, which included small and large pedagogical changes. The primary school bill of 1924 lengthened primary education to seven grades by adding three complementary grades to the four previously mandated in the Old Kingdom. It reemphasized the obligatory nature of elementary education and made adult courses for illiterates compulsory up to the age of eighteen.[69] The private education bill of 1925 concerned mainly minority denominational schools, although all private schools using a language of instruction other than Romanian were under its purvue.[70] The 1928 secondary education bill reduced secondary schooling from eight to seven grades, changed a trifurcated lycée to a single-track one, and limited the maximum number of pupils in gymnasium and lycée classes.[71]

The three pieces of legislation also formalized the piecemeal decrees and administrative measures introduced since 1918 to deal with the exigencies of expansion. These included inter alia articles on the school committees and on the "cultural zone" instituted in 1920 to provide higher salaries and benefits for teachers willing to take jobs in Romania's new multilingual regions. The "cultural zone" required more intensive work from teachers both in class and in extracurricular activities. The zone nearly formed a half-circle from the northwest to the southeast (southern Dobrudja) of Romania. Encompassing mostly border areas, it was likened in one memo to a "cultural cordon"—an analogy perhaps to the *cordon sanitaire* with which Western statesmen had wanted to surround revolutionary Russia.[72] The bills devoted attention to the teaching (in Romanian) of Romanian language, history, geography and civics in non-Romanian schools, and to school instruction in languages other than that of the state, the concern

[67] Ibid.

[68] "Expunere de motive."

[69] Ministerul instrucţiunii, *Lege,* p. 3, and MIC/1924/211/159–160, 164, n.d.

[70] Board of Education, *Draft of Act concerning Private Teaching* (Bucharest: Editura Cartea românească, 1927).

[71] Ministerul instrucţiunii, *Proect de lege asupra învăţământului secundar teoretic* (Bucharest: Editura Cartea românească, 1928).

[72] MIC/1924/211/97, April 21, 1924; Ministerul instrucţiunii, MIC/1923/464/53, October 16, 1920; *Lege,* p. 278; and Ministerul instrucţiunii, *Proect de lege,* p. 102.

being the competition of the Hungarian, German, and Russian languages beyond their "natural" ethnic pool.

Most important for this book, all three bills addressed themselves to the effect of the political changes of 1918 on education. Although pedagogical points were also at stake, the debates of the 1920s reveal that the main objective of this legislation was to eradicate the variations among the four school systems from the assembled Romanian territories. Consequently, each of the main political parties competed to leave its stamp on the national education system. The Liberal Party—and Constantin Angelescu as the Liberal minister of education—was victorious in this contest.

Already during the brief Liberal cabinet of 1919, a unification initiative— which was ultimately aborted—had been on the agenda. The projected bill announcing "reform through unification" in March 1919 had aimed to standardize schools from the four provinces by September of that year. Onisifor Ghibu viewed Angelescu's 1919 project as devoid of content and uninformed about the new provinces. He argued that a Romanian "consolidation committed to the unitary Romanian point of view" was more urgently needed than a unification of external forms. Ghibu compared the situation in the schools with that of the Romanian army in 1919. "At that date, the Romanian army . . . was getting ready to go on the offensive against the Hungarians. Although its soldiers wore very different uniforms: Romanian, Hungarian, and Russian—as they had come out of the revolu- tion—[the army] was spiritually completely unified. That general would have had to be mad, who in those moments would have figured that the first thing [to do] was to unify the soldiers' uniforms."[73] According to Ghibu, in the cultural realm Romanians also had unity after 1918 by virtue of their shared language and spirituality, trustworthy teaching staff, and leadership. These essential elements made the lack of external uniformity insignificant. Ghibu lauded Angelescu for postponing the 1919 reform plan when he met with Transylvanian resistance.[74]

By 1922, however, when the Liberals resumed power and Angelescu returned to the Ministry of Education, the autonomist tendencies had been weakened by the dissolution of the Directing Council in 1920 and by the subsequent liquidation of the general secretariats and directorates. Angelescu could therefore abandon his conciliatory stance toward the provincials. He was anxious to promulgate a reform as soon as possible, since his predecessor, P. P. Negulescu, had failed to pass the bill he had been hurrying to complete.[75] Negulescu's fear that the Averescan People's Party to which he belonged might lose power before he could draft his

[73] Ghibu, "Consideraţii," pp. 4, 5.
[74] Ibid., pp. 5, 7.
[75] Ibid., p. 8. Negulescu, *Reforma,* presents the reforms he had wanted to introduce.

education reform had come true. Angelescu may have determined not to suffer a similar fate. His political ego would have impelled him to propound the "great" school reform and add this to the Liberal Party's list of achievements,[76] though Angelescu himself would certainly have denied any such suggestions. He claimed that the unification stipulated by the Primary School Bill of 1924 was absolutely necessary and had to be accomplished "as quickly as possible" because the institution of the primary school was essential to cementing Romanians' spiritual unity.[77]

Angelescu's reasons notwithstanding, some of the provincials, particularly the Transylvanians, found the reforms of the 1920s premature, if not superfluous. Their reaction owed partly to having felt excluded from the drafting process. In notes written in 1925 "in the margin of the draft bill on secondary education," Onisifor Ghibu wondered indignantly about the authorship of the "monstrous" draft, asking why he had not been asked to collaborate on the reform despite the ministry's recognition of his expertise.[78] Elsewhere, Ghibu suggested that a depoliticized pedagogical constituent assembly—a body of national unity—consisting of former ministers of education, former general secretaries of education, and church and minority representatives should write the reforms.[79] In part, the Transylvanians perceived Angelescu's reforms as assertions of Liberal Party strength and of the Regat's ascendancy over Transylvanian traditions and institutions.

Particularly sensitive was the issue of the Uniate and Orthodox churches, which had kept Romanian schools alive through centuries of Austrian and Hungarian domination. According to Ghibu, the 1924 reform struck "at the forces that had given Transylvania and Bessarabia a Romanian school system without any assistance from the State.[80] He charged that Angelescu, enmeshed in "Byzantine" corruption, did not represent the Greater Romanian state, standing only for himself and the Liberal Party. (The word "Byzantine" is a barbed reference to the historical tradition of the Regat, as distinguished from Transylvania's Habsburg inheritance.) "With parvenu ministers who know only how to blunder and to get rich, raising all the parvenus to undeserved positions, with all the teachers enmeshed in politics, . . . with Byzantine ministers, you can keep making reforms on paper— paper will be the only thing left of everything you did, Dr. Angelescu," wrote Ghibu.[81] He was not alone in his dissatisfaction with Angelescu's

---

[76] Ghibu, "Consideraţii," p. 10.
[77] Angelescu, *Evoluţia,* p. 42.
[78] Onisifor Ghibu, "Note pe marginea 'Anteproiectului de lege pentru învăţământul secundar, teoretic şi aplicat (practic),' " 1925, Ms., Arhiva O. Ghibu.
[79] Ghibu, "Consideraţii," pp. 14–15.
[80] Ghibu, "Reforma?" p. 3.
[81] Ibid.

reforms. The Orthodox Transylvanian metropolitan, Nicolae Bălan, Uniate Bishop Hossu, and Vasile Goldiş, a leading member of the National Party and the first head of the Education Department during the Directing Council also protested the etatization of Transylvania's Orthodox and Uniate confessional schools.

Supporters of the reform argued that because the state now really represented the Romanian people or (as was said elsewhere during those debates) because the state was now "nothing but the organized kin," autonomous denominational schools no longer made sense; they charged moreover that such autonomy implied a perverse distinction of purposes dividing "sons of the same country who should have the same ideals and aspirations."[82] In the Senate, Angelescu stressed that, "the interests of the State, the interests of the Romanian people, stand above individual interests, be they even [those] of the communities. . . . [O]ur churches have to realize that the Romanian State that is ours, all of ours, must be strengthened and that this State can only be strengthened by . . . letting the State mold the souls of all its citizens."[83] To Bishop Hossu's wish to at least "sing an honest requiem at the death of the confessional school," Angelescu responded by asking His Holiness "to sing a Te Deum of gratitude to God for having given us . . . what our fathers and grandfathers had wanted without believing that it could happen: the Union of all Romanians. . . . God has granted for us to see the entire Romanian plain strewn with Romanian schools in which Romanian is spoken and thought."[84]

What emerges from these parliamentary debates on school reform is a sense that the Greater Romanian state, like the education reforms, belonged more to some than to others, more to the Liberals based in the Regat than to the historic Romanian churches and patriots of Transylvania. In order to defeat those forms of Romanian patriotism not congenial to the Old Kingdom–based state, the Liberals polemicized against regional and confessional particularism and hailed the state as the essence of "the organized kin." The Transylvanians had difficulty responding to this supreme nationalist argument, because they too had endeavored to organize the kin by cultural means, chief among which were the Uniate and Orthodox schools. The education reform bills attempted to usurp the regional and institutional base of Transylvanian patriotism on behalf of the Greater Romanian state.

Angelescu defended his course of action repeatedly, but perhaps most eloquently on June 28, 1924, in the Chamber of Deputies.

Our church had identified itself with the school and with the aspirations of our kin. But, Gentlemen, we must recognize that times have changed now

[82] Ministerul instrucţiunii, *Lege,* pp. 167, 191, 198–200.
[83] Ibid., p. 167.
[84] Ibid., p. 200.

and [that] they have changed for the better, both for the church and for the country and kin. The union of all Romanians has been made, this country is ours, all of ours, and [we are] in a modern State. The State has certain obligations. It is not admissible that the soul of the people, the mind of the child, the molding of this mind and this soul, not be in the hands of the State which forms tomorrow's citizens. . . . [M]oreover, our churches . . . are Romanian churches, they are no longer denominations.

We want, Gentlemen, that the school be one and the same for the whole kin. It is not admissible that in Ardeal there should remain denominational schools, while here in Vechiul Regat we should have State schools, and similarly in Bukovina and Bessarabia, State schools.[85]

Constantin Angelescu's ambitious program for school expansion and for unifying the four school systems of Greater Romania had both democratizing and centralizing tendencies. From Angelescu's point of view the two were not contradictory, since the objective of both was to consolidate the Romanian nation-state. The expansion of the school system meant Romanian culture might reach ethnic foreigners or estranged Romanians in the new provinces, as well as, more deeply, the poor, downtrodden, hitherto uneducated ethnic Romanians, whose mobility to elite status the state now encouraged. The rather rapid unification of the four school systems—at times over the federalist or gradualist preferences of the provincials—was intended to enforce uniformity among the various school systems in the united Romanian provinces in and after 1918. Those who, like Onisifor Ghibu or Nicolae Bălan, resented the centralization policies started by Bucharest Liberals claimed that they were not opposed to unification as such, but to a unification that was insensitive to local needs and to institutions like the Orthodox and Uniate churches—the heroic bearers of Romanian culture in Transylvania. This approach accused the centralizers themselves of acting parochially, in light of their own special interests, and of doing so by abusing the state. To the centralizers, the very existence of the Greater Romanian state made obsolete the previous autonomy of such national institutions as the churches and confessional schools. Although they had had previously to defend the kin against hostile foreign rule, the Greater Romanian state, which was "nothing but the organized kin," should now transcend and subsume all Romanian institutions.

As primus inter pares among the united Romanian provinces, the Old Kingdom assumed the task of consolidating the Romanian state. It operated, however, from a position of weakness because of large numbers of non-Romanians and because of the local solidarities of the Romanians in the new provinces. The "cultural offensive" aimed to consolidate nation and state by drawing an increased number of Romanian peasants into the ranks of a national elite and by imposing centralized cultural institutions.

[85] Ibid., p. 194.

2

Bukovina: An Austrian Heritage
in Greater Romania

Today, when the national principle is celebrating its great triumph, when the old states are tumbling down, and in their ruins are arising rejuvenated national states within the ethnic boundaries of each nation, "Bukovinism" has to disappear. ... Bukovina has reunited with Romania, within whose boundaries there is no room for *homo bucovinensis,* but only for *civis Romaniae.*

—Ion Nistor, 1918

O f the three provinces newly incorporated by Romania in 1918, Bukovina was the least ethnically Romanian. The northern half of the territory was compactly inhabited by a Ukrainian population that outnumbered the area's Romanians.[1] (See map.) In 1910, the Ukrainians formed the largest group in Bukovina, with 38.4 percent of the population. Ethnic Romanians came second with 34.4 percent, followed by the Jews and Germans with 12 and 9.3 percent, respectively.

Although most historians do not dispute these figures, some attribute the high concentration of Ukrainians to Austrian policies.[2] They argue that

[1] I use the term Ukrainian more than Ruthenian in this chapter, although Romanian and Austrian sources and much of the literature on the Habsburg Empire often prefer the latter. Before the middle of the 19th century Ruthenian was the more commonly accepted term. But after that, nationally conscious West Ukrainians adopted Ukrainian terminology and identity to link themselves to their co-nationals in Eastern Ukraine and differentiate themselves from the Russians. See Orest Subtelny, *Ukraine: A History* (Toronto: University of Toronto Press, 1988), p. 307. An earlier name for Ukrainians, especially in the Russian Empire, was Little Russians.

[2] See Ion Nistor, *Bessarabia and Bukowina* (Bucharest: Rumanian Academy, 1939), p. 36; Nistor, *Problema ucraineană în lumina istoriei* (Czernowitz: Institutul de arte grafice şi Editura Glasul Bucovinei, 1934), pp. 65–76, 173–174; and Ministère des affaires étrangères, Archives diplomatiques, Paris, Quai d'Orsay, Série Z, Roumanie (hereafter QD), 62/206–223, "Mémoire sur la situation des ruthènes en Roumanie" [1927].

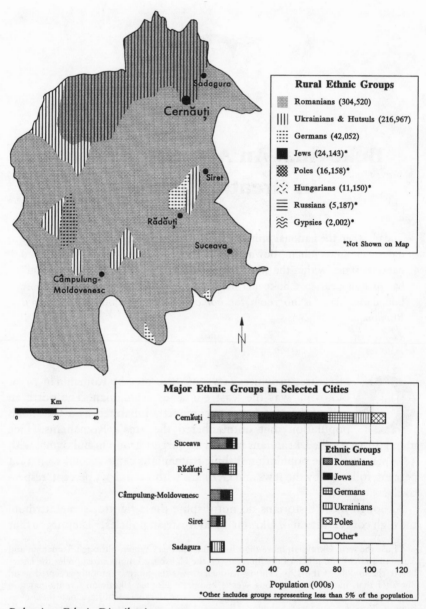

Rural Ethnic Groups

- Romanians (304,520)
- Ukrainians & Hutsuls (216,967)
- Germans (42,052)
- Jews (24,143)*
- Poles (16,158)*
- Hungarians (11,150)*
- Russians (5,187)*
- Gypsies (2,002)*

*Not Shown on Map

Major Ethnic Groups in Selected Cities

Cernăuți
Suceava
Rădăuți
Câmpulung-Moldovenesc
Siret
Sadagura

0   20   40   60   80   100   120
Population (000s)

Ethnic Groups
- Romanians
- Jews
- Germans
- Ukrainians
- Poles
- Other*

*Other includes groups representing less than 5% of the population

Km
0   20   40

Bukovina, Ethnic Distribution

Romanians initially dominated, but that their concentration was altered by the massive immigration of Ukrainians from neighboring Galicia, the linguistic assimilation of Romanians to Ukrainian, and the Slavicization of Romanian names.[3] Others assert, however, that the Ukrainians preceded the Romanians in Bukovina (and in Bessarabia and northern Transylvania as well). They lay claim to Bukovina, or at least its northern section, on the basis of Ukrainian numerical superiority since the nineteenth century.[4] In many ways the relationship between Ukrainians and Romanians in Bukovina parallels that between Ukrainians and Poles in Galicia.

Austrian Bukovina

Studied little by Western scholars, Bukovina receives insufficient understanding in the literature from which one might expect an objective rendition. A. J. P. Taylor, for example, dismisses Bukovina as "a forgotten province," writing that "Bukovina could not be claimed by any one nationality as their national home and had no history over which they could fight. The Roumanians and Little Russians," he continues, "were peoples without a past; the Germans, despite a touch of German mission, were made humble by the arrogance of their Polish neighbours in Galicia and of their Magyar neighbours in Hungary."[5] Behind such summary statements lies a complex reality differently appreciated by the major ethnic groups inhabiting Bukovina and by the Austrian imperial power. The Habsburgs saw in the 1775 acquisition of Bukovina, which connected two other Habsburg territories, Galicia and Transylvania, an advantage over Turkey and Russia in the evolving Eastern question.[6] As part of the Austrian

[3] Robert A. Kann and Zdeněk V. David, *The Peoples of the Eastern Habsburg Lands, 1526–1918* (Seattle: University of Washington Press, 1984), p. 275; and Ion Nistor, *Românii și rutenii în Bucovina: Studiu istoric și statistic* (Bucharest: Librăriile Socec, 1915), pp. 146–167. Other explanations of the "Ruthenization" of parts of Bukovina stress the influx of Ruthenians as laborers for the landed Romanian population. Their cohabitation at the side of the Romanians resulted in the Romanians' linguistic assimilation to Ukrainian—rather than the other way around—because of the Romanians' superiority and their consequent ability to adapt to a new language. AA IX/ Varia 10, December 20, 1922.

[4] See, for example, *Ukraine: A Concise Encyclopaedia,* vol. 1 (Toronto: University of Toronto Press, 1963), pp. 17–18, 242, and Iwan M. Nowosiwsky, *Bukovinian Ukrainians: A Historical Background and Their Self-Determination in 1918,* trans. Walter Dushnyck (New York: Association of Bukovinian Ukrainians, 1970). In the medieval period Bukovina was first part of the Galician-Volhynian appanage and became part of the Moldavian Principality in the 14th century. Wolfdieter Bihl, "Die Ruthenen," in *Die Habsburgermonarchie, 1848–1918,* ed. Adam Wandruszka and Peter Urbanitsch, vol. 3 (Vienna: Verlag der Österreichischen Akademie der Wissenschaften, 1980), p. 558.

[5] A. J. P. Taylor, *The Habsburg Monarchy, 1908–1918: A History of the Austrian Empire and Austria-Hungary* (New York: Harper and Row, 1965), pp. 200–201.

[6] Robert A. Kann, *A History of the Habsburg Empire, 1526–1918* (Berkeley: University of California Press, 1974), p. 164, and Alexandru D. Xenopol, *Istoria Românilor din Dacia Traiană,* 3d ed., vol. 9 (Bucharest: Editura Cartea românească, 1925), p. 152.

Empire, Bukovina gained other political meanings as well. Merged with Galicia until the second half of the nineteenth century, it gained self-governing status after 1848, and witnessed the growing national aspirations of both Romanians and Ukrainians who struggled increasingly against each other, and against Austria within local and imperial institutions, for stakes in politics, society, and culture.

The importance of Bukovina to both Romanians and Ukrainians remains evident: to this day each people considers it an essential part of its national home. Nicholas Dima's estimation of Bukovina as "the cradle of Moldavia"[7] typifies the Romanian view, and the Ukrainian perspective is encapsulated in Iwan M. Nowosiwsky's statement that "Bukovina is essentially a compact Ukrainian land dating back to the fourth century A.D."[8] In the nineteenth century, Bukovina's Germans—and its Jews, with whom the Germans were closely allied—dominated the urban, bureaucratic, and cultural landscape of this imperial outpost—the neighboring Magyars and Poles mentioned by Taylor notwithstanding.

In the century and a half between the 1775 partition of the Moldavian Principality by Austria and the Ottoman Empire and the return of Bukovina to modern Romania in 1918, the province changed significantly. Austria's economic and nationality policies prompted a distinct shift in Bukovina's ethnic balance, in time making this the Habsburg Empire's "most multinational crownland" (table 5).[9]

Bukovina was one of the least literate of the Dual Monarchy's provinces: 32.4 percent of the total population (45.2 percent of the population over ten years of age) in 1910 knew how to read and write. The Ukrainian and Romanian population suffered the highest rates of illiteracy at 70.6 and 60.4 percent of the population over ten, respectively.[10] This situation appeared demeaning to the Romanians, but it was substantially superior to that of their compatriots in Bessarabia.

During Bukovina's administrative dependence on neighboring Galicia in the first half of the nineteenth century, many Ukrainian peasants came to settle in Bukovina. They found the availability of land, and until 1830, the exemption from military service, attractive. Immigration contributed to increasing Bukovina's population from an estimated 71,750 in 1774 (though that estimate may have been low) to 190,000 in 1801 and 337,000 in 1848. By 1880 there were 239,000 Ukrainians and 190,000 Romanians

---

[7] Nicholas Dima, "Bucovina, Romania, and the Ukraine," in *The Tragic Plight of a Border Area: Bassarabia and Bucovina,* ed. Maria Manoliu-Manea (Los Angeles: Humboldt State University Press, 1983), p. 19.

[8] Nowosiwsky, *Bukovinian Ukrainians,* p. 13.

[9] Kann and David, *Peoples,* p. 420.

[10] Calculated from K. K. Statistische Zentralkommission, *Bewegung der Bevölkerung der im Reichsrate Vertretenen Königsreiche und Länder im Jahre 1910* (Vienna: K. K. Hof- und Staatsdruckerei, 1912), vol. 8, pt. 1, p. 11, and vol. 1, pt. 3, pp. 98–99.

Table 5. The population of Bukovina, by ethnicity, 1930

		Romanians	Ukrainians	Jews	Germans
Total	853,009	379,691	248,567[a]	92,492	75,533
(%)		44.5	29.1	10.8	8.9
Urban	228,056	75,171	31,600	68,349	33,481
(%)		33.0	13.9	30.0	14.7

Sources: Ion Nistor, *Românii și rutenii în Bucovina,* pp. 23, 156, Institutul central de statistică, *Anuarul statistic al României 1937 și 1938,* pp. 60–61; idem, *Recensământul general al populației României din 29* decemvrie *1930,* vol. 2; Erich Beck "Das Buchenland-deutschtum in Zahlen," in *Buchenland: Hundertfünfzig Jahre Deutschtum in der Bukowina,* p. 78; and Constantin Lacea, *La Bucovine,* p. 15.
[a] This figure includes the Hutsuls.

in Bukovina.[11] The heaviest concentration of Ukrainians lay north of the Siret River. Unlike in Transylvania and Bessarabia, in Bukovina, Romanians were neither the largest nor the most oppressed nationality. Here they were better off, enjoyed more political representation, and had a more complete class structure than the Ukrainian population, which consisted almost exclusively of peasants. After 1787, when Bukovina became a *Kreis* of Galicia, the Ukrainians, lacking a native nobility, had to contend with the Polish upper class, the German imperial administration, and the local Romanian nobility. A Ukrainian national intelligentsia—chiefly clergymen—began to form from the peasantry in the nineteenth century.[12]

By contrast, from the beginning of the Austrian annexation of Bukovina, the Romanian population had a complex make-up consisting of enserfed and free peasants, artisans, merchants, clergy, teachers, noble landowners, and state servants.[13] Whereas Romanian remained a subsidiary official language alongside the main state language, German, Ukrainian had no official status until 1860. As of 1869, German and Romanian were both used in the local Diet.[14] After 1775, although some Romanian boyars refused to serve the Habsburgs and crossed the border back into Turkish Moldavia, many stayed, received Austrian titles of nobility, and were coopted into the Austrian bureaucracy. Thus, some of the Romanian nobility benefited from the province's new imperial affiliation, an option not open to the Ukrainians who, by and large, lacked a noble class. After a provincial Diet was formed in 1867, its head was always a Romanian nobleman. Both the Landtag and the Reichsrat delegation from Bukovina

[11] An earlier and more modest Romanian migration to Bukovina mostly from neighboring Transylvania and Moldavia accounted for the increase in the province's population from 117,000 in 1778 to 190,000 in 1801. Kann and David, *Peoples,* pp. 275, 288, 441.
[12] Ibid, p. 275, and Subtelny, *Ukraine,* pp. 215, 238, 333.
[13] Aurel Morariu, *Bucovina, 1774–1914* (Bucharest: P. Suru, [1914?]), pp. 25, 26.
[14] Kann and David, *Peoples,* pp. 275, 419.

were dominated by Romanians. This policy brought some Romanians to evaluate Austrian rule positively.[15] Eudoxius Hurmuzaki, for example, expressed the following sentiments in the Diet in 1863:

> Since Bukovina ceased to be a part of the vast oriental empire [and] . . . entered the great Middle-European Empire . . . its material and spiritual conditions have changed considerably in its favour; the Western civilization has spread over it beneficially; freedom and equality, law and order, have profoundly permeated all its relationships; the [principle of] equality was extended not only to individuals but also to classes and estates, nations and religions.[16]

Nevertheless, by the mid–nineteenth century a national movement was afoot among the Romanians of Bukovina, led by descendants of the Hurmuzaki family.[17] During the 1848 revolution some nationalists called for the unification of all the Romanians in the Habsburg Monarchy in an autonomous crownland, and others for a unification of Romanians in Transylvania, Moldavia, and Wallachia within a federalized Habsburg Empire. This idea alarmed the Ukrainians who preferred to retain Bukovina's administration as part of Galicia with its substantial Ukrainian population.[18] Habsburg authorities, increasingly mindful of the rising nationalism of the monarchy's Romanians (particularly those in Transylvania) tried to pit Bukovinian Ukrainians against them. In the second half of the nineteenth century, therefore, Ukrainians gained more rights and schools, and in the context of the Ukrainian national movement in Russia and Galicia they also developed a higher degree of national consciousness.[19]

The postwar Romanian state inherited the social and demographic structure of Bukovina which had been shaped during the Austrian period. In Bukovina the Ukrainian and Romanian populations were mostly rural, while the German and Jewish populations were highly urban. According to Ion Nistor, the Germans (8.9 percent of the region's population in 1930) were "spread over differents [sic] parts of Bucovina," and "the Jews

---

[15] Ibid., pp. 273, 275, 287–289, 438–440, and Theodore Ciuciura, "Romanian Views on Bessarabia and Bukovina: A Ukrainian Perspective," *Nationalities Papers* 13 (Spring, 1985): 109–110.

[16] *Stenographische Protokolle des Bukowinaer Landtags,* I. Diet (Wahlperiode), 2. Session; January 12, 1863, p. 4, cited in Ciuciura, "Romanian Views," p. 110.

[17] Keith Hitchins, "Die Rumänen," in *Die Habsburgermonarchie, 1848–1918,* ed. Adam Wandruszka and Peter Urbanitsch (Vienna: Verlag der Österreichischen Akademie der Wissenschaften, 1980), p. 615.

[18] Ibid., p. 616, and Kann and David, *Peoples,* pp. 417, 438–439. As in Galicia and Transcarpathia, the Ukrainians in Bukovina failed to join the insurgents—Poles, Hungarians, Romanians—but became effective allies of the empire. See Subtelny, *Ukraine,* pp. 247–251.

[19] Kann and David, *Peoples,* pp. 419–420, and Subtelny, *Ukraine,* p. 334.

form[ed] mostly city inhabitants.[20] But although Bukovina's urban elites and bureaucracy were largely German and Jewish, Romanians and Ukrainians also enjoyed opportunities for upward mobility. Bukovina's less polarized climate and the possibility of social and political cooptation in turn affected the nature of Austrian authority, which was never (before 1918) as seriously challenged as in other parts of the Habsburg Empire.

These factors tempered relations among nationalities. The generally moderate attitude of the Romanians vis-à-vis the Kaiser meant that Bukovina's acculturated Jewish community, which increasingly gravitated toward the capital city of Czernowitz, could assimilate unimpeded into German culture. Moreover, the extreme ethnic fragmentation of Bukovina's population and the almost even split between the two most numerous nationalities made ethnic political collaboration necessary; the German and Jewish communities became potential, and at times actual, allies of the predominantly rural Romanians and Ukrainians. In Austrian Bukovina, Jews enjoyed not only social and economic prominence, but also political importance. Czernowitz had several Jewish mayors during the last two decades of Austrian rule.[21] Eighty-six percent of the lawyers in 1914 were Jewish, as was the president of the law board. Large numbers of Jews attended the German University of Czernowitz. Some, even among the Jews, felt that influential Germanized Jews "contributed much more than the Germans [themselves] to the German character of the region."[22]

Bukovina's Romanian elite had not developed the strong identity of the Polish nobility in neighboring Galicia, or the sense of national mission of the Romanian intelligentsia in Transylvania.[23] Mild Austrian policies had produced a Romanian educated elite that was less assimilated than its Russified counterpart in Bessarabia and more complacent than its nationalistic counterpart in Transylvania. Austria's relative liberalism toward the nationalities had engendered an accommodationist spirit and a fairly strong provincial solidarity even among ethnic groups. Among Romanians ethnic collaboration was first advocated by the Centralist Party under the leadership of the Hurmuzaki brothers in the 1870s. Although in 1892 the purely nationalist Romanian National Party was founded, in 1900 Aurel Onciul's National Democratic Party again provided an accommodationist alternative. It brought together liberal Romanians who favored ethnic compromise

---

[20] Ion I. Nistor, *The Union of Bucovina with Rumania* (Bucharest: Editions Bucovina–I. E. Torouțiu, 1940), pp. 12–13.

[21] William O. McCagg, Jr., *A History of Habsburg Jews, 1670–1918* (Bloomington: Indiana University Press, 1989), pp. 172–173.

[22] See Hermann Sternberg, "Zur Geschichte der Juden in Czernowitz," in *Geschichte der Juden in der Bukowina,* ed. Hugo Gold, vol. 2 (Tel Aviv: Olamenu, 1962), p. 46.

[23] Ilie E. Torouțiu, *Românii și clasa intelectuală din Bucovina: Notițe statistice* (Czernowitz: Editura societății academice Junimea, 1911), and Kann and David, *Peoples,* p. 442. See McCagg, *Habsburg Jews,* p. 173, for the comparison to Galicia.

and opposed the social conservatism of the National Party. The Romanian National Democrats cooperated with the Ukrainian National Democrats and with Jewish and Polish parties. In 1903, a "Free-Thinking Union" comprised of Ukrainian, Romanian, Jewish, Armenian, and German deputies from Bukovina was organized in the Vienna parliament.[24] Hence, in 1918, the Romanians in Bukovina were not, like those of Transylvania, united behind a single "National Party," but were active in several competing parties—irredentist nationalists, anti-Semitic Christian Socialists, pro-Austrian liberals, and social democrats.

The Romanian National Revolution

Paradoxically, the Romanian nationalists who were least impressed with the pluralist tradition of Bukovina under Habsburg rule carried the day in 1918. They came from the local Romanian intelligentsia—doctors, lawyers, teachers, professors, and journalists—and they tended to disagree with the Romanian delegates to the Vienna parliament at war's end over the issue of conciliation with the now reform-bent Austrian state and with the Ukrainian nation. Romanian intellectuals living in Bukovina proper, and those who had sought refuge in the Regat, Bessarabia, or Russia during the war, were more intransigently nationalistic than their compatriots in Vienna. Their idea of uniting all of historic Bukovina with Romania coincided with the aspirations of the Old Kingdom and the program of the Romanian premier Ion Brătianu. Thus their pan-Romanian politics set the tone for later developments.

During secret negotiations with the Allies, Bukovina had been promised to Romania in exchange for joining the war against the Central Powers. In 1916, Romania declared war on Austria-Hungary. Near the end of the war, Romanian claims to Bukovina came into conflict with Ukrainian projects to form an independent Ukraine outside the Soviet state or at least a Ukrainian province—including Eastern Galicia and Northern Bukovina—as a crownland of Austria.[25] Bolstering his pleas with arguments that

---

[24] Hitchins, "Die Rumänen," pp. 616–617; Kann and David, *Peoples,* pp. 440–441; and Nowosiwsky, *Bukovinian Ukrainians,* p. 78.

[25] See Sherman David Spector, *Rumania at the Peace Conference: A Study of the Diplomacy of Ioan I. C. Brătianu* (New York: Bookman, 1962), pp. 25–26; John S. Reshetar, Jr., *The Ukrainian Revolution, 1917–1920: A Study in Nationalism* (Princeton, N.J.: Princeton University Press, 1982), pp. 181, 212–213; Anna Cienciala and Titus Komarnicki, *From Versailles to Locarno: Keys to Polish Foreign Policy, 1919–1925* (Lawrence: University Press of Kansas, 1984), p. 153; John W. Wheeler-Bennett, *Brest-Litovsk: The Forgotten Peace, March 1918* (New York: Norton, 1971), pp. 154, 168, 171; "Texts of the Ukraine 'Peace', " in *The Inquiry Handbooks,* vol. 19 (1918; reprint, Wilmington, Del.: Scholarly Resources, [1974]), p. 141.

"Rumania was defending Europe against Bolshevism," Brătianu managed to obtain all of Bukovina for Romania.[26] The Romanian national movement in Bukovina had helped set the stage for this diplomatic success.

Romanian nationalist intellectuals had begun to meet in small conspiratorial circles in the late summer and fall of 1918. They later remembered the charmed, mystical character of their secret activities.[27] On October 22, 1918, the Romanian propaganda organ, *Glasul Bucovinei* (Bukovina's Voice) began to appear. Its lead editorial indicated that the editorial board, the *glasişti*, did not wish to become just another political party, but were instead seeking to close ranks among the parties representing ethnic Romanians. Only with such solidarity could Romanians achieve sovereignty in their ancestral land and secure the possibility of deciding their fate together with the Romanians in Transylvania and Hungary in a pan-Romanian framework.[28] The *glasişti* thus attempted to change Bukovina's "Austrian" pluralist tradition by demanding that the Romanians unify behind the Romanian idea and bury their other political differences.[29]

On October 17, 1918, a Romanian National Council had formed in Vienna in response to the emperor's manifesto calling for the federalization of Austria on the basis of all the constituent nationalities. In his last imperial audience, on October 18, the president of the council told the monarch that the Romanians would vote even against a reformed monarchy. During the last session of the Austrian parliament, Romanian members called for the emancipation and self-determination of the Romanians in Austria-Hungary.[30] On October 27, a Constituent Assembly of the Romanians of Bukovina met in Cernăuţi, (Czernowitz, Chernivtsi) and voted for the "union of integral Bukovina with the other Romanian lands in a national

---

[26] Spector, *Rumania*, pp. 316, 140–141.

[27] Ion I. Nistor, ed., *Amintiri răzleţe din timpul Unirii* (Czernowitz: Glasul Bucovinei, 1938).

[28] Maximilian Hacman, "Primul sfat pentru unire la doctorul I. Bodea," in Nistor, ed., *Amintiri răzleţe*, pp. 157–158.

[29] That this idea was a revolutionary departure from the more flexible politics practiced under Habsburg rule is suggested by debates even within the *Glas* group when the signed editorial was drafted. Some of the original group, fearful of breaking totally with the Austro-Hungarian Empire, wanted to downplay the goal of self-determination "in the framework of Romanianism as a whole." In the end, the resolution reflected the mood of irreversibility expressed by Puşcariu in his ironic response to the cautious ones: "Gentlemen, we started by express train toward a goal from which we will not waver. You stuck your heads out the window to see which way we were going, and the wind swept away your hats. Now you want to pull the emergency brake in order to stop the train for the sake of your hats? To make people think that our engine is faulty? Better get off quickly at the next stop, go back and let us go forward!" Sextil Puşcariu, "Cum a luat fiinţă 'Glasul Bucovinei': Pagini de ziar," in Nistor, ed., *Amintiri răzleţe*, p. 336.

[30] Their speeches were well received except by the Ukrainian leader Mykola Vasyl'ko, who demanded northern Bukovina for the Ukrainians. Kann and David, *Peoples*, pp. 180–182.

independent state."[31] It elected a fifty-member National Council headed by Iancu Flondor, a Romanian landowner and member of the National Party.[32]

The Romanians were not alone in claiming Bukovina. Like most nationalities of Austria-Hungary, the Ukrainians wished to obtain independence from the debacle of the empire. Unlike other groups, however, they did not constitute an irredenta of a prewar state, nor had they the protection of one of the victorious powers. The new East Ukrainian state, federated with revolutionary Russia, further complicated matters, and the West Ukrainians were resigned to gaining substantial national rights only within an Austrian framework. Thus the West Ukrainian state that proclaimed its independence on October 19, 1918, in L'viv (Lemberg, Lwów), resolved to remain "mit Anschluss an Österreich."[33] Like the Ukrainian National Rada of L'viv, the Ukrainian National Committee for Bukovina formed on October 25 made claims to northern Bukovina, where Ukrainians outnumbered Romanians.[34]

No compromise to the Ukrainian-Romanian dispute in Bukovina was achieved, in part because the Romanian negotiator, Aurel Onciul, a former member of the Viennese parliament, no longer spoke for a significant current of Romanian public opinion, nor did he possess the credentials of an appointed or elected delegate.[35] The conflict received a military solution—in favor of the Romanian claims—later approved by the Paris Peace Conference. But at first, from November 6 to November 11, Ukrainian military units had the upper hand.[36] This situation prompted the Romanian National Council to call in Romanian troops, an intervention that returned power to the Romanian National Council.[37]

[31] Dimitrie Marmeliuc, "În preajma unirii: file de carnet," in Nistor, ed., Amintiri răzleţe, p. 209. The assembly, as its name indicated, did not include Ukrainian and Jewish delegates. Ciuciura, "Romanian Views," p. 112.

[32] Radu Sbiera, "Clipe de mare înfrigurare şi de aleasă înălţare," in Nistor, ed., Amintiri răzleţe, p. 382, and Hitchins, "Die Rumänen," p. 625.

[33] I.e., the West Ukrainian state intended to remain part of Austria. Evidently this dissatisfied some Ukrainians. Nistor, Problema ucraineană, pp. 206, 245, and Nowosiwsky, Bukovinian Ukrainians, p. 111.

[34] Nowosiwsky, Bukovinian Ukrainians, app. 2, p. 156, and app. 4, pp. 159–160; Kann and David, Peoples, p. 446; and Ion Nistor, Românii şi rutenii în Bucovina (Bucharest: Ediţiunea Academiei Române, 1915), p. 158. Ukrainians initially claimed the capital of Bukovina as well, but on November 6, they agreed, in negotiations with Aurel Onciul, to a Ukrainian-Romanian condominium over Cernăuţi. In fact the problem of the capital and of two other disputed Bukovinian towns, Siret and Storojineţ, was that though having predominantly Ukrainian hinterlands their largest urban ethnic contingent was neither Ukrainian nor Romanian, but Jewish. Nowosiwsky, Bukovinian Ukrainians, pp. 110, 118, 119.

[35] Nistor, Problema ucraineană, p. 212; idem, Union, pp. 19–21; and Nowosiwsky, Bukovinian Ukrainians, p. 120.

[36] According to one observer, three of Archduke Wilhelm's regiments were in the Cernăuţi district in the fall of 1918. See Petre Popescul, "Amintiri din viaţă în jurul zilei de unire, anul 1918 ziua 28 noembrie," in Nistor, ed., Amintiri răzleţe, p. 310.

[37] Nistor, Problema ucraineană, pp. 209–214; idem, Union, pp. 22–24; and idem, Bessarabia and Bukowina, p. 41.

At a General Congress on November 28, Romanian, German, and Polish delegates voted unanimously for the union of Bukovina and Romania.[38] Missing from this important decision, however, were the voices of Bukovina's organized Ukrainian and Jewish communities which witheld from participation.[39] The opening speaker of the congress greeted first the Romanian army, then Romanians from Bessarabia, Transylvania, and Hungary, then the "leaders of the Romanian race in Bukovina," and only lastly the minorities in the hall.[40] He, of course, did not address the Ukrainian National Council, nor the Jewish representatives boycotting the congress.[41] The lack of substantial ethnic representation at the General Congress did not bode well for the social peace of Romanian Bukovina.

After the union with Romania, the struggle among Romanians, Ukrainians, and Jews continued. A related conflict raged between nationalist Romanians opposed to the Austrian tradition of ethnic collaboration and their more flexible co-nationals. In an article of December 10, 1918, Ion Nistor, a Bukovinian Romanian historian who had taken refuge in Bucharest and Bessarabia during the war and had joined the struggle for Greater Romania, criticized what he disdainfully called "Bukovinism" and "homo bucovinensis," a species of Romanian renegades grown "in the political nursery of the former Austrian regime."[42] Nistor's condemnation of these Romanians, whom he considered traitors, and of the foreigners in Bukovina, expressed deep revulsion:

[The Austrians] sought by all means at their disposal to erase all traces of the past and to smother the national consciousness of the native population. In these aspirations the previous regime also found support in our alien compatriots, who . . . had an obvious interest in supporting a doctrine that tended to erase the distinction between foreigners and natives. Since some of them had no homeland, and others had one elsewhere, they began to preach the doctrine of "Bukovinism" (Bukowinärthum) a favorite of both the Vienna and the Cernăuţi governments. According to the principles of this doctrine, all the peoples in Bukovina, especially the Romanians, had to rid themselves of their national convictions, to break all ties with their co-nationals in other countries, to abandon their language, and to forget their ancestral traditions and mores so as to melt together with the other peoples into an exotic Bukovinian species, having German as the language of conversation.[43]

[38] Nistor, *Problema ucraineană*, p. 214.
[39] The thirteen Ukrainians present at the Congress "represented no Ukrainian groups or organizations." See Nistor, *Union*, pp. 32–34, and Nowosiwsky, *Bukovinian Ukrainians*, p. 130.
[40] Nistor, *Union*, p. 35.
[41] Grigore Nandriş, "Zile trăite în Bucovina," in Nistor, ed., *Amintiri răzleţe*, p. 256.
[42] Ion Nistor, "Homo bucovinensis," in Nistor, ed. *Amintiri răzleţe*, p. 285.
[43] Ibid.

Nistor and other nationalists wanted to fight Bukovina's spirit of ethnic collaboration and moderation because it represented the Austrian heritage of compromise. In its place they wished to put Romanian integral nationalism.

The Educational Pyramid

When Bukovina joined Romania the stratification of Bukovinian society was reflected in the province's educational system. Romanians and Ukrainians together formed a majority of the overall population, but a minority of the urbanites and elites. Their representation in the province's schools followed the same pattern: they were a majority in the elementary schools and a minority in the mostly urban secondary schools, where Jewish and German pupils predominated, as a result of their demographic position as an urban elite.[44] In 1910, for example, there were 5,682 boys attending elite academic gymnasia in Bukovina, of which 3,196, or 56.2 percent, spoke German as their native language. Of these, 2,295, or 71.8 percent, were Jewish. In these schools there were 2,100 boys whose mother language was Romanian or Ukrainian, accounting for only 37 percent of academic pupils.[45]

In the interwar period Romanian authorities made an effort to halt what they perceived as a process of "Ruthenization" in the countryside of the northern districts by giving the Romanians of Bukovina more of the horizontal base of the educational pyramid they shared with the Ukrainians. Other policies attempted to modify the traditional educational pyramid vertically, by reducing the number of Jewish youths able to receive secondary and higher schooling, thereby making room for a larger number of Romanian youths to receive the training necessary for participating in an expanding national elite. Institutionally, this *Kulturkampf* had a dual locus—rural primary schools and urban secondary schools. The rural Ukrainian grammar schools operated in the largely Ukrainian northern counties of Cernăuți, Sadagura, Coțmani, Siret, Storojineț, Stănești, Văș-căuți, Putila, Vijnița, Zastavna.[46] In the urban high schools, German and Germanized pupils, mostly Jews, predominated. Ethnic and regional struggles in the schools reached violent proportions in the mid-1920s.

---

[44] On the Jewish movement toward education in Bukovina, see McCagg, *Habsburg Jews*, p. 172.
[45] Bureau der K. K. Statistischen Zentralkommission, *Statistik der Unterrichtsanstalten in den in Reichsrate vertretenen Königreichen und Ländern für das Jahr 1909/1910*, vol. 7, pt. 3 (Vienna: K. K. Hof- und Staatsdruckerei, 1913), pp. 65–66, 84–85.
[46] Nistor, *Românii și rutenii*, p. 158.

Bukovina's Schools before World War I

When Bukovina was annexed by Austria in 1775, six Romanian urban schools operated in the province: one Greek, one Latin, several monastery-affiliated schools, and a "goodly" number of rural schools.[47] In the first decade of Austrian rule, some German schools were also added, bringing the total number of schools to thirty-two, of which six were purely Romanian. A decline in the province's school system began when Bukovina united with Galicia. This brought about administrative subordination to Lemberg—the capital of Galicia-Bukovina—in 1786. Thereafter Bukovina's provincialness was accentuated by its status as a *Kreis* of Galicia; people perceived Bukovina as not only one of the most remote areas of the empire, but as more of a backwater than even Galicia, famed for its backwardness. A decline in autonomy led to an institutional drain as government offices moved to Lemberg. The number of schools fell to fourteen, of which only three remained Romanian.[48] In 1816, school administration shifted to the Roman Catholic Consistory in Lemberg, and the Polish language extended its influence to Bukovina through Catholic Polish teachers sent to instruct in Bukovina's schools. Until 1850, the Lemberg Consistory opened just eighteen new schools, of which only ten were destined for Romanian children. None of these schools, however, featured Romanian as the language of instruction.[49] Among other reasons, these developments account for Bukovina's lack of a class of nationally conscious clerics and teachers such as those of Transylvania in the nineteenth century. In Bukovina few Romanians popularized "the sentiment of a national right."[50]

During the 1848 revolution the Romanian population voiced educational demands along with ones for political autonomy and participation.[51] In 1850, Bukovina's schools reverted to the jurisdiction of the Czernowitz Orthodox Consistory. Many new schools were built and some textbooks written.[52] Although Romanian instruction became more available, purely Romanian schools still did not exist.[53] Bukovina's brief reannexation to the neighboring province of Galicia in 1860 coincided with the introduction

---

[47] Onisifor Ghibu, "Şcoala românească în anul 1912," *I Anuar pedagogic (1913)* (Sibiu, 1912 [*sic*]), p. 225, and Morariu, *Bucovina,* p. 27.

[48] Ghibu, "Şcoala românească," p. 225, and Morariu, *Bucovina,* p. 51.

[49] Ministerul instrucţiunii, *Lege pentru învăţământul primar al statului şi învăţământul normal-primar* (Bucharest: Editura Cartea românească, 1925), p. 11.

[50] Nicolae Iorga, *Histoire des Roumains de Bucovine à partir de l'annexion autrichienne, 1775–1914* (Jassy, 1917), p. 71.

[51] Ibid., p. 83; Vlad Georgescu, *Istoria ideilor politice româneşti* (Munich: Ion Dumitru Verlag, 1987), p. 226; and "Bukovina," in Great Britain, Foreign Office, Historical Section, *Peace Handbooks* (London: HMSO, 1920), p. 16.

[52] Ministerul instrucţiunii, *Lege,* p. 11.

[53] Ibid., p. 12, and Morariu, *Bucovina,* p. 53.

of more liberal educational legislation throughout Austria. Romanians, however, widely regarded such liberalization as intended to give non-Romanians an advantage over Romanians, who had already lost political ground through reannexation to Galicia and demographic ground through the immigration of Ukrainians. Ukrainians did become the beneficiaries of a "well-organized Ukrainian school system,"[54] but, after the new legislation, the Romanian community received some new church-sponsored schools as well. In line with these changes, the German language teacher-training college in Czernowitz split in 1909 into three linguistic tracks to accommodate Romanian and Ukrainian. By 1912, 717, or almost 40 percent, of the 1,801 primary school teachers in Bukovina were Romanian. Of them, 646 held teaching posts in Romanian schools.[55]

The first secondary school in Bukovina was a German gymnasium that opened in 1809.[56] In the next hundred years four "Romanian" secondary schools opened as well, but these were in fact bilingual schools, in which German was more important than Romanian, and where half or fewer of the students were ethnic Romanians. For example, in 1910, at the Greek Orthodox *Realschule* in Czernowitz, only 69 of the 694 pupils attending were Romanian, and 280 were Jewish.[57] As late as 1912, none of the fifteen secondary schools in Bukovina had Romanian as the sole language of instruction. In four lycées there were Romanian sections, but even there some of the teaching was in German. The lack of any purely Romanian secondary school may have discouraged some Romanian youths from pursuing an education at all.[58] Secondary schools multiplied rapidly in the late nineteenth century in Bukovina partly because they were stakes in ethnic-political rivalries. In one instance, a Ukrainian secondary school was opened up in the northern town of Vijniţa because the Polish community in nearby Galicia did not want it in their province.[59]

In general, Ukrainians did not enjoy a healthy school system at any level until the 1860s, when the situation improved dramatically. By the outbreak of World War I Bukovina had 202 Ukrainian grade schools,[60] two Ukrainian gymnasia, two Ukrainian-German gymnasia, and one German-Romanian-Ukrainian gymnasium.[61] Naturally, in the interwar period Ukrainian

[54] Subtelny, *Ukraine*, p. 334.
[55] Ghibu, "Şcoala românească," p. 225.
[56] Morariu, *Bucovina*, p. 56.
[57] Statistischen Zentralkommission, *Statistik der Unterrichtsanstalten*, pp. 84–85, and Onisifor Ghibu, "Naţionalizarea învăţământului românesc în Bucovina," I *Anuar pedagogic (1913)*, p. 62.
[58] Ghibu, "Naţionalizarea," pp. 61–62.
[59] Morariu, *Bucovina*, pp. 57–60.
[60] Thus more than the 179 Romanian ones. Ghibu, "Şcoala românească," p. 225.
[61] Bihl, "Die Ruthenen," p. 574.

leaders focused on their achievements and "the flourishing state of their development" during the period of Austrian rule.[62]

Bukovinian Jews, too, looked back fondly on their successes under the Austrian regime, including in the realm of education. Although they focused primarily on the secondary schools, they also prided themselves on the large number of Jewish children in the province's grade schools.[63] In certain urban centers—Cernăuţi, Suceava, Rădăuţi, Sadagura, Storojineţ, Vijniţa—where Jews formed a majority of the population, Jewish children were the absolute majority of the primary school population.[64]

By the twentieth century, the province's primary school population reflected its general demography; at the secondary school level, school statistics reflected Bukovina's urban demography. Romanians and Ukrainians were here underrepresented relative to their frequency in the general population, whereas German and, even more significantly, Jewish high school pupils far outweighed their proportions in the general population. This pattern was exacerbated in the university, where the proportion of Jews fluctuated between 24 percent in 1886, 48.8 percent in 1896, 41.5 percent in 1906, and 38.5 percent in 1914.[65] This educational stratification might be imagined as a pyramid resting on a mixed, prevalently Ukrainian and Romanian base; as the pyramid narrows toward its point, Jews and Germans account for more of the fewer places left toward the top.

The Nationalization of Primary Schools

After 1918 Romanian nationalists wished to counter the inroads of "Ruthenization" to which they attributed the large number of Ukrainians in Bukovina. Romanians blamed the schools for having functioned as instruments of the old regime's "Slavicization" policies, carried out by "fervent propagandists of Slavism from Galicia."[66] Their solution was a vigorous program of Romanization which included increasing the overall number of schools and the proportion of Romanian schools. Overall, the number of Romanian primary schools rose from 179 in 1912, to 257 in

[62] See "Plainte," QD 62/185 and passim, July 11, 1927.

[63] The figure cited in "Memoriu asupra raporturilor pedagogice ale evreilor din Bucovina" is—at 10,927—slightly smaller than Ghibu's 11,324. See the Central Archives for the History of the Jewish People, Jerusalem (hereafter CA), RM 134, n.d., and Ghibu, "Naţionalizarea," p. 61.

[64] CA/RM 134, n.d.

[65] Sternberg, "Zur Geschichte," pp. 34, 46. In 1906, 53 percent of law students were Jewish. According to Sternberg, many Jewish professors also taught at the University of Czernowitz.

[66] The success of this relentless process seemed evident to the Ministry of Education from the "Ruthenization" of previously pure Romanian areas adjacent to the Old Kingdom. AA IX/ Varia 5, November 22, 1922.

Table 6. Primary school capacity in rural Cernăuţi County,
by language of instruction, 1918 and 1922

	1918		1922	
	Number of schools	Number of classes	Number of schools	Number of classes
Romanian	20	59	38	138
Ukrainian	35	109	17	55
German	7	31	2	7
Polish	1	2	2	6
	63	201	59	206

Source: AA IX/ Varia 5, November 22, 1922.

1919–1920, and 319 in 1922–1923. At the same time, the number of Ukrainian primary schools fell from 202 in 1912 to 157 in 1919–1920, and to 155 in 1922–1923.[67] Romanian schools advanced at the expense of schools of other ethnic groups in Bukovina with the collaboration of Romanian communal authorities.[68] In the rural district of Cernăuţi, despite a lack of teaching aids and libraries, the number of Romanian schools increased between 1918 and 1922 as dramatically as the number of Ukrainian and German schools decreased (table 6). Similar changes took place in the northwestern county of Văşcăuţi between 1918 and 1922. Here the total number of schools increased only slightly, from 36 to 37, but the balance between Ukrainian and Romanian establishments shifted decisively. On the one hand, the number of Romanian schools went from 0 in 1918 to 17 in 1922. On the other hand, only 13 of 29 Ukrainian schools active in 1918 were still functioning in 1922. The few Polish and German-Jewish schools in Văşcăuţi County were left untouched.[69]

But Romanization proved neither a smooth, uniform process nor a real cure to the Ukrainian problem as conceived by the Romanians. For example, by 1923 the mainly Ukrainian Hotin County, bordering Bessarabia, had sixty-five Romanian schools, and only four Ukrainian ones. After reporting on the large number of Romanian schools in this largely Ukrainian area, military authorities inspecting the county's primary schools in 1923 remarked that nevertheless "the result . . . was not the expected one," given that many teachers and priests were still Ukrainians. Even more worrisome were the counties of Coţmani, Zastavna, and Vijniţa, which

[67] Ghibu, "Naţionalizarea," p. 225, and *Lege pentru învăţământul primar,* p. 12. In 1912, besides the 179 Romanian schools, 26 other schools had Romanian sections, and besides the 202 Ukrainian schools, 8 other schools had Ukrainian sections. According to Ukrainian sources, there were 216 or 218 Ukrainian primary schools in Bukovina before the war. *Ukraine: A Concise Encyclopedia,* vol. 2, p. 338, and QD 62/184, July 11, 1927.
[68] AA IX/ Varia 5, November 22, 1922, and Varia 10, December 20, 1922.
[69] Ibid., / Varia 10, December 20, 1922.

had 16, 23, and 28 Ukrainian schools, respectively, in 1923 and no Romanian ones at all. These districts were close to Bukovina's frontier with solidly Ukrainian Galicia. Romanian officials warned that unless drastic steps were taken, Romanian schools in the whole region would be irreversibly subverted by the Ukrainian irredenta.[70]

Ukrainian statements from the late 1920s indicate that Romanian efforts succeeded in severely restricting Ukrainian schools and other cultural outlets. Despite its international obligations to respect non-Romanians' rights to schools in their native tongue, Romania circumvented the Minority Protection Treaty by claiming that the Ukrainians were Ruthenized Romanians who needed to be returned to their true Romanian identity. Besides transforming all Ukrainian public schools into Romanian ones and depriving Ukrainian private schools of accreditation by 1927, Romanian authorities suppressed such cultural and national societies as the Chytal'nia Rus'koi Besidy and Sich clubs. Ukrainian demands for the reinstatement of Ukrainian as the language of instruction were repeatedly denied, and Ukrainian disappeared even as a subject of instruction.[71]

These measures sowed dissatisfaction among the Ukrainians without, however, really allaying the apprehensions of the Romanians. Ukrainians of course felt linguistically disenfranchised; the fact that prohibitions on Ukrainian extended even to religious instruction may well have politicized even the older, more passive population.[72] The suppression of Ukrainian language and schools fits into a broader pattern of political and social disenfranchisement which included gerrymandering administrative districts and prohibiting the use of Ukrainian in local government, courts, and commerce. An ordinance in spring 1927, for instance, demanded that all advertisements, posters, cinema, theatre, and concert programs be published either in Romanian or bilingually.[73]

From the Romanian viewpoint, however, the linguistic balance in northern Bukovina did not swing quickly and decisively enough from Ukrainian to Romanian. Although schools were massively Romanized on paper, many

---

[70] AA IX/ Varia 10, September 11, 1923.

[71] QD 62/187–192, July 11, 1927; MIC/1926/324/9, July 28, 1926; MIC/1929/87/22–23, May 28, 1929; Subtelny, *Ukraine*, p. 447; and *Ukraine: A Concise Encyclopedia*, vol. 1, p. 857.

[72] In 1924, Dr. Dutczak complained to the League of Nations that for the first time since 1595 Ukrainian Uniates in Cernăuţi had to use Romanian books and language. QD 61/49–53, December 28, 1924. The Romanian government responded that the Ukrainian Uniates were receiving texts from Galicia, and refused to submit them to the Ministry of Instruction for inspection. QD 61/55–58, n.d. In 1927, the Ukrainian inhabitants of Zamostea submitted a plea requesting that the minister of education relent to allow at least the teaching of religion in their mother tongue, so that their children might fully understand their religion, since the parents only knew one language. MIC 1929/87/27, September 30, 1927.

[73] QD 62/187, July 11, 1927.

teachers could not actually speak the new language of instruction.[74] By the mid-1930s, the strong-arm methods used in northern Bukovina certainly had not produced Romanization. Perhaps they had even backfired. An inspection in the environs of Cernăuți in 1934 yielded reports of "manifestations [that are] unhealthy and dangerous to the State [and which had] tried to crush the school and Romanian education."[75] The report cited "alarming" statistics on non-Romanian teachers: of 339 teachers in Storojineț county, 110 belonged to national minorities, and almost half of that number "knew the Romanian language hardly at all." In Cernăuți County, where 180 of 508 teachers belonged to national minorities, 105 did not know Romanian. Although the delinquent teachers were summoned to a Romanian language exam,[76] to Romanian authorities the very need for this examination indicated failure, for those to be tested had been teaching for years, sabotaging the patriotic education of their pupils through their ignorance of the state language.

Despite these discouraging signs, many Romanians convinced themselves that though the elites were dangerous, the masses of Ukrainians were innocuous. School officials tended to distinguish between the "good" common people and the "bad" intellectuals. A statement made in 1926 by the director of the Lycée No. 4 in Cernăuți exemplifies this view that, in its own way, reflects the important role of priests and other intelligentsia members in the national awakening of the Ukrainians in Eastern Galicia and Bukovina:[77]

> The population understands this moment and wishes to learn Romanian. But the Ruthenian intellectuals, especially the Greek-Catholics, most of whom have come from Galicia at the time of Coco Vasilco and Stocki [Baron Mykola Vasil'ko and Stepan Smal-Stotsky], do not want to accommodate themselves to the new structure of the Romanian state, and entertain an intense agitation not only in the villages beyond the Pruth, but also this side of the Pruth [where the Romanian population was denser], and they strive to maintain the unfair and unnatural situation from before the war created by the Austrian school and Austrian rulers, the clear adversaries of the Romanians.[78]

[74] Inspections from Vijnița County in the early 1920s suggested that not many teachers knew Romanian, even when the entire school system was about to be completely Romanized. AA IX/ Varia 6, November 30, 1922; and MIC/1925/124/237–241, Report on 1923–1924.
[75] AA XV/ Varia 5, December 20, 1934.
[76] Ibid.
[77] See Subtelny, Ukraine, pp. 238–240, 335.
[78] MIC/1926/324/9, July 28, 1926. Smal-Stotsky was from Galicia, he studied at Cernowitz University, and then, in 1885, he became professor of Ukrainian there. He was part of the "influx of the Galician intelligentsia" to Bukovina which greatly influenced the process of Ukrainian nation-building. Vasil'ko was a local landowner. (See Subtelny, Ukraine, p. 334.) Both were leaders in the Ukrainian movement beginning in the 1880s and effective politicians at the turn of the century. Nowosiwsky, Bukovinian Ukrainians, pp. 69–80.

Other education officials expressed similar views. They claimed that local Ukrainians would support Romanian nationalization measures were it not for the few recalcitrant intellectuals and strongly advised replacing Ukrainian teachers and priests with Romanians.[79]

Romanian authorities worried that, given the large numbers of Ukrainians, a few irredentist "troublemakers" could arouse a mass movement. Romanian efforts at cultural repression must be seen in this context. The embattled tone of these reports mirrored the state of siege reigning in northern Bukovina from 1918 to 1928. The authorities used martial law to impose even more arbitrary measures, which did not, however, completely intimidate the Ukrainians: when the state of siege was lifted, cultural clubs and national agitation quickly reemerged. In societies such as Chytal'nia Rus'koi Besidy, Ukrainians discussed strategies for reintroducing their language in schools. This group also demanded the removal of Romanian civil servants from Ukrainian regions and staged weekly theatre performances, which many Ukrainian peasants attended. In 1929, Ukrainian groups organized a boycott of the schools. It was to have continued until the Ukrainian language was reinstated, but the leaders of the movement were put on trial.[80]

New reports of Ukrainian subversion surfaced in the mid-1930s. A school director who had worked eight years in the district of Vășcăuți reported that the overwhelming majority of the teachers there still did not know Romanian and "worked openly against our state interests." He blamed the "priests, mayors, notaries, [and] retired teachers [for] perpetuating the Ukrainian consciousness of the Ruthenized population," and he estimated that one-quarter to one-half of the school children in Vășcăuți County did not attend the Romanized state schools but went to clandestine Ukrainian ones.[81] Other accounts from the same period concur, suggesting

[79] One inspector in 1923 reported that "for the most part, the rural Ruthenian-speaking population hardly participates at all in the Ukrainian political movements, but rather considers itself of Romanian nationality." MIC/1923/568/54. In Vășcăuți County in 1923, another school inspector blamed Ukrainian intellectual subversives for paralyzing Romanian actions, for the problems in Romanizing all the minority schools, and for influencing the population's views on the peace treaties and the legitimacy of Romanian institutions. In Romanian eyes, the Ukrainians here seemed to lead a broader block of national minorities: "Priests, civil servants of all categories, and even gendarmes are of Ukrainian, German, Jewish, etc. nationality. In all business dealings they use the Ukrainian language, and so the population is not obliged to learn the Romanian language." The inspector recommended that minority priests, teachers, and clerks be replaced by ethnic Romanians, or, at the very least, that politically dubious minority teachers be replaced by Romanian teachers. These latter should receive a substantial salary increase since their living expenses would be 30 percent higher than those of their Ukrainian counterparts in this Ukrainian area. The inspector was sanguine that "with these [Ukrainian] intellectuals out of the way, progress would be made in huge steps on the terrain of Romanian culture and of the re-Romanization of the population." AA IX/ Varia 10, December 20, 1922.
[80] MIC/1929/87/22–23, May 28, 1929.
[81] AA XV/ Varia 5, April 20, 1934.

that the Romanians in Bukovina were worse off in the mid-thirties than before the Great War and even that some Romanian teachers and children had been Ruthenized recently due to the militance of minority priests and teachers and to official indifference. One report blamed this situation on the overbidding of the minority population by the political parties, an indictment of Romania's imperfect, demagogic democracy. The author recommended an immediate purge of Ukrainian priests and teachers as "the most ardent adversaries of everything that is Romanian."[82]

Although parallel concerns existed with regard to German primary schools and the German population, Romanian authorities worried far less about them, both because the German population was considerably smaller and more geographically restricted and because ever since November 1918 the German community had asserted its allegiance to the new regime. In Gura-Humorului, the erstwhile "Germans' citadel in the south of Bukovina," Romanian had been introduced as the language of instruction in the schools by 1923. German children were still able to study their native language four to five hours a week with German teachers. Although inspectors felt that the Germans "had made their peace" with the new situation,[83] Germans were not entirely happy with their place in the new order of things. They too preferred separate schools, "only for German children," having "a German direction," and taught by German teachers in German.[84] These demands, however, were subject to negotiation, and they did not give rise to fears of irresolvable conflict.

The Nationalization of Secondary Schools

The nationalization of Bukovina's high schools pitted Romanians against urban Germanized Jews more than any other national minority because, Jews (and German culture) dominated in the urban areas where secondary schools were concentrated. In 1912, three of Bukovina's fifteen state secondary schools were in Cernăuţi, Bukovina's political and cultural capital. In Lycée No. 1 the language of instruction was German, and the majority of the students were Jewish. Lycée No. 2 had a basic program in German, with bilingual Ukrainian-German parallel classes, and Lycée No. 3 had bilingual Romanian-German classes.[85]

In December 1918 the new Romanian administration of Bukovina split the three Cernăuţi high schools, according to nationality, into five lycées.[86]

---

[82] AA xv/ Varia 5, December 20, 1934.
[83] AA ix/ Varia 10, December 27, 1923.
[84] MIC/1927/4/30–31, December 5, 1926.
[85] MIC/1923/568/21, 22, n.d.
[86] Ibid.

In 1922 the Romanian Lycée No. 1, "Aron Pumnul," had 15 classes and 359 pupils;[87] the German Lycée No. 2 had 9 classes and 238 pupils; the Jewish Lycée No. 3 had 28 classes and 1,054 pupils; the Ukrainian Lycée No. 4 had 13 classes and 650 pupils; and the Polish Lycée No. 5 had 7 classes and 166 pupils.[88] In addition there were an Orthodox *Realschule* with 12 classes and 260 pupils (in three grades parallel classes were taught in German); a state *Realschule* with 11 classes; and an Orthodox Girls' Lycée divided into Romanian and Ukrainian sections with 16 classes. Other boys' lycées existed in Suceava, Siret, Coţmani, and Vijniţa. There were girls' lycées in Rădăuţi and Suceava, and additional municipal girls' lycées existed in Cernăuţi and Rădăuţi.[89]

Two Views of the Jewish Question

On a tour of Cernăuţi high schools in 1922, Bukovina's secondary school inspector was struck by the size of the Jewish lycée. Whereas the school had functioned as only a section of the German state lycée before the war, it had become autonomous in 1918 "thanks to a broad spirit of liberty on the part of Bukovinian Romanian leaders."[90] Moreover, the lycée was huge by comparison to all the others in the region; the inspector doubted that any other high school in the whole country had twenty-eight classes and a monthly budget of 170,000 *lei*. His report to the Ministry of Public Instruction recommended reducing both the number of students and the budget.[91] The Jewish population of Cernăuţi had not only a much larger lycée than the other ethnic groups in the city and province, but Jewish youths also predominated in the *Real* Lycée No. 2, where 305 of 449 registered pupils in 1928 were Jews. Of the remaining 144 pupils only 28 were Orthodox Romanians and Ukrainians, a fact the authorities ascribed to insufficient dormitory space. Only one private facility existed in Cernăuţi to service all the city's high schools.[92] The scarcity of dormitory space naturally affected rural children, namely Romanians and Ukrainians.

[87] AA IX/ Varia 5, August 7, 1922. "Aron Pumnul" was named for a renowned nineteenth-century Transylvanian teacher who took refuge in Bukovina after the 1848 revolution and influenced the formation of the small nationally conscious Romanian elite in Bukovina.

[88] Ibid., and MIC/1923/568/54, n.d. According to Benno Straucher, a Jewish MP, the Jewish lycée had been founded in 1919 with 31 classes. In 1923–1924 it had already been reduced from the 1922 student body of 1,054 to one of less than 900 pupils and 23 classes. See CA/RM/6, August 8, 1925.

[89] AA IX/ Varia 5, August 7, 1922, and Victor Morariu, "Unirea la Suceava," in Nistor, ed., *Amintiri răzleţe*, p. 243.

[90] AA IX/ Varia 5, August 7, 1922.

[91] Ibid. He suggested that the local school committee could pick up the extra expense, following the example of the Old Kingdom, where this kind of financial decentralization had worked quite well.

[92] AA VI/ Varia 17, [n.d.], 1928.

Although Romanian authorities may not have worried about the opportunities of Ukrainians, they were not indifferent to the fate of Romanians.

To many Romanians in Bukovina, Jewish preponderance in urban secondary schools, and especially in the provincial capital's lycées, flew in the face of national pride and nationalist goals. To the Jewish community, however, efforts to undercut its prewar position were clearly anti-Semitic. The Jews remembered fondly their prewar situation as one "in the most beautiful full bloom."[93] That desirable *statu quo ante* was now being whittled away. Where once Jews had had free access to all Austrian schools, they were now ghettoized into Jewish schools that were in turn being Romanized and cut back. Jewish leaders complained of harrassment and persecution of Jewish pupils, teachers, and school officials. By the mid-1920s the Cernăuți Jewish community was angry about anti-Semitic measures in other areas as well. Its grievances ranged from discrimination against Jewish civil servants to the problem of the Jewish *Heimatslose* rendered stateless by the malicious misapplication of postwar laws.[94] Most complaints, however, arose in regard to education.

One of Bukovina's Jewish MPs, Benno Straucher, in correspondence with Prime Minister Ion Brătianu and Wilhelm Filderman, the Jewish leader from Bucharest, charged that Jewish primary school administrators were being fired or demoted to teacher rank. Straucher claimed that primary schools in Cernăuți, a city where Jews made up 50 percent of the population and paid 90 percent of the taxes, were being "purged" of Jewish teachers through pensionings and suspensions. Similar changes were occurring in secondary schools. Jews were usually replaced by gentiles—generally Romanians, but also Germans and Ukrainians—but younger Jews were also hired over the heads of the community to replace teachers of religion whom the community had chosen previously and was content with. Furthermore, the state was refusing normal financial support for the reconstruction of Jewish schools and other public buildings.[95]

The story of the Jewish Lycée No. 3 in Cernăuți exemplifies dramatically the institutional loss of power which Bukovina's Jewish community experienced. The school had been established in 1919 by royal decree. According to the principle of national lycées, Jewish pupils from schools all over Cernăuți had had to transfer there, forming a large student body of 1,300, attending 31 classes.[96] Bukovinian Jews viewed this segregation of high

[93] CA/RM 134, n.d. [1928]

[94] CA/RM/6, August 8, 1925. On the succession of treaties, decrees, and laws affecting Jewish citizenship in interwar Romania see Joshua Starr, "Jewish Citizenship in Rumania," *Jewish Social Studies* 3 (January 1941): 64–68. Bukovina's Jews were most adversely affected by the new legislation, which was applied differently in each province.

[95] CA/RM/6, August 8, 1925.

[96] Ibid., and CA/RM/134, n.d. [1928].

schools into nationalities primarily as the separation of their children from Bukovina's Germans.[97] Previously, Jews and Germans together had dominated the city's lycées; lycée education had been, virtually by definition, a German one, and was imbibed together with German culture. Romanian authorities hoped to separate the Jews from their German/Austrian identity and to give them a Romanian orientation, setting a transition period of ten years, after which all instruction would be only in Romanian or Hebrew. In the meantime, both Romanian and Hebrew subjects were to be taught.[98]

The capacity of the Jewish lycée suffered successive reductions: from 1,300 students and 31 classes in 1919, to 28 classes and 1,054 pupils in 1922, to over 800 pupils and 23 classes in 1923–1924.[99] In 1924–1925, 20 classes were allotted for the same number of students, and in 1925–1926 there were 17 classes for 534 students. In six years, then, the number of students and classes was cut by approximately half. The alarming significance of this trend did not elude the Jewish community, especially since most Jewish high school students in Cernăuţi were concentrated in one institution. Over the protests of local Jewish leaders, Jewish youths were being progressively squeezed out of the Cernăuţi school system. The contraction was achieved in great part by diverting Jewish pupils to private schools, whose number soared after Bulkovina's incorporation with Romania.[100]

As table 7 indicates, Jewish youngsters were the main clients of private secondary institutions both before and after World War I. Although the percentages suggest a drop in the Jewish use of private schools, the large growth of the private school system creates a different context. A total of 363 pupils attended private secondary schools in 1913, 300 of them Jews. By 1923–1924, private secondary schools had expanded to accommodate 1,953 pupils in all, of whom 1,522 were Jews. Some Jewish youths, like the gifted Wolf Goldmann of Gregor von Rezzori's *Memoirs of an Anti-Semite*, went to study in Viennese high schools, fleeing Bukovina's Romanization,[101] but most took refuge from the nationalized public school system in the local network of private schools. Not that private Jewish high schools were a safe haven. To members of the Jewish community it appeared that these were also suffering "true martyrdom," due to the "hostility and persecutions of the authorities." Jewish advocates charged that examining committees had "shown a manifestly anti-Semitic attitude," failing in some

[97] CA/RM/134, n.d.
[98] Ibid. In 1928, the teachers at Lycée No. 3 still barely spoke Romanian, and some of them conducted class in German. See AA VI/ Varia 17, n.d. [1928].
[99] AA IX/ Varia 5, August 7, 1922.
[100] Board of Education, *Draft of Act concerning Private Teaching* (Bucharest: Editura Cartea românească, 1927), pp. 69–70.
[101] "*Skushno*," in Gregor von Rezzori, *Memoirs of an Anti-Semite: A Novel in Five Stories* (New York: Viking, 1981).

Table 7.   Profile of private school pupils, by ethnicity, Bukovina,
1913 and 1923–1924

	Jewish	German	Romanian	Ukrainian	Polish	Total
1913	300	28	24	4	3	359
(%)	83.6	7.8	6.7	1.1	0.8	100
1923–1924	1,522	251	31	140	9	1,953
(%)	77.9	12.8	1.6	7.2	0.5	100

Source: Board of Education, Draft of Act concerning Private Teaching, pp. 69–70.

cases three-quarters of the Jewish candidates, and that private Jewish lycées were being unfairly closed down and decertified.[102]

Certain educational measures strained Jewish teachers in particular. The concentration of state Jewish secondary education in the Lycée No. 3 in Cernăuţi was accompanied by the transfer of many Jewish teachers from other parts of Bukovina to that school.[103] But beginning in 1921–1922, with the progressive reductions at the lycée, some of the staff was assigned to different schools within the city, others were laid off or moved "to the most distant corners of the Old Kingdom," Transylvania, and elsewhere.[104] Many were sent to all-Romanian areas for total immersion in the state language. These Jewish teachers objected vehemently to their uprooting from their homes, familiar surroundings, and networks in the still powerful Jewish community of Bukovina. Some preferred to stay and change professions, claiming that living and housing conditions made such "a transfer . . . equal to economic disaster."[105] These teachers were sometimes sent to posts in all-gentile areas, where they could not properly practice their religion nor benefit from the support of the community in case of hardship.[106] To add insult to injury, Jewish teachers who had made the effort to learn Romanian and take the proper exams were occasionally replaced by gentiles anyway.[107]

Pupils of the Jewish lycée had to pay much higher tuition fees than their gentile peers.[108] In a further injustice, the building that had housed Lycée No. 3 was taken over by a new conservatory, the Jewish lycée being given

[102] CA/RM/6, August 8, 1925, and Alliance Israélite Universelle, Paris, Archives Roumanie (hereafter AIU), III/B/52, May 5, 1927.
[103] CA/RM/134, n.d.
[104] Ibid.
[105] CA/RM 6, August 8, 1925.
[106] Ibid.
[107] Ibid.
[108] Jewish students paid an annual fee of 1,000 lei in the lower lycée grades, and 1,600 lei in the upper grades, compared with the 300 and 500 lei, respectively, paid at other lycées. CA/RM 6, August 8, 1925.

"two small buildings" in which both morning and afternoon sessions were necessary. Jewish parents were forced to contribute an additional tax to raise funds for the construction of a new building, and they wondered why they were singled out among all nationalities for this expense. Dr. Straucher protested these injustices and one more: Jewish children attending state schools were forced to write on Saturday, the Jewish Sabbath, in spite of Romania's guarantees to its national and religious minorities of full religious, cultural, and linguistic rights.[109]

Other grievances followed related injustices. Jewish educators gradually saw themselves excluded from Cernăuți schools, and Jewish civil servants, no longer trusted, gradually lost their positions in public administration. Not only did Jewish parents have to pay for the construction of Jewish schools, but the Jewish community did not receive its fair share of taxes for rebuilding prayer houses damaged during the war. The Jewish community also lost the right to impose its own tax on its members. Not only were Jewish pupils judged with unfair harshness by examining commissions, but Jewish university students became the targets of anti-Semitic attacks. All this signalled the end of an era in which Jews had enjoyed both equal rights and social privilege.

In fighting for the restoration of their previous status, Bukovina's Jews invoked their loyalty to the Romanian regime and pointed to the country's constitution, which promised equal treatment to all of its citizens. For example, in Straucher's parliamentary speech of November 1924, he declared that "Bukovina has been in several respects like a stepchild . . . [to Romania], although Bukovina with its civilized population—patriotic, obedient, grateful, and full of feelings—today forms an integral part of Greater Romania, and therefore our population without distinction has the right to be treated in all regards on an equal footing with the population from the Old Kingdom.[110]

But Bukovinian Jews also made an appeal to the regionalist sentiments of other ethnic and social groups in Bukovina. In the same speech, Straucher focused on the decline of Cernăuți from its previous status of a capital under Austrian rule. "The flowering city of Cernăuți," he said, "with a very patriotic and loyal, civilized, and prudent population, has lost the function and position of a capital, has suffered various economic, moral, and political damages, in a word . . . it is losing its significance day by day."[111] The bulk of Straucher's speech set forth specific Jewish complaints in Bukovina, but the regionalist lament formed a subtext. Happier times had preceded Bukovina's stepchildhood, and the Jews had been the benefi-

---

[109] Ibid.
[110] CA/RM/134, [November 28 and 29, 1924].
[111] Ibid.

ciaries of that more auspicious, more autonomous past. The better fortune of Bukovina in general as an Austrian province appeared in Straucher's argument as a corollary to the prosperity of the Jews and the flourishing of their schools.

Many of the issues raised by Bukovinian Jews in the mid-1920s were two-sided. Measures that they interpreted as punitively anti-Semitic may have been adopted not so much against the Jews as for the Romanians, although the negative, sometimes brutal, effect on Jews is undeniable. The Romanization of Bukovina's school system was thorough, it transgressed the Minorities Protection Treaty of 1919, and it impinged on all non-Romanian ethnic groups, as we saw in detail in the case of the Ukrainians, and even on Romanians whose loyalty to the center may have been questionable.

Nation- and state-building strategies were implemented through such educational policies as those that determined the transfers of teachers from Bukovina to the Old Kingdom. In 1921 the General Secretary of Education in Cernăuți identified to the Ministry of Education in Bucharest the two groups whose transfer to the Old Kingdom had first priority: (1) Ruthenian teachers whose political agitation had made them "impossible" in their Bukovina posts, and (2) teachers made "superfluous" by the Romanization of their schools, and who, being tenured, could not legally be dismissed.[112] While the "Ruthenians" were identified specifically as a dangerous group whose transplantation was desirable, the Jews were not. It is likely, however, that the second category of teachers were mostly Jews, for Jewish teachers were being rendered superfluous, "*supranumerari,*" by the Romanization of their schools. Logically, the second category could include neither Romanians nor Ukrainians, but had to consist of German, Jewish, or Polish teachers, probably some of each. The ethnicity of the "superfluous" group may not have been mentioned because of its very heterogeneity. By the same token, as Jewish leaders argued, Jews were adversely affected by the transfer policy. They may well have been more affected than all the other groups because of their numerical preponderance. Indeed, a striking lexical similarity exists between the official formulation of the problem and the Jewish protests advanced in the mid-1920s. The unusual term "*supranumerari*" ("superfluous") was also used by Straucher in his correspondence and speeches from the 1920s to refer to the pretext on which Jewish teachers were being laid off or transferred.[113] The point is that, unlike the Ukrainians, the Jews were not named by name, and Education Secretariat officials may well have thought of them as part of a general category of educators associated with the old order, a category rendered superfluous by Romanization.

[112] MIC/1921/275/227, March 9, 1921.
[113] See CA/RM/6, August 8, 1925.

When teachers were transferred to the Old Kingdom, the ministry wanted to keep them there as long as possible, arguing that it was "in the interest of the cause" that non-Romanians serve for as long as possible in exclusively Romanian environments.[114] Petitions for transfers back to Bukovina were often curtly rejected on ostensible grounds of no vacancies.[115] But the ministerial correspondence about the petitions reveals the real reasons for these rejections. One school inspector, for example, wrote the General Directorate for Education in 1922 that, "Considering that in our district, we have an important number of non-Romanian superfluous (*supranumerari*) teachers, and since our district is a minority (*eteroglot*) district in which a non-Romanian does not have the possibility to learn the Romanian language, we cannot declare ourselves for the petitioner's transfer to our district [Cernăuţi]."[116]

In an exception that proved the rule, a petition was granted to a young teacher named Maria Isar, an ethnic Romanian from a *răzeş* (free peasant) family that had been among the "pillars of Romanianism" in Văşcăuţi county. Isar had been appointed to a school in Buzău county in the Old Kingdom. She argued convincingly that in her native Bukovina she would perform her teaching duties "zealously," living up to her patriotic lineage by reawakening those who had been "alienated from their ancestral language and customs," her "Ruthenized brothers." For her to remain in Buzău, Isar wrote, would be like "pouring water into a full fountain."[117] The ministry approved her request.

Official correspondence and reports from Bukovina in the 1920s betray unease over the abilities and loyalties of nearly all teachers, regardless of ethnicity, sometimes even including Romanians.[118] In documents referring to teachers' resistance to learning Romanian and to taking the Romanian language, history, and geography exams,[119] Jews appear not to have been singled out as an object of concern. Nor were Jews alone in their protests.

---

[114] MIC/1922/285/64, n.d.

[115] MIC/1922/285/60–66, n.d.

[116] MIC/1922/285/61, n.d.

[117] MIC/1922/285/81–82, September 1922, n.d.

[118] The Organization of Young Teachers of Romania (Organizaţia Tineretului Învăţătoresc din România) struggled against the "danger of foreignism" in Bukovina in the 1930s, focusing specifically on Bukovina's Regional Association of Teachers, whose leaders, they said, "out of a narrow spirit of regionalism and petty material interests have joined in solidarity with their brothers from before, the minorities. . . . The protests of the minorities were immediately backed by the *regionalist* leaders of the Association, [who were] offended in their national dignity because they were curtly asked to prove their *Românism*." Here too, the writer stresses the regionalism of both Romanians and minorities in Bukovina, to such an extent that it is hard to know whose "national dignity" he means, that of the minorities or that of the regionalist Romanians. AA IX/ Varia 6, February 20, 1935.

[119] AA IX/ Varia 6, November 30, 1922; MIC/1924/408/56, August 16, 1923; MIC/1924/408/75, September 2, 1923; MIC/1923/464/76, June 2, 1923; and MIC/1924/408/53–55, September 2, 1923.

The Roman Catholic church, for instance, disagreed with the single authority of the Ministry of Public Instruction.[120] The president of the Christian German Society of Bukovina argued that the requalifying exam under the new regime should be limited to language, lest non-Romanian pedagogues feel "injured in their state of citizenship and in the guarantee of their profession vis-à-vis Romanian [colleagues] from whom no proof of special knowledge was expected at all."[121]

Neither Ukrainian, nor Polish, nor German lycées were spared the Romanization measures imposed on the Jewish high schools. In 1923, the Ukrainian Lycée in Cernăuţi adopted Romanian as the language of instruction and from then on offered Ukrainian only as an elective language course.[122] Although three years later the director of the lycée recalled that the Romanization measures had gone smoothly, in fact the process was marred by some anti-Romanian incidents in 1923.[123] "Subversive and antipatriotic tendencies" emerged again in 1924 and 1925 when Ukrainian pupils participated in irredentist societies and destroyed the coronation trees.[124]

The Polish Lycée in Cernăuţi also lasted only a few years. This school had been promised to Bukovina's Polish population in 1918 in exchange for its acquiescence to the province's union with Romania.[125] Polish and Romanian interests converged in opposition to a Western Ukrainian state in eastern Galicia and northern Bukovina. Later, Romanian officials surmised that the lycée had been an unnecessary concession, arguing that even without it "the Poles would have found themselves on our side, because of their resentments for the Ukrainians."[126] By 1922–1923, the fluid frontiers of that area had solidified, shutting out Ukrainian territorial claims. Relations between Poland and Romania remained cordial as both states focused their attentions internally on their considerable nationalities problems.

Although never regarded with the intense suspicion reserved for Ukrainian or Jewish institutions, the Polish Lycée was also restricted by the

[120] MIC/1924/408/56, August 16, 1923, and MIC/1924/408/75, September 2, 1923.
[121] MIC/1923/464/76, June 2, 1923.
[122] MIC/1923/568/53, n.d., and MIC/1926/324/9, July 28, 1926.
[123] MIC/1926/324/9, July 28, 1926. In 1923, the inspector general for the Cernăuţi region wanted to believe that this change would be easily accepted by most parents who were "sick of the sterile and antipatriotic politics of a few small circles of Ukrainian intellectuals brought by the Austrians from Galicia;" but he reported that some "sad incidents" occurred at Lycée No. 4 involving the destruction of Romanian royal symbols—the coronation tree and the king's proclamation to the schools. MIC/1923/568/54, n.d.
[124] MIC/1925/417/111, April 10, 1925.
[125] In Bukovina there were approximately 30,000 Poles in 1922, of which about half lived in Cernăuţi. They constituted a sizable minority of the provincial capital's population of 87,128 (in 1910). Ibid. and Statistischen Zentralkommission, Bewegung der Bevölkerung, vol. 8, pt. 1, p. 11.
[126] MIC/1923/568/21, 22, n.d.

Romanian nationalist code. At a school show in 1922, when the Polish students and faculty hung Polish symbols and flags and performed a tableau vivant of Poland's apotheosis, the Directorate of Public Education was shocked by what it called an "inadmissible incident from a patriotic point of view." The episode assumed added significance because the Polish consul had attended the performance; the diplomat was accused of engaging in nationalist agitation.[127] Although no territorial disputes existed between Poland and Romania, and although Poles were a negligibly small minority, such competing nationalisms could not continue side by side within the Romanian state of the early 1920s. When the need for Polish cooperation disappeared with the consolidation of a Romanian order in Bukovina, the Polish Lycée was no longer tolerated in Cernăuţi. In 1923, the pupils of that school were incorporated in the Romanian Lycée No. 1.[128]

Other evidence, too, suggests that the mistreatment of the Jews in Bukovina was part of a larger pattern of national suppression. In 1923, the president of the examining commission for minority secondary teachers reported a rather optimistic picture of the state of Bukovinian education. (That year, 142 of the 167 candidates examined passed.) The president considered the results "quite satisfactory" and attributed them to the system of transfers of non-Romanian teachers to Romanian areas.[129] He wanted the system to continue, specifying that the Ruthenian and Jewish teachers who had been sent to other parts of the country had learned Romanian quite well: in fact, some of them were ready to be reappointed to Bukovina, given their improved knowledge and loyal attitude toward the state.[130] Other inspectors were certainly less sanguine about the Romanization of Bukovina's teaching cadre, but their disapproval reflected equally on all ethnic groups. Even many Romanian teachers did not know Romanian well and could benefit from time in the Old Kingdom.[131] Jews and Ukrainians, however, were treated comparably—and positively—in the 1923 report. The author reproached Roman Catholics most harshly. He condemned Catholic teachers of religion—most probably Germans and Poles—for attempting to escape Romanian language, history, and geography exams. Having thus mentioned all the main ethnic and religious minorities in Bukovina—Ukrainians, Jews, and Catholics—he concluded:

[127] Ibid.

[128] MIC/1923/568/54, n.d.

[129] MIC/1924/408/53–55, September 2, 1923. Evhen Petrushevytch's "Complaint" of July 1927 mentioned that most Ukrainian teachers of primary, secondary, and professional schools had been transferred from Bukovina "to the end of Romania." To Petrushevytch, who was the president of the Western Ukrainian National Republic, Bukovina was not properly part of Romania. In his terms "Romania" must have referred to the Old Kingdom. QD 62/193, July 11, 1927.

[130] MIC/1924/408/53–55, September 2, 1923.

[131] See AA VI/ Varia 17, n.d. [1928], and AA XV/ Varia 5, April 20, 1934.

The teachers from Region No. XIV, almost all of them raised in submission to the Austrian state, have started to realize that the Romanian state has a durability that no one can overturn. They have started to reconcile themeselves to the idea of a Romanian state and they bow before the authority of this state the more decisive the measures which the government takes vis-à-vis any citizen in order to defend the prestige of this state and to remind everyone that one has obligations toward the state which one cannot evade.[132]

This concluding passage was no longer concerned with any one ethnic or religious group. The emphasis here fell on Bukovina's Austrian inheritance, which had left its imprint on "almost all" teachers, Romanians presumably included. In this man's view, the Romanian state, depicted here as antiparticularist, democratic, and centralist, had to assert itself not so much against non-Romanian ethnic groups as against the regionalism Bukovina derived from its Austrian heritage. Although this report referred to efforts at integrating different national and religious minorities into the Greater Romanian state, it was not concerned with the national issue per se. Its emphasis, rather, was on integration as such. Consequently, it paid as much attention to unifying Bukovina with the mother country as to dislodging the Austrian mentality and loyalties from all the Romanian citizens in Bukovina.

Jews were nevertheless most affected by the policies of centralization and integration enforced in the 1920s for several reasons. Because Jews had what Romanians coveted most, education and urban status, and because they occupied an elite position in the Austrian system, it was important to unseat the Jews as a symbol of Romanian achievement. Anti-Semitism was thus in one sense a by-product of Romania's efforts to assert its interests in formerly Austrian Bukovina. Nonetheless, even if only a by-product of more general nationalization policies, anti-Semitism was hard to control. It had its own momentum, and it operated not only provincewide but on the broader stage of Greater Romania where extreme nationalists were mounting an increasingly effective nationwide campaign. Understandably, Bukovina's Jews interpreted the attempts at Romanizing the province as anti-Semitism.

In the mid-1920s, the tensions between Romanians and Jews surfaced in the Jewish-dominated capital of Bukovina. The tragic events that occurred in Cernăuți in 1926, which involved both local and national actors, took place against this particular local backdrop of educational struggles.

[132] MIC/1924/408/53–55, September 2, 1923.

A Violent Baccalaureate

The year 1926 was the second year that a baccalaureate examination was administered in Greater Romania. The exam, last given in 1908, was reinstituted in 1925 under Constantin Angelescu's Ministry of Education, perhaps in response to foreign universities' complaints about the low level of Romanian students' preparation.[133] But Angelescu also envisaged the exam as a way to stop the rise of an intellectual proletariat by screening high school seniors for entrance to universities.[134] Exam sessions took place in the summer and early fall.[135] For many youths the baccalaureate became an extra hurdle on the road to higher education and a career.

Political and ethnic camps judged the baccalaureate to be discriminatory according to differing criteria. An article in the weekly of the Union of Independent Students asserted that about 80 percent of the examinees had failed the baccalaureate in 1925 and charged that the exam was corruptly administered and had a class bias. "The baccalaureate exam thus appears as a means of selection only for the poor, those starting from below, in order to throw them into an even darker misery, while the sons of the rich are not subjected with equal severity to such a sieve."[136] Others saw the baccalaureate being used primarily against the minority nationalities and the new provinces. The German minority disliked the exam and campaigned to have it suppressed.[137] The Ukrainian minority also found the baccalaureate unfair, while Romul Boilă, a Romanian Transylvanian senator, charged that the baccalaureate sought to "cut the future of young lives from the annexed provinces."[138] Jewish observers felt that the uneven administration of the exams amounted to a roundabout way of introducing the otherwise illegal *numerus clausus* policy. A Romanian Jew from Galaţi in a December 1927 report characterized the baccalaureate in these terms:

> For the purpose of excluding the Jews as far as possible from university studies and in order to create a virtual *Numerus Clausus,* the so-called Baccalaureate Law was passed. This enables the government to "plough" Jewish would-be matriculants at will. The matriculation examiners, according to this law, are

[133] Zsombor de Szasz, *The Minorities in Roumanian Transylvania* (London: Richards Press, 1927), p. 271.

[134] AA VI/ Varia 5, n.d.

[135] Iosif I. Gabrea, *Şcoala românească: structura şi politica ei 1921–1932* (Bucharest: Tip. Bucovina, n.d.), p. 31.

[136] *Viaţa universitară,* October 18, 1925.

[137] QD 62/259, 260, March 28, 1929. According to Szasz, *Minorities,* p. 280, the baccalaureate was used as a "veiled numerus clausus."

[138] QD 62/192–193, July 11, 1927, and George Silviu, "Tragedia învăţământului secundar," *Lupta,* October 22, 1927.

appointed by the Minister, who sends examiners to the schools of the Minorities carefully selected to ensure the failure of as many candidates as may be agreeable to the anti-Semitic party. This law and these examination methods have resulted during the last three years in the failure of from 60 to 70 percent of the Jewish candidates sent up from the Minorities' schools.[139]

The fall 1926 session of the baccalaureate in Cernăuți stirred up minority protests and the arrest of over twenty Jewish youths.[140] These incidents, in turn, engendered a nationalist backlash and the murder of a Jewish youth.

One hundred eighty-two candidates presented themselves for the baccalaureate exam in Cernăuți in the fall of 1926. Significantly, only 15 of them (or 8.2 percent) seem to have been ethnic Romanians; the remaining 167 (or 91.8 percent) had graduated from the German, Jewish, Ukrainian, Jewish-German, and private lycées.[141] A clear ethnic breakdown of the minority candidates is not available, but it is likely, given the demographic structure of Cernăuți and the shape of the ensuing protest, that most of them were Jewish. Of the 182 candidates, 142 passed the written exam, but only 60 also passed the second, oral, and decisive part of the exam. Two-thirds of all the examinees and 80 percent of the Jewish candidates failed the baccalaureate in October 1926.[142] The Minister of Public Education was apparently convinced "that the examiners drew up the questions intentionally to the end that it should be impossible for the boys to pass."[143]

In notes prepared for a session of parliament, Bukovinian Zionist deputy Mayer Ebner commented on the atmosphere created around the exam.

[139] The Joint Foreign Committee of the Board of Deputies of British Jews and the Anglo-Jewish Association, *The Jewish Minority in Roumania: Further Correspondence with the Roumanian Government respecting the Grievances of the Jews,* Presented to the Board of Deputies of British Jews and the Council of the Anglo-Jewish Association, April 1928 (London: Joint Foreign Committee of the Board of Deputies of British Jews and the Anglo-Jewish Association, 1928), p. 7. In 1929, the exam was "simplified," the written exam was shortened and minorities could take the science part in their native language. QD 62/263/4, May 3, 1929.

[140] The Joint Foreign Committee of the Board of Deputies of British Jews and the Anglo-Jewish Association, *Correspondence with the Roumanian Government respecting the Grievances of the Jews,* 2d ed., Presented to the Board of Deputies of British Jews and the Council of the Anglo-Jewish Association, June 1927 (London: Joint Foreign Committee of the Board of Deputies of British Jews and the Anglo-Jewish Association, 1928), p. 41.

[141] MIC/1926/324/90–105, October 19, 1926.

[142] Ibid.; and Joint Foreign Committee, *Jewish Minority,* 2d ed., p. 41. Inspector Marinescu's report to the Ministry of Education does not give the ethnic breakdown of the minority candidates. Evhen Petrushevytch contends that there were 61 Romanian candidates and 29 Ukrainians. Berthold Brandmarker gives an accounting of the baccalaureate candidates at Aron Pumnul lycée, where apparently the conflict in October 1926 erupted. According to him 106 students had registered for the baccalaureate there, out of which 94 were Jews; 92 of the Jewish candidates failed. See QD 62/193, July 11, 1927, and Berthold Brandmarker, "David Fallik," in *Geschichte der Juden in der Bukowina,* ed. Hugo Gold, vol. 2 (Tel Aviv: Olamenu, 1962), pp. 174–175.

[143] The Joint Foreign Committee, *Jewish Minority,* 2d ed., p. 42.

The large number of failed candidates, Ebner wrote, "agitated profoundly and enormously the entire population of the city of Cernăuți without distinction to creed or nationality. The population cannot understand that pupils who attended the lycée during eight years, fulfilling their studies successfully, graduating up to the eighth [final] grade of the lycée, might be declared unfit to attend a university."[144] The Ukrainian leader Evhen Petrushevytch also complained of the high number of Ukrainian candidates who had failed the baccalaureate in October 1926.[145] The proportion of successful baccalaureate candidates nationally was substantially higher than the 33 percent cited by Inspector Marinescu, and particularly higher than the proportions of Ukrainians and Jews cited by Petrushevytch and Brandmarker respectively: in 1926, 50.2 percent of the candidates passed the exam nationally.[146]

According to some sources, the troubles in Cernăuți began before the disappointing results had been posted. This may be explained by the fact that a large number of non-Romanian candidates had failed the exam the previous sessions because of what they perceived as a biased commission, and these minority baccalaureate candidates again anticipated unfairness. The previous year at one high school in Cernăuți all the Romanian pupils had passed, but only 30 percent of the German and Ukrainian pupils, and 15 percent of the Jewish pupils.[147]

According to Berthold Brandmarker, the results were announced on the evening of October 7, the last day of exams.[148] Even if the results were only posted the next day, some or all candidates may already have been aware of their status on the evening of October 7. In his report, the Inspector General wrote that "the main provocateurs were the rejected candidates D. Fallik and B. Schächter," implying that the results were indeed out.[149] A crowd joined by people coming out of stores surrounded the members of the examining commission—a mixed group of local and Old Kingdom teachers—and attacked them aggressively while they were

---

[144] Ebner cited a different set of figures: he wrote that 213 out of 352 failed the baccalaureate. Ebner's figures may have included both the summer and fall sessions of the baccalaureate examination in Cernăuți, or possibly his figures were simply inaccurate. Although his total number of candidates is larger, his proportion of failures is somewhat smaller than that which emerges from the inspector's figures—60.5 percent vs. 66 percent. Thus, he is not trying to exaggerate the number of students who failed. I use the official inspector's figures. MIC/1926/324/119–120.

[145] According to him, 26 out of 29 Ukrainians failed, as opposed to 2 out of 61 Romanians. QD 62/193, July 11, 1927. The source of numerical inconsistency may be the counting of candidates registered for the baccalaureate at different high schools.

[146] Calculated from Ministerul instrucțiunii, *Proect de lege asupra învățământului secundar teoretic* (Bucharest: Editura Cartea românească, 1928), p. 98.

[147] The Jewish Telegraphic Agency, October 21, 1926, cited in Joint Foreign Committee, *Jewish Minority,* 2d ed., p. 41.

[148] Brandmarker, "David Fallik," p. 175.

[149] MIC/1926/324/90–105, October 19, 1926.

on their way to supper in a restaurant. The police, who did not intervene immediately, eventually made some arrests. Among those arrested were five pupils from the Jewish Lycée No. 3, including David Fallik and Benno Schächter.[150]

A slightly different account of these events describes the protest as specifically directed at the history examiner Diaconescu, who emerged alone out of the lycée building. The leader of the protest, David Fallik, approached Diaconescu spontaneously and asked, "Why did you do that?" During the confrontation the crowd began to shout "Down with Diaconescu!" An angry mob chased Diaconescu in his horse-drawn cab around town and roughed him up. Ironically, he was rescued by a Jewish policeman. Fallik and 23 others were arrested and charged with abuse of a public employee in the exercise of his duties.[151]

The incident produced a sense of righteous indignation among members of the examining commission and local educators. After an investigation, the Inspector General found that the commission had "worked conscientiously and impartially," and that there had been "no tendency toward or hint of anti-Semitism." The commission had found most of the minority students to be insufficiently prepared, and all the decisions about passes and failures were unanimous.[152] The president of the commission was Professor Traian Brăileanu, a native of Bukovina who taught sociology at Cernăuți University and was one of the first academics to adhere to the Legion of the Archangel Michael after its foundation in 1927.[153] In his report, he wrote that the commission found "the height of ignorance . . . in the history and geography of the fatherland." The inspector also pointed to the better results obtained by another baccalaureate commission in the region, which had examined candidates from lycées in Storojineţ, Briceni, and Dorohoi; he concluded that in the Cernăuți setting, with its frequent evening dances and superficial learning, young people lived a more frivolous life.[154]

While casting aspersions on the corrupt, unhealthy, cosmopolitan atmosphere of Cernăuți and on the rebel examinees, the inspector hinted at larger forces looming behind the latter. He intimated that the "demonstration of the minority youths" was no spontaneous act but "the result of premeditation, the goal of which was simply to repeal the baccalaureate." In a

[150] Ibid.
[151] Brandmarker, "David Fallik," p. 175. The Marinescu report describes a broader protest but also mentions that the crowd pursued Diaconescu. MIC/1926/324/90–105, October 19, 1926.
[152] MIC/1926/324/90–105, October 19, 1926.
[153] Leon Volovici, *Nationalist Ideology and Antisemitism: The Case of Romanian Intellectuals in the 1930s* (Oxford: Pergamon, 1991), pp. 70, 162–163.
[154] MIC/1926/324/90–105, October 19, 1926.

meeting with Marinescu, representatives of the minorities[155] had said that
the baccalaureate was pointless, and should be administered, if at all, by
a lycée's own teachers, not by outside examiners. Marinescu concluded
that "Romanian public opinion had been outraged; the teachers who bore
no guilt other than that of conscientiously fulfilling their duty were insulted
and brutalized."[156] No matter what verdict the courts of law might reach,
the inspector wanted some satisfaction on behalf of the schools, to uphold
the institution of the baccalaureate and the authority of teachers and
examiners. The offending youths were disciplined: their right to compete
in the exams again during the next two sessions was taken from them.
Participants in the melee who were too young for the baccalaureate were
penalized by expulsion from school.

The polemics over the baccalaureate session in Cernăuţi had begun
before October 7. Right after the written part of the exam and before the
results had been posted, Mayer Ebner had written an article in the *Ost
Jüdische Zeitung* condemning the appointment of Professor Brăileanu as
president of the examining commission on the grounds of his membership
in the right-wing anti-Semitic organization Liga Apărării Naţional Creştine
(LANC, the League of National Christian Defense). Ebner had thus stood
up for the rights of the minorities, but some took his stance as a euphemistic
defense of the rights of "Yids." Ebner's prophecy, however, that Brăileanu
would persecute candidates of "another law"—that is, non-Christians—
may well have brought about Brăileanu's dismissal.[157]

According to Nicolae Gheorghiu, a geography professor on the baccalaureate commission, Jews had intervened in other ways too in preparation
for the 1926 baccalaureate. Mayer Ebner and a man named Gerner had
offered Gheorghiu and Diaconescu lodgings at their houses, so that the
two Old Kingdom teachers might not have to stay in hotels. Four examiners
were told suggestively that certain candidates' parents would show their
appreciation in exchange for leniency. Household objects and large sums
of money were mentioned as possible payoffs. The attempts to bribe were
directed significantly at the nonlocal members of the commission, who
were feared as the "hangmen." On the other hand, the Jewish parents to
whom Gheorghiu's report seems to refer had confidence in the local teachers with whom they felt they "could easily get along."[158] And, in fact,

---

[155] Mayer Ebner, Karl Klüger, Alfred Kohlruss, and Anton von Lukasiewicz.

[156] MIC/1926/324/90–105, October 19, 1926.

[157] MIC/1926/324/106–118, October 17, 1926. Sources here are inconsistent. While
Gheorghiu reports that Brăileanu was subsequently replaced as president of the commission,
Marinescu quotes Brăileanu's report as president of the commission. Cf. MIC/1926/324/
90–105, October 19, 1926. It is possible that Brăileanu wrote a report as president after the
written portion of the exam and was only then replaced, or that his replacement was to take
effect for the next exam session.

[158] MIC/1926/324/106–118, October 17, 1926.

while Inspector Marinescu's report to the ministry alluded to the unanimity of all the grading decisions and the concurrence of the one Jewish teacher on the commission, Gheorghiu's report to Marinescu indicated that local members of the baccalaureate commission had actually been unduly lenient at times. They probably feared the consequences of grading strictly, thus their "frequent repetition of the words 'we are staying back here with them.' "[159]

In the baccalaureate incident, the still powerful Bukovinian Jewish community confronted the Romanian state in the persons of the outside examiners: The incident illustrates the force of Bukovinian regionalism, complicated by ethnic tensions. In Bukovina, ethnic questions were embedded in a struggle for national integration of the region as a whole and in the local resistance to centralization. The minority demonstrators in October 1926 protested the baccalaureate, because, they felt, it was intended to limit their educational opportunities and, thereby, their social and economic futures. The baccalaureate itself, instituted throughout Greater Romania perhaps as a covert *numerus clausus,* represented Bucharest's dominion. Bukovina's minorities resented particularly the Old Kingdom members of the baccalaureate commission, whom they saw as the real agents of Bucharest much more than local Romanians with whom a modus vivendi had been worked out.

A range of frustrations exploded the night of the October 7 demonstration. The slogans provide important clues. As reported by Gheorghiu, the crowd shouted, "Down with Diaconescu, down with Gheorghiu, down with the Regăţeni [those from the Old Kingdom], down with the Romanians, down with science, down with bacşiş,[160] long live those who flunked the baccalaureate, down with the Regăţeni crooks."[161] Of these eight slogans, one hailed the ignorant victims of the baccalaureate, one denounced "Romanians" per se, and one condemned "science," (i.e., the knowledge the baccalaureate was supposed to test). The other five, however, all expressed regionalist resentment of the undesirable intruders from the Old Kingdom.[162] Indeed, even "Down with the Romanians" may have carried

[159] Ibid., and MIC/1926/324/90–105, October 19, 1926.
[160] The *bacşiş,* originally a Turkish institution somewhere between a tip and a bribe, was practiced in the Old Kingdom, where Turkish influences have prevailed into the 20th century.
[161] MIC/1926/324/106–118, October 17, 1929.
[162] Four slogans were directed at the *Regăţeni* in general, or at two particular examiners from the Regat, Diaconescu and Gheorghiu. The fifth decries the *bacşiş* identified with the Old Kingdom. Another variant of that evening's slogans is in MIC/1926/324/90–105, October 19, 1926: "Down with the baccalaureate! Down with Diaconescu! Down with science! Down with Gheorghiu! Down with the commission!" Although quite similar, this seems to be the cleaned-up version reported by the inspector general to the ministry on October 19. By eliminating all regionalist references, the inspector may have been trying to emphasize the antibaccalaureate nature of the protest, which would have been most objectionable to the ministry as a challenge to its explicit authority. The inspector's own report seems to have been based at least partially on Gheorghiu's report to him, dated October 17.

a regionalist note, referring to the "real" Romanians rather than to Bukovinians.

The trial of the minority offenders opened on November 10 "in an extremely stormy atmosphere."[163] After a setback the prosecutor asked for an adjournment and the removal of the trial to Câmpulung, a town Jews considered to be a center of anti-Semitism.[164] Just after this request had been granted, Neculai Totu, a 21-year-old Romanian student from the University of Iaşi, who was active in the protofascist Brotherhood of the Cross and a close associate of Corneliu Zelea Codreanu, shot and killed the Jewish youth David Fallik.[165]

The crime brought the nationalist, regionalist, and ethnic issues underlying the Cernăuţi events into national public debate. Nationalist politicians from Octavian Goga—a prominent Transylvanian poet, journalist, and politician, member of the People's Party, and Minister of Interior at the time—to A. C. Cuza, a law professor at the University of Iaşi, the leader of LANC and a member of parliament, rose to Totu's defense.[166] Goga blamed the murder on the "unsuitable atmosphere" in Cernăuţi, and suggested that the October protest and the November murder were equivalent, stating that he disapproved of excesses no matter who was responsible for them. Since the "unsuitable atmosphere" created by the rebellious minorities had provoked Totu's wrath, final responsibility for the crime implicitly fell on the victim's shoulders. To bolster his argument in parliament, Goga cited passages from several Cernăuţi minority newspapers that had sympathized with the protesters and had offended Romanian national pride. "The settlement of the Regăţeni in Bukovina has been likened to that of the British in the African colonies. Allusions to the native land have been made, as if others were more native than Stephen the Great [applause]. Well, Gentlemen, in this situation came the deed of the wretched Totu."[167] The minister of interior furthermore endorsed the student movement of which Totu was a member, by saying that he, Goga, did not "side with those who represented the student movement as collective madness. It is an organic action of this people and it is a continuation of trench psychology. [Our youth should] keep in its soul the altar of the national idea, and pray to it morning and night."[168] Continuing the same mystical imagery of nationalism, A. C. Cuza went even further, proposing the exclusion from Romania's parliament of the Jewish deputies condemning Fallik's

---

[163] *Dimineaţa*, November 12, 1926, cited in Joint Foreign Committee, *Jewish Minority*, 2d ed., p. 42.

[164] Brandmarker, "David Fallik," p. 175.

[165] *Paix et droit*, November 1926, and Lucian Predescu, *Enciclopedia Cugetarea* (Bucharest: Cugetarea-Georgescu Delafras, 1939–1940), p. 959.

[166] See articles in *Îndreptarea* and *Universul*, December 4, 1926.

[167] *Îndreptarea*, December 4, 1926.

[168] *Universul*, December 4, 1926.

murderer. Cuza compared "the parliament with a national temple on whose platform those insulting us, who are called to serve here, have no business being."[169]

Neculai Totu was tried in Câmpulung on February 21, 1927, in an atmosphere of public exaltation in favor of the defendant. According to the Alliance Israélite Universelle paper *Paix et droit,* about 3,000 lawyers had volunteered for the honor of defending Totu. Anti-Semitic students and leaders, including A. C. Cuza and Corneliu Zelea Codreanu, had worked over the town. They brought with them anti-Semitic propaganda and a national folk costume for the accused to wear at his trial. The Jewish inhabitants of Câmpulung left the town or shut themselves in their homes for safety. During the trial, Totu confessed to the premeditated murder of the Jew Fallik, "since the latter had struck a teacher, and in striking a teacher he had struck the State itself."[170]

The lawyer for the defense gave Totu a symbolic grade of "A" for patriotic conduct. His plea to the jurors praised the crime as a moral act, and the criminal as a hero: "David Falik [sic] has been killed by the bullet of Totu, and so will die all the country's enemies, by innumerable bullets which will be fired against the filthy beasts. Gentlemen of the jury, . . . Totu is a martyr and a hero. You must declare him free, . . . and you should deliberate no longer than the moment necessary for dipping your pens in ink." The well-known Cuza also spoke for the defense. The jury deliberated for ten minutes and acquitted Totu, eight to two.[171]

Totu's career did not suffer as a result of the murder he committed. He received a law degree from the University of Iaşi and became a leader in the Legionnaire movement. Later, he participated in the Iron Guard plot to kill Prime Minister Ion G. Duca, for which crime he was again acquitted. He fought in the Spanish civil war on the Franchist side.[172] Totu is archetypal of the radical nationalist youth of the interwar period.

The incidents which occurred in the fall of 1926 in Cernăuţi were symptomatic of the tensions which existed in Bukovinian society as a result of the Romanization of the province. Romanian cultural policies affected the schools of all the minorities in Bukovina, including the Ukrainians—not really a minority since they were the largest population of the province—and the Jews, a smaller urban group who suffered disproportionately by

[169] *Îndreptarea,* December 4, 1926.

[170] Jerusalem, Yad Vashem Archives, P/6/13, p. 14; "Le général Averesco et l'antisémitisme," *Paix et droit,* March 1927, p. 4; and *Adevărul,* February 22, 1927, cited in Joint Foreign Committee, *Jewish Minority,* 2d ed., p. 43.

[171] *Adevărul,* February 22, 1927, cited in Joint Foreign Committee, *Jewish Minority,* 2d ed., p. 43.

[172] Predescu, *Enciclopedia Cugetarea,* p. 959.

the Romanization of secondary schools. In 1926 in the capital of Bukovina, the minorities—and especially the highly urban Jews—still constituted an entrenched elite, despite efforts to cordon them off into separate schools and lycées, and to reduce their resources and influence. (The list of candidates at the fall 1926 baccalaureate exam reflected this: 91.8 percent belonged to the minorities, while only 8.2 percent were ethnic Romanians.) At the same time political power rested ultimately with the Greater Romanian state, among whose primary goals was that of nurturing a Romanian elite and culture. For purposes of the baccalaureate, the examining commission represented the state. This connection was indeed made explicit by Neculai Totu, who justified his assassination of Fallik as a deed in defense of the state. Within the state, authority tended to revert to the Old Kingdom, the kernel around which the dispersed territories, Bukovina among them, had been gathered in 1918. The regional dimension of Bukovina's union with the Regat played an important part in the conflicts over the baccalaureate. Both the vengefulness of the radical nationalist youth, Totu, and his defense in court and parliament by his elders, Goga and Cuza, resonate with an assertive Romanian nationalism on the offensive against the resilient particularisms of Bukovina's ethnic minorities and regionalist outlook.

3

Bessarabia: Nationalism in an Archaic Province

The ethnographic character of Bessarabia is Romanian, since even the physical lay-out of the Bessarabian land is akin to the rest of the land which forms the *territorial unity of the Romanian people.*

—L. T. Boga, 1925

If the geographic distance between Bucharest and this village [Corjeuți, Hotin County] can be traversed in ten or fifteen hours, by contrast two to three centuries, or even more, are necessary, going back in time, in order to reach the living reality, the archaic and mystical plasma out of which the people of these places are made.

—Geo Bogza, 1934

Of all the territories Romania gained in 1918, Bessarabia posed the most difficulties for Romania's policy of cultural nationalism, sanguine assessments of the essentially Romanian character of the area notwithstanding. Romanian authorities were deeply suspicious about the loyalty of the local population. The fact that Bessarabia was torn from neighboring Soviet Russia in 1918 partly explains this insecurity, but fear of Soviet aggression does not tell the whole story. After 106 years of separation from the Romanian heartland, the region had in some ways adjusted to its place in the Russian imperial order and had grown apart from the "mother country."

Romanian fears about Bessarabia were based in part on the ethnic and linguistic profile of the Bessarabian population itself. In 1897, at the time

89

of the first imperial Russian census, the population of Bessarabia was 1,936,012, of which 47.6 percent was Romanian, 19.6 percent Ukrainian, 11.8 percent Jewish, and 8 percent Russian, other ethnic groups being represented in lower proportions.[1] Whereas Romanians and Ukrainians together accounted for almost three-quarters of the rural population, the urban areas were dominated by Yiddish and Russian speakers. The capital, Kishinev (Chişinău), was 45.9 percent Jewish and 27 percent Russian.[2] In cities and towns, many of which had Jewish majorities, Russian was considered the only acceptable, "polite" language.[3] Even in 1930, Russians and Jews together accounted for a majority of Bessarabia's urban population (see map 4 and table 8).

A French diplomat noted after a visit to Bessarabia in 1922 that the town population was "purely Russian and Israelite and violently anti-Romanian."[4] Non-Romanian aspects of Bessarabia's cities were a sore point with Romanian nationalists after 1918, as the following introduction to Ştefan Ciobanu's essay "Oraşele" (The towns) reveals:

> If one wanted to form an impression about Bessarabia by its towns, one would commit the most grievous error. Bessarabian towns, generally speaking, are not the natural emanation of the villages surrounding them, [nor] the logical expression of the villagers' lives, having only different social and economic forms, but sharing the same soul, the same tongue, and the same traditions and customs. The great majority of the towns [are rather] the artificial creations of the Russian regime, [and] are completely at odds with the life of the surrounding villages.[5]

The rural and even suburban environments, rarely inspected by foreign visitors, represented the non-Russian side of the Bessarabian coin. Andrei Popovici described the contrast:

[1] "Prilozhenie k obshchemu svodu dannykh pervoi vseobshchei perepisi naseleniya 1897g. Po imperii, Kartogrammy i diagrammy," in *Pervaya vseobshchaya perepis' naseleniya rossiskoi imperii 1897 g.,* vol. 3 (St. Petersburg: Izdatel'stvo Tsentral'nago statisticheskago komiteta Ministerstva vnutrennikh diel, 1905), pp. 226–227. The 1897 census figures represent native language measurement, rather than nationality per se.

[2] Ibid.

[3] Irina Livezeanu, "Urbanization in a Low Key and Linguistic Change in Soviet Moldavia, Part 1," *Soviet Studies* 33 (July 1981): 330–331.

[4] He also reported, however, that "the [Romanian] military administration [which is] almost omnipotent in Bessarabia, is perhaps not always able to rise to the height of its tasks" committing abuses and violent acts against which the population had no recourse. QD 68/84–85, June 13, 1922.

[5] Ştefan Ciobanu, "Oraşele," in *Basarabia: Monographie,* ed. Ştefan Ciobanu (Chişinău: Impr. Statului, 1925), p. 76.

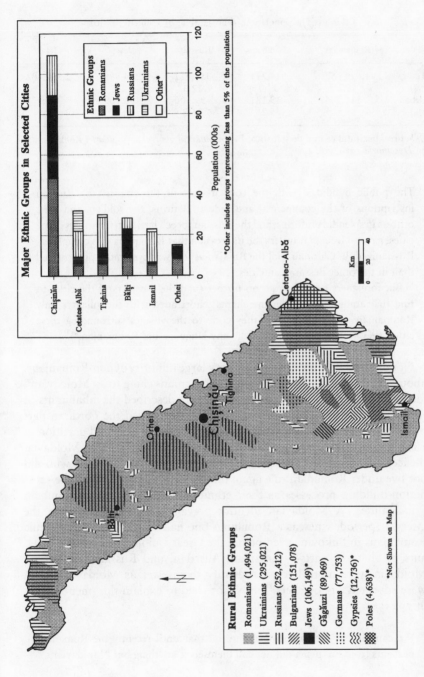

Major Ethnic Groups in Selected Cities

Ethnic Groups
- Romanians
- Jews
- Russians
- Ukrainians
- Other*

*Other includes groups representing less than 5% of the population

Population (000s)

Chişinău
Cetatea-Albă
Tighina
Bălţi
Ismail
Orhei

Rural Ethnic Groups

- Romanians (1,494,021)
- Ukrainians (295,021)
- Russians (252,412)
- Bulgarians (151,078)
- Jews (106,149)*
- Găgăuzi (89,969)
- Germans (77,753)
- Gypsies (12,736)*
- Poles (4,638)*

*Not Shown on Map

Km
0   20   40

Bălţi
Orhei
Chişinău
Tighina
Ismail
Cetatea-Albă

Bessarabia, Ethnic Distribution

Table 8.   The population of Bessarabia, by ethnicity, 1930.

	Romanians	Ukrainians	Russians	Jews	Total
Total	1,610,757	314,211	351,912	204,858	2,864,402
(%)	56.2	11.0	12.3	7.2	
Urban	116,736	19,181	99,500	98,709	370,971
(%)	31.5	5.2	26.8	26.6	

Source: Institutul central de statistică, Recensământul general al populaţiei României din 29 Decemvrie 1930, vol. 2.

The public buildings, with the coat-of-arms of the empire, the Russian inscriptions of the commercial and industrial firms, the soldiers and their officers in splendid uniforms, and the Russian speech heard on the streets of the cities, gave to foreign travelers the impression that Bessarabia was completely Russianized. In Chisinau [sic] the Russian aspect was even more pronounced than in the other Bessarabian cities.

But foreigners needed to go no further than the outskirts of the cities to find that among the smaller merchants who traded with the villagers only Roumanian was spoken. Had they gone to the villages surrounding these cities, they would have heard hardly any language but Roumanian.[6]

Not only did Bessarabia contain a very large minority of non-Romanians, about 44 percent even in 1930, but its Romanians clung to a "Moldavian" identity. The term "Moldavian" had initially described the inhabitants of the Moldavian Principality. In 1775, Austria annexed the northern part of the principality, thenceforth known as Bukovina; a second partition in 1812 resulted in Russia's annexation of the eastern part of Moldavia, thenceforth known as Bessarabia. The partitioned Moldavians, who did not live under Romanian rule again until 1918, did not undergo the same nation-building processes as their ethnic counterparts in the Danubian Principalities. A Moldavian identity prevailed in Bessarabia into the interwar period, whereas a Romanian one had developed among ethnic Romanians in Bukovina even before the Great Union. Furthermore, peasants in all three parts—Romanian, Austrian, and Russian—of historic Moldavia were more likely to identify themselves as Moldavians than were educated city dwellers. Ion Nistor tried to explain this phenomenon in 1915:

We can all very well remember after all that until recently the Romanian peasants from Bukovina did not call themselves anything but "Moldavians,"

[6] Andrei Popovici, The Political Status of Bessarabia (Washington, D.C.: School of Foreign Service, Georgetown University, 1931), p. 101.

and their language "Moldavian." Influenced by the literary language the term "Moldavian" was subsequently replaced by that of "Romanian." In Bessarabia this literary influence has not yet penetrated, and because of that our brothers from across the Pruth still today call themselves "Moldavians."[7]

In 1919, the geographer Emmanuel de Martonne commented after a trip to Bessarabia that all Bessarabian peasants, "still called themselves "Moldavians.' "[8]

Bessarabia's Moldavians were divided roughly into two elements: a small urban elite that had been Russified to a high degree,[9] and a very large but unschooled and inert peasantry. Romanian nationalists looked upon the Moldavian peasants as "unspoiled," but in fact the task of making them into nationally conscious, educated Romanians who could take over from the Russianized Moldavians and the urban minorities proved difficult.

Russian Bessarabia

The Russification of eastern Moldavia, or Bessarabia, did not begin immediately after Moldavia's partition in 1812. Hoping to prove the superiority of Russian Orthodox rule over that of the infidel Turks for Russia's new Christian subjects, the relatively liberal regime of Alexander I initially granted Bessarabia privileges and a high degree of autonomy within the Russian Empire. The province benefited from certain tax exemptions until 1817, and the ancient local laws and administration remained in effect until 1818, when Alexander signed the statute that reconfirmed Bessarabia's federal relationship to the Russian Empire. For a decade after 1812, Bessarabia had "the highest degree of autonomy of any province or district in the Empire." Both Romanian and Russian were used as languages of administration and justice, in law courts preference was given to the Roma-

---

[7] Ion Nistor, *Românii şi rutenii în Bucovina: Studiu istoric şi statistic* (Bucharest: Librăriile Socec, 1915), p. 73.

[8] Emmanuel de Martonne, "En Bessarabie," *Journal des débats,* July 19, 1919, p. 2. "Moldavian" can also sometimes refer to the inhabitants of Old Kingdom, Western Moldavia, as will be clear from the context.

[9] Almost all accounts of Bessarabia in 1917–1920 portray a Russified Moldavian elite. One witness described the recalcitrance of Moldavian bureaucrats who had functioned in *zemstva,* the local government institutions of the Russian empire, to adapt to the Romanian order: "Never mind the Russians, who did not want to speak Romanian even if they knew [it], but these Moldavians of ours who were provincial *chinovniki* only after much insistence [from us] admitted that they knew Moldavian too, even though they knew this language of ours as well as we do." See Eugeniu N. Giurgea, *Din trecutul şi prezentul Basarabiei* (Bucharest: Institutul de arte grafice Bucovina, I. E. Torouţiu, 1928), p. 111.

nian language, and Moldavian customary law was used in judging civil cases.[10]

As the Russian state became more highly centralized, it began to encroach on Bessarabian autonomy, not least by denationalizing Bessarabia's elite. The Romanian ruling class was gradually replaced or Russified.[11] The onset of fairly rapid urbanization in the nineteenth century signalled the rising prominence of another urban ethnic group: the Jews became the dominant trading and manufacturing class, despite the fact that many of them were very poor. Russian bureaucrats and Jewish petit bourgeois were the urban elites while the Moldavian peasantry labored in the countryside.[12]

After 1822, imperial measures aimed also to suppress the official use of the Romanian language. At first this tendency was tempered by the Russian government's realistic need to communicate with and enforce its will on the Moldavian population. As Russification extended to the school system, however, Romanian disappeared from administration as well. Moldavian and Russian had both been taught at first, but by 1867 no Moldavian language schools remained in the province.[13]

Even so, the Russification policies of the regime did not greatly affect the identity of most Moldavians, the overwhelming majority of whom were illiterate peasants. In 1897, 15.6 percent of Bessarabia's total population could read.[14] Moldavians were the most rural and least educated nationality in Bessarabia; clearly, literacy had to have been extremely rare among Moldavian peasants. Statistics compiled in 1905–1907 by the local *zemstvo* indicate that the Moldavians were 6.1 percent literate, thus the least literate, next to the Gypsies, in the province. Given these circum-

---

[10] Ladis Kristof, "Russian Colonialism and Bessarabia: A Confrontation of Cultures," *Nationalities Papers* 2, no. 2, (1974): 27, 29; Ion Pelivan, *Bessarabia under the Russian Rule* (Paris: Impr. J. Charpentier, 1920), pp. 7–9; and George Jewsbury, *The Russian Annexation of Bessarabia, 1774–1828: A Study of Imperial Expansion* (Boulder, Colo.: East European Monographs, 1976), pp. 11–13, 107.

[11] See Kristof, "Russian Colonialism," p. 31. In his monograph, *The Russian Annexation of Bessarabia,* George Jewsbury has recast the question of Bessarabia's shrinking autonomy, suggesting that the Russification of Bessarabia after 1822 arose from the failure of the earlier autonomist regimes to represent the general interests of the population: the local boyars were driven by corruption, rapaciousness, and self-interest. According to Jewsbury, Alexander I and his statesmen, steeped in rationalist ideas, had wanted to leave Bessarabia's autonomous institutions in place, hoping for the province's prosperity and efficient administration; they were, however, forced to take Bessarabia in hand and revoke the Statute of 1818 in exasperation over the inefficiency and oppressiveness of the autonomous Moldavian administration.

[12] Kristof, "Russian Colonialism," p. 31; Livezeanu, "Urbanization in a Low Key," p. 329; and Ezra Mendelsohn, *The Jews of East Central Europe between the World Wars* (Bloomington: Indiana University Press, 1983), p. 179.

[13] Kristof, "Russian Colonialism," p. 29; Pelivan, *Bessarabia,* pp. 15–16; Ştefan Ciobanu, *Cultura românească în Basarabia sub stăpânirea rusă* (Chişinău: Asociaţiei uniunea culturală bisericească, 1923), pp. 126, 131, 150–158, 172–175; and Ion Nistor, *Istoria Basarabiei,* 3d ed. (Cernowitz: Glasul Bucovinei, 1923), p. 373.

[14] "Priolozhenie k obshchemu," *Pervaya vseobshchaya perepis',* p. 38.

stances, Romanian authorities could conclude with some satisfaction after 1918 that "the Romanian population has been indifferent toward the school and has remained almost untouched by Russian culture."[15]

The reverse, however, was true of the Moldavian intelligentsia: imperial assimilation measures deeply transformed Moldavia's small but influential native elite. Near the end of the nineteenth century Russian authorities could suppress Romanian language instruction without eliciting much protest, and Romanian language sections and courses in secondary schools were shutting down partly because of a lack of demand.[16] The higher one went up the educational ladder, the less one encountered Romanian culture. Since no local higher educational institutions existed at all, young Bessarabians who had studied in local Russian high schools went to imperial universities in Odessa, Kiev, Kharkov, Moscow, and St. Petersburg.[17] As a result, the local Romanian intelligentsia was extremely Russified.

Romanian also declined as a language of the Moldavians' Orthodox church, particularly under the ruthless Archbishop Pavel (1871–1882), who led a campaign of Russification which closed down many churches where services were not held in Russian, dismissed priests who did not know Russian, and suppressed the Romanian Parish's printing press. Such measures, including the elimination of seminaries that taught in Romanian, produced many priests "who could not preach two words of Romanian . . . nor even read the Gospel." The bulletin of the Orthodox church stopped printing articles in Romanian in 1871.[18] Moldavian clergy, therefore, had been largely stripped of its potential for Romanian nationalism.

Although imperial policies did not Russify Bessarabia through and through, they relegated the Moldavian language to the rural and less educated native population, and they stunted the normal growth of a literary Moldavian/Romanian language. In his book on the Romanian culture in Bessarabia, Ştefan Ciobanu remarks that, "The Romanian language of Bessarabia, the beautiful Moldavian language, survived intact only in the villages; [on the other hand] it degenerated in the mouths of the intellectuals who had gone through Russian culture. The books put together by the intellectuals bear this same stamp of Russian culture, they are printed in Russian letters."[19]

[15] Ministerul instrucţiunii, *Lege pentru învăţămăntul primar al statului* (Bucharest: Editura Cartea românească, 1925), pp. 19, 79.

[16] This is the testimony of Ion Doncev, a Moldavian writer, teacher, and patriot, in his 1865 preface to the last Romanian language textbook to be published before 1918 in the Latin alphabet in Bessarabia, where he expresses regret that a school in Hotin was liquidating its Romanian courses for lack of interested students. In Nistor, *Istoria Basarabiei*, p. 376.

[17] C. Filipescu and Eugeniu N. Giurgea, *Consideraţiuni generale, agricole, economice şi statistice* (Chişinău: România nouă, 1919), p. 323.

[18] The semi-monthly bulletin was *Kishinevskiia eparkhial'nyia vedomosti*. Pelivan, *Bessarabia*, pp. 22, 23, 26, and Ciobanu, *Cultura românească*, pp. 286–287.

[19] Ciobanu, *Cultura românească*, p. 134.

The Cyrillic alphabet, which Romanians in the Principalities wrote until the second half of the nineteenth century,[20] had continued to be used in Bessarabia until the Romanian annexation. Given the Latin structure of the Romanian language, it has been hard for Romanian and Moldavian nationalists to remember that the Cyrillic alphabet was not initially imposed on Romanians by alien imperialists, unless one wants to consider the medieval Orthodox church in that guise. The alphabet had been introduced in the tenth century with Old Church Slavonic, the written language which Romanians had used in the Orthodox church, the princely courts, and places of high culture, much as Catholic Western and Central Europe had used Latin.[21]

The linguistic and cultural Russification of most of the Moldavian intelligentsia, the high level of political repression, and the large proportion of unmobilized peasants in the Moldavian population meant that nationalism was not a mighty force in Bessarabia before the twentieth century. The Moldavians had their first brief inkling of national liberation with the Russian revolution of 1905, and those studying at Russian universities were in the vanguard of their national movement.[22] But the flurry of open national activity was short-lived, followed by a wave of reaction which left only a few brave veterans to carry the torch to 1917. In the years before the Great War, Moldavian nationalism in Bessarabia was again very restricted.[23] Onisifor Ghibu was a Transylvanian who took refuge in Bessarabia in 1917 and became one of the main organizers and the best memoirist of the national movement there. In 1916, Ghibu recalls, Bessarabia "was still tsarist Russia in full force. Everything seemed Russian between the Pruth and the Dniester. There was no wind blowing of Romanian cultural awakening. With few exceptions Bessarabia felt very well under 'the tsar's yoke.' The 'Moldavians' were the most loyal subjects of Nicholas II."[24] In 1917, there were still practically no Romanian books in Bessarabia; and even in the capital, Chişinău, there was no Romanian library nor any bookstore that carried Romanian books.[25] During and immediately after World War I, pan-Romanian nationalism was almost

[20] Gheorghe Ivănescu, *Istoria limbii române* (Jassy: Editura Junimea, 1980), pp. 678–679.

[21] Ibid., p. 517.

[22] Ion Pelivan, *The Union of Bessarabia with Her Mother-Country Roumania* (Paris: Impr. des arts et des sports, 1919), p. 7.

[23] Moldavian nationalist activity found voice in the periodical *Cuvânt moldovenesc* (Moldavian Word) started in 1913 under the direction of Pantelimon Halippa. Nistor, *Istoria Basarabiei*, pp. 394–403. One other short-lived Moldavian publication, *Glasul Basarabiei* (Bessarabia's Voice), also saw the light.

[24] Onisifor Ghibu, "În Basarabia, după patru ani," *Adevărul*, September 9, 1923, reprinted in *Călătorind prin Basarabia: Impresiile unui român ardelean* (Chişinău: Tip. Eparhială, 1923), p. 1.

[25] Onisifor Ghibu, *Pe baricadele vieţii IV: În Basarabia revoluţionară (1917–1918) Amintiri*, Ms., p. 370.

wholly imported to Bessarabia by Transylvanians, Bukovinians, and propagandists from the Old Kingdom, while many Moldavians in Bessarabia, educated in Russian schools and universities, or part of the demoralized Russian army, were initially swept up in the *social* revolution of 1917.

Rejoining Romania

The Moldavian National Party (MNP) was founded in spring 1917 at the suggestion of the Transylvanian Ghibu, who had come to Bessarabia rather than fight with Hungary against Romania. To his dismay, Ghibu encountered both inertia and opposition: many Moldavians felt that cultural work was sufficient and considered direct political activity dangerous and unnecessary; socialists, meanwhile, put the social question first. The MNP's April 4 program, drafted by Ghibu, placed the national question at the core of the party's work, but it was much challenged, almost splitting the party.[26]

The Moldavian nationalist independence movement would most likely have taken many more years to develop had it not benefited from the convergence of a number of external factors. The threat of annexation by newly independent Ukraine, the fear of being engulfed into Russia's civil war, and the peace Romania signed with the Central Powers in May 1918, in which Bessarabia's annexation was in effect granted in exchange for Romania's agreeing to the Central Powers' "complete economic control" over Romania all contributed to Bessarabia's return to Romania in 1918.[27]

Simultaneously with the Bolshevik seizure of power in November 1917, a soldiers' congress in Chişinău called for Bessarabia's autonomy within the democratized Russian state. A Moldavian Democratic Republic was officially declared on December 2, 1917, by a provisional parliament called Sfatul Ţării (the National Council). To try to stave off civil war and the area's Bolshevization as anarchic bands of soldiers wreaked havoc across Bessarabia on their return from the front, Sfatul Ţării invited the help of the Romanian army. On January 24, 1918, soon after the arrival of Romanian troops and after the declaration of Ukrainian independence, Sfatul Ţării proclaimed the independence of the Moldavian Republic. On April 9, Sfatul Ţării voted for maintaining semi-autonomy while proceeding with a conditional union with Romania. The process of union between Bessara-

---

[26] Ibid., pp. 62–65. See also Irina Livezeanu, "Moldavia, 1917–1990: Nationalism and Internationalism Then and Now," *Armenian Review* 43 (Summer–Autumn 1990): 160 and n. 30.

[27] Carlile A. Macartney and Alan W. Palmer, *Independent Eastern Europe* (London: Macmillan/St. Martin's Press, 1962), p. 77. Even once the threat of annexation by Ukraine was averted, the new Ukrainian state cut off Bessarabia from the territory of Russia.

bia and the Romanian Kingdom was completed on November 27, 1918, when Sfatul Țării voted to cancel these conditions and then dissolved itself.[28]

The annexation of Bessarabia in 1918 did not allay the fear that Bessarabia might remain an "indigestible" part of Greater Romania, for this concern derived partly from the proximity of revolutionary Russia and the potential for Bolshevik infiltration. In 1919, the Romanian command in Bessarabia expected insurrections provoked by Bolshevik agitation.[29] Prime Minister Ion Brătianu observed that famine and the threat of Bolshevism made Romania's situation serious and warned further that external difficulties could render it *"sans issue."*[30] Such alarm was sounded repeatedly, whether over the creation in Moscow of a "League for the Liberation of Bessarabia" led by Christian Rakovsky,[31] or over local communist activity deemed threatening in the context of postwar instability.[32]

Romanian authorities and their French allies were also concerned with the national heterogeneity of Bessarabia and the hostile reactions of the Moldavians to Romanian intervention and high-handedness. A French report of May 15, 1919, emphasized the Romanians' tenuous hold on Bessarabia:

> South of Kishinev the majority of the population is plainly hostile to the Romanians [and] Russian in their language and interests. The small Romanian element there is represented by poor peasants who are themselves hardly disposed in favor of their compatriots. The rest—Jews, Bulgarians, Russians, German settlers—detest and despise the Romanians, who, on their part, do everything to deserve that. This population goes so far as to prefer the ruble over the *leu*. In many places the *leu* is refused, or two *lei* are accepted in place of a ruble. The peasants, who have all their savings in rubles, have a lot of interest in this artificial rate of exchange.
>
> The Romanians are alienating these populations by all means at their disposal: too harsh a police that thrashes the citizen with sticks . . . , inquisition, venality, extortion, organized theft under pretext of requisitions, etc.[33]

[28] See Henry L. Roberts, *Rumania: Political Problems of an Agrarian State* (New Haven, Conn.: Yale University Press, 1951), pp. 33–34, and Livezeanu, "Moldavia, 1917–1990," pp. 161, 165–169.

[29] Ministère de la guerre, Direction de l'armée de terre, Vincennes (hereafter V), 7N 1458/2, n.d.

[30] QD 3 27/63, January 7, 1919.

[31] V 7N 3043, January [n.d.], 1920.

[32] QD 55/3–4RV, 5R, March 1, 1920; QD 22 27/250r, December 15, 1920; QD 55/156–160, May 28, 1921; and V 37N 1459/6, May 15, 1919.

[33] V 7N 1459/6, Report of Captain de Valence on his trip to Bucharest on May 6–15, 1919.

This report by the French military, which generally sympathized with the Romanians against the Bolsheviks, was not unique. Others were equally critical of Romanian practice and fearful of the good prospects thus being created for the Bolsheviks in Bessarabia. In February 1920, the military attaché, General Pétin, reported on the situation in Bessarabia just as the first Bolsheviks were settling on the shore of the Dniester, an area recaptured from the Volunteer Army:

> Russians, Bulgarians, Turks, Germans have their spirits stretched to the limit. . . . For all, in any case, the arrival of the Soviets on the shores of the Dniester marks the possible opening of a new era.
>
> On several occasions, I have signalled . . . the blunders of the Romanian administration toward all the [different] Bessarabian populations, even toward the Moldavians. It was in order to tell you . . . how much the arrival of the Bolsheviks revives their hopes and may be capable of evoking disorders in Bessarabia later.
>
> One could be astonished that even the bourgeoisies of these foreign elements wish to see the arrival of the soldiers of the Russian revolution . . . Only the Jewish elements observe a prudent silence not knowing what to prefer: the . . . anti-Jewish Romanians or an invasion of the Bolsheviks who do not respect the Jews any more than the others.[34]

Fears, whether French or Romanian, about Bessarabia's smooth integration into the Romanian order focused also on schools, which everyone recognized as politically important. In 1921, an official of the Romanian Ministry of Interior concluded his inspection tour of Cetatea Albă, Tighina, Ismail, Cahul, and Chişinău counties with foreboding, writing that:

> The population [here] is almost unanimously hostile to us . . . The separatist tendency that exists in Bessarabia contributes to this very much; every nationality beginning with the Bulgarians and the Germans invokes the principle of minorities [and] wants to make a state within a state, demanding purely Bulgarian and German schools with a separate program from the one set by the inspectorate. The other nations, seeing what is happening, will not hesitate to imitate them, thus making Romanization impossible.[35]

The very newness of Bessarabia's postwar partnership with Romania and the tenuousness of Romanian national consciousness in Bessarabia formed the basis for such worries. The solution seemed to lie in cultural

---

[34] V 7N 3043, February 21, 1920, Report of Général Pétin, Military Attaché in Romania, to the Minister of War.
[35] MIC/1921/273/17.

propaganda and, longer range, in the development of a Romanian school system to break the monopoly of the Russian educational establishments.

Cultural Propaganda

In this process of cultural assimilation, however, the Russian legacy made itself felt at every step. Although the peasant population had not lost its "Moldavian" identity, Russian was considered the proper public language of the educated and urban elites and of the bureaucracy. Moldavians who had become part of these elites under Russian rule, while not necessarily forgetting their native language, suppressed it in nondomestic contexts. Moldavians' weak sense of Romanian cultural identity was reflected in their low esteem for Romania, a country many of them regarded as "uncivilized." They also held Romanian high culture in disdain, although or because they were little acquainted with it.

Moldavian teachers are a case in point of the distance between Romanian and Moldavian identities. In spring 1917, teachers who agreed to join a Moldavian teachers' association still signed its statutes with Cyrillic letters, they approached Romanian books with awe and read Romanian slowly and haltingly, and most of them said that they did "not know Romanian, only Moldavian."[36] Although differences between the Moldavian dialect and literary Romanian certainly existed (deepened by the political separation imposed in 1812), from a strictly linguistic point of view the idiom of Bessarabian Moldavians is not a language apart.[37] Thus the teachers' inability to see Moldavian and Romanian as one and the same was not principally a linguistic problem but a psychological one. Moldavian had effectively been "demoted" to a noninstitutional language in the tsarist empire, and educated Moldavians continued to perceive it as inappropriate for public discourse. People commonly referred to Moldavian as *limba prostimei,* the language of simple people.[38]

---

[36] Onisifor Ghibu, "În vîltoarea revoluţiei ruseşti: Însemnări zilnice ale unui ardelean, martor ocular—şi mai mult decît atît—al revoluţiei ruseşti în anii 1917–1918, începînd cu ziua de 12 Martie şi pînă în ziua de 6 August 1917," Ms., April 30, 1917.

[37] See Kenneth Rogers, "Moldavian, Romanian, and the Question of a National Language," in *The Tragic Plight of a Border Area: Bassarabia and Bucovina,* ed. Maria Manoliu-Manea (Los Angeles: Humboldt State University Press, 1983).

[38] The word *prostime* in Romanian is pejorative, connoting both low status and lack of intelligence. (In Moldavian usage it conveys the sense of "popular" or "folkish," as in "the language of the simple people.") Romanian activists in Bessarabia found it necessary to "translate" their speeches and propaganda into the local "popular" idiom after first producing them in standard Romanian. Onisifor Ghibu translated his draft of the MNP program, and presumably other articles and speeches, into the " 'popular' Moldavian form," i.e., *limba prostească,* before publishing it in the local press. See Ghibu's entry of April 5, 1917, in his diary, "În vîltoarea revoluţiei ruseşti."

Given the categorization of Moldavian as uncultured, it is no wonder
that many educated Moldavians wanted nothing of it. In his diary, Ghibu
recorded his observations of the Moldavians' alienation from their native
tongue and their resistance to Romanian. At a *zemstvo* meeting, a Moldavian teacher told Ghibu that she had become completely Russian and liked
it that way. Ghibu recorded their exchange:

> I say [to her]: these were the circumstances under the old regime, but now
> things are going to change. [She answered:] "Yes, but I don't want to make
> myself Moldavian any more; I'm staying Russian. There is nothing greater
> or more beautiful than Russia! The Moldavians have no literature." I tell her
> that they do, and even a very beautiful one, but she says that that [literature]
> is Romanian. I tell her that there is only one people, one language, etc. . . .
> All these female teachers are resistant to Moldavian tendencies, in which they
> see separatism. They say that if they think in Russian, then they are Russian.[39]

To attempt to change this mentality and to train local teachers, pedagogical courses were held in Chişinău during the summers of 1917 and 1918.
The teachers were to learn enough Romanian to be able to establish and
staff Romanian schools together with propagandists from the Old Kingdom. The courses were organized by Moldavians with the help of Romanians from across the Pruth and local *zemstvo* funds. Moldavian school
teachers and students of philology, natural sciences, medicine, and law in
Russian universities composed the prospective audience of the summer
courses.[40] The first steps in establishing a Moldavian school system, then,
took place when Bessarabia still belonged to Russia. The local *zemstvo*,
prodded by Moldavian and Romanian patriots, officially sponsored these
beginnings.[41] On April 17, 1917, the *zemstvo* appointed a Moldavian
School Commission that took charge of producing textbooks.[42]

On May 3, 1917, the Moldavian School Commission began preparing
the nationalization of schools. Ghibu and Romulus Cioflec were invited
to help and Ghibu's role was especially important.[43] Given the need to
print textbooks rapidly, they had first to decide whether to use the tradi-

---

[39] Ibid., April 30, 1917.
[40] Ghibu, *Pe baricadele vieţii,* pp. 247–248.
[41] The Bessarabian *zemstvo* was closed down, and its responsibilities, budget, and funds
were taken over by the Romanian bureaucracy in October 1918. See Giurgea, *Din trecutul,*
pp. 105–107. The schools, however, remained under *zemstvo* jurisdiction until January 1919.
See AA IX/Varia 10.
[42] The Moldavian School Commission had only 2,000 rubles to use, as opposed to the
30,000 that the Russian School Commission received. Ghibu, *Pe baricadele vieţii,* p. 150.
[43] Cioflec was, like Ghibu, Transylvanian-born, but he had lived in the Regat from the
age of fourteen. Lucian Predescu, *Enciclopedia Cugetarea* (Bucharest: Cugetarea–Georgescu
Delafras, 1939–1940), p. 195. On Ghibu in this context, see Sever Bocu, "Semănători de
idei," *România mare,* September 21, 1917, p. 1.

tional Cyrillic or the Latin alphabet used in the other Romanian lands. Initially, most of the members of the commission, including all the clergy, favored keeping the Cyrillic alphabet, but many changed their minds in the ensuing discussion and voted for the Latin script.[44] At the Moldavian teachers' congress on May 25, the alphabet issue was raised again, eliciting "struggles of Homeric proportions." The Cyrillicists even wanted a secret ballot, in fear that they could not otherwise express themselves freely. In fact, most of them left the hall before the open vote, and the Latinists won again unanimously.[45] This incident suggests that the Moldavian community was ambivalent about the extent and methods of cultural nationalization.

Disagreements also erupted over the political content of the teacher-training courses. One member of the Moldavian School Commission proposed bringing Russian teachers from Kiev and Odessa to give the political lectures. Ghibu opposed this idea vehemently, afraid that under Russian influence Bessarabia might erupt in full-blooded social revolution, and he convinced his collaborators to invite Romanians from Bukovina and Transylvania instead.[46] Overall, the Teachers' Congress in May was a victory for the nationalists, for it resolved to open as many Moldavian schools as necessary in fall 1917, including several secondary schools in Chişinău and elsewhere, to make Moldavian the language of instruction in teachers' and priests' seminaries, and to introduce the Latin alphabet in all Moldavian schools.[47]

One problem with this revolutionary conversion to a Moldavian school system was the lack of properly qualified teachers. Indeed, the purpose of the summer courses was precisely to prepare teachers for the all-new Moldavian school network scheduled to open within months of the May congress. The summer school offered not only courses in Moldavian language, but also in the literature, history, and geography of the Romanian lands, teaching methods, Moldavian songs, and extracurricular activity. It may seem strange for a crash course like this to devote precious time to "extracurricular activity," but nationalists viewed it as a fundamental element of the curriculum, à la Haret, through which teachers would contribute to the social and civic development of the Moldavians.[48] The expectation that teachers should fulfill civic and national responsibilities especially in their extracurricular activities was common in Bessarabia and was in fact one of the reasons the role of the teacher was such a crucial and highly politicized one.

[44] Ghibu, *Pe baricadele vieţii*, pp. 236–237.
[45] Ibid., pp. 265–266.
[46] Ibid., p. 237.
[47] The direction and inspection of all the Moldavian schools was to be done by Moldavians in Moldavian. Moldavian schools were also to open in Moldavian communities across the Dniester and in the Caucasus. Ibid., pp. 262–263.
[48] Ibid., pp. 263–264, 326.

Much of Bessarabia's cultural life took place outside the school, in institutions of popular culture which strove to reach the mostly rural, literate and illiterate adult population. Although this cultural life had a spontaneous side, it also had an official obligatory side that was often included in the duties of school authorities and local teachers. School inspectors, for example, had to visit popular culture societies and make recommendations for their endowment to Casa şcoalelor.[49] The societies needed books, national pictures, folk costumes, embroidery patterns, artistic companies on tour, post cards, and portraits of the royal family. Representatives of cultural circles pleaded with inspectors who in turn pleaded with Casa şcoalelor (an institution that supplied funds and teaching materials in the interwar period) or with the Ministry of Education for these resources.

The Department of Extracurricular Activity published and distributed books, pamphlets, calendars, periodicals, pictures, and maps to rural audiences. In 1919 and 1920, ten titles were published in editions of 15,000 for teachers' free distribution to villagers. From February 1919 to February 1920, the department distributed 794,835 books, 449,900 periodicals, 4,950 pictures, and 820 maps. The army also contributed to popular education by dispensing books from Casa şcoalelor to the villages where they were quartered or starting local libraries and reading circles.[50] Troops sometimes initiated *cămine culturale* or *cercuri culturale* (cultural hearths or circles) by publicizing the concept and mobilizing the notables of a given village. These societies then took on their own life, but when they sought funding they reverted to such military metaphors as "spiritually conquering the estranged population." Some popular culture institutions also had an important spontaneous component. Citizens forming cultural societies, reading groups, and libraries wrote to Casa şcoalelor asking for money or books, invoking the "light" and the national culture they were bringing the people.[51]

Known as "*cursişti*," the teachers who graduated from the Chişinău summer courses in 1917–1918 were certified to teach in Moldavian schools. In 1917, close to five hundred teachers, most of them Moldavian,

[49] CS/1920/7/298/299, n.d.

[50] Ştefan Ciobanu, the General Director of Education in Bessarabia, was in charge of the Department of Extracurricular Activity that opened on February 1, 1919. CS/1920/7/178, CS/1920/417/7–10, both n.d. Some of these texts were still entirely in Cyrillic or contained Cyrillic and Latin facing texts. The newspaper *Cuvânt moldovenesc* (Moldavian Word) appeared in editions of 6,000 twice weekly. It had started out in Cyrillic print and, after a transitional stage in which both Cyrillic and Latin were used, it came to be published entirely in Latin letters. The magazine *Şcoala Basarabiei* (Bessarabia's School), a monthly organ of pedagogic culture and national education, was distributed free to all schools. Other more local papers, such as *Tighina* (from Tighina) and *Unirea* (The Union from Bălţi), received subsidies from the Department of Extracurricular Activity as well.

[51] CS/1920/7/298,299, CS/1920/334/37, CS/1920/7/273, and CS/1920/7/60, all n.d.

attended. Anxious to keep their jobs in Moldavian villages, some Russians attended as well. The majority of the Moldavian *cursişti* were completely estranged from Romanian culture. According to Ghibu, who organized and taught some of the courses, they were "not only devoid of any Romanian culture—they did not even know the Latin alphabet—but they also lacked a national consciousness." This alienation may explain why many of the Moldavians were nearly as hostile to the compulsory courses as their Russian colleagues who sat in the back of the classroom and grumbled their displeasure audibly.[52] In 1918, there were 537 participants in the course (363 Moldavians, 95 Russians, 34 Ukrainians, 13 Bulgarians, and 34 from other ethnic groups). Two classes comprising seventy persons taught those who knew no Romanian at all; others were for "beginners" and "advanced" students of Romanian. The session was taught by twenty six instructors under conditions of scarce textbooks, insufficient food, and a general shortage of funds.[53] In a country devastated by war, this situation is not surprising. What is striking, however, is the extent of the pedagogical task exemplified by the large contingent of ethnic Moldavians who needed language training.

The two summer sessions produced many successes. Although some teachers dropped out, the ones who stayed learned to read and write Romanian using the Latin alphabet, they acquired a command of Romanian grammar, they imbibed a version of Romanian history that emphasized the great Roman ancestry of the Moldavians and strengthened the teachers' weak national sentiments, and they picked up something about Romanian literature. The courses brought them to understand that the Moldavian and Romanian language were identical.[54] Undoubtedly, many *cursişti* became more aware of the shared culture and history of Moldavians and Romanians and thereby more nationally conscious as well.

The summer teacher-training courses of 1917 and 1918, established to alleviate the dearth of qualified Moldavian teachers, themselves had difficulty finding qualified and available cadre.[55] Staffing was a lesser problem the second year, but the magnitude of the task still struck some of the instructors as daunting. Petru Bogdan, a professor at the University of Iaşi, taught a course in scientific terminology in Chişinău.[56] Bogdan found that his summer students profoundly lacked confidence in their ability to use Moldavian to lecture on scientific subjects.[57] They told Bogdan that Mol-

---

[52] Ghibu, *Pe baricadele vieţii*, pp. 338–339, 361–362.
[53] MIC/1918/199b/400 (156–158), n.d.
[54] Ghibu, *Pe baricadele vieţii*, pp. 361–362.
[55] Ibid., pp. 326–327, 335–337.
[56] MIC/1918/193/12–15, August 6, 1918.
[57] According to Octavian Ghibu, the problems encountered by Bogdan in 1918 were less severe than those of 1917, the year that his father, Onisifor Ghibu, began cultural work in Bessarabia. Personal communication, 1984.

davian was "limba prostimei," the language of simple folk. They were convinced that Moldavian was so different from literary Romanian "that they *did not understand . . . Romanian.*" These teachers could not fathom Moldavian as a learned language, and were certain they could not use literary Romanian.[58]

Petru Bogdan was eventually able to change the minds of his students, partly because, he claimed, his spoken Romanian was close to the language they understood: he had been born and raised in western Moldavia, the part of the Old Kingdom adjacent to Bessarabia. He also openly admired the language of the Bessarabians. Although they formulated their thoughts in Russian first, they translated them into the language called "old and wise" by Eminescu, Romania's greatest romantic poet, himself a native of neighboring Bukovina. Bogdan found this somewhat archaic prose refreshing, for it was not burdened by the gallicisms and neologisms that had crept into the Old Kingdom's idiom. Bogdan idealized the language and folkways that Bessarabia, of all the Romanian lands, had been best able to preserve in its hundred-year political exile. He encouraged the rediscovery of Bessarabia's "priceless treasure" and extolled the beneficent influence it would have in the "purification of our scientific language."[59]

In attempting to explain the extreme lack of confidence he found among the Moldavians, Bogdan invoked their cultural oppression under Russian rule and the powerful influence of Russian literature. But he also rued the fact that during the war Romanian propaganda came to Bessarabia with the wrong people, that is, Transylvanians and Bukovinians who "spoke a language which was more distant, more motley, and . . . included neologisms and dialectal elements."[60] The implied comparison was with the Moldavian Romanian that Bogdan himself spoke and which he viewed as a less distant, purer language untainted by neologisms and free of nonstandard features—a truer, more worthy Romanian closer to the Moldavian spoken by the Bessarabians. Bogdan waxed nostalgic as he described the idiom he had learned as a child on the shores of Moldavia's Siret River, among the peasant children with whom he played in the fields or took the cows to pasture.[61] With such emotional references, Bogdan unwittingly defined a Greater Moldavian space that included Bessarabia and western Moldavia. Although Bogdan thought it necessary to change the environment of the Russified Moldavian intellectuals, he felt that only Moldavians from the Old Kingdom, like himself, should help guide the process.[62]

---

[58] MIC/1918/193/12–15, August 6, 1918. It is interesting in this context to note that the national liberation movement of the Moldavians in the 1980s has demanded and won official recognition of the identity between the Moldavian and Romanian languages.

[59] Ibid.

[60] Ibid.

[61] Ibid.

[62] Ibid. Bogdan also considered the theater a productive force in countering the influence

Petru Bogdan expressed important aspects of the Bessarabian problem as it appeared in 1918 in his letter to the minister of education. He embodies the genuine enthusiasm of Old Kingdom intellectuals engaged in cultural work in this most archaic province—the most and, at the same time, the least Romanian. They saw in the Moldavians from Bessarabia, who had missed out on modern national development, the romantic possibility of their own rejuvenation, of access to an otherwise lost national innocence. Against the backdrop of Russian literature, which was the point of cultural reference for many Bessarabian intellectuals, nationalists from the Old Kingdom struggled to persuade them that *limba prostimei,* the idiom of the village, of the household, of the fields, of the lower classes could—in the new political context—become the language of science, school, theatre, poetry, and state. This cultural and psychological revolution coincided with the political realignment. Army and school were partners in 1918.

Bogdan's opinions also testify to the phenomenon of regionalism in Greater Romania. In his eagerness to absorb the Moldavian teachers into the nation, the Iaşi professor was quick to assert a hierarchy of merit among the Romanians of the different reunited regions, with Old Kingdom Moldavians in this case at the top. He discounted the wartime propaganda work of the Transylvanians and Bukovinians[63] as counterproductive. At the very moment that Romania made claims to Bukovina and Transylvania, the Romanians from these provinces were being judged inferior in the endeavor of national propaganda—the most national of national tasks. Bogdan was not alone in expressing regionalism in the performance of Bessarabian cultural work. Onisifor Ghibu presented the perspective that it was the Transylvanians and Bukovinians who had achieved superior work in the awakening of the Moldavians before the arrival of corrupt politicians from the Regat.[64] The tensions among the peoples comprising the Romanian nation is an abiding theme throughout the relatively short life of Greater Romania. Paradoxically, the intense cultural work undertaken in common sometimes heightened these tensions.

Beginning in 1919, the Department of Extracurricular Activity of Bessarabia's Directorate of Education offered adult language courses to non-

---

of Russian literature. He meant especially the 19th-century Romanian-Moldavian dramatist Vasile Alecsandri, whose plays, exemplars of a sometimes xenophobic patriotism, were social satire targeted at the superficially Westernized upper classes who flaunted a tortured version of French and spoiled their native language in the process.

[63] In 1917 and 1918, Bukovinian officers, priests, professors, teachers, and students, along with Transylvanians, were involved in all of Bessarabia's economic, political, and cultural institutions. Bogdan himself taught at teacher-training courses in Bălţi in summer 1918. See Filaret Doboş, "În preajma zilei de 28 noiembrie 1918," in Ion Nistor, *Amintiri răzleţe din timpul unirii* (Czernowitz: Glasul Bucovinei, 1938), pp. 110–111.

[64] Ghibu, *Pe baricadele vieţii,* pp. 18–19, 23 .

teachers. Between February and July, two series of adult courses taught eight or nine hundred persons each in Chişinău. Tighina, Bălţi, Orhei, Soroca, Cahul, Reni, Leava, Chilia, Ismail, Bolgrad, and Cetatea Albă also offered classes whose goal was to help local civil servants become proficient in the new state language. Besides language, literature, history, and geography, these courses also taught bookkeeping and correspondence.

Village audiences received their share of adult courses, taught by teachers, officers, and regiment priests. During 1920, extracurricular activity intensified: twenty-one adult courses four to six months long were taught in many towns. An aggregate audience of ten thousand heard five hundred courses taught in the countryside. Although attendance was uneven among villagers, young people and army recruits came relatively regularly. A report surveying extracurricular activity in Bessarabia for 1919–1920 concluded that the adult courses were "satisfactory," citing as progress the fact that young readers from the countryside were now asking for books and newspapers with "Romanian lettering" (Latin alphabet), rather than Cyrillic.[65]

Aside from these less traditional channels of Romanian cultural propaganda in Bessarabia, the main work of cultural nationalization took place in regular children's schools. In September 1917, eight hundred primary schools and some secondary schools were slated for nationalization.[66] School expansion was also underway: the number of primary schools in Bessarabia grew from 1,383 in 1916 to 1,878 in 1917.[67] Even after the summer teacher-training courses, however, local cadre were insufficient. Additional teachers came from the ranks of Romanian refugees and prisoners of war finding themselves in need of employment and on Russian territory.[68] Because of staff shortages, conversion to Romanian as the language of instruction had to be postponed in many schools, and a majority continued instruction in Russian or stayed shut.[69]

More teachers and school administrators were sent to Bessarabia by the Ministry of Education in Bucharest. In the spring of 1918, the ministry began receiving a deluge of requests from teachers and other professionals applying for positions in Bessarabia as school inspectors, teachers, lecturers, and propagandists.[70] This interest may be explained by the fact that

---

[65] CS/1920/417/7–10, February 7, 1920. When funds were left over in the "extracurricular" budget, guest performers could be invited. But in 1921 the budget was so tight and the demand for adult courses so high that the teachers of "hundreds" of courses already under way remained unpaid. Many requests for books from villages also went unmet. MIC/1921/273/2, January 22, 1921.

[66] Ghibu, *Pe baricadele vieţii*, pp. 369–379.

[67] Liviu Marian, "Cultura şi şcoala," in Ciobanu, ed., *Basarabia: Monografie*, pp. 263–264.

[68] See *Ardealul* advertisement no. 7, November 19, 1917, cited in Ghibu, *Pe baricadele vieţii*, p. 395.

[69] "Memoriu despre învăţământul primar din judeţul Chişinău," AA IX/ Varia 10, n.d.

[70] MIC/1918/196, n.d.

much of Romania was suffering economic hardship and unemployment under German occupation. By comparison, Bessarabia was a free Romanian territory. Although refugees from German-occupied Bucharest may have simply wanted jobs at a time of economic chaos, they summoned up motives tied to the national cause.[71] Some applicants wanted to do propaganda work in Bessarabia in lieu of military duty,[72] but most of them advanced patriotic concerns as their main motive. Typically, they pointed to their knowledge of the country, their participation in the war, and their wish to contribute to the "development of national consciousness."[73] Some invoked old ties to the area,[74] others owed their interest in Bessarabia to the circumstances of the war,[75] and many claimed no other connection to Bessarabia than their devotion to the province's spiritual homecoming.

Some of those eager for appointments in Bessarabia's budding Romanian cultural establishment in 1918 had particularly distinguished credentials, having earned science degrees, doctorates, or tenure at ranking secondary schools.[76] A graduate of the Sorbonne with a doctorate in philology was one of the most illustrious applicants for a teaching job in Bessarabia in 1918. He had been teaching Italian in the west Moldavian town of Bârlad (population 26,000) and complained that the provincial atmosphere and the lack of libraries had stifled his intellect. Yet, as both "fighter" and "intellectual" he felt attracted to newly annexed Bessarabia where he yearned to teach French and Italian. He argued that familiarity with French would bring Russified Romanians and the Russian bourgeoisie of the region closer to the language and culture of modern Romania, so deeply influenced by French civilization, while "the Italian language, so close to the Latin and to the Romanian, could serve toward the affirmation of our Latinity, [which is] so necessary [in Bessarabia] where the struggle against Slavism does not promise to be particularly easy."[77] Thus in the very first months of the Bessarabian revolution, job seekers began advancing nationalist arguments in their quest for jobs.

Local cultural workers who were already active in Bessarabia also sought support from the Ministry of Education after 1918. Relying on their limited resources, this spontaneous vanguard of Romanian culture weathered the

[71] See, for example, MIC/1918/199b/459, n.d.
[72] MIC/1918/107/114, n.d.
[73] MIC/1918/199b/324, March 21, 1918.
[74] They may have been born there, or had families of Bessarabian descent, or known Russian. MIC/1918/199b/316, April 3, 1918, and MIC/1918/199b/324, March 21, 1918.
[75] One graduate of the University of Bucharest in literature and philosophy, who had been mobilized and garrisoned in Chişinău, had "created his own circle of nationalist activity [there]." MIC/1918/199b/304, May 30, 1918.
[76] MIC/1918/199b/305, May 14, 1918; MIC/1918/199b/309, May 21, 1918; MIC/1918/199b/327, March 14, 1918; and MIC/1918/199b/459, n.d.
[77] MIC/1918/199b/327, March 14, 1918.

revolution and the short period of Bessarabian autonomy and started courses, performing groups, and libraries on their own. Now however, they turned to Bucharest for authorization, funding, and the sense of power that comes from association with the state.[78] Romanian sovereignty over the new province, especially at a time when the rest of the country was in disarray because of the German occupation after the Treaty of Bucharest, meant new employment and financial opportunities for teachers, humanists, and, generally, for all those committed in different degrees to Romanian nationalism.

The state clearly had its own reason for encouraging an outpouring of cultural nationalism in Bessarabia: The Romanization of the province required cadre. Although non-Romanians could not be counted on, many educated native Moldavians did not prove to be very reliable either. Many Moldavian-born bureaucrats declined to speak or write Romanian, and even refused to take the oath to the Romanian king and state.[79] The Ministry of Education thus actively recruited a propaganda staff for Bessarabia beginning in 1918.[80] As already indicated, the response seems to have been overwhelming; in fact, at one point, the ministry felt that too many people were heading to Bessarabia.[81]

The Romanian army had come to Bessarabia beginning in January 1918, before the annexation of the province, and its cultural role continued into the next decade. Teachers previously mobilized for military service were demobilized and assigned to teaching posts in Bessarabia under military administration. They were distributed among army zones determined by the military authority.[82] The Ministry of Education and the military collaborated in the recruitment of the propagandists who fanned out through Bessarabia. By summer 1918, over two hundred people were part of the "propaganda staff" of the province. Some of these functioned as teachers,

[78] For example, Nicolae Totu and Dumitru Stroia, two Transylvanian theology students, refugees in Bessarabia, had been distributing books to peasants and teachers, and they had organized a 10,000-volume library, paid for by a local Popular University that was running out of money. In June 1918, they wanted to be "paid by the central government as propagandists." MIC/1918/199b/416. George Florescu, a self-described "dramatic artist" already in the midst of teaching drama to a group of Bessarabian students, wanted to establish an amateur theater group at state expense. MIC/1918/199b/417.

[79] Giurgea, *Din Trecutul*, pp. 111–112, 116.

[80] MIC/1918/107/112. The ministry advertised in the newspaper *România*, an official daily published in Iași while the government was exiled there.

[81] MIC/1918/199b/359, 360, May 2, 1918.

[82] This was the *Marele pretorat de pe lângă Marele Cartier General*. A memo sent by the Ministry of Education on February 6, 1918, to Infantry Regiment 43/59 informs it of its responsibilities toward members of the regiment now assigned to Bessarabia. It states that "all teachers of all grades who are sent to Bessarabia are considered as if mobilized and detached, keeping the rights they have within the military units to which they belong; they are to be given their military or civilian pay as before." See MIC/1918/107/118, February 6, 1918.

others as secondary school professors, and many more were at-large "propagandists without appointments" working in various capacities on newspapers; as school administrators; as substitute teachers; in libraries, theatres, museums; and at special training courses for Bessarabians. Periodic transfusions of school personnel from the Old Kingdom occurred in the early 1920s.[83]

In addition to supervising the propaganda staff, the military itself conducted extensive educational activity in Bessarabia partly in order to promote Romanian literacy and political loyalty among army recruits. It also set up adult schools intended for national propaganda in the frontier zones, near the Soviet border,[84] and sponsored periodical publications in conjunction with the Ministry of Education.[85] Professional educators were not always pleased to collaborate with the military in cultural work.[86]

The Ministry of Education's relationship to the propaganda staff in Bessarabia was mediated through the office of the "Technical Delegate for Schooling" based in Chişinău. This agency had functioned under the short-lived autonomous Moldavian Democratic Republic and continued after Bessarabia's union with Romania. A poster-manifesto issued by the delegate office on March 3, 1918, defined the role of the propagandists. The announcement, addressed to the "teachers and schoolmasters from Romania, who find themselves in the Moldavian Republic," instructed them on their "cultural and national activity" in Bessarabia: They were to organize choirs, festivities, and skits with school children, villagers, and local teachers; stimulate the population's interest in the Moldavian school and language which would begin to serve in justice, administration, church, schools, and other areas of public relations; and foster "pride in 'being Moldavian' " by teaching about this people's glorious past. Teachers were asked to emphasize the great qualities of the Romanian people inherited from that most virtuous ancient people, the Romans, and to describe

[83] MIC/1918/199b/148–149, 150–155, n.d. In 1921, for example, twenty-five grade school teachers were "transferred" to Bessarabia, fifty-five were "detached," and fifty were "appointed" there. The ministry looked upon most of these assignments to Bessarabia as temporary. After a year or two of service, Old Kingdom teachers were supposed to return to their original posts, but not all did. MIC/1921/275/42–47, MIC/1921/275/91, both n.d.

[84] AA IX/ Varia 10, April 13, 1922, and April 25, 1923; Octavian Ghibu, personal communication, 1984.

[85] In the summer of 1918, for instance, the First Division of Cavalry sponsored the newspaper *Glasul moldovenesc* (The Moldavian Voice) published in Bălţi, in editions of two to three thousand, and distributed free in Bălţi and Soroca counties. The editor was planning to expand to a larger format if the Ministry of War lowered the cost of paper. At the same time, the editor solicited an additional contribution from the Ministry of Education in order to hire a journalist who, he argued, would benefit the nationalization of labor under way. *Glasul moldovenesc* thus obtained the modest sum of 600 lei monthly from the Ministry of Education's propaganda fund, in addition to its military financial sponsorship. MIC/1918/199b/425 (181).

[86] AA IX/ Varia 10, February 20, 1923, and March 7, 1923.

the great economic and military progress made by the other Romanian provinces—the Old Kingdom, Bukovina, Transylvania, Dobrudja. The Romanian teachers were expected to help their Moldavian colleagues, who were "struggling with great hardships" to establish Moldavian schools, and to organize lectures where such schools were still lacking. The cultural and national duties of these propagandists also included advising peasants about hygiene, folk medicine, veterinary medicine, agriculture, and animal husbandry. Finally, they were responsible for gathering folkloric, ethnographic, paleographic, and geological material.[87]

This many-point program made Old Kingdom teachers in Bessarabia an essential link to the Moldavian population, especially to the peasantry, to whom the Romanian army and state had few other means of access. The teachers did not merely function in their traditional professional capacity of teaching children the three R's; rather, they were expected to convince the entire Moldavian population that it was Romanian, and instruct it how best to be so.[88]

Although the army of outsiders addressed by these announcements may have descended on Bessarabia with the best intentions, they occasionally offended local teachers and authorities who saw them as meddlers. In June 1918, for example, the Bălți district *zemstvo* was up in arms over a high-handed propagandist who forced his way into a school and filed a complaint voicing the anxiety that regular local teachers would resent the "advice" of the propaganda staff as intrusive. Such outside intervention, the *zemstvo* argued, might then interfere with the smooth functioning of the school system of Bessarabia just at the critical moment of its "nationalization and crystallization," defeating the very purpose of cultural propaganda.[89] The Ministry of Education insisted that the Bălți *zemstvo* exaggerated and generalized from an isolated incident, thus denigrating the laudable work of the self-sacrificing propagandists.[90] But the strained relationship continued between propagandists from the Regat and local teachers, and even between the Ministry of Education in Bucharest and local organs in Chișinău.

[87] The teachers functioned within units called "circles" whose radius included several villages. All ethnic Moldavian villages were to receive equal attention. The announcement was signed by Dumitru M. Cădere, the Technical Delegate for Schooling. MIC/1918/199b/ 428 (184), n.d.

[88] Other documents carried the same message. One memo from the Cultural Service of Bessarabia's General Commissariate reminded the propagandists that their "mission [was] to awaken the Romanian consciousness in the Moldavian people of Bessarabia" where "national consciousness [was] weak," though Romanian ethnicity and language were still alive. The propagandists also had the task of researching the level and manifestations of national consciousness of villagers in their circle. Arhiva O. Ghibu, document signed by Gh. D. Mugur, [1918].

[89] MIC/1918/199b/430, June 23, 1918.

[90] MIC/1918/199b/429, August 16, 1918.

The nationalization of schools was a sensitive process that spawned conflicts at other levels too. Students and parents initially resisted Romanian education, which had no status in the old Bessarabian framework. Emmanuel de Martonne's observations from Cahul County in 1919 indicate these early difficulties:

> Enters the head of the secondary school. He has recently come from the Kingdom. . . . Since the act of union, the majority of the board of managers, made up of teachers and parents, decided to introduce Roumanian into the school: the Russian officials and the non-Roumanians withdrew. The boys themselves refused at first to attend classes conducted in Roumanian. The notion that Russian alone could be a learned and literary language had sunk deep in those young minds. Roumanian, a peasants' tongue, could lead to nothing! All over Bessarabia the same incidents took place.[91]

The Schools

The first stage in the appropriation of Bessarabian schools focused on training teachers. It also saw the establishment of some Romanian schools, periodicals, libraries, and popular-cultural institutions for the Romanian rural population. A second stage of cultural consolidation began in 1919–1920. The nationalization of primary schools was completed, and the local administrators became increasingly concerned with obtaining cultural materials from Bucharest. The demands made by Bessarabia's school administrators to Bucharest for endowing local schools with pedagogical materials were echoed and amplified in a popular, grassroots insistence on the construction of more, better, and higher level schools.

School inspectors and administrators sent requests to Casa școalelor for pedagogical materials such as textbooks, folk-art books, teaching aids, brochures, lesson plans, maps, library books, and laboratory equipment. The typical request reminded Casa școalelor bureaucrats of the hardship and poverty with which Romanian culture in Bessarabia had to contend and of the dearth of cultural objects, particularly Romanian books, thus emphasizing the embattled atmosphere of Bessarabia's Romanian schools.[92] A theological seminary from Ismail couched its plea for books in martial phrases, claiming that it was "the school that bore the brunt in the most estranged part of Bessarabia," in a struggle in which the most powerful

---

[91] Emmanuel de Martonne, *What I Have Seen in Bessarabia* (Paris: Impr. des arts et des sports, 1919), p. 12.
[92] CS/1921/33/1, n.d.

weapon was the book.[93] Similarly, the headmaster of a new military lycée in Chişinău, Lt. Col. Hristescu, prefaced his demand for a shipment of books with the following battle cry: "This lycée will be a new hotbed of culture which will fill a void felt in Bessarabia's secondary education and which has to fulfill an important cultural role. We are taking part in the great work of nationalization of the native population."[94]

Indeed, the desire for schooling in Bessarabia in the 1920s is impressive, particularly considering the Moldavians' previous low literacy rates. Their interest may have been encouraged by the potential availability, for the first time since the mid–nineteenth century, of instruction in the native language of the majority poulation. The school committees established in 1919 decentralized some of the decision making and alloted the bulk of the financial burden to local constituencies, which may also help explain this phenomenon. The committees became responsible for raising money for school construction and for funding extrabudgetary classes. In Bessarabia, they were especially important in the primary schools. In the process of bringing the school issue "home," by raising a local tax and a volunteer labor force to build and staff a local grammar school everyone came to know, the rural Bessarabian population became involved in education in unprecedented ways. In some cases, of course, school committee meetings were explosive occasions where villagers and clergy expressed their displeasure at the schools, which were, among other things, an intrusive arm of the state. A school inspector from Tighina County reported in 1924, for example, on a meeting called in the commune of Cimişlia to discuss the budget: "There was no question in which we were not attacked with insults: [that we are] 'skinning the people alive,' [that] 'the school is the poor peasant's misfortune,' [that] 'the teachers are the milkers of this cow—the people'."[95] Through the committees (already discussed in Chapter 2), public meetings, and thick state-sponsored propaganda portraying education as the school of the reunited nation, the rural public seems to have become sensitized to its educational rights and to the benefits and prestige of education at the higher level as well. Many of the schools rural Bessarabians were asking for were not the compulsory grammar schools, but middle schools, gymnasia, and lycées. Furthermore, they tended to plead for the transfer of schools from urban to rural settings.

People requested new schools on various grounds. Petitions mentioned both the inferiority of the Romanians vis-à-vis the minority populations that had more solid schools[96] and the great distance peasant children had

---

[93] CS/1920/7/114, March [n.d.], 1920.

[94] CS/1920/7/20, October 29, 1919.

[95] AA IX/ Varia 10, November 10, 1924. The priest was the principal attacker, and strange as it may seem, the inspector accused him, in the report, of Bolshevism.

[96] CS/1921/33/1, n.d., and CS/1921/33/9, April 28, 1922.

to travel to existing secondary schools, located mostly in towns. Some Bessarabians had been deprived of secondary schools by the redrawing of national boundaries.[97] In one instance, the inhabitants of Cimişlia, a village in Tighina county in southern Bessarabia, had collected three hundred thousand *lei* to contribute toward the opening of a lycée. The nearest town, the county capital Tighina, was about ninety kilometers away. The consensus expressed in the letter to the Ministry of Education was that in Tighina County only the minorities drank "at [the fountain of] lycée culture,"[98] presumably because in Tighina, as in most of Bessarabia, the urban population that had convenient access to secondary schools was predominantly non-Romanian. Similarly, the mayor of Volontirovca, in Cetatea Albă County, requested the state to upgrade the local middle school into a lycée, protesting that the Germans had a lycée at Tarutino, the Bulgarians had one at Comrat, and the Jews of Tatar-Bunar had a Russian lycée. Romanian lycées, went the complaint, were all urban, thus precluding the attendance of village children.[99]

A request from the market town of Râşcani in the county of Bălţi voiced a fear of isolation from Romanian culture, saying that, "The market town of Râşcani is in the center of a purely Romanian region, surrounded by about 180 very rich villages that, however, lack railways or other means of communication."[100] The notable who wrote the letter went on to speculate about integrating this insular but thoroughly Romanian area by means of a lycée: "Half of a county—the whole north of the Bălţi—prays, begs for light. . . . Mr. Minister, give us light over here in the country, where nothing has yet been touched and from where—who knows—if a new, better, healthier current might not start for our nation and for our country, which we feel today needs bright and conscious sons."[101]

The "Romanian regeneration" argument marshalled in this plea for a local lycée belied the multiethnic backing of the Râşcani campaign. A majority of the 101 signatures on the petition received in this case were Russian and Jewish names.[102] It is possible that many potential Romanian supporters may have been illiterate and unable to sign their names, while Russians and Jews, as elsewhere in Bessarabia, constituted the more literate class and could sign. In any case, Râşcani, or at least the population of Râşcani actively supporting this petition, was not as ethnically pure as its

[97] For example, the children of Atachi had gone before the war to middle schools and lycées in Mogilev, a town across the Dniester River, which had meanwhile become the international frontier between Soviet Russia and Romania. MIC/1923/477/7, October 15, 1922.

[98] MIC/1923/476/24, received May 28, 1923.

[99] MIC/1923/477/147–148, January 17, 1923.

[100] MIC/1923/477/108, December 15, 1922.

[101] Ibid.

[102] MIC/1923/477/109, December 4, 1922.

notables claimed. Chances are that the priest and subprefect, in collusion
with the literate citizens of the village, drafted a letter which reflected
their understanding of what the ministry wanted to hear. The petitioners
certainly wanted a lycée, although they were not in their majority ethnically
Romanian. But culture, inseparable from nationalist discourse, and
schools, as a vehicle of ethnic purification, had become a kind of currency
of words in the negotiations between Bucharest and the multiethnic borderlands.

Bessarabia's Ukrainian enclaves also produced loyalist arguments tinged
with nationalism. The mostly Ukrainian population of the northeastern
part of Hotin County wanted a gymnasium built in Clişcăuţi, which they
regarded as the center of "Bessarabian Bukovina."[103] The Ukrainians justified their need for a secondary school in somewhat stilted Romanian. They
needed the school:

> due to the fact that Bessarabia was for a long time torn away from the body
> of the Mother country; in our region a weak knowledge of the State language
> [exists. It] has remained undeveloped . . . [but] for us it is absolutely
> indispensable since we encounter great difficulties . . . in getting a State or
> county job, and mainly in the Military service as well as in various necessities
> of contact with the Authorities, Traders, and Manufacturers. Also for this
> reason a book, a newspaper, a magazine and all official ordinances remain
> unknown and ununderstood by us. Because of this we have a big, [and] hard-
> to-overcome obstacle [that is] in the way of [our] complete fusion with the
> culture of our Country.[104]

The letter also emphasized the financial straits of rural residents faced with
sending their children to be schooled in town. Under the circumstances,
"urban elements" were better prepared for admission to the lycée: "As a
result of this state of affairs, in our opinion, . . . last year out of eighteen
Pupils graduated from the lycée in the Town of Hotin, sixteen . . . were
Jewish, which is fully understandable since we, the peasant layer, lack the
possibility of competition with them in this regard."[105] By drawing attention
to their underpriviledged status as rural residents, the Ukrainians were
appealing—perhaps unconsciously—to the Romanian state in an implicit
anti-Jewish anti-urban solidarity, offering an alliance based on a kind of
populist "rural nationalism" in which the otherness of the urban Jews
could contribute to a Romanian-Ukrainian identification.

The Romanian state's attempts to use cultural policies to cement Bessarabia's union with Romania helped legitimize a nationalist vocabulary. Many

---

[103] MIC/1923/476/75, August 8, 1923.
[104] MIC/1923/476/157, 158, September 25, 1923.
[105] Ibid.

groups of Bessarabians, regardless of ethnicity, used this terminology in formulating their demands for resources from Bucharest. One result of this rhetorical process was the "bidding up" of nationalist discourse. Another result, of course, was that the secondary school network expanded substantially, and many schools were transferred to rural areas. Writing in 1926 about Bessarabia's school situation since the union, Liviu Marian posited as one sign of progress "the establishment and transfer of almost all middle schools [i.e. lower secondary schools] from the towns [that are] county seats to urban and rural communes." He commented that "the latter were until recently treated unfairly relative to the cities, where all categories of secondary schools were concentrated, thus hampering very much plowmen's children's access to secondary schools."[106]

Language, Ethnos, Region

The Romanization of the school system had been officially completed by 1922,[107] but that de jure accomplishment only partially corresponded to the actual situation. By 1922, forty-eight primary schools in the city of Chişinău were Romanian. This number included eleven schools that previously had been Russian and nine that had been Jewish. The national minorities in the city were free to attend private Jewish, Russian, French, Armenian, and Baptist schools, or minority state schools—for Russians and Jews—in which the language of instruction was Romanian after 1922 (except for religion and maternal language classes).[108] In Chişinău County, 181 of the 184 primary schools were Romanian and 3 were Ukrainian. Even in the latter, in the first and second grades the language of instruction was Ukrainian, but from the third grade on all subjects except Ukrainian language were taught in Romanian.[109]

In Hotin County in 1922, the Romanian language had been introduced successfully in primary schools without incurring hostile reactions from the minority population. "On the contrary," a report claimed, "Ukrainian villages have asked to have only Romanian schools, [saying] that they don't want Ukrainian ones."[110] This is no small feat, for Hotin County was one of the least Romanian in Bessarabia, containing a large minority of Ukrainians and many Jews and other minorities.[111] An inspector of primary schools in Lăpuşna, Tighina, and Cetatea Albă Counties found

[106] Marian, "Cultura şi şcoala," p. 268.
[107] Ibid.
[108] AA IX/ Varia 10, October 14, 1924, and December 30, 1922.
[109] AA IX/ Varia 10, [n.d.], 1921/22.
[110] AA IX/ Varia 10, December 21, 1922.
[111] John Kaba, *Politico-Economic Review of Basarabia* (n.p., 1919), p. 28.

in 1926 that non-Romanian pupils and teachers "spoke the Romanian language satisfactorily," though the cultivation of Romanian nationalism left something to be desired.[112] An inspector of primary schools in the Cetatea Albă county in 1924–1925 commented on the degree of progress made in Romanian language acquisition even in many schools with "pure minority" populations.[113]

Such successes were achieved in part through well-designed measures. Romanian kindergartens were introduced to facilitate the transition to Romanian primary schools, with good results.[114] As Romanian facilities were opened, corresponding Russian ones were closed down. In 1922, for instance, the Ministry of Education ordered the closing down of Russian school libraries.[115] The school inspectorate in the city of Chişinău reported in 1922 that there was a greater shortage of non-Romanian books than the previous year. As the writer of the report speculated, pupils may have been pushed toward Romanian schools by the book situation and by their recognition of the need to learn the state language. The year 1922 seemed to signal a turn toward Romanian schools, the reverse of the phenomenon of 1918, when Romanian schools had stayed empty while pupils had crowded the minority schools.[116]

According to these inspectors' reports, after a difficult start, the Romanian language received broad acceptance in Bessarabia's schools in the early and mid-1920s. These results, however, were neither uniform nor enduring; in the late twenties and in the thirties, the status of Romanian as a lingua franca in Bessarabia seems to have been tentative still, eliciting Romanian officials' alarm.

In 1936, an inspector in the county of Cetatea Albă concluded that "The 20 years of Romanian rule . . . and of the nationalization of minority villages through the school have not borne fruit." The same inspector also took a dim view of the teachers in Cetatea Albă's minority schools; he found many to be "if not in fact dangerous, at least harmful."[117] Clearly, the persistence of the Russian language among teachers and school staff was an obstacle to the nationalization of Bessarabia's schools. In October 1922, Constantin Angelescu, the Minister of Education, expressed concern over the stubborn use of Russian by Bessarabian school directors, professors, and supporting staff. He attempted to eliminate the problem by issuing directives making Romanian the compulsory language of communication

---

[112] MIC/1926/5/25, May 31, 1926.

[113] MIC/1925/124/127–132, n.d.

[114] MIC/1926/5/23, March 18, 1926.

[115] MIC/1922/572/68, October 19, 1922. In 1920, school libraries in Soroca County were ordered to get rid of tendentious Russian books from their shelves. See S. K. Brysiakin, *Kul'tura bessarabii, 1918–1940* (Chişinău: Shtiintsa, 1978), p. 29.

[116] AA IX/ Varia 10, August [n.d.], 1922. See also AA IX/ Varia 10, October 14, 1924.

[117] AA IX/ Varia 10, August 3, 1936.

for headmasters, teachers, teaching aides, and pupils, and by closing Russian school libraries in favor of Romanian ones. Romanian pupils caught speaking Russian faced expulsion. Teachers who had not yet mastered the state language were given an ultimatum to pass a language proficiency exam by the end of the school year or risk being fired.[118] In February 1923, the Ministry of Education sent a memo to all Romanian schools in Bessarabia which again forbade the use of Russian.[119]

The language competency exams, though undoubtedly necessary, were applied as if ethnic competency were at stake. One school director from Soroca asked which of his teachers should register for the exam; he was told that not only must all teachers who did not know Romanian be examined, but also Russians, even if they knew Romanian, as well as other minority teachers who were automatically "all considered foreigners."[120] This way of handling the language issue offended the professional dignity of Bessarabian teachers, regardless of ethnicity, and reinforced the regionalist solidarity of Bessarabians against the "true Romanians" of the Old Kingdom. In June 1923, Bessarabia's faculty protested the "humiliating" language exams that denied them their previous rights. In a public statement, they expressed a preference for individual inspections and "a more parental treatment from the highest school authorities."[121]

Extracurricular cultural activities also experienced the law of diminishing returns in the mid- and late twenties. An inspector of cultural and extracurricular activity in Lăpuşna County reported in 1928 that adult courses and public libraries had poor attendance, and that people had to be practically dragged to cultural festivities. He speculated that a mutual distrust existed between the population and the notables in charge, which he explained as residue from the time when local peasants were confronted by foreigners in positions of power. Although the officials were now Romanian, the mistrustful attitude had carried over.[122] Other peasants were merely indifferent. An inspector in Tighina County in 1925 was shocked to find that "on the walls of [villagers'] rooms were nailed portraits of the former Imperial Russian family and scenes from the Russo-Japanese war."[123] He failed to convince the peasants to remove the pictures they were using as

[118] MIC/1922/572/68, October 19, 1922.
[119] AA IX/ Varia 9, February [n.d.], 1923. Of 123 teachers registered to take the language exam administered in 1923, 56 were absent, 25 passed with "satisfactory," 34 were graded "insufficient," and 8 failed outright. Those absent and those who failed were dismissed from the schools, while the 34 with "insufficient" grades were allowed to take the exam again the following year. MIC/1923/464/144, n.d. A report filed in 1923, however, again rued Bessarabia's teachers' scant knowledge of Romanian. MIC/1923/232/72, March [n.d.], 1923.
[120] MIC/1923/463/163, May 2, 1923.
[121] Scânteia, June 20, 1923.
[122] MIC/1928/32/163, February 1928, n.d.
[123] MIC/1925/124/215, June 1, 1925. See also CS/1921/213/1, n.d.

decorations; they simply did not want bare walls. The inspector recommended that Casa şcoalelor print up Romanian royal portraits and historic scenes to be distributed to the population free of charge.[124]

An inspector's report from 1922 may provide a key for interpreting the uneven success of the Romanization of Bessarabia. In Soroca County, where all the teachers knew Romanian and the Romanian schools all taught in the Romanian language, where there were 243 Romanian schools, 9 Jewish schools, 5 Ukrainian schools, and 3 Russian schools, and where the minority schools were gradually becoming Romanized, nationalization seemed to be making good progress. A "regrettable fact," however, tempered the inspector's sanguine judgment, namely, his observation "that the majority of the teachers in their private conversations and at get-togethers—even official ones, but especially family ones—spoke only the Russian language."[125] He recommended that those teachers be relocated to the interior of the province where the population was purely Romanian and replaced with teachers who were well fortified pedagogically and nationally. It seems that while the letter of Romanization was being followed, its spirit often was not. The educated elites and the peasants were alike content to retain remnants of Russian culture in their private lives. This fact was particularly painful to Romanian nationalists because of the emphasis they placed on the spiritual aspects of the process. The solutions suggested here, of replacing unreliable minority or local teachers with "solid" Romanians, or that of automatically testing all ethnic non-Romanians for language competency, are part of an underlying integral nationalist program for dealing with ethnic diversity. Though not official government policy in the 1920s, this working program was developed "on the ground" in response to the needs and frustrations of nation building.

Apparently, Russians and Moldavians could not quite be trusted with the Romanian language; furthermore, their political loyalty was in question. In 1925, the Ministry of War alerted the Ministry of Education about the activities of communist students at the lycée in Hotin, blaming the administration and staff of the school for the students' misdirection: "The High Command deems that this state of affairs is the result of the fact that a majority of the professors from that lycée, and first of all its Director, are originally Russians or Bessarabians, who give the young people an education damaging to our State interests, and [the High Command] solicits their replacement with elements from the Old Kingdom."[126] In this instance, the Romanian authorities put the Russians and Bessarabians (Moldavians) together in the same untrustworthy category. The solution to troublesome

---

[124] MIC/1925/124/215, June 1, 1925.
[125] AA IX/ Varia 10, October 22, 1922.
[126] MIC/1925/417/277, December 3, 1925.

ethnic Russians and regionalist Bessarabians was again an integral nationalist one: to import "good Romanians" from the Old Kingdom.

In the 1930s, there are indications that Russian persisted or perhaps
reemerged in official contexts, including schools, possibly in reaction to
Bucharest's mistrustful attitude. In 1931, the Ismail County prefecture
ordered its employees to use Romanian, for they acted as if Russian was
still the official language.[127] In 1936, a confidential inspector's report from
Cetatea Albă sounded the alarm about "undesirable . . . , dangerous, or,
in any case, harmful" minority teachers. The report observed further that
"the twenty years of Romanian rule and of nationalization of the minority
villages through the school in the Cetatea Albă County have not born
fruit."[128]

Looking at Bessarabia in the 1920s and 30s, Romanian nationalists
might well have worried about the weakness of the Romanian press. Bessarabia's youth was being steadily converted to Romanian culture by means
of the Romanized schools—but was that orientation properly nurtured by
a high-quality, richly differentiated press? The three Romanian dailies
that had begun publication in 1917 had long since died.[129] Except for
1926–1927, when *România nouă* reemerged briefly, there was not a local
Romanian-language daily after 1918. In 1928, according to one calcula-
tion, only 4 percent of Bessarabia's daily press was Romanian; the rest
was Russian and Jewish. In fact, there was not even one Romanian daily—
only three Russian dailies in Cetatea Albă with sections in Romanian.[130]

Charles Upson Clark judiciously observed the qualified progress made
in Romanizing Bessarabia in the 1920s: "Kishineff in 1919 seemed quite
like any Russian provincial city; the Roumanian element still seemed intrusive, though entirely at home in the country villages. But Kishineff in 1925
was clearly a Roumanian provincial capital, though still with a certain
Russian flavor."[131]

Nationalism and Anti-Semitism

In the interwar period, Bessarabia's cultural landscape was changed
by the proliferation of Romanian schools and other cultural institutions.

---

[127] *Cuvânt moldovenesc,* August 16, 1931, cited in Brysiakin, *Kul'tura bessarabii,* p. 31.
[128] AA IX/ Varia 10, August 3, 1936.
[129] *Cuvânt moldovenesc, Ardealul* (which was first a weekly, and whose name later changed
to *România nouă*), and *Sfatul Țarii.*
[130] Onisifor Ghibu, *Ardealul în Basarabia—O Pagină de istorie contimporană* (Cluj: Institutul de arte grafice Ardealul, 1928), pp. 236–239. This general estimate is confirmed by a
Soviet source, which asserts that in 1930, two Romanian weeklies and four Russian dailies
were published in Chișinău. Brysiakin, *Kul'tura bessarabii,* p. 89.
[131] Charles Upson Clark, *Bessarabia: Russia and Roumania on the Black Sea* (New York:
Dodd, Mead, 1927), p. 221.

Group of honor roll pupils of the Primary School for Girls in Chişinău (June 1926). They are posing in front of an exhibit of their folk art embroidery. Courtesy of Arhivele Statului, Bucharest

Whereas the state was concerned with establishing a network of Romanian *elementary* schools which would bind the province to the mother country, the decentralized rural network of *secondary* schools was created largely by popular demand. To be sure, this demand was in part a by-product of the early Romanization campaign that had attempted to use culture and education to appropriate Bessarabia. Apparently, that campaign inculcated the "nationalization" code successfully. Rural Bessarabians were only drawing the obvious conclusion in insisting that Romanian culture be taken one step further to make secondary education available to Bessarabian peasants. Their interest in secondary schools was not, however, merely cultural. Culture, in this case, schools, promised a social mobility previously denied to the rural population. In the interwar period such mobility was inextricably bound with urban realities and images to which Moldavian and other Bessarabian villagers had an ambivalent relationship.

Bessarabian peasants found towns threatening and alien, but also regarded them with a certain envy and ambition. In some towns, urban dormitories and boarding schools opened their doors to peasant young-sters, offering hospitable, controlled environments where they could begin their acquaintance with the city world but be spared its alienation and "horrors." The society "Public Assistance," which was in charge of a boarding facility for country girls in Chişinău, claimed to shelter them from the "temptations that are offered by life as a lodger." In the dormitory they could "live in a moral environment" which was "at the same time also a hotbed of national propaganda." The society "Vatra Şcolii" (the School Hearth) opened in Bălţi in 1919 to help Romanian pupils with lodging. Located in an old army barracks, it accommodated more boarders each year.[132] The organization prided itself on its large contribution to the Romanization of education in Bălţi: the dormitory allowed the rural Romanian element to be well represented in the local boys' lycée and commercial school. (By contrast, no girls' dormitory existed in Bălţi in 1926, and few Romanian girls, particularly from the country, attended the local girls' lycée.) But such dormitories were few and far between. In general, rural groups preferred to petition the transfer of secondary schools from urban to village settings.[133] Nonetheless, the ruralization of education was not the ultimate goal, but the means to another end. Little interest existed in an agriculturally oriented education; the longer-range, implicit objective of much of the rural population (an objective shared by the state) was to overcome the historic domination of the towns by the traditional urban "foreign"—often Jewish—elites.

In the historic settling of accounts that followed unification, the Romanization and ruralization of education and the elites was a logical goal. Yet the process was accompanied not only by resistance from both Romanians and non-Romanians, but also by "excesses" against Bessarabia's Jews. Bessarabia's anti-Semitic tradition, dating back to Russian rule, fuelled the animosities of the province's gentile population. In 1903, Chişinău, immortalized by the Hebrew poet Hayyim N. Bialik as "The City of Slaughter," had been the site of one of the bloodiest pogroms in modern history.[134] According to both Jewish and Romanian sources, some of the Black Hundreds who organized it were of Moldavian extraction, as were many of the participants.[135] Another pogrom took place in Chişinău during the 1905 revolution.

To this tradition of manipulated popular anti-Semitism was added the peculiar social and economic stratification of Bessarabia, which persisted

[132] MIC/1925/362/1, 2, n.d. The number of boarders of Vatra Şcolii went from 40 in 1919 to 140 in 1926. MIC/1926/360/9–10, February 17, 1926. Not all their boarders were Romanian: in 1926, 14 were Ukrainian, 6 were Russian. See MIC/1926/360/16–18, n.d.

[133] Thus the inhabitants of Văşcăuţi, in Soroca County, and Clişcăuţi, in Hotin County, aided by school inspectors, clamored for moving a Jewish middle school from the town of Soroca to their village, since, they argued, Soroca already had two boys' lycées, one girls' lycée, and one private Jewish *tarbut*. MIC/1923/477/65, 76, September 25, 1923.

[134] Mendelsohn, *Jews*, p. 176.

[135] AIU/VII/C/50 and Gheorghe Bogdan-Duică, *Românii şi ovreii* (Bucharest: Institutul de arte grafice Tip. românească, 1913), p. 60. See also R. W. Seton-Watson, *A History of the Roumanians from Roman Times to the Completion of Unity* (Cambridge: Cambridge University Press, 1934), p. 563.

into the Romanian period. The Jews constituted 37 percent of the urban population, although half of Bessarabia's Jews lived in small towns and shtetls. Although not prosperous themselves, the Jews made up the lower middle class of this economically poor and nationally heterogeneous province, working as traders, craftsmen, and professionals. During the interwar period, many Jews left commercial occupations for the free professions in response to economic insecurity, and, at least initially, to expanded educational opportunities. According to Jewish sources, half the doctors and over 90 percent of the dentists in Chişinău, for example, were Jewish.[136] In addition, the Jews of Bessarabia were very much a community apart, not just religiously and occupationally, but linguistically as well. Of Bessarabia's 206,958 Jews, 201,278 declared Yiddish their native language in 1930.[137] Nationalists noticed with envy that while there was no regular Romanian daily in Chişinău, a Yiddish one appeared alongside other Jewish papers.[138]

During Bessarabia's brief period of independence from both Russia and Romania in 1918, the Jews enjoyed equality as citizens for the first time. As the union of Bessarabia with Romania was forged, the Jews initially rejoiced at the relative safety offered by the Romanian state, come to protect the area from chaos, Bolshevism, and potential pogroms. Although the Jews' status did not change formally after Romanian troops occupied the area, they were once again subject to harassment. This situation was exacerbated by the authorities' suspicions of Jews as Bolsheviks and the influx of Ukrainian Jewish refugees (discussed in Chapter 7).[139]

Despite Romania's obligation to naturalize its minority populations, and thus its Jews, en masse, Bessarabian Jewry remained highly vulnerable to the corruption of Romanian officials in the granting of Romanian citizenship.[140] Even after the citizenship law of 1924, 80,000 Romanian Jews remained unnaturalized. In 1928, a majority of these lived in Bessarabia. Their precarious citizenship status left them prey to arbitrary officials who could use their *Heimatlose* status to deny Jews professional and residence rights and their children admission to state schools.[141]

---

[136] AIU/VIII/C/56, June 12, 1932, and Yankev Leschinski, *Yahadut besarabiya,* p. 27 cited in Mendelsohn, *Jews,* p. 277.

[137] Mendelsohn, *Jews,* p. 182.

[138] See Ghibu, *Ardealul,* pp. 237, 243, 245–426.

[139] Lucien Wolf papers, YIVO Institute Archives, New York (hereafter LW), 3/80/10528–9, July 10, 1918.

[140] In 1923, 30 percent of Romania's Jewish population was still not naturalized. See LW/4/137/19925–8, March 12, 1923, and Wilhelm Filderman, "My Life," Ms., YV/P 6 2–III, p. 302.

[141] Theodor Lavi, "Activitatea parlamentară a lui Michael Landau," *Toladot* 6 (May 1977): 5.

Jewish schools also encountered harassment, though private ones managed to flourish nonetheless.[142] Michael Landau, a Zionist deputy from Chişinău, had a long list of grievances to raise in 1930: Some of the Jewish schools established by royal decree in 1918 and Jewish teacher-training courses in Chişinău were Romanized in 1922 when Constantin Angelescu became the Minister of Education. Thus, the government was not living up to the Minority Protection Treaty that guaranteed national minorities an education at state expense and in their own language. Private Jewish schools were also closed down by local authorities on suspicion of subversion and Bolshevism or on pretexts of insufficiently large quarters. Hebrew textbooks were unfairly censored. The ministry did not give to Jewish schools the full amount of their allocated subsidy, charged excessive exam taxes, and was unable to find the funds to open a Jewish teacher-training seminar in Chişinău. The Minister of Education in 1930, Neculai Costăchescu, defended himself in part by claiming that the government did not have the money to give to Jewish schools any more than to the rest of the population.[143]

This disclaimer may have been plausible in the crisis-ridden Romania of 1930, but anti-Semitic episodes occurring both in the 1920s and 1930s in Bessarabia, while the province was under martial law and thus well supervised by Romanian authorities,[144] suggest that anti-Semitism and cultural nationalism were flip sides of one coin. The cultural propaganda and nationalization campaigns created an atmosphere inimical to the Jews, who, despite their formal emancipation, were often not accepted as part of the province's legitimate population. On December 2, 1926, the Bessarabian Jewish deputy Aron Ghendrich sounded the alarm over the anti-Semitic agitation that was spreading in "the province between the Pruth and the Dniester." He was especially disturbed by the apparent complicity of the authorities: "In Bessarabia's towns and villages the agents of anti-Semitic propaganda incite to hatred and provoke disturbances. The impunity that they enjoy constitutes an example and encouragement for the elements of disorder. Under the eyes of the authorities [they] are asking for the expulsion and murder of the Jews. Under the eyes of the authorities plunder and crime are being urged."[145]

Ghendrich went on to cite a particular incident that occurred that winter. Following the murder of David Fallik in Cernăuţi,[146] the director of a

---

[142] Mendelsohn, *Jews,* pp. 200–201.
[143] Desbaterile Adunării Deputaţilor, *Monitorul oficial,* no. 76, September 24, 1930. See also Lavi, "Activitatea," pp. 10–11. For a similar list of grievances earlier, in 1923, see LW/ 4/137/19925–8, March 13, 1923.
[144] CA/RM 132, "Extras din Monitorul oficial," no. 7 din 2 decembrie 1926.
[145] Ibid., no. 10 din 11 decembrie 1926.
[146] See Chapter 2.

seminary in the Bessarabian town of Ediniţa, a priest named N. Georgescu, cancelled classes and led a demonstration of his students through the town. The group shouted "Down with the Kikes," and "Death to the Kikes," and stopped in different locations to hear the director's speeches. These, according to Ghendrich, constituted incitements to riot. Georgescu urged peasants who were on their way home from the market to burn down Jewish houses. When the authorities did not react, the terrorized Jewish population shut itself in. Finally called to account before the communal council, of which he was himself a member, Georgescu did not deny his actions; the authorities still did nothing. Although in this case the gentile population apparently did not respond to the incitement, since Ghendrich would certainly have mentioned any violence that had occurred, the Jewish politician did make the connection between such anti-Semitic expressions and the kind of nationalist crime committed against the Jewish student Fallik in Cernăuţi. He charged the Bessarabian authorities with being "moral authors" of the Fallik murder. Ghendrich made his speech amidst anti-Semitic comments from fellow deputies.[147]

Dimitrie V. Ţoni, a prominent pedagogue and politician,[148] responded to Ghendrich's speech in parliament on December 11, 1926. His strategy was to clear Georgescu's name by describing his patriotic work. Georgescu had held the position of Subdirector of Religious Education at the Ministry of Education. He was then appointed the Director of the Ediniţa Seminary and given the "special mission of completely Romanizing it" and of elevating its standards. Ţoni said that "In one year the priest Georgescu fulfilled his mission with such competence and zeal, that the Ministry . . . had to recognize the great . . . Romanian *oeuvre* accomplished in such a short time by the new director."[149] As a result of this leadership, the seminary was now supposedly "from a moral point of view in a flourishing state." Georgescu had undertaken not only to organize the seminary itself, but also to create an economically and spiritually Romanian environment around it. A popular bank, a regional museum, a popular atheneum and three cultural hearths had sprung up in the area—precisely the kind of extracurricular institutions that the Ministry of Education, the army, and local patriots

---

[147] CA/RM 132, "Extras," no. 10 din 11 decembrie 1926.

[148] As a young teacher, Ţoni was an "instigator" in the 1907 peasant uprising but was then decorated by Haret for his part in bringing the peasants under control. He was an activist in the nationalist movement and headed the Cultural League in Galaţi. He did cultural work in Bessarabia at the end of the war, for which he was again decorated. He was a school inspector, a prefect, and was several times elected to Parliament from Covurlui and Cetatea Albă counties. In 1929, he became President of the Romanian General Association of Teachers. In 1938, during the ministry of Petre Andrei, he became Undersecretary of State for National Education. See *Şcoala şi vieaţa: Revista Asociaţiei generale a învăţătorilor din România* 10, (September–November 1939), esp. Teodor Iacobescu, "Celui mai bun învăţător, închinare!"

[149] CA/RM 132, "Extras," no. 10 din 11 decembrie 1926.

The faculty and pupils of the Theological Seminary in Edinița, Bessarabia, photographed in front of the school (October 1923). Courtesy of Arhivele Statului, Bucharest

were striving for in Bessarabia. Țoni concluded to the applause of the League of National Christian Defense delegates. In his finale, he asked the ministry to put an end to the groundless chatter about the "distinguished cleric" and to the attempts to push him aside as director of the seminary, "only because his Romanian *oeuvre* is a thorn in the side" of those nostalgic for pre-1918 conditions.[150] Țoni did not directly address the charges of anti-Semitic provocation imputed to Georgescu, but his implicit line of defense against that accusation was to uphold the record of cultural nationalism that made the priest a Romanian hero beyond suspicion or reproach. By implication, the Jews accusing Georgescu were themselves antipatriotic, and if the charges they raised were true, Georgescu's anti-Semitism, part and parcel of his irreproachable nationalism, was justified.

Georgescu's defense continued with the speech of the Bessarabian nationalist poet and deputy Ion Buzdugan.[151] His oratory was studded with anti-Semitic buzzwords. Buzdugan alleged that the Jews had no right to desecrate the Romanian parliament "the altar of our fatherland" with their "paws," that they were agents of foreign governments and internationals, and that their false claims of anti-Semitic agitation in Romania were provo-

[150] Ibid.
[151] Predescu, *Enciclopedia Cugetarea*, p. 149.

cations meant to harm Romania. Although no such agitation had taken place yet, Buzdugan threatened that they might in the future, sparked off by the Jewish provocateurs themselves, because of the peasantry's hard times and "because in the soul of the people there are great dissatisfactions against the profiteering of the townspeople." Buzdugan ended his speech, so full of racist commonplaces, by warning that "if in the soul of the people of Bessarabia and in the soul of our people in general, there is a dissatisfaction fermenting, which has not yet taken any concrete form, that ferment exists that much more in the fiery soul of our Romanian youth, in the soul of our students."[152] Buzdugan's invocation of nationalist student youth—who had been carrying out anti-Semitic agitation since 1922— clarified the connection between this local incident and the wider right-wing radicalism engulfing Romania's campuses.

The Georgescu episode was not unique in interwar Bessarabia. Violence against Jewish train travellers was reported beginning in 1926; the student disturbances that plagued Romania beginning in 1922 affected Chişinău directly once the Theology School opened there in 1926; Jewish actors were forced to resign from the National Theatre in Chişinău in 1927; peasants in Soroca and Bălţi counties followed incitement to anti-Jewish violence in 1930; members of the Jewish community in Cetatea Albă County reported in 1935 that they were the subject of a "propagande des massacres" made in the dangerous atmosphere of a general famine.[153] But the seminary incident of 1926 best illustrates the early relationship between the sometimes aggressive cultural nationalism fostered by the Romanian state and nationalist elites and its radical, anti-Semitic underside.

[152] CA/RM 132, "Extras," no. 10 din 11 decembrie 1926.
[153] YV/P 6 13, pp. 12 (150), 15 (153), 16 (154), 67 (181), 75 (189), 77 (191). See also MIC/1930/557/31, June 26, 1930; AIU/ix/C/59, November 10, 1935; AIU/ix/C/59, [n.d.], 1935; and Wilhelm Filderman, "My Life," Ms. YV/P 6 211, p. 380. He cites anti-Semitic violence in various Romanian towns and villages, including Chişinău, Bălţi, and Cahul in Bessarabia.

4

Transylvania:
Regionalism and Ethnic Strife

The province of Transylvania is the core of Romania. The map of Romania
... makes this assertion obvious. Without Transylvania, Romania would be
like France without the Auvergne, without the region of Paris or the Île de
France; or like Russia without Moscow and its surroundings. ... To quote
an example from historic Europe, without Transylvania, Romania would be
like Italy without Latium and Toscana.

—Simion Mehedinţi, 1940

Transylvania, the largest of the three provinces to join Romania in
1918, brought with it the most developed and mature Romanian
national movement. The long-term exclusion of Romanians from
political rights, and the late–nineteenth century efforts at Magyarization combined with certain vigorous Romanian cultural institutions to
foster a national consciousness and define a tradition of struggle.[1] The
strong Romanian element in Transylvania did, however, have to contend
with the large and, after 1918, deeply disgruntled Hungarian minority, as
well as with the German and Jewish minorities, all more urban and historically more privileged than the Romanians. Furthermore, as elsewhere in the
new territories, regionalism also interfered with Romanian national goals.

---

[1] See Keith Hitchins, *The Rumanian National Movement in Transylvania, 1780–1849*
(Cambridge, Mass.: Harvard University Press, 1969), idem, *Orthodoxy and Nationality:
Andreiu Şaguna and the Rumanians of Transylvania, 1846–1873* (Cambridge, Mass.: Harvard
University Press, 1977), and his essays collected in *Studies on Romanian National Conscious-
ness* (Rome: Nagard, 1983); R. W. Seton-Watson, *A History of the Roumanians from Roman
Times to the Completion of Unity* (Cambridge: Cambridge University Press, 1934), pp.
409–415; and Vasile Popeangă, *Aradul, centru politic al luptei naţionale din perioada dualismului (1867–1918)* (Timişoara: Editura Facla, 1978), pp. 19–20 and chaps. 4, 5.

Transylvania had belonged to Hungary and the Habsburg Empire since the Middle Ages but its commercial and cultural ties with Moldavia and Wallachia remained vital. The province was intermittently autonomous, and parts of it came temporarily under Wallachian and Moldavian rule. For a brief moment in 1599–1600, Transylvania, Wallachia, and Moldavia were united under Michael the Brave.[2]

The Trianon Treaty awarded Romania not just historic Transylvania, the sometime independent medieval *voievodat,* but also parts of eastern Hungary where large numbers of Romanians lived: Crişana, Satu-Mare, Maramureş, and part of the Banat. These contiguous territories together were known in interwar Romania as Transylvania or Ardeal; the same terminology will be used here unless otherwise noted.

The Romanian National Revolution

After 1867, Transylvania was incorporated with the Hungarian part of the Dual Monarchy. Transylvania was promised to Romania by the Entente powers, first to obtain Romania's neutrality and then to entice Romania to join the Allies against the Central Powers.[3] Romania joined the Entente in 1916; the later union with Transylvania became possible partly because of this deal, and partly because of the revolutionary situation that obtained in 1917–1918 in Hungary, where the war had radicalized political life. In the wake of the Central Powers' defeat, Count Mihaly Karolyi came to power on October 31, 1918. His government instituted democratic reforms and concessions to the national minorities. These changes came too late, however, to stem the national revolutions of Hungary's minorities, including the Romanians. The appeal of the motherland was so magnetic that even the socialists opted for Romania, pledging to struggle for the democratization of its monarchy rather than stay within the newly established Hungarian republic.[4]

On October 31, 1918, the Central Romanian National Council (CRNC) was formed in Arad. Consisting of six Social Democrats and six Romanian National Party members, the CRNC coordinated local revolutionary activities through National Councils and National Guards. Land seizures and

---

[2] Cornelia Bodea and Virgil Cândea, *Transylvania in the History of the Romanians* (Boulder, Colo.: East European Monographs, 1982), pp. 11–14, 22–23, and Vlad Georgescu, *The Romanians: A History* (Columbus: Ohio State University Press, 1991), pp. 41–42.

[3] See document 181 in Direcţia generală a arhivelor statului, *1918 la Români: Desăvîrşirea unităţii naţional-statale a poporului român. Documente externe, 1879–1916,* vol. 1, pp. 631–632, and Georgescu, *Romanians,* pp. 167–168.

[4] Keith Hitchins, "The Rumanian Socialists and the Hungarian Soviet Republic," in *Studies,* pp. 212–213.

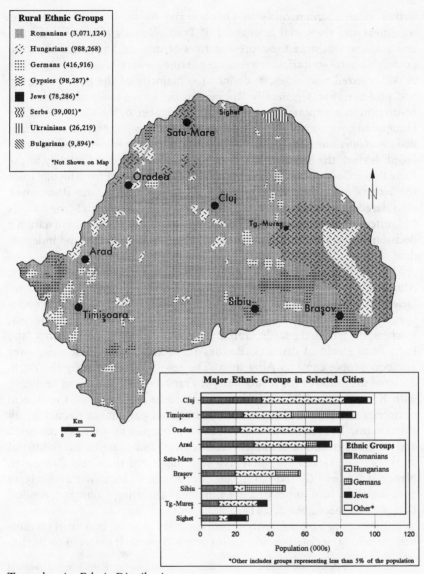

Rural Ethnic Groups

Romanians (3,071,124)
Hungarians (988,268)
Germans (416,916)
Gypsies (98,287)*
Jews (78,286)*
Serbs (39,001)*
Ukrainians (26,219)
Bulgarians (9,894)*

*Not Shown on Map

Sighet
Satu-Mare
Oradea
Cluj
Tg.-Mureș
Arad
Sibiu
Brașov
Timișoara

Km
0   20   40

Major Ethnic Groups in Selected Cities

Cluj
Timișoara
Oradea
Arad
Satu-Mare
Brașov
Sibiu
Tg.-Mureș
Sighet

0   20   40   60   80   100   120
Population (000s)

Ethnic Groups
Romanians
Hungarians
Germans
Jews
Other*

*Other includes groups representing less than 5% of the population

Transylvania, Ethnic Distribution

strikes arose spontaneously in October and November, reflecting war-weariness and the social grievances of Transylvania's peasants, workers, and soldiers. But since the representatives of state authority and the local power brokers—notaries, mayors, gendarmes—were largely Hungarians or Magyarized minorities, and since the majority of the poor peasantry and proletariat was generally Romanian, the CRNC easily channeled the revolution in a national direction.[5] On November 9, the CRNC asked the Hungarian government for "full power to govern over the territories inhabited by Romanians in Ardeal and Hungary."[6] The ensuing negotiations failed, leaving the Transylvanian question to be settled definitively at the Paris Peace Conference. Whereas the Hungarians hoped for leniency from the victors after their break from the Central Powers, the Romanians considered self-determination the only path. On November 18, the CRNC's "Manifesto to the Peoples of the World" proclaimed the Romanian nation's decision "to establish on the territory it inhabits its own free and independent state."[7]

The council then called a Grand National Assembly for December 1 at Alba-Iulia; it was to serve as a plebiscite for union with the Old Kingdom. Delegates to the assembly represented Romanian churches, cultural societies, women's organizations, schools and seminaries, university students, teachers, the national guards, craft guilds, the Romanian Social Democratic Party, and electoral districts. Besides the 1,228 official delegates, over 100,000 people came to Alba Iulia. The resolution drafted by the CRNC declared the union of the Romanians of Transylvania, Banat, and Hungary with Romania, and it asserted the provisional autonomy of the Ardeal territories until the meeting of a constitutional parliament elected by all Romanians. The resolution also set forth principles of political, national, and religious freedom, of radical land reform, and of rights for industrial workers.[8] The Grand National Assembly instituted the Great Romanian National Council (Marele Sfat Naţional Român), an unwieldy body of 250, which in turn appointed a 15-member Directing Council, Consiliul Dirigent, on December 2, 1918.[9]

The Directing Council, with its headquarters in Sibiu, had nearly unlimited governing, legislative, and enforcement powers. It deferred to Bucha-

[5] Ion Popescu-Puţuri and Augustin Deac, *Unirea Transilvaniei cu România; 1 decembrie 1918* (Bucharest: Editura Politică, 1970), pp. 559–576.

[6] Ibid., p. 623.

[7] Ibid., p. 654, and Popeangă, *Aradul*, pp. 258–261.

[8] Popescu-Puţuri and Deac, *Unirea*, pp. 657–658, 687, 680, 689–691.

[9] Ibid., p. 295; Mircea Muşat and Ion Ardeleanu, *Political Life in Romania, 1918–1921* (Bucharest: Editura Academiei R.S.R., 1982), p. 106; Carlile A. Macartney, *Hungary and Her Successors: The Treaty of Trianon and Its Consequences, 1919–1937* (London: Oxford University Press, 1937), p. 276; and Gheorghe Iancu, *Contribuţia Consiliului Dirigent la consolidarea statului naţional unitar român (1918–1920)* (Cluj: Editura Dacia, 1985), pp. 14–16.

rest only in relation to foreign and military affairs, the railroads, and a few other areas of national jurisdiction.[10] The council consisted of two Social Democrats, three independents, and ten Romanian National Party members. Together, the fifteen heads of departments formed a kind of cabinet or provisional government. Iuliu Maniu, chairman of the Romanian National Party, became the president of the council and head of the Interior Department. Vasile Goldiş, another Romanian National Party leader, became head of the Department of Public Education and Religions, (later also of Relations with the Co-inhabiting National and Religious Minorities); he delegated to Onisifor Ghibu, a prominent educator and nationalist militant, most of the practical educational and cultural work of the department. Ghibu maintained his post of Secretary General under Goldiş's successor, Valeriu Branişte.[11]

Issues relating to the Directing Council underline the importance of problems of regionalism in Transylvania. In the early post-union years, Transylvanian politicians and patriots wished to act somewhat independently of the political parties, power structures, and institutions based in Bucharest.[12] The Directing Council clashed with Bucharest over economic, political, administrative, and cultural matters.[13] The conflict between the council and the "center" may be traced to the question of "conditions" for union which arose during the period preceding the Alba Iulia Assembly.

[10] Aurel Galea, "Consiliul Dirigent: Organizarea, atribuţiile şi cauzele desfiinţării sale," *Studii: Revista de istorie* 26 (1973): 300, 308.

[11] Ibid.; Romul Boilă, "Consiliul Dirigent," in *Transilvania, Banatul, Crişana, Maramureşul, 1918–1928*, vol. 1 (Bucharest: Cultura naţională, 1929), p. 90; Iancu, *Contribuţia*, pp. 19, 254; and Vasile Popa, "Aspecte din activitatea lui Onisifor Ghibu la Consiliul Dirigent," *Studia universitatis Babeş-Bolyai, Historia* 31, no. 1 (1986): 62–66. Ghibu was an extremely prolific writer who documented his pedagogical and national activities painstakingly. See Onisifor Ghibu, *Viaţa şi organizaţia bisericească şi şcolară în Transilvania şi Ungaria* (Bucharest: Inst. de arte grafice N. Stroilă, 1915); idem, *Puncte cardinale pentru o concepţie românească a educaţiei* (Sibiu: Inst. de arte grafice Dacia Traiană, 1944); idem, *Pe baricadele vieţii: Anii mei de învăţătură* (Cluj: Dacia, 1981); idem, *Nu din partea aceea* (Bucharest: Editura Eminescu, 1985); idem, *Pentru o pedagogie românească* (Bucharest: Editura didactică şi pedagogică, 1977). About Ghibu, see Traian Vedinaş, *Onisifor Ghibu educator şi memorialist* (Cluj: Dacia, 1983), and Biblioteca centrală pedagogică, *Onisifor Ghibu: 100 de ani de la naştere* (Bucharest, 1984). Ghibu's activities were at the center of the cultural transformations going on in Transylvania before and after World War I (as well as in Bessarabia, see Chapter 3), thus Ghibu's writings are a valuable source for this book. Wherever possible I have tried to balance them with other sources.

[12] See Iancu, *Contribuţia*, pp. 12–13, 292.

[13] Galea's argument is that this conflict owed to the fact that the Directing Council represented mainly the interests of the Transylvanian bourgeoisie, whose economic and financial interests conflicted with those of its counterpart in the Old Kingdom. The Directing Council wanted to maintain customs duties between the two provinces, for example. Conflicts also arose over the formula for nationalizing enterprises formerly owned by the Hungarian state and Magyar entrepreneurs, and over the conversion of the Hungarian to the Romanian currency. The Transylvanians felt that the rate of exchange was set unrealistically low, so as to favor the Old Kingdom's financial supremacy. Galea, "Consiliul Dirigent."

Was the union to be unconditional and unreserved, or was it to be a conditional "marriage" on equal, clearly defined terms, in which Transylvania remained an autonomous partner? Iuliu Maniu initially favored the autonomous or conditional solution. But this position, even if explicable by the tradition of adversarial struggle in the Austro-Hungarian Empire, would have struck a false note in the enthusiastic chorus singing the praises of unity for all Romanians. Maniu's opponents campaigned for unconditional union. A compromise was reached in the formula of "provisional autonomy," a transitional stage intended to eradicate the vestiges of Habsburg domination and thus enable the ultimate goal of total unity within a centralized Romanian state.[14]

Although this compromise allowed the Alba-Iulia Assembly to be consecrated as a festive occasion, the issue of conditions was not truly resolved to everybody's satisfaction. Some Transylvanians became involved in Greater Romanian politics, joining parties based in the Regat. For this, however, they were sometimes accused of "*politicianism*", that is, of playing the unsavory game of corrupt politics. The accusers, men like Iuliu Maniu or Onisifor Ghibu, were notable for their honesty and correctness. Believers in ideals fathomed during years of heroic preunion struggle, they sought the true, clean, "perfect" Romanian politics. But if their criticism reflected the outraged "national conscience," it also contained a regionalist component. The Transylvanian purists perceived the pettiness, indiscipline, and sloppiness of the bureaucracy as the baggage of Balkan Romania and were reluctant to help carry it. They saw themselves as more skilled and morally superior, an outlook which made for a certain ideological compatibility between this group of Transylvanians and a younger generation of radical Romanian nationalists.

Maniu's formula of transitional autonomy referred graciously to Transylvania's oppressive Habsburg inheritance and the need to outgrow it during the transition period. One senses, nevertheless, that the Ardeal's political leaders were waiting impatiently for the Regat to catch up to more civilized Transylvania. Moreover, the "transitional period" was a somewhat indeterminate concept implying a state of readiness for a more perfect union, the timing of which not all would necessarily agree about. The stated condition for ending Transylvania's semi-autonomy was the election of a national parliament by universal suffrage. But when the Averescu government dissolved the Directing Council on April 2, 1920, the Transylvanian polity underwent a crisis.[15]

[14] Pamfil Șeicaru, *Istoria partidelor Național, Țărănist și Național Țărănist,* vol. 1 (Madrid: Editura Carpații, 1963), pp. 288, 290.
[15] Iancu, *Contribuția,* pp. 293–301.

Table 9. The population of Transylvania, by ethnicity, 1910 and 1930

		Romanians	Hungarians	Germans	Jews
		1910			
Total	5,446,326	2,830,040	1,664,296	565,116	182,724
(%)		51.9	30.6	10.4	3.4
Urban	865,986	152,790	481,466	122,866	82,724
(%)		17.6	55.6	14.2	9.6
		1930			
Total	5,549,806	3,208,767	1,353,288	544,278	178,810
(%)		57.8	24.4	9.8	3.2
Urban	963,418	336,756	365,008	126,936	100,413
(%)		35.0	37.9	13.2	10.4

Source: Sabin Manuilă, "Aspects démographiques de la Transylvanie," pp. 70–73.

The Romanian Nation and Foreign Enclaves

In 1918, Transylvania was peopled by a complex array of ethnic, linguistic, and religious groups including Romanians, Magyars, Szeklers, Germans, Jews, Ukrainians, Gypsies, and Serbs. Over half the population was Romanian, but the Romanians were overwhelmingly rural (see map 5 and table 9). In 1910, they constituted 59.7 percent of the rural population, but only 19.7 percent of the town dwellers. Together, the Hungarians, Germans, and Jews formed 88.5 percent of Transylvania's urban population (table 9).[16] The Romanians had all been Eastern Orthodox until the end of the seventeenth century, when part of the clergy and lay population accepted union with Rome, thereby forming the Uniate or Greek Catholic church.[17] In the interwar period, 58.2 percent of Ardeal Romanians were Orthodox, and the rest Uniates.[18] Paradoxically, therefore, the union of Ardeal with Romania brought an additional measure of fragmentation of the Romanians, by virtue of a second, Uniate, national church. The Magyars and Germans of Transylvania, meanwhile, belonged to the Catholic, Lutheran, Reformed, and Unitarian churches.

Culturally, Transylvanian urban elites were in large part Hungarian and German, with many Magyarized Jews included among them. In 1910, Hungarians were 31.6 percent of the province's population but they constituted 62 percent of the urban population; the Germans were 10.7 percent

[16] Roumanian University of Cluj, Study and Research Center for Transylvania, *Transylvania* (Paris: Boivin, 1946), p. 91.

[17] See Hitchins, *Rumanian National Movement*, pp. 15–20.

[18] Institutul central de statistică, *Anuarul statistic al României 1937 și 1938* (Bucharest: M. O., Imprimeria națională, 1939), p. 72.

of Transylvania's population, and 15.8 percent of the urban population; the Jews were only 3.5 percent of the province's population, but they represented 10.7 percent in towns.[19]

While almost 20 percent of the Romanians of Transylvania lived in towns at the turn of the century,[20] they had little cultural impact on the urban environment. A Romanian living in Cluj but working in a menial job, as a servant in a bourgeois household, for example, was still considered a peasant. She or he had relatives in the village and would probably eventually return there. Romanian high school students were forced to give up peasant dress to wear "civilized European" clothes and suffered pressure to shed their ethnic identity as well. Significantly, Romanians constituted larger proportions of smaller towns and smaller proportions of larger, more culturally important towns. The Jews, although not a large segment of Transylvania's population, constituted a large number in certain counties and in the major towns. Linguistically, urban Jews were largely assimilated to Magyar, thus enhancing the Hungarian aspect of Transylvania's towns, except in the Banat where Jews were more assimilated to German, the prevalent urban tongue there.[21]

Just as the Jews added to the Magyar presence in urban areas, the Szeklers augmented the Hungarian presence in rural areas in Ardeal. In 1920, there were about six hundred thousand Szeklers in Transylvania.[22] The Szeklers, an ethnic group related to the Magyars, had been brought to Transylvania at the beginning of the eleventh century to guard the eastern frontiers of the Hungarian-dominated lands. They settled in compact masses in the areas of Transylvania bordering on Moldavia. The Szeklers became one of Transylvania's three privileged nations, along with the Magyars and the Saxons. Whatever the ethnic origin of the Szeklers and their early relationship to the Magyars, in time they had become basically indistinguishable from the latter. Romanians claimed that many of their co-nationals living in the Szekler area had been "denationalized" to the point where only the vague memory of Wallachian ancestry survived.[23]

[19] Roumanian University of Cluj, *Transylvania*, pp. 92–95.

[20] See Sabin Manuilă, *Aspects démographiques de la Transylvanie*, extrait de *La Transylvanie* (Bucharest: n.p., 1938), p. 15.

[21] See Bela Vago, "The Destruction of the Jews of Transylvania," in *Hungarian Jewish Studies*, ed. R. L. Braham, 1 (1966): 172–174.

[22] Elemér Illyés, *National Minorities in Romania: Change in Transylvania* (Boulder, Colo.: East European Monographs, 1982), p. 11.

[23] Gheorghe Popa-Lisseanu, *Sicules et Roumains: Un procès de dénationalisation* (Bucharest: Socec, 1933), and Ion I. Rusu, *Românii și secuii* (Bucharest: Editura științifică, 1990), pp. 120–127. This essentialist view of ethnic identity has most recently been challenged by Liah Greenfeld: "An essential characteristic of any identity is that it is necessarily the view the concerned actor has of himself or herself. It therefore either exists or does not. . . . Identity

In 1910, the Germans of Transylvania numbered 556,009.[24] Transylvanian Saxons maintained contacts with German high culture as it developed in Germany by sending their sons to study or be apprenticed in Germany. They appeared to have a highly organized communal life, financed from property owned by the "Universitas Saxonum," an institution representing the Saxon nation.[25] Good management, an urban and artisanal tradition, sustained contact with Germany, and a strong civil society revolving around the Lutheran church lent Saxon communities an air of prosperity, civilization, and orderliness much envied by Romanians even in the interwar period.

Between 1910 and 1930, the proportion of Romanians in Ardeal increased from 53.8 percent to 57.8 percent of the population. This relative increase is partly due to the exodus of Hungarians after 1918. About one-fifth of Transylvanian Magyars, or 197,000 people, "repatriated to Hungary."[26] Some of these self-exiles were loath to accept Romanian rule before, and even after the Trianon Treaty. The number of Hungarians in Transylvania dropped from 1,664,324 (Magyar speakers) in 1910 to 1,353,276 in 1930, or from 31.6 percent to 24.4 percent of the region's population. Although most Transylvanian Jews continued to identify with Hungarian culture,[27] some adopted the state language and became loyal Romanians during the interwar period. This change may also help account for the decrease in the number of "Hungarians" between 1910 and 1930.[28]

The Romanian elite had started to form in Transylvania in the eighteenth century around the institution of the Uniate church, which gave the Roma-

---

is perception. If a particular identity does not mean anything to the population in question, this population does not have this particular identity." *Nationalism: Five Roads to Modernity* (Cambridge, Mass.: Harvard University Press, 1992), p. 13. Whatever their ancestors had been generations earlier, these "denationalized" Romanians were now Szeklers.

[24] Modern-day Transylvanian Germans are descendants of two groups of migrants: the Saxons, who had been brought into Transylvania beginning in the 12th century to protect the southern borders and to settle the area around Sibiu (Hermannstadt) and Braşov (Kronstadt), and the much later immigrant group of the Schwabs (or Swabians), whom the Habsburgs invited to settle in the Banat in the 18th century to repopulate areas liberated from the Turks and counter the rebellious Hungarians. The Saxons belonged to the Lutheran church after 1550, whereas the Schwabs were mainly Catholics. G. C. Paikert, *The Danube Swabians* (The Hague: Martinus Nijhoff, 1967), pp. 13–17; Illyes, *National Minorities*, pp. 12–14, 18–19, 22; Georges Castellan, "The Germans of Rumania," *Journal of Contemporary History* 6 (1971): 52–53; and Marilyn McArthur, "The Saxon Germans: Political Fate of an Ethnic Identity," *Dialectical Anthropology* 1 (September 1976): 351–352.

[25] McArthur, "Saxon Germans," p. 352.

[26] Macartney, *Hungary and Her Successors*, p. 253, cited in Katherine Verdery, *Transylvanian Villagers: Three Centuries of Political, Economic, and Ethnic Change* (Berkeley: University of California Press, 1983), p. 287.

[27] Vago, "Destruction of the Jews," p. 173.

[28] The 1910 figures were a measure of linguistic assimilation rather than ethnicity and thus included Magyarized non-Magyars.

nians a measure of recognition, privileges, and contact with the West. In the nineteenth century, especially after 1848, this elite expanded into lay society at the edges of the bureaucratic and bourgeois classes that were still overwhelmingly composed of ethnic Magyars and Germans. New opportunities opened up to Romanians in a growing and diversifying middle class. Romanians, often educated as lawyers in Hungarian or German institutions, joined Hungarians and Saxons as bureaucrats, intellectuals, merchants, bankers, manufacturers, and traders. Disadvantaged by their previous exclusion from the middle stratum, however, these new members of the elite were still few and somewhat peripheral. These Romanians tended to be just one generation away from the village, schooled in the foreign cities of Transylvania, Hungary, or Austria, practicing their professions either in the rural environment or as representatives of their village communities in an urban world they perceived as hostile and cunning. Unlike Magyars and Germans who lived in the countryside, rural Romanians were poorly connected to the urban, commercial, and administrative spheres. By contrast, those Saxons who lived in rural settings used their ties to a regionwide Saxon community and had, even at the village level, a more cosmopolitan orientation.[29]

The Romanization of Transylvania met further difficulties after 1918 in nationalizing important foreign enclaves in the three overlapping categories of geographic areas, cultural institutions, and cities.

Szeklers in the East, Magyars in the West

Two Hungarian-dominated zones in Transylvania caused the Romanians grave concern. The first trouble spot was in eastern Ardeal, where Szekler settlements abounded. Although they were not socially, economically, or culturally superior to the Romanians, the Szeklers had a history of privilege since the Middle Ages. Furthermore, their compact presence over whole districts challenged the legitimacy of Romanian territorial claims. To further complicate matters, the Szekler districts were located in the middle of the newly unified country, making territorial restructuring inconceivable. The second worrisome area was in northwestern Transylvania, on the border with Hungary, where "true" Magyars, rather than Szeklers, lived. Romanians always emphasized the difference between the two groups, viewing the Szeklers with less hostility than the Magyars.[30]

[29] Verdery, *Transylvanian Villagers*, pp. 182, 206, 225, 243–245, 255, and Keith Hitchins, "Rumanian Intellectuals in Transylvania: The West and National Consciousness, 1830–1848," in *Studies*, pp. 75–80.

[30] Popa-Lisseanu said that although Szeklers "spoke the Magyar language, like all other Hungarians . . . they differed from the latter by [their] nature and way of life." *Sicules et Roumains*, p. 5.

Policies and initiatives for dealing with the Szeklers rested on the assumption that they could be Romanized and that many Szeklers were really "hidden" Romanians. Authorities attempted to count the presumed Szekler Romanians and to educate them gently back toward Romanian culture.[31] Thus Sabin Manuilă, the Director of the Demographic Institute in Bucharest, suggested to the minister of education that what was needed was "not a policy of aggression, but one of peaceful assimilation. The sacrosanct dogma toward the Szeklers should be that of assimilation. The roads ought to be built in such a way as to bring the Szeklers easily toward Bucharest and other Romanian centers. They should not be left in isolation. Bucharest will swallow them up (*mistui*) easily."[32]

In 1935, Gheorghe Popa-Lisseanu estimated the number of Szeklers in Romania at approximately 500,000,[33] but he also disputed their numbers and ethnic purity. He argued that the "bloc sicule" was a fiction of post-1848 vintage, created by the Hungarians in need of a great "power in the interior of Transylvania and in the midst of the Romanians, who, delivered from serfdom, were a menacing threat for the recent union of Transylvania with Hungary."[34] Popa-Lisseanu based his arguments on the absence of exclusively Szekler villages and on the distortions of the Hungarian census of 1910, which recorded the language and religion—rather than the nationality—of the country's inhabitants.[35]

Popa-Lisseanu's thesis was that denationalization had caused the Romanian population in the Ciuc, Odorhei, Trei Scaune, and Mureş districts to fall dramatically between the eighteenth century and the twentieth century.[36] According to most Romanians writing about this question, the denationalization was carried out by the church and, from 1867, also by the army, administration, justice, and economy. On all these levels Popa-Lisseanu saw Magyarization policies as both relentless and successful in the Szekler area, where, he stated:

> The [Hungarian] state power has acted by all means, legal and illegal, to the detriment of the Romanians who, little by little, have abandoned the language

[31] A report filed with the Ministry of Education in 1927 mentioned such a census in the Ciuc and Treiscaune counties, where very few Romanian villages had survived. MIC/1928/32/54–55, December [n.d.] 1927. In the effort to reclaim denationalized Romanians, the inspector requested books and magazines from Casa şcoalelor, night courses for denationalized Romanians and for Hungarians, prizes for those willing to teach the courses, and the opening of movie theaters.

[32] AA II/Ms. 8, November 19, 1935.

[33] According to R. W. Seton-Watson there were 458,307 Szeklers in Transylvania in 1908. See his *Racial Problems in Hungary* (1908; repr. New York: Howard Fertig, 1972), p. 6.

[34] Ibid.

[35] Ibid., pp. 7–8.

[36] By 125–130 thousand people, or from 30 percent to 5 percent of the population. Ibid., p. 39.

and faith of their ancestors, thereby augmenting the number of Szeklers. This is why today we meet at each step in all the towns and in all the villages denationalized Romanians, representatives of Magyar public life: here, as notables of the bar, there, as distinguished educators, elsewhere, as leaders of Hungarian political organizations, etc.—none of them wishing to own up to their origins.[37]

What is important about this view of a malignant process of denationalization is not so much whether and to what extent "Szeklerization" happened, but that it was noticed, theorized, and "deconstructed" by Romanians unwilling to simply accept a Szekler presence in eastern Transylvania. Denationalization theories became the basis of educational policy. In a conference held in 1935, the Szekler question was taken up by the Ministry of Education, which generally concurred with Popa-Lisseanu's views: The process of denationalization had intensified in the nineteenth century and accelerated after 1910 when the Magyar language was imposed upon the Romanian Uniate church with the establishment of the Hajdudorog diocese (*episcopie*). The Romanian Orthodox church had kept its language, but it had lost its priests. Some Romanians did not speak Romanian, but they were still conscious of their ancestry and belonged to one of the Romanian churches. Others belonged to the Hungarian churches and had completely melded with the Szeklers.[38] The Ministry of Education estimated that "public administrative, judicial, military, and school institutions give Romanian coloring [and] surface to the Szekler towns, but the foundation has remained unRomanian." Few Romanian artisans and merchants had settled in Szekler towns. But from the Romanian point of view, the villages suffered even more from the Szeklers' "disastrous influence," for they lacked even the few Romanian state institutions that the towns had.[39]

After 1918, new schools and Uniate and Orthodox parishes were established in the Szekler areas. In the Counties of Mureş, Ciuc, Odorhei, and Treiscaune, seventy-five schools were opened between 1919 and 1928, thirty-four more between 1929 and 1933, and another fifteen in 1934–1935. In addition, the state schools in which Hungarian had been the language of instruction switched to Romanian after 1919. In these same counties, eleven Uniate and fourteen Orthodox parishes were constituted between 1919 and 1935. All this activity enabled Romanian officials to conclude that, "there existed almost no denationalized settlement today not provided with a Romanian school [in 1935]."[40] It is therefore curious

[37] Ibid., p. 51.
[38] AA II/Ms. 8, November 19, 1935.
[39] Ibid.
[40] Ibid.

that the 1935 progress report presenting these achievements is followed by the acknowledgment that, despite the many new schools and the efforts of private individuals and of cultural societies, "not enough has been done for the Romanians of Szeklerdom, and their situation has changed little, [that is,] compared to what it should be."[41]

Such contradictions may be explained by the social reality behind these achievements. August Caliani, General Director at the Ministry of Education, conveyed the opinions of local church officials and school inspectors on the Szekler region when he reported on the hostility of the population of the Szekler area toward state schools "regardless of their [ethnic] origin."[42] Especially hostile, to be sure, were the Szeklers who were forced to contribute financially to the construction of state schools for "denationalized" Romanians, even when they themselves formed a majority of a commune, and already had a school. Caliani wrote:

> The construction of new sites meets with great difficulties in the mixed villages, where the minority population has its own buildings for confessional schools. The difficulties are not only material, but also moral. The material impositions provoke dissatisfactions exploited by minority intellectuals, by their priests, teachers, lawyers, and especially by their politicians, not only against the State but also against the dominant Romanian element.[43]

Caliani recognized the need for sensitivity not only in school construction campaigns, but also in the hiring of competent teachers with some knowledge of Hungarian, even if the goal was Romanization. At the very least, the school director and the first grade teachers had to know Hungarian, in order to be able to teach little children and to establish a proper relationship with the adults:

> If the teacher does not know the language of the adult population, he cannot make and keep contact with the population. And, without this contact, his role is reduced to the school's four walls, the field being left prey to the agitations of elements [who are] recalcitrant to the Romanian language and state. . . . [W]ithout knowing the [Magyar] language . . . [the Romanian teacher] can develop almost no extracurricular activity in the midst of the denationalized population whom [his mission is] to draw near to the Romanian schools and culture, in all ways and by all available cultural weapons.[44]

[41] Ibid.
[42] Ibid., August 17, 1935.
[43] Ibid.
[44] Ibid.

Caliani recommended other measures as well: that teachers recruited from the local elite undertake intense extracurricular activity, including adult Romanian language courses and popular history and geography conferences, "of course in the language understood by the people," (that is, Hungarian). He also advocated that they join choirs, take trips to the Old Kingdom, and start cooperatives and popular banks that could help the denationalized Romanians. He proposed that these teachers establish libraries—possibly even with books in Magyar—about geography, history, agriculture, and finance "to counter the activity of Hungarian libraries." Caliani thought that a "religious offensive ought to have gone hand in hand with the Romanian cultural offensive among the Szeklers after a well thought out plan," and he recommended salary increases for the Romanian priests of the region as well as scholarships for seminary students from Szeklerdom who knew Magyar. Denationalized Romanians were to be given preference in all jobs. Caliani finally suggested economic aid and the colonization of Romanian craftsmen and merchants from other regions in the Szekler areas.[45]

The approach that Caliani and Manuilă both suggested for the Szekler areas contrasts with the one recommended for the areas at the western border of Transylvania with Hungary. As unRomanian as the Szekler region, the state deemed the western frontier zone to be endangered by irredentism. It was a strategic area, within easy reach of Budapest by road, train, and radio. Moreover, the non-Romanian population in the west was mainly Hungarian, not Szekler. The Romanians deeply mistrusted the Hungarians, who still held some bureaucratic jobs and were unreconciled to the prospect of losing their 1,000-year position as the ruling elite. Mixed marriages between Romanian men and Hungarian women still took place, resulting in off-spring raised in a "foreign spirit, language, and even religion." According to Sabin Manuilă, the border area had to be purified along one hundred kilometers "through the eradication (*extirparea*) of the Hungarian element."[46] He recommended colonizing the frontier zone with Romanians repatriated from Trianon Hungary, thus solving two problems at one stroke. He intended such drastic measures to correct intolerable conditions:

Too many posters are hanging on the doors and walls of public institutions, saying "Speak only Romanian." [This admonishment] is, however, not respected. Everywhere, but everywhere—in the train station, on the train, in the town hall, the prefecture, etc.—you only hear Hungarian, with some honorable exceptions. Let this tolerance be done with! If in all the public

[45] Ibid.
[46] Ibid., November 19, 1935.

institutions everyone would speak Romanian, they would get used to our language, imperceptibly, and we would really seem as if we were in a Romanian country. The decree on the use of the Romanian language should be reissued.[47]

If the official state language was ignored in the western borderlands, so too was the requisite school curriculum, as school inspectors' reports reveal. In 1928, in a secondary school in Baia Mare, some of the teachers still used "a strange idiom—reminiscenses of Magyar culture." Inspectors believed the cure lay in importing "two or three good elements," Romanians, no doubt, who might "bring a breath of fresh air into the life of this school."[48] At the same time, Magyarized children would be sent to Romanian summer camps "to awaken them to a new life," while their parents were to become familiarized with Romanian life and language through school shows.[49]

The proposed solutions to the educational problems Romanian authorities perceived in the Szekler and western borderland areas reflect their view of school, culture, and religion as the most important weapons in an all-encompassing arsenal of nationalizing practices and institutions. The cultural offensive was carried out very differently in the two Hungarian geographic enclaves. In the east, Romanizing measures were tempered by sensitivity to local conditions and by the Romanians' belief that many Szeklers were originally Romanian and thus receptive to renationalization. In the west, Romanization was applied more harshly, in keeping with the memory of Hungarians as an overbearing elite and with the fear of Hungarian revisionism.

Cultural Institutions

Transylvanian schools had witnessed struggles for cultural supremacy long before 1918. After the *Ausgleich* of 1867 which relegated Transylvania and other Habsburg lands to Hungarian rule, Hungary intensified the pressure to assimilate the non-Magyar nationalities through the schools. Although the Primary Education Act of 1868 and the Law of Nationalities of 1869 enshrined the liberal principle of instruction in the mother tongue, the education laws of 1879, 1883, 1891, and 1907 were intended to Magyarize the teaching staff, expand schooling in Hungarian, and utterly

[47] Ibid.

[48] AA xv/Varia 11, March 12, 1928. Others also recommended that teachers from this area be transferred and replaced by Regat teachers. See Onisifor Ghibu, "Primele inspecţii la şcolile de stat din Transilvania românească (martie-aprilie 1920)," in *Pentru o pedagogie românească: Antologie de scrieri pedagogice* (Bucharest: Editura didactică şi pedagogică, 1977), p. 222. He suggested similar measures for Maramureş and Bihor (pp. 220–221, 225).

[49] Ghibu, "Primele inspecţii," p. 225.

restrict teaching in the minority languages.[50] R. W. Seton-Watson cogently summarizes the situation: "The state pledged itself to provide primary and secondary education for all its citizens in the mother tongue. In practice, however, the state schools were made the medium of unrestrained Magyarization."[51]

Although assiduous, and at the secondary level quite efficient, these efforts were not entirely successful, indeed, they backfired. In the words of the prominent Hungarian sociologist Oscar Jászi, who served as Minister of Nationalities in the Karolyi government, "non-Magyar youth, recruited from these schools, became the most ardent supporters of the claims of their races, and the mechanical drill of Magyarization had as its result the embittered fight of these 'Magyarized elements' against the school system of assimilation and sometimes against the Hungarian state itself, which they identified with the system of forcible Magyarization."[52] Moreover, despite these pressures, the Romanians of Transylvania held on to a large number of confessional schools. In 1914, 2,392 Orthodox, Uniate, and parochial schools taught primarily in Romanian.[53] These schools continued to strengthen Romanian national consciousness by providing a comfortable and nurturing environment and by popularizing patriotic and religious Romanian literature and songs, which fired the pupils' anti-Hungarian imagination. Ghibu notes, for instance, that *Arion,* a popular collection of songs and carols,[54]

> enjoyed a wide distribution in all of the Ardeal's larger villages, being considered a handbook for [one's] whole education. . . . Quite a few of these poems would be learned in school, as part of the program . . . A large part of the songs . . . had a revolutionary character, which awakened and kept alive in children a spiritual state of permanent national pride and revolt, embroidered on the consciousness of our Latinity, of the necessity of the unification of all Romanians, and of the great historic destiny of our people.[55]

Most Romanian youths lived in villages, and if they chose to get more than a primary education, they normally had to move to a Hungarian or

---

[50] Seton-Watson, *Racial Problems in Hungary,* chap. 11 ("The Education Laws of Hungary and the Nationalities"), and Oscar Jászi, *The Dissolution of the Habsburg Monarchy* (Chicago: University of Chicago Press, 1961), p. 328. See also Seton-Watson, *History of the Roumanians,* chap. 13 ("Transylvania under the Dual System").

[51] Seton-Watson, *History of the Roumanians,* p. 399.

[52] Jászi, *Dissolution of the Habsburg Monarchy,* pp. 330–331.

[53] There were as well 4 lycées, 6 middle schools, 1 commercial school, 8 normal schools, and 2 industrial schools. Roumanian University of Cluj, *Transylvania,* pp. 151, 153.

[54] *Arion, sau culegere de cânturi naționale, de stea și colinde,* cited in Ghibu, *Pe baricadele vieții,* p. 63.

[55] Ibid., pp. 64–65.

German school away from home. Adult memories of the shift from the familiar Romanian environment of home and village school to urban foreign schools suggest the cultural and psychological trauma involved. Both of Onisifor Ghibu's elder brothers went to secondary urban schools but dropped out before graduating. When Onisifor set out for Sibiu (Szeben) in fall 1893, the prospect provoked such revulsion in the boy that he threw a tantrum and held on to the horse cart in which his parents were driving back to Săliște. He was persuaded to remain in Sibiu only when his elder brother accompanied him and spent some time with him "to initiate [him] in the mysteries of urban life."[56] Octavian Goga's experience in separating from his home environment in nearby Rășinari to attend the lycée was similarly disorienting.[57]

In the Hungarian high schools, Romanian pupils faced a politicized atmosphere charged with ethnic tensions. The teachers here had the dual responsibility of teaching their pupils and of making them into Magyars.[58] The pressure toward Magyarization was unabated. Romanians were the object of strong suggestions from their teachers to give up traditional village costume and adopt "German" or "European" dress. One by one, Romanian students abandoned peasant clothes, making it that much more difficult for others to persevere in their symbolic resistence. Onisifor Ghibu was the last in his class to give in. In his memoirs he remembers his teacher's ultimatum:

"If after Easter you too don't show up in European clothes, don't even come back to school, because you'll be thrown out. I won't stand you any more in this smelly sheepskin." [H]e ended by grabbing me by the collar of the sleeveless lamb coat, which my father had made for me with his own hands and which I greatly enjoyed wearing. I was speechless at the prospects which lay before me. Give up my dress? But why? How could he force me into something like this? A glaring injustice! But since all my classmates gave up theirs and the teacher threatened to throw me out of school, could there be any escape?[59]

Ghibu finally resigned himself to the "German" clothes, which "delighted" his teacher but "demoralized" him. He changed into his Romanian outfit as soon as he returned from school every day. The poet and politician Octavian Goga, who attended the same lycée as Ghibu, commented on the lack of nurturing offered to Romanians educated in the Magyar high school: "For what happens, for example, in a lycée in which

[56] Ibid., p. 69, and Vedinaș, *Onisifor Ghibu,* p. 14.
[57] Ion Dodu Bălan, *Octavian Goga* (Bucharest: Editura Minerva, 1971), pp. 36–37.
[58] Ibid., p. 38.
[59] Ghibu, *Pe baricadele vieții,* p. 81.

Maramureş peasant family. The mother and two younger children are wearing normal peasant clothes, while the older son is dressed in a pre–World War I Hungarian lycée uniform. Private collection

the students are in great part of Romanian nationality? Most of the teachers completely lack that bright humanitarian sentiment, that parental good will toward their pupils, without which a true education cannot be imagined."[60] It is interesting to compare these recollections of alienation and humiliation at a Hungarian state lycée with the warm memories of another patriot, Vasile Goldiş, of the extremely modest Romanian parochial primary school he attended in the village of Cermei, Arad County, in 1869–1871:

> I had my first class in the little house covered by straw. One room facing the street, a little kitchen in the middle; from here you went into the room facing the garden: this was the Romanian Orthodox confessional school. In the yard a shed, in the garden a goat, to feed the teacher. His pay was 40 zloty a year, as I found out later. But how wonderful that school was!
>
> There were about twenty of us pranksters, and nobody had heard of compulsory education. We were taking Romanian and old Nicolae Albu . . . would teach us the Cyrillic alphabet one day, reading the Latin alphabet another, 'rythmetic' . . . , liturgy, and everything there was to learn, but he went around summers without socks on and he kept all the fasts; only the goat sweetened his existence. That is where my soul came into being, and it has remained the same from then until today. In mother's arms, in the whining of the cradle, in the smoke filled with incense,[61] in the teacher's first lessons, the soul of each of us takes shape.[62]

The emotional comparison between the cold, disapproving atmosphere of the Magyar schools and the nurturing ambience of the Romanian ones illustrates the "impermeability" of Hungarian cultural institutions to most Romanians in Transylvania before 1918. These institutions offered upward mobility only to the assimilated. In general, the majority of Romanians did not get far in the Magyar system. Those Romanians who did succeed had to assimilate, and did so, in fact, so well that they passed for Magyars and then were lost as Romanians.

The reasons for most Romanians' reluctance to Magyarize are complex. Romanians constituted a majority of the population; they were the poorest stratum of Transylvanian society; they had been consistently denied national political rights; and they had been almost exclusively a rural population, ill-at-ease with the urban and cultural environments into which

[60] Bălan, *Goga,* p. 38.

[61] This is a reference to the fragrant incense burned in Romanian Orthodox churches.

[62] Vasile Goldiş, "Discurs pe marginea legii învăţămîntului primar," *Patria,* September 14, 1924, cited in Mircea Popa and Gheorghe Şora, "Studiu introductiv," in *Scrieri social-politice şi literare,* ed. Vasile Goldiş ([Timişoara]: Editura Facla, 1976), p. 11.

upward social and ethnic mobility generally took place. All these factors contributed to their ethnic conservatism.

Perhaps the most representative reaction was neither assimilation nor self-conscious nationalism, but rather that of Onisifor Ghibu's elder brothers, who after only two years in foreign schools returned to their village with some knowledge of Magyar and German that would serve them later in life, but who easily rejoined the family business in sheepskins and stayed in the traditional Romanian world. Onisifor Ghibu himself represents a third alternative. An obviously bright and gifted youth educated in Romanian, Hungarian, and German schools, sensitive to the national issues that these schools also exemplify, he succeeded in completing his education and became politicized in the process of observing his experience and the differences between the foreign and Romanian schools.[63] Neither assimilating nor giving up, Ghibu reacted to his schooling by turning Magyarization on its head. He devoted his life to the Romanian national project.[64]

The school system of old Hungary provoked in Romanians a hurt national pride that sought to avenge itself after 1918. Ghibu's youthful experience is worth detailing not only because it typifies that of a whole generation, but also because he was instrumental in forging Transylvania's school system after 1918. The legacy of the Hungarian period also left its mark on the Romanian confessional schools. These institutions were relatively numerous, but economic and cultural inequalities evolved over hundreds of years afflicted them with an inferiority complex vis-à-vis their German and Hungarian counterparts. This sense of an overall imbalance persisted under the Romanian regime, as communicated in a 1926 inspection report from the Velţ and Saroş districts, in Târnava-Mică County,[65] which suggests that the legacy of the Hungarian period was not easily overcome. In Velţ, a village of mixed population, the inspector visited a Romanian school on the outskirts of the village which he found miserable, poorly managed, and lacking in books. His next stop, in the central Saxon area of the village, underlined the painful contrast between the two milieux:

[63] For other cases of Romanian nationalists nurtured by the Hungarian educational system, see Verdery, *Transylvanian Villagers*, pp. 206, 226–227.

[64] Ghibu's professional interest in pedagogy also stems from these same years and experiences. It is somehow fitting that he went on to study theology, pedagogy, and philosophy, crowning his education at the University of Jena with a doctoral dissertation on bilingualism in education. He carefully avoided as much as possible the Magyar universities of Cluj (Koloszvár) and Budapest; he went to the Orthodox Seminary in Sibiu, and to the Universities of Bucharest, Strasbourg, and Jena. Ghibu was forced by a Transylvanian Orthodox Church fellowship to spend one year in Budapest. He accepted the fellowship on condition that he would then be able to study in Germany, and he spent the year writing for and editing the Romanian Budapest newspaper *Lupta* (The Struggle). Ghibu, *Pe baricadele vieţii*, pp. 131–164. Despite his Romanian aspirations, he had to get a German higher degree to be able to work in Transylvania.

[65] MIC/1927/4/4–10, November 4, 1926.

These are two altogether different worlds: on one side light, on the other darkness; on one side prosperity, on the other poverty; on one side disorganization, on the other discipline and order. How could the Saxons and Romanians live side by side so many hundreds of years without the former influencing the latter for the better? . . .

Looking around me, I see [Saxon] households built to last thousands of years, veritable fortresses with high gates dug out of the walls, oxen coming to water with blankets on their backs, although it is only November. The Saxon school! Right next to and touching the church, a real fortress, stands together with the parish house, with the teachers' dwellings, with the amphitheater for shows and assemblies, with the *chilii*[66] (cells) surrounding it; it is the heart of the Saxons. The treasury is in the altar, the school in the front porch. Orders leave from here which are executed exactly. The assets of the community are administered here with honesty which sets an example. Here is the culture, here is the faith.[67]

The inspector found the Saxon school clean, its teacher industrious, its supplies ample. The school was dutifully executing the directives both of the church and of the Ministry of Education. The inspector mused again on the unfavorable contrast to Romanian schools. "I compare in my mind our labors in the Romanian school, the large expenditures versus the small results we obtain, with the incomparably smaller labors versus the sizable results [of the Saxon school], and I wonder. Everything comes from the fact that they have duty in their conscience, a conscience with which they are born and die; [while] we, figuring that we can cheat, only cheat ourselves."[68]

The village of Saroş, with mixed Hungarian and Romanian populations, next on the inspector's trail, did not present as clear-cut a contrast between the two ethnic communities. Here the Hungarian Unitarian school was not following ministry requirements, the teacher did not know Romanian well enough, and the priest not at all. If not exemplary, the Hungarians' situation was still better than that of the Romanians, whose church was up on the hill, "wooden, blackened by time, a poor bond of the kin and law of the oppressed. Next to it the little school: a little hallway divides a low-ceilinged small room—the classroom—from a little toy of a cell, the teacher's dwelling. [The teacher who is young, the son of a priest, with a

---

[66] *Chilie* is the Romanian word for a monastery cell.

[67] The report made a further ethnic and social comment, noting that Saxon youth "have their own vineyard [for wine] without needing to enrich the Jewish merchant, who, if he is not to be pitied, has our little Romanians to thank for it." MIC/1927/4/4–10, November 4, 1926.

[68] Ibid.

Mass in the yard of a wooden church in southern Transylvania. From Albumul
Fischer (1920). Courtesy of Cabinetul de Stampe. Biblioteca Academiei
Române, Bucharest

sense of duty] is trying as much as he can to hold the candle of Romanianism
in this Magyar center [although he does not have everything he needs]."[69]

A look at the situation of books in Transylvania illustrates the hardship
facing Romanian schools and culture there. Upon inspecting the library
of a lycée in Gherla in 1920, the Ministry of Public Instruction found
13,830 Hungarian books and 49 Romanian ones. A middle school in Aiud
had only 100 Romanian volumes. A boys' normal school had not a single
Romanian book.[70] A school in Baia Mare led by an enthusiastic Romanian
school director had "not even the beginnings of a Romanian library."[71]
Requests for Romanian-language books and materials speak to the short-

---

[69] Ibid.
[70] CS/1920/7/160, July 21, 1920; CS/1920/7/211, September 15, 1920; and CS/1920/7/
263, November 8, 1920.
[71] Onisifor Ghibu, "Primele inspecţii," in Pentru o pedagogie, pp. 221–222.

age of the Romanian printed word and of maps, pictures and charts due to the successes of Magyarization (though some libraries had rich holdings in German books as well.)[72] Cultural activists viewed an increase in Romanian books as a primary means of reestablishing a cultural equilibrium,[73] while the lack of Romanian books was seen as a particular problem for Romanian intellectuals in Ardeal, who, living among Hungarians and in areas where non-Romanian cultural institutions were strong, had been forced to imbibe Magyar culture. They had trouble letting go of Hungarian intellectual life, because "they [did not] have anything to put in its place."[74] Thus many requests for Romanian (and sometimes French) books came from teachers' societies not just for their use in the classroom, but even more for the teachers themselves.[75] Some Romanian intellectuals in Satu-Mare writing to Casa şcoalelor used a somewhat forced but telling metaphor: "With every volume you give [to us] you contribute another brick to erecting the wall [being] built against Magyar attacks in our souls [that are being] steeled at the fire of our national culture."[76]

Urban Areas

Before 1918, the towns and cities throughout the province of Transylvania were overwhelmingly Hungarian in linguistic and cultural orientation. The second most dominant urban language and culture of the region was German. In 1910, the 776,262 urbanites of Transylvania were 72.7 percent Hungarian and Jewish, 19.7 percent Romanian, and 15 percent German.[77] Ardeal's towns, however, were more culturally than ethnically Hungarian; Jews, among others, were partly responsible for the Magyar appearance of Transylvania's towns. The urban hegemony of Hungarian (and to some extent German) culture lasted well into the interwar period.

Because of France's rivalry with Germany for influence in East Central Europe, French diplomats and French Jewish organizations were painfully

---

[72] CS/1920/7/266, November 10, 1920.

[73] CS/1920/7/288, November 10, 1920.

[74] CS/1921/215/3, April 24, 1921.

[75] CS/1920/252/4, February 9, 1920; CS/1920/7/190, April 5, 1920; and CS/1920/7/264, n.d.

[76] CS/1920/7/190, April 5, 1920. Another issue concerned the need for textbooks to instruct Romanian language and culture to the Romanians and non-Romanians, including teachers, of Ardeal. See CS/1920/7/163, July 29, 1920. In 1920, there was a request for textbooks usable for instructing Saxon teachers in the Romanian language. We find authors or prospective authors for guidebooks to the Transylvanian (Romanian) dialect, and for school textbooks geared specifically to the population in the Szekler area. See CS/1920/6/201, n.d. There were inspectors who suggested the publication of bilingual textbooks for the schools in the Szekler areas and magazines geared especially to minority youth. See MIC/1928/772/34, June 21, 1929.

[77] Manuilă, *Aspects démographiques,* pp. 15–17, 70.

aware of the Hungarian and German cultural affinities of Transylvania's elites. France had supported Romania's territorial claims during and after the war and hoped to profit from Romania's expansion by extending French influence into former Habsburg territories. Representatives of L'Alliance Israélite Universelle, the Paris-based Jewish organization, looked at Transylvanian Jewry in terms of competing German and French dominance, as did French statesmen. An Alliance report in 1930 rued the fact that in Transylvania and Bukovina, France did not have the cultural and moral clout it enjoyed in the Regat: in these provinces, German (rather than French) was the major second language, German and even English newspapers were sold, but not French ones, and minority youth went to study in Austria, Germany, and Czechoslovakia, but never to France, the traditional mecca for the youth of the Regat. In Transylvania, it was Germany that counted as a civilized country. Minority high school students (i.e., Jews) were more interested in German than in the state language they had to study in school, and French intrigued them not at all. Lastly, the Jewish lycées themselves favored German as a foreign language.[78]

The Alliance saw the problem of Jewish youth in Ardeal in the context of Transylvanian Jewry in general, the native language and culture of which was overwhelmingly Hungarian and continuing to Magyarize in spite of the Romanian schools established since 1918.[79] Jewish predominance in the liberal professions, particularly in law and medicine,[80] made Ardeal Jews, according to an Alliance report, the most significant urban elite group, since it was they who largely determined the cultural orientation of the whole province. This preponderance of Jews in prominent liberal professions gave the towns their Hungarian character, "since it was they who read Hungarian newspapers . . . [and] books, and who frequented Hungarian theatres." Moreover, their second language was German, not French. When the government closed down many Hungarian schools, the Jews started sending their children to Saxon schools, to avoid the Romanian ones.[81]

The report proposed to establish French schools for the Jews of Transylvania in order to begin to de-Magyarize and de-Germanize the Jewish elite of this province along with the towns and cities whose elites the Jews formed. The Alliance may indeed have overstated the Jewish importance in Ardeal to transmitting one or another world culture in the interest of

[78] AIU/II/B/18, June 8, 1930.
[79] Ibid.
[80] The report (ibid.) quoted the following statistics: In Cluj there were 88 Jewish doctors versus 4 or 5 Magyars; in Oradea there were 70 Jewish doctors versus 1 or 2 Magyars; the proportion of lawyers was about the same in Arad, Timişoara, Turda, Dej, Diciosânmărtin, Braşov, Deva, Satmar, Sighet, Baia Mare, Sălaj, and other places.
[81] Ibid.

persuading French leaders to sponsor French-language Jewish schools in Transylvania. The Romanians, however, corroborated the singular importance of the Jews, albeit in a negative fashion. After the 1867 compromise, Hungary's Jews had assimilated, unlike most Romanians. The Romanians thus viewed Transylvanian Jews as subversives, as an insidious group of "hidden Magyars," "worse" than the Magyars themselves, whose orientation toward their own national culture was, after all, to be expected, a natural, unavoidable consequence of their ethnic origin. Modern assimilated Jews, on the other hand, did not have a necessary culture of their own, and therefore their choice of the Hungarian one together with a certain cultural Germanophilism was that much more heinous.

Although 152,790 Romanians lived in urban areas in 1910, they tended to live in smaller, and therefore "less urban," towns. Romanians represented only 12.4 percent of the population of large cities of over 100,000 but 38.4 percent of the population of small towns of under 5,000.[82] In addition, two other tendencies diluted and qualified the Romanian urban presence: many Romanian urbanites were either "ghettoized" or Magyarized. Romanians who were part of the urban elites often worked in specifically Romanian cultural or religious institutions and thus had little impact outside of the Romanian community. They lived and worked as "professional Romanians," as lawyers representing the rights and economic concerns of the rural and largely isolated Romanian population before hostile Hungarian authorities; as school inspectors of the Romanian schools; as teachers and priests in the Orthodox and Uniate schools and churches; and as journalists, writers, and politicians for the Romanian constituency. Even members of the Romanian bourgeoisie who had capital assets typically geared their investments to serve the Romanian community.[83]

Like Onisifor Ghibu, many Romanian intellectuals in Transylvania reacted to Magyarization efforts by becoming fervent Romanian nationalists. Others, however, embraced Magyarization. After 1918, education officials tried to address this problem, for it also affected Romanian teachers. Teachers played a crucial role in the nationalization of Transylvania, and their alienation from the ancestral culture caused serious concern. In one instance, the inspectorate of the Satu Mare district applied for funds to publish a local pedagogical journal to tackle the issue of Magyarization. The request was justified in the following way:

---

[82] Manuilă, "Aspects démographiques," pp. 16, 17, 70.
[83] See Verdery's example of Ioan Mihu, a Romanian lawyer "typical of the Romanian bourgeoisie," who was quite wealthy and chose to use his fortune to open a Romanian bank that catered particularly to the Romanian middle class and peasantry. *Transylvanian Villagers*, pp. 206–207.

The Romanian teachers of this county have earned their professional culture partly in state normal schools, partly in Greek Catholic normal schools in Gherla and Ordea-Mare, where very little weight used to be placed on Romanian national culture. Upon entering [a regular] daily life, they were assaulted by Hungarian cultural and social currents, between the banks of which streamed their entire life. To read a Romanian book, or to speak Romanian in public, was considered a crime. The intellectuals from these parts, feeling that they were regarded with suspicion and spied upon, abandoned Romanian life in all of its forms, even in their families, conforming entirely to the Hungarian influences and environment.[84]

Romanian elites were partially responsible for the staying power of the Hungarian language in Transylvanian urban settings, or, put another way, Magyarization was so successful in places that it was not easily shed with the change from Hungarian to Romanian political rule. In 1926, the Cluj magazine *Țara noastră* published an article that expressed concern that Romanians in Cluj did not read Romanian newspapers and had not been decisively "won over."[85] It claimed that other towns were even worse off: "In Satmar, Oradea, Sighet, the situation is even sadder. Hungarian is spoken often; . . . in the family, in society, in stores, on the 'corso', at parties the language of the Romanian 'elițe' is Magyar . . . in the Lord's year 1926, eight years after union." According to Corneliu Codarcea, the Romanization of the Romanians was yet to come.[86]

The rural identity of most Romanians in Transylvania meant that those who were not part of the elite and who migrated to and found work in urban areas confronted a more or less hostile environment, where they did not truly master the language. They tended to work in lower-class jobs as servants and unskilled laborers. In short, Transylvania's towns and cities constituted a stronghold of Magyarism against the Romanian populace, a citadel which the Romanians naturally wished to conquer after 1918. The protracted battle for the urban areas exacerbated the Romanians' sense of inferiority, even though the state was on their side.

In Transylvania, as in the other new provinces, a transformation of the social and professional structure of the Romanians was needed, for only such change could empower them to replace the elites and change the face and sound of the *urbs*. The schools therefore became the object of great concern, and the desire to orient them toward producing a Romanian middle class became one of the rallying cries of the Transylvanian national vanguard. Without a viable middle class, the Romanian patriots feared

[84] CS/1920/261/150, December 13, 1920.
[85] Corneliu Codarcea, "Kolozsvar-Cluj: Problema rŏmânizării oraşelor din Ardeal," *Țara noastră*, June 27, 1926.
[86] Ibid.

that they would remain isolated and never make good on the political victory won in 1918.

For the Romanians, the enclaves—i.e. cities, foreign populated zones, and cultural institutions—represented different, though overlapping, aspects of the national problem in Transylvania and the biggest and most urgent issue posed by the union of Ardeal with the Old Kingdom. But questions of regionalism also made themselves felt, crisscrossing the national problem at unexpected junctures. The regionalist dimension, subject of the next section, came as a surprise to interwar Romanian participants in cultural work and has remained poorly understood to this day.

Educational Work and the Struggle
over Transylvanian Autonomy

The period inaugurated by the Grand National Assembly at Alba Iulia in 1918 began on a sanguine note for Ardeal educators. A political dream had been achieved, and schools could now develop in an unfettered way, not only free from Magyar constraints, but also free to contribute to the new political order. Some educators thought that the schools would be able to tilt Romanian society in the right direction after centuries of straying. Onisifor Ghibu, one of the designers of the new course of Transylvania's schools, celebrated the moment:

> The day of December 1, 1918, inaugurates a new world: *Românism* has become free and its own master. It must build for itself its own state and set its own mission in this world. In this historic work, what role belongs to school and education? . . . The oppression of the Magyar language, . . . history, and . . . geography has fallen. . . . In high schools and the University instead of the Magyar language the French, English, and Italian languages [will be taught]. Romanian language, . . . history, . . . [and] geography [will serve] the purpose of consolidating a new state and founding a nation.[87]

At this heady moment, provincial leaders deemed unification desirable—in the long run—but problematic and nothing to rush into.[88] Ghibu's own vision of the "new world" included merging the four school systems (the old Romanian one, the Hungarian one from Transylvania, the Austrian one from Bukovina, and the Russian one from Bessarabia), but not immi-

[87] Onisifor Ghibu, "Două zeci de ani de şcoală românească în Transilvania (1919–1939)" in *Prolegomena la o educaţie românească* (Bucharest: Editura Cultura românească, 1941), p. 855.
[88] Interview with Onisifor Ghibu, *Patria*, Sibiu, March 30, 1919, reprinted in *Prolegomena*, p. 313.

nently. His position emerges from the following passage: "The unification of the school system in the entire country . . . is . . . our goal. A process of transformation this radical, however, can't be rushed. We must be patient until out of the four school organizations that we have today in the whole country—the dowry of a cruel past—a single whole, sound in its foundations and in all of its joints, can be made. We must work every moment for unification, but we must not force it against the nature of things."[89]

In this framework, the Directing Council's Public Education and Religion Department set about nationalizing existing schools and establishing new ones, organizing teacher training courses to cover up inherent staff shortages, and courses in Romanian language, literature, history, geography, and civics for reeducating minority teachers. From December 1918 to September 1919 the department prepared to open, in the fall of 1919, the confessional schools of the Orthodox and Uniate churches, as well as 1,306 primary state schools with Romanian as the language of instruction, 20 Romanian lycées (taught by teachers brought from the Old Kingdom and by *cursişti* educated during the summer courses of that year), 40 Romanian civil schools, and 8 normal schools. It nationalized 11 schools for arts and crafts, opened 6 state commercial schools, and reorganized the University of Cluj and Transylvania's educational administration. According to Ghibu, "the best [people] of both Ardeal and the Old Kingdom collaborated in this labor, which we initiated and led, so that we, for good reason, considered it not our labor, but an accomplishment of the whole generation to which Providence had reserved the happiness of putting new foundations to the life of this country."[90]

Nothing seemed to daunt Ghibu in those first months, neither the lack of teachers, nor the lack of books, nor the expected, if temporary, decrease in quality.[91] He met difficulties cheerfully, sure they could be overcome. By and large in this "breathless" period of home rule, the administration was local under the autonomous government of the Directing Council: an important morale factor for Transylvania's Romanian educators. Ghibu later reminisced that the Education Department was initially "infused by a high spirit. Not bureaucracy. Decentralization. Regional directorates; our own creations, not taken from the Hungarians. The appointments of regional directors and inspectors [were] determined exclusively by higher interests." In 1918–1920 the region's school system seemed to be "going slowly and methodically toward an organized unification."[92]

[89] Onisifor Ghibu, "De vorbă cu învăţătorimea din Ardeal," in *Prolegomena*, p. 322.
[90] Onisifor Ghibu, "După cinci ani de la Unire: Scrisoare deschisă d-lui Octavian Goga," in *Pentru o pedagogie*, p. 68.
[91] Interview with Onisifor Ghibu, *Patria*, Sibiu, March 30, 1919, reprinted in *Prolegomena*, pp. 314–315.
[92] "Două zeci de ani de şcoală românească în Transilvania (1919–1939)" in *Prolegomena*, p. 856.

The first decree passed by the Directing Council on January 24, 1919, established Romanian as the official language and redirected the 1868 Hungarian law of nationalities at the new minorities. This decree also prescribed the language of instruction in the various types of Transylvanian schools.[93] In non-state schools, the sponsor would decide the teaching language. In state primary schools, the language of the majority within a community would serve as the language of instruction, but parallel classes could be set up for minority pupils in their native tongue, if a sufficient number existed. Instruction in secondary schools would be in the language of the majority of the county, while the teaching language of higher educational institutions would correspond to the language of the majority in the whole region.

During the reign of the Directing Council, its Religion and Education Department reorganized and nationalized 1,611 schools of all levels and orientations and took over and Romanized Cluj University (for this see Chapter 6) and the National Theater in Cluj.[94] Romanizing schools and other cultural institutions in Ardeal was a difficult task, given the previous Hungarian hegemony. Some Romanian leaders considered that the very heritage of Magyar domination demanded as quick and radical a Romanization as possible; others believed that a more gradual approach made sense. These alternative views were propounded by the secretary general, Onisisfor Ghibu, and by Vasile Goldiş, the head of the council's Department of Education, respectively. Asked about the nationalization of secondary education in Transylvania, Goldiş suggested nationalizing one grade at a time beginning in fall 1919; Romanization could be completed within eight years.[95] Ghibu, however, felt that the "exceptional straits" of Transylvania's secondary schools required more drastic action. He argued that "the lycées made by the Hungarians for our Magyarization could not rightly be left Hungarian for another seven or eight years."[96]

One practical objection to Ghibu's idea was that insufficient teachers were available to staff a large number of new Romanian schools. Under the circumstances, the Directing Council retained Hungarian teachers if they swore loyalty to the new regime, while recruiting new Romanian cadre. Many Hungarians refused to take the oath.[97] In winter 1919, Ghibu appealed to Romanian Ardeleni teachers then serving in Hungarian second-

[93] Boilă, "Consiliul Dirigent," p. 93.
[94] Ibid., p. 100.
[95] Onisifor Ghibu, "O pagină din istoria învăţământului nostru," in *Prolegomena*, p. 390.
[96] Ibid. Given that there were only 3 Romanian lycées, versus 22 Hungarian ones, immediate wholesale nationalization was the only proper solution to the secondary school riddle, no matter how much effort was required, according to Ghibu.
[97] In Braşov County, teachers were fired for not appearing for the oath-taking ceremony, or for appearing and declaring their opposition publicly, but they were allowed to continue in their posts until the end of the school year. One Romanian Uniate Teacher from Maramureş

ary schools to "come home." He urged "all the sons of our people thrown by the wicked circumstances of the past in the service of foreign schools" to come where they were needed.[98] In addition, as earlier in Bessarabia, teacher-training courses were offered in the summer of 1919 which almost anybody was welcome to attend. The graduates, known as *profesori cur-siṣti*,[99] were often disparaged. One unsympathetic observer wrote that, "People of no previous education, village notaries, railway guards, etc., offered themselves and, after a superficial training and merely formal examination, were appointed as secondary-school teachers."[100]

In defense of this ad hoc category of teachers, Ghibu later wrote that no one had intended them to serve in the schools permanently, unless they subsequently completed more training. But for the 1919–1920 school year, they were to serve a kind of internship while helping Romanian secondary schools proliferate and proving themselves worthy of attending more advanced courses the following year, after the reorganization of Cluj University.[101] Ghibu's plan never achieved full fruition, for the Directing Council was dismissed in the spring of 1920. A second series of *cursiṣti* was trained in the summer of 1920 at Cluj University. These students, Ghibu felt, were worse than those of the previous year. Most of them remained in Transylvania's school system permanently, without additional training. Paid less than regularly trained teachers, they were generally regarded as inferior in their professional qualifications.[102] In Ghibu's view, the Bucharest-led education bureaucracy had thoughtlessly institutionalized a revolutionary measure meant to rescue Transylvania in an emergency.

The problem escaped neither Hungarian nor Romanian critics from Transylvania, to whom Bucharest's centralization tactics seemed both premature and careless. Minority spokesmen regarded the *cursiṣti* as "instruments of Romanization."[103] Ghibu, on the other hand, felt that the *cursiṣti*

---

also refused to take the oath, giving his answer in Hungarian, "*nem,*" to the satisfaction of his Hungarian colleagues, who cheered him with shouts of "*eljen*" (hurrah). (Subsequently he repented, was forgiven, and took the oath.) According to Pompiliu Dan, the school inspector for Braşov County, Hungarian teachers' refusal to swear allegiance to the Romanian state had "very painful consequences" for the Magyar community and "precious advantages for Romanian education and culture, [since] primary schools and kindergartens, which had until then been populated by Magyar pupils, were flooded by Romanian school-age youth, while Magyar school teachers were replaced by Romanian ones or by other Magyars who subsequently took the oath." AA IX/ Varia 2, December 30, 1922.

[98] Onisifor Ghibu, "Dascăli pribegi, întoarceţi-vă acasă!" January 4, 1919, in *Prolegomena*, pp. 303–304.

[99] Ghibu, "O pagină," pp. 390, 391.

[100] Zsombor de Szasz, *The Minorities in Roumanian Transylvania* (London: Richards Press, 1927), pp. 272–273.

[101] Ghibu, "O pagină," p. 392.

[102] Ibid., p. 395.

[103] Szasz, *Minorities in Transylvania*, p. 274.

ultimately did Transylvanian education a great disservice. In the mid-1920s, he declared that "Romanian education in Ardeal was weaker than when we had there only three confessional Romanian lycées and relatively weaker than even in Bessarabia,"[104] and in an article of March 1924 in *Patria* he accused the *cursişti* of being "simple electoral agents who received their posts for political services" and of being "adventurers without a moral compass, who believe in no God and have no convictions."[105]

Although the Romanian state maintained Magyar language schools with Magyar teachers in the communities with larger Hungarian populations, the Hungarian churches began organizing a growing number of confessional grade schools, effectively boycotting the state schools.[106] In Braşov County, the number of Magyar confessional schools rose from two in 1919 to fifteen a year later. Romanians thought that these schools were supported by illicit funds from Hungary and the United States and by parishioners' taxes. In the nearby communities of Crizbav, Satu Nou, and Satulung-Suseni, meanwhile, the Magyar population did not maintain confessional grade schools and went along with the Magyar-language state schools.[107]

The experiments introduced in pursuit of Romanian national ideals, and the attendant injustices to the Magyar population, elicited Magyar complaints. To many Hungarians, Romanian measures of nationalization appeared arbitrary and unfair. The director of the National Lycée for Girls in Oradea Mare (Nagyvarad, Grosswardein), Adalbert Gajda, complained bitterly to the Inter-Allied Military Commission in the fall of 1919.[108] That summer, Romanian authorities had fired Hungarian teachers who had refused to pledge the loyalty oath at his lycée and at the Real High School. The Reformed Church petitioned to establish two new schools, employing the fired teachers, but by November the Directing Council in Sibiu had not yet responded. While waiting, the unemployed teachers had organized their own private courses. Gajda reported that the new Romanian schools had only forty and one hundred pupils apiece, although both had boarding facilities. The student body, concentrated in the first grade, was recruited from the peasant population by "noisy propaganda and dazzling promises." The teachers (probably *cursişti*) lacked diplomas. Most of the former pupils preferred to go to the private, unaccredited courses taught by the fired Hungarian teachers. Exasperated by this competition, Romanian authorities ordered all Hungarian teachers who had refused to take the

[104] Ghibu, "O pagină," pp. 393–394.
[105] Quoted in Szasz, *Minorities in Transylvania*, p. 274.
[106] See, for instance, Louis C. Cornish and the Anglo-American Commission of 1924, *The Religious Minorities in Transylvania* (Boston: Beacon Press, 1925), p. 56.
[107] AA IX/ Varia 2, December 30, 1922.
[108] QD 41/78–80R, November 26, 1919.

oath to leave town, regardless of proof of residence, property ownership, or birthplace. The director was also expelled. Protests brought about a change in the expatriation order, but the wealthier teachers were forced to give up their homes and move to cottages.[109]

Gajda felt that the expulsion measure was calculated to eliminate the qualified Hungarian teaching cadre from Oradea, only to be followed up hypocritically with an apparently liberal measure allowing Hungarian secondary schools to open when they no longer had the proper resources. Several hundred Hungarian pupils would then have to register in the Romanian schools, in a town where the population consisted of 58,421 Hungarians and 3,604 Romanians. In the wake of these measures, only one Hungarian secondary school, a confessional lycée, was left in Oradea. It, too, however, was being admonished by the Romanian authorities for teaching Hungarian history, geography, and literature and for allowing the singing of the Hungarian anthem; as a result, its director and three teachers faced possible arrest.[110]

The Romanization measures in Transylvania involved a major effort of cultural and social mobilization among the Romanians. As Gajda mentions in his memorandum, the difficulty of recruiting Romanian pupils was in some places as serious as finding qualified teachers. Lycées found enrollments most problematic, because they had been strongholds of Magyarism. Faced with apathy, the Directing Council's Education Department mounted a campaign to enlist pupils for the new Romanian schools. Unless the schools filled up quickly, their raison d'être could be subject to question. More importantly, the project of creating a Romanian elite to wrest Transylvania away from Magyarism and its elites could be derailed. Decree No. 7185, S. VI, was promulgated in March 1920 to stimulate school recruitment.[111] The decree urged all local Romanian notables in Transylvania, the Banat, and Hungary "to carry out a systematic propaganda among villagers [to determine them] to educate their children in nearby towns, in order to prepare them for various careers." During Pentecost, each priest was expected to preach a sermon on the benefits of education and the parents' obligation to educate their children. Later the local priest, teacher, notary or communal secretary (if Romanian), and other "caring Romanian

[109] Ibid.
[110] Ibid.
[111] Its *exposé de motifs* stated: "In order to be able to satisfy all the needs of our national and state life, we have an urgent need for as large a number as possible of Romanians specially prepared for all branches of employment. The solution of this problem cannot be left to time alone. If we do not accelerate it by all the means at our disposal, we will not become masters in our own country even in the distant future; rather we will continue our subservience to the foreigners, who, thanks to a long and auspicious past, are still our masters today." Onisifor Ghibu, "Selecțiunea sistematică a copiilor dela țară, în vederea îndrumării lor spre diferitele ramuri ale vieții și activității naționale," in *Prolegomena*, p. 317.

intellectuals—were to confer to decide on the unmet economic and cultural needs of the community" and write down the statistics of potential and actual young people—students or practitioners of trades or professions— who could be encouraged to go to town for schooling either at their family's expense or with the aid of the commune.[112] On the second day of Pentecost, following church services, the School Council was supposed to call a public meeting during which the situation of the village would be presented to all inhabitants: the council was to describe the community's needs for more educated people, urge parents to send their offspring to school, and organize a scholarship fund for the poor and orphans.[113]

Centralization and Resistance

On April 2, 1920, the recently appointed Averescu government dissolved Transylvania's Directing Council.[114] The decree, a result of a stand-off between Averescu and the National Party came suddenly and without a parliamentary debate or vote (although the National Party that dominated the council had been discussing it).[115] The dissolution of the Directing Council produced deep disappointment among local Romanian elites, which felt that their labor, expertise, and traditions were disregarded. The measures of April 1920 were perceived in Transylvania as heavy-handed, and this approach to centralization caused a general malaise.

The French government took note of the reactions in Transylvania. A report to the French Ministry of War in May 1920 stated that the Bucharest take-over of the council's powers had "stirred up the most ardent dissatisfaction" among former members, the decision having been accepted only out of deference to the Crown. The National Party of Transylvania was calling ominously for a new assembly at Alba Iulia where the Great Union had been proclaimed less than two years earlier.[116] Another French report, quoting a "seemingly well informed" source, declared that the suppression of the Directing Council had been ill-received, adding to the general disillusionment with Romanian rule in Ardeal:

> Accustomed for a long time to its own political life, distinct from the rest of
> Romania by virtue of its [different] intellectual culture, customs, and economic

[112] Ibid.

[113] Examples were to be given from other ethnic groups, whose enlightened representatives were benefiting them. Ibid., p. 319.

[114] Even before the dissolution of the Directing Council, Ghibu, among others, greeted speculation about this possibility with apprehension. In an article in February 1920, he objected that such a measure was premature and that it "threatened with true disaster the only just hatched (*înjghebat*) Transylvanian school system." *Patria* (VI/47).

[115] Iancu, *Contribuţia,* pp. 296–301.

[116] V 7N/3043.

interests, the Ardeal expected a different treatment from the Old Kingdom. . . . The dissatisfaction is constantly fed by the continuation of the intensified state of siege, by arrests, by numerous expulsions, and by the closing of many schools where the teaching staff has refused to pledge allegiance. Finally, life becomes more and more expensive as a result of the windfalls made by Bucharest merchants who come to buy back in Transylvania at an advantageous rate the merchandise that they had sold there several months ago.[117]

Dissolution of the Great Union even seems to have been considered. The revered historian (and politician) Nicolae Iorga notes in his memoirs a discussion with Iuliu Maniu and Alexandru Vaida-Voevod on April 25, 1920 in which he told them, "neither do we want the dissolution of the political union of the Romanians of Ardeal" from the rest of Romania.[118] This comment suggests that, however vaguely, secession was in the air. While the Transylvanians stayed in the union, they added the Directing Council's liquidation by royal decree to their list of grievances.

Among other things, obligatory centralization measures interrupted the multifaceted work of the of the Directing Council's Education Department, which responded to its own liquidation with dismay. Remembering that moment of shock, Ghibu wrote, "Unexpectedly . . . came *the unification.* The unification was identical with centralization, bureaucratization, politicianization, and 'cultural' inflation. Unification 'by pitchfork' "[119] resulted in a "lack of any clear aim with regard to the functioning of the schools and of education from a national and moral point of view."[120] Although Ghibu was asked to take a leadership position in the new system, he refused to go to Bucharest to work in the Averescu government.[121] He argued, along with most of the higher functionaries of the Education Department, that Transylvania's schools should be administered locally "for years to come." He denied any "separatist" component to this conviction. The previously autonomous departments could well merge with the central ministry, he allowed, but they needed to remain physically on location in Cluj. His denials notwithstanding, his stance does indicate a kind of Transylvanian autonomism based on the conviction that a particular local experience differed substantially from the general Romanian or Bucharest variety, and that the incorporation of regional traditions into a general unification plan was absolutely essential. In later years he felt vindicated,

---

[117] QD 41/139, June 8, 1920.
[118] Nicolae Iorga, *Memorii*, vol. 3 ([Bucharest]: "Naționala" S. Ciornei, [1939]), p. 16.
[119] Ghibu, "Două zeci de ani de școală românească," in *Prolegomena*, p. 856.
[120] Ibid.
[121] This was not the first time that Ghibu had turned down a Bucharest position. He had already refused to be Secretary General of the Ministry of Education in the fall of 1919.

citing that even though the unification was proclaimed in 1920, the actual unification took place only in 1923.[122]

At first, the successors of Branişte and Ghibu praised their work and made an implicit promise to continue it.[123] But bitter polemics broke out between the old and the new guard. Ghibu accused his replacements of *politicianism* and inconsistent and chaotic policies. In turn, the Directing Council was blamed retroactively for its leniency toward minority confessional schools.[124] Not denying that minority school authorities in Transylvania had resisted Directing Council directives, Ghibu argued that measures the council initiated should have been continued after April 1920. The liquidation of the Directing Council had caused discontinuity and inconsistency of action; the Averescu government's representatives in Ardeal even failed to administer the sanctions promised in case of noncompliance. In 1919, the council had organized courses for minority teachers for the first time, but after the liquidation of the Directing Council Bucharest allowed the courses to lapse. The minorities had themselves filled the gap by establishing their own summer courses (taught on occasion by teachers from Germany).[125] Ghibu intimated that this kind of negligence could foster potentially dangerous practices among the minorities.

Even more important than the actual arguments in this debate are the terms on which it took place. Clearly, the cultural tasks of *any* Romanian administration in Transylvania were enormous, making criticism of their imperfect execution very likely. It is interesting, however, that regionalist tensions framed the debate, of which localism and centralism became the main terms; the same conflict was repeated several times over essentially the same issues. Some of the Transylvanians who had made their peace with Bucharest early on and had become part of the educational power structure eventually became themselves disappointed with the "center," and made their own localist critiques. Ion Mateiu's experience provides a case in point.

Ion Mateiu, a Transylvanian Liberal, became the director general of Transylvanian education in 1922 under a Liberal government. His allegiance in itself is significant, as the Liberal Party was based in the Old Kingdom and had to struggle to gain adherents in Transylvania. One can safely assume that Transylvanian Liberals were receptive to centralist policies. After only a few months on the job, Mateiu became involved in

---

[122] *Patria*, March 4, 1924.
[123] Ibid.
[124] Onisifor Ghibu, "Politca şcolară faţă de minorităţi: o acuzaţie nedreaptă adusă fostului Consiliu Dirigent al Transilvaniei," *Adevărul*, 1925, Nr. 12721, reprinted in *Prolegomena*, p. 767.
[125] Onisifor Ghibu, "Neajunsurile învăţământului nostru primar," *Vremea şcolii*, Iaşi, no. 4 (1930), reprinted in *Prolegomena*, p. 473.

a conflict with other Liberals over the course of Transylvanian education. Mateiu became indignant when the Ministry of Education removed all normal schools from under his supervision. The decision proceeded via the directors of the schools, completely bypassing Mateiu in the Cluj office of the director general. In protest, Mateiu argued that teacher-training education in Ardeal was extremely complex, as it included several different types of schools. While recognizing that a unitary direction for all Romania was necessary in the long run, Mateiu warned that the new guidelines "would have damaging repercussions on the course of local education."[126]

A faction of Liberal MPs lobbied Bucharest to dissolve Mateiu's Directorate of Education, claiming it fostered separatism and thwarted unification.[127] By the end of 1922, Mateiu had lost the fight, and the Cluj Directorate of Education had been dissolved.[128] Mateiu wrote to Ion Brătianu, the head of the National Liberal Party and president of the Council of Ministers, to advise on future policies and draw the government's attention to "the worrisome state of Transylvanian schools." Clearly, Mateiu had a political stake in defending the views that had lost him his job, but nevertheless, his pitch is worth citing. Mateiu explained that as director general of Transylvanian education he had tried

> to avoid any measure . . . which might have produced shocks in the normal evolution of education, dissatisfaction among the teaching staff, reaction among the minorities, and disappointments in the prestige and competence of our [Liberal] administration. [He had believed that] only the continuation of the old Transylvanian school tradition, with its honesty, precision, and dignity would serve fruitfully our work of consolidation and unification, and again [that] only this way would we definitively win over the sympathies of the Transylvanian teaching staff for our party, [which was] so broadly supported in the general elections.[129]

Mateiu believed that he had attracted teachers to the Liberal Party, and he regretted the Liberals' centralizing tendencies—their wish to "replace"

[126] AA xv/ Varia 1, October 3, 1922.

[127] In October 1922, they wrote a memo to the Minister of Education insisting on the necessity of dismantling the General Directorate of Education for Transylvania. They charged that the director's office was working "as an organ almost independent of central authority" and was "delaying," and "sometimes thwarting decisions taken in the general interest, thus contributing to the accentuation of separatism—so dangerous in Ardeal." AA xv/ Varia 1, October 23, 1922. In their view, liquidating the director's office would further the unification of education begun in 1919, continued by the dissolution of the Directing Council in 1920, and culminating in the transformation of the General Secretariates into General Directorates that were "totally dependent on the Ministry." Not only was the work of unification "not progressing" in Ardeal, it was actually "becoming illusory" and "the very idea of unification" was endangered there. Ibid.; see also AA xv/ Varia 1, November 25, 1922.

[128] The Finance and Agriculture Directorates remained, however. Ibid., May 23, 1923.

[129] Ibid.

the Transylvanian school organization that he felt was "in very many respects superior to the one in the Old Kingdom." Such methods and the dissolution of the Directorate, he felt, alienated the teachers. To make matters worse Bucharest sent Lupu Antonescu to direct Transylvanian education, who, though a "venerable man ... [was] absolutely unacquainted with the mysteries of school life in Ardeal."[130] According to Mateiu, great chaos ensued, the teaching staff did not know whether to address its queries to Cluj or to Bucharest, and the planned "liquidation" had not really been completed even after five months. Mateiu concluded his recommendations with the imperative of appointing Transylvanians to key positions for reasons of "local pride." Mateiu repeatedly recommended that the government collaborate with Transylvanian experts, teachers, and politicians in all aspects of education policy, as well as with Liberal Transylvanian intellectuals.[131] Accordingly, he wrote, "unification should no longer be imposed by hurried and mistaken measures, which overturn through simple ministerial decisions a rightful order based on laws which are still in force ... [for an] orderly life, even when it has at its basis a foreign legislation, must not be disturbed for the sake of ill-applied patriotism." Finally, Mateiu's comment on policy toward the minorities implied that Old Kingdom Romanians were ignorant of Transylvania's multiethnic reality. His opinion was that "school policy toward the minorities must change the concept it presently practices, as it is bringing us to a bitter cultural war that severely impinges on the work of quiet consolidation of the state.[132]

Mateiu and Ghibu seem to be part of a "Transylvanian" pattern. They both initially took administrative positions made possible by the inclusion of Transylvania in Greater Romania, Ghibu under the Directing Council in 1919–1920 and Mateiu under the Liberal government in 1921–1922. They were both Romanian patriots with Transylvanian sensibilities that were finally offended by efforts at centralization, and they were both displaced in power struggles with the "center." Their regionalism prevented them from maintaining power; the stated terms of their struggle were nation versus region, and those were the grounds on which both ostensibly lost.[133]

Nevertheless, most Transylvanians made their peace with centralization, which after all represented the Romanian idea they had long aspired to, and the cultural project continued very much in the same vein it had

---

[130] Ibid.

[131] Ibid.

[132] Ibid.

[133] Octavian Prie, Ghibu's immediate successor, also expressed dissatisfaction with the lack of consideration granted to the Transylvanian educational tradition. He criticized the 1924 primary school reform bill for its regressive measures. He cited the example of the communities, rather than the state, being responsible for school construction. See Țara noastră, June 1, 1924, pp. 674–679.

followed during the Directing Council's brief reign. Against the grain of relatively well-established Magyar and German cultural institutions, the Ministry of Education pursued the work of school construction, the opening of new schools, and the Romanization of Magyar schools begun under the Directing Council, indeed, the ministry proceeded perhaps even more harshly than the council had. Although regionalism was sometimes expressed in bureaucratic struggles over administration and personnel (and in the political sphere per se), in school matters the correspondence and reports from inspectors and other school officials indicate an interest in centralization, Romanization, and the homogenization of the curriculum with that of the Old Kingdom. This spirit is captured by an inspector from Târnava-Mică who, in support of unifying the curriculum, asked indignantly: "Until when shall we, Ardeleni, learn certain things, while our brothers from the Regat, [learn] others? We believe that the time has come for the new school generations to be raised with the same thoughts and feelings; in this we can more easily succeed in the framework of a single uniform curriculum."[134]

Nationalizing Transylvania's Schools

The construction and opening of new Romanian schools in Transylvania and the conversion of Magyar schools into Romanian ones was an uneven process, engaging urban and rural inhabitants, Hungarian, German, and Romanian speakers, and common people and members of elites very differently. Efforts took place against different ethnic and cultural backdrops: in areas where Magyarization had made inroads even among the Romanian population, which now had to be brought back to the "true" national fold;[135] in places where Magyars or Szeklers were in a majority and tried to hold their own before the advance of Romanian culture and the consolidation of the Romanian state; in areas peopled by Germans, Ruthenians, and Magyarized Jews who had never before had to reckon seriously with Romanian culture. Archival reports and other sources tell the story of a mostly uphill battle, coupled with some successes.[136]

[134] MIC/1923/96/16, June 15, 1923. Another inspector from Braşov County was concerned about the unmodified version of the geography curriculum. This program lacked a geography of Greater Romania to replace that of Austria-Hungary taught previously. MIC/1923/95/36, October 27, 1923.

[135] In 1920, for instance, in primary schools in Satu-Mare, the majority of Romanian children did not know Romanian; the teachers themselves spoke the language poorly. See Onisifor Ghibu, "Primele inspecţii," in *Pentru o pedagogie românească*, p. 222–225.

[136] For this section, the Archive of Constantin Angelescu, who was the National Liberal Party's expert on educational affairs and who served as Minister of Public Instruction several times during the interwar period, was very useful, as were the Archives of the Ministry of Public Instruction.

In Transylvania's urban areas, the Romanians and the state shared an interest in expanding the network of Romanian schools as hotbeds of *Românism*. On the whole, the difficulties were more staggering in rural areas, where attempts to mobilize interest, resources, and teachers ran up against poverty and apathy. In the Transylvanian countryside, the incentive to dislodge the Magyar language from its leading position was rather weak,[137] and the population resisted having to make financial contributions to school construction, something they had never had to do before.[138]

Cultural Work in the Transylvanian Countryside

In the countryside of Ardeal, substantial effort went into introducing a school system that would serve a national purpose. Indeed, initiatives at times proceeded ahead of ministerial approval; local leaders asked for sanction and funding from the Ministry of Education only after the fact. A truly grassroots initiative, however, did not arise among Romanian peasants; rather, the drive belonged to the literate Romanian elite involved with school administration. An inspector from Mureş-Turda County offers an eloquent example of such activism. In 1922, he wrote,

[We] would have committed the greatest sin, were this people—delivered from slavery after so much suffering but finding itself in agony—to remain even one more day without the life-giving light of school. Thus, I hurried, Your Excellency, to rent by agreement or requisition a house here and there, often quite dilapidated, and seating the little children on wooden boards set on two tree stumps, or on bricks, holding their little writing boards on their knees, to start with all the burning fire of love for our people (*neam*), in addition to the teaching of elementary notions and the learning of our forgotten language; to instill both in the children and in the grown-ups the sentiments of love of country, love for the Dynasty, and pride of belonging to the Romanian people (*neam*).[139]

[137] Thus, the Regional Director of Education in Timişoara asked the Minister of Education in March 1923 to order all minority primary schools to teach Romanian at least an hour a day in the third and fourth grades, since only urban schools had taught Romanian until that time, leaving the rural minority pupils ignorant and unable to follow secondary school instruction in Romanian. MIC/1923/96/6, March 30, 1923.

[138] In Bihor, school committees charged with collecting funds and materials for the building of schools from the population still encountered landless peasants (the land reform, though legislated, had not yet been implemented), as well as the "specific mentality of the Bihorian people, accustomed to schools erected for them by the state." AA/ Varia 2, February 24, 1923. An inspector's report from Mureş-Turda County spoke of the "ravages" left by the Hungarians' concerted policies of denationalization, such as the closing of Romanian schools. But the school committees were "totally ineffective" in collecting funds for school construction because the population was used to leaving this to the state, and because the Romanians were very poor. AA IX/ Varia 2, November 1, 1922.

[139] AA IX/ Varia 2, November 1, 1922.

The material difficulties of this area, as of others—insufficient buildings and monies for repairs—were compounded by the lack of Romanian teachers: half of the 166 positions reserved for Romanian teachers in 1922 went unfilled or attracted only substitutes. Few Romanian teachers wished to go there; the area was considered so thoroughly Hungarian that Romanian teachers' work was bound to be hard. Local authorities were understandably disturbed. Between 1919 and 1923, they had managed to increase the number of Romanian schools from 56 to 138 and the number of Romanian teachers' posts from 58 to 188, to try to reverse the overwhelming trend of Magyarization.[140] But with the difficulty of getting enough qualified Romanian cadre, one report declared rhetorically, "Anyone can imagine what our chances for victory are in a struggle in which we have leading the schools on our side church cantors, mayors, ex-gendarmes, children [who are] graduates of [only] three or four secondary [school] grades." Under the circumstances, the writer concluded glumly, "the Romanian school is compromising itself . . . Romanians being Magyarized even in Greater Romania."[141]

Similar problems prevailed in the western county of Bihor, where very few children knew Romanian. Here a teacher's tasks were reportedly "doubled by the special labor of nationalization. He must . . . first teach . . . [the children] their mother tongue, so that he may later introduce them into the mysteries of science."[142] The apathy characteristic of denationalized rural Romanians was still apparent in the late twenties. A primary school inspector in the village of Vetiş near Satu Mare found one school dirty, neglected, unheated, with its archive and registers in disorder. Of the 150 registered pupils, 43 were in attendance on the day of his visit, and none, not even the Romanians, knew the state language after ten years of Romanian rule.[143]

Educational nationalization measures were possibly least successful in the Szekler zone, judging by the reports not only of educators, but also of local prefects and the Ministry of the Interior. Even when Magyar schools were Romanized, the language of instruction remained Hungarian. Writing about Treiscaune County, one observer noted that essentially nothing had changed: "The teachers are still the old ones, the pupils are all Hungarians, the spirit and color are still the same."[144] In 1928, state schools in Odorhei

---

[140] Ibid. and MIC/1923/263/6, August 10, 1923.

[141] MIC/1923/263/6, August 10, 1923.

[142] AA IX/ Varia 2, December 18, 1922.

[143] MIC/1928/4/77, October 19, 1928.

[144] MIC/1923/477/37. (Received August 16, 1923.) Another inspector in the Szekler region took a slightly different view: although the area appeared to be "all Szekler," a considerable number of Romanians lived there who no longer spoke the ancestral language but kept the memory of Romanian ancestry and sometimes bore characteristic Romanian names. The church and the school should be responsible for reawakening these lost Romanian brothers. MIC/1923/476/161, October 9, 1923.

County still employed primarily minority teachers, making it hard to distinguish their activity from that of Magyar confessional schools. Extracurricular activities followed an entirely Magyar program, though the Romanian Royal Hymn was sung pro forma at the end of meetings. To boost the poor results of Romanization there, the Ministry of the Interior proposed hiring Romanian teachers and sending the present teachers to more Romanian areas to hone their language skills and their enthusiasm for things Romanian.[145]

Romanian officials and local notables debated another issue: the viability of schools as seminal institutions, rather than as instruments serving a specific present need. For example, the German middle school in the commune of Periamos (Periam) in Timiş-Torontal County had added a Romanian section in 1919, which briefly taught twelve pupils from a neighboring commune. Their numbers gradually dwindled to two, the teacher was transferred, and the school petered out. The local Romanian elite—teachers, priests, notaries, mayors, and lawyers—protested the closing, but both the regional director for education in Cluj and the secondary education director in Timişoara felt that a Romanian school there did not make sense. The director did not "understand to what end certain gentlemen force the establishment of a Romanian section just in Periamos, where the pupils cannot be placed [in lodging], and where the teachers do not like to go, seeing as this is a purely German commune. It is a childish idea that the Schwabs might be Romanized with a Romanian staff."[146] He argued sensibly that if one wished to establish a Romanian middle school, the place for it was Pesac, a nearby Romanian commune "where the primary Greek Orthodox school was rented out as a tavern."[147]

Of course, in many places progress was being made, or at least reported.[148] A 1927 inspection of the state primary school in Sf. Gheorghe, Treiscaune County, for instance, yielded a very positive evaluation. An energetic director led the school, and it had grown from 18 to 140 pupils since 1923. Although located in the heart of the Szekler lands, even the school's Magyar section showed an "almost Romanian character," while the teachers were trying to teach the children "to feel and to speak Romanian."[149] Thus, although apathy prevailed, it did not uniformly characterize rural Romanians' involvement with their schools.

---

[145] MIC/1928/6/143, Registered May 29, 1928.
[146] MIC/1923/477/1–3, December 30, 1922.
[147] Ibid.
[148] There is no way to control for the subjectivity of these inspectors' reports. As such these data are certainly impressionistic, but they do tell us how a range of school officials saw the progress of the schools. These perceptions are important in themselves, since it was the *perceived* difficulties and successes that contributed to the political mood of the country.
[149] MIC/1928/32/33–34, December 7, 1927.

Cultural Work in Urban Transylvania

In the Ardeal countryside, Romanian teachers formed part of an isolated, sparse elite spread among the somewhat indifferent Romanian peasants. The educated upper layer alone seemed to care about cultural development and nationalization. In towns by contrast, school officials, parents, and pupils belonged to the same class. Together they formed a struggling Romanian elite attempting to appropriate the historically and culturally alien territory of urban Transylvania. Urban Romanians seeking to carve out a livable niche in Transylvanian towns took a decided interest in the social mobility symbolized and facilitated by Romanian schools, especially at the secondary level. When tensions arose, they most frequently occurred between the state, which wanted the schools to produce a solid *lower* middle class by training teachers and artisans, and local Romanians, who preferred to rise through academically tracked schools to white-collar positions.[150]

In Transylvania, the cultural conquest of the cities was more than a metaphor, it was a physical process. Romanians aspired to occupy the downtowns of cities, rather than be relegated to the countryside or even city outskirts. A report about cultural advances in Oradea Mare expresses this concern: "In 1919, when the Romanian army entered this non-Romanian city, we had 3 teachers and a total of 100 Romanian children. Today after three years we have 25 Romanian teachers and 734 Romanian children in Oradea Mare. This is incontestably progress, and is evidence of the rapidity with which we are growing and taking our deserved place in the interior of this city."[151] The Romanian children living in the slums on the periphery of Oradea who had previously gone to Hungarian schools were now attending Romanian schools.[152]

An important issue in the urban cultural struggle was the question of which sort of education best suited Romanian interests: academic or vocational. Many people valued academic training as the only path to a cultured, urban life in the Romanian elite. In a typical instance, Ministry of Education officials clashed with the local population from Abrud and the Apuseni Mountains over what type of secondary school to establish. Whereas the ministry wanted to open a normal school, the local community's "natural

---

[150] Discord arose over the particular sense of the "middle-class project" in individual cases. Thus we have examples of vocational school graduates trying to avoid employment in the trade of their training, preferring to try to find clerical white-collar jobs. AA IX/ Varia 2, February 7, 1934.

[151] AA IX/ Varia 2, December 18, 1922.

[152] Ibid. The generally optimistic report from Bihor also praises the efforts of Magyar teachers working in state schools to conform to the "changed situation" by taking courses and exams in Romanian language, geography, history, and constitution.

leaders"—doctor, priest, mine manager, merchants, lawyers, mayor—favored a regular middle school, or, even better, a lycée.[153]

Twenty-one inhabitants from the northwestern city of Satu Mare signed a petition opposing the replacement of a civil school for girls with a vocational one; they argued that a vocational school preparing girls for their roles as mothers and housewives was a luxury Romania could not then afford. Least of all should such a frivolous education be "the primordial goal" in the Satu Mare region "where all the functions are in the hands of Magyars because of a lack of educated Romanians." In fact the petitioners wanted the civil school to be upgraded to a girls' gymnasium to enable many Romanian girls to abandon Magyar secondary schools. The Romanian elite in Satu Mare was outraged at the continued Hungarian hegemony over academic education and at the resulting Magyarization of their daughters.[154] Similar requests were made for boys' academic secondary schools. Thus the inspector general, responding to repeated pleas from a senator and a prefect from Târnava-Mare County, asked the minister of education in 1923 for permission to open a boys' lycée in the predominantly Saxon town of Sighişoara. "Considering . . . that the town of Sighişoara like the towns around it, Ibaşfalău and Mediaş, are compact Saxon centers with powerful cultural organizations, I believe that the deeper penetration into these masses by the Romanian element imposes itself as a national necessity. *To this end, I beg permission, Your Excellency, to ask you to admit in principle the establishment in Sighişoara of a boys' lycée.*"[155]

The most common argument in such requests was the national one: that monies for the schools funded the defense and development of the national culture and thus served the national interest. Such reasoning projected the interests of the Romanian urban constituency onto the Romanian state, which supposedly had an equal interest in penetrating the ethnically alien power structures embodied by foreign schools, foreign cities, and the foreign middle class of Transylvania. Although referring to real inequities and the wish to redress them, these requests generally employed a rhetorical leap in portraying local conditions as intrinsically connected to larger state and national interests.

Requests for opening or upgrading secondary schools reflected Romanians' desire for social mobility and the perceived role of schools in furthering it. In towns where Romanians were outnumbered, schools fulfilled the need of a fairly restricted interest group, but, so the argument went, such schools were necessary even in these areas in order to plant (and nurture) the seed of Romanian culture. An inspector from the Sibiu region recom-

[153] MIC/1923/477/41–42, August 26, 1923.
[154] MIC/1923/478/122–123, September 15, 1923.
[155] MIC/1923/476/8, March 6, 1923.

mended transforming a civil school for girls in the industrial city of Deva into a lycée. He argued that the inhabitants of Deva wanted their daughters to receive the superior form of culture which was unavailable because the closest lycées were very far away (in Arad, Sibiu, and Blaj); furthermore, the lycée would be, "a new hotbed of culture in . . . Deva, which, although located in a region where the majority of the population is Romanian, is nevertheless a foreign city whose inhabitants are for the most part Magyars and Jews."[156]

This perception of a hostile environment comes across in many reports from predominantly Magyar areas. In Odorhei, for instance, which was conceivably a difficult challenge to Romanian *Kulturkampf*, an attempted exchange of teachers with the Old Kingdom had failed because the Regăţeni were reluctant to move there.[157] The inspector had hopes for opening a Romanian lycée in Odorhei, to "strengthen that handful of brave employees who are today maintaining and spreading the Romanian interests in this estranged town, [and to] weaken the two Hungarian lycées in this town— causing to disappear two nurseries of Hungarian propaganda." The project included bringing thirty to forty scholarship pupils from the Old Kingdom to live among local villagers in the dormitories. The villagers would undergo a "spiritual transformation" and carry Romanian culture back to their homes. The local Romanian elite was so interested in the possibility of a Romanian lycée in Odorhei that they volunteered to fund the school themselves until it could be incorporated into the state budget. Some of them also offered to teach free of charge, leaving only the director's salary to be paid.[158]

School administrators saw vocational schools as the means to expand the Romanian class of craftsmen, an important goal in Transylvania. In Oradea Mare one vocational school, under the direction of one Juliu Muth—"Romanian by nationality"—had 1,672 pupils, the majority of them Romanian and the rest Hungarian, Jewish, and German. The school

---

[156] MIC/1923/478/128, July 27, 1923. Similarly, a secondary school for girls was on its way to being established in 1923 in Cristur, even though the great majority of the commune's inhabitants were Magyar. Cristur, a large rural commune in the Szekler region, resembled a small provincial town by virtue of its intellectual, professional, and white-collar population. Reports about the projected school mentioned its creation as a "hotbed of Romanian culture," in what one can deduce was a very hostile environment for the Romanian elite. The Ministry of Education was urged to send its own architect to Cristur in order to carry out the necessary repairs, since the local architects could not be trusted: as foreigners they might view the lycée with "enmity" and sabotage its renovation. MIC/1923/478/104–107, n.d.

[157] In 1928, an inspector complained that the town leaders were not paying "proper attention to state primary education." This neglect resulted in the housing of the state primary school in an old building, even though a special lot had been set aside especially for a new school; the Magyar schools were all ensconced in large and beautiful buildings. MIC/1928/6/173, May 29, 1928.

[158] MIC/1923/476/161, October 9, 1923.

functioned with the Hungarian curriculum of 1884 translated into Romanian, but it left a very favorable impression upon one inspector in 1926.[159] Nevertheless, a report in January 1926 reviewing the situations of Arts and Crafts schools in Arad, Timişoara, and Oradea Mare objected to the teaching of night courses in Hungarian language. The regional inspectorate and the Ministry of Education were indignant, the ministry claiming that if the present system continued, "the Romanians would find themselves always, and increasingly, foreigners in the country which is, after all, theirs and [and not that of] the foreigners."[160] Although the state was undoubtedly Romanian, the large majority of workers in Transylvania, especially among the older generation, came from minority groups. Thus it made sense to introduce the Romanian language gradually and to set an example within the school for the desired ethnic composition of Ardeal's society.[161]

Looking to Bucharest

If Romanian schools assumed the role of redressing Hungarian policies toward the Romanian population of the Ardeal, they also took on the more challenging task of reorienting non-Romanians and non-Hungarians toward Bucharest. In northern cities like Sighetul Marmaţiei, important Ukrainian and Jewish populations had always attended Hungarian schools. In the spring of 1920, when Onisifor Ghibu went on a school inspection tour, he noted the large number of Jews, Ukrainians, and Romanians in Hungarian language state and confessional schools, remarking in one instance that the only reason to maintain a Hungarian state school in Satu Mare would be for the benefit of the Jews.[162] In Sighetul Marmaţiei, he addressed "the cultural situation of Jews and Ruthenians" who were "all Magyarized," and declared that steps had to be taken to remove the Hungarian administrators of the Ruthenian pupils' boarding school, a school directed "in the Hungarian spirit, while the Jews must be attracted out of Hungarian into Romanian schools, in parallel classes." He stressed the need for "*a totally clear, systematic, and energetic school policy*" with which "to counter the artificial Hungarian influence."[163] To this end, he proposed to distribute teachers from the Old Kingdom to needy schools throughout Ardeal, while local teachers who were replaced would go to

[159] MIC/1926/5/86–87, October 15, 1926.
[160] MIC/1926/574/8, January 23, 1926.
[161] MIC/1926/574/18, February 13, 1926.
[162] Ghibu, "Primele inspecţii," in *Pentru o pedagogie*, p. 223.
[163] Ibid., p. 225.

the Old Kingdom to strengthen their national consciousness and Romanian language skills.[164]

The Magyarization of non-Magyar groups was evident not only in linguistic terms, but also in the national sympathies of minority youth. The Jews, the most thoroughly Magyarized ethnic minority in Ardeal, tended to maintain that loyalty. A fictionalized account of this phenomenon appears in Mihail Sebastian's 1934 novel *For Two Thousand Years*. A young Transylvanian Jew, Pierre Dogany, persists in his loyalty to Hungary and its culture long after Hungary had stopped being a hospitable place for Jewish students.[165] In real life, Romanian school authorities also encountered expressions of Magyar nationalism from their Jewish students. Frequent Romanian national celebrations provided one occasion for such confrontations.[166]

Although some of the many school problems we have mentioned were transitional, others were abiding, and some even worsened with the economic depression that hit heavily the Romanian peasantry who were the reservoir of recruits for many of the new schools established after 1918. Under budgetary difficulties, governments closed down many schools, affecting ethnic Romanian teachers and pupils disproportionately, according to some school inspectors. In Banat between 1928 and 1933, the number of Romanian secondary school pupils dropped, while the number of minority pupils rose, by 30 percent and the ethnic Romanian faculty suffered a 7 percent reduction.[167] The number of pupils at a boarding school lycée in Maramureş dropped from one hundred to forty in 1934; the normal school there was also in trouble.[168] The inspector said that the drop was due to the poverty of the local peasants, as evidenced by the fact that not a single villager had attended either school in the previous two years.[169]

---

[164] Ibid., p. 222. Unfortunately, incentives for minority teachers "detached" to the Old Kingdom were lacking. Besides the disruption that such a move entailed, the teachers were often not fully remunerated during their time of transfer. They were supposed to draw their full salary, but they sometimes received only 25 percent of it. See MIC/1929/86, esp. MIC/1929/86/35, June–July 1935.

[165] Mihail Sebastian, *De două mii de ani,* 2d ed. (Bucharest: Fundaţia regală pentru literatură şi artă, 1946).

[166] For example, two Jewish lycée students in the school district of Sibiu were punished with expulsion from all state schools when they behaved disrespectfully during the visit to the house of Avram Iancu, a Transylvanian Romanian hero of the 1848 revolution. MIC/1924/404/234–237, June 18, 1924.

[167] AA VI/ Varia 4, n.d. Another way to look at the situation, which the report does as well, is in urban-rural terms: the rural element dropped, and the urban element rose by 30 percent.

[168] AA IX/ Varia 2, February 7, 1934.

[169] A similar situation prevailed at the town's girls' lycée, where the student body was mainly Jewish. Accordingly, the inspector recommended that only a gymnasium (that is, a

The large minority student body of academic schools was matched by a "large number of minority teachers inherited from the Hungarian state." Many of these still did not know much Romanian in 1934, and their "souls" were still "foreign," according to Romanian inspectors. They warned in their reports to the ministry that such "conditions do not make for a Romanian education, which is necessary for consolidating our ethnic frontiers," and they recommended continued support for dormitories, which some claimed "were of great importance for national education," though others felt that they had proved ineffective.[170]

The financial crisis of the early 1930s also threatened to close various successful schools that had attracted a large body of Romanians as well as minorities. The Romanian state lycée in Braşov provides a case in point. Its teaching staff defended the school in 1933:

> Keeping the [Romanian] lycée in Braşov, a city where no fewer than four Saxon high schools and three Hungarian high schools are functioning, is a cultural and national necessity. If this does not happen, there will then be fewer state Romanian secondary schools for boys in Braşov ... than the Romanians had when struggling with untold hardships [in the bad old days of] Hungarian domination. It would be painful for Romanian education that Romanian pupils might have to enroll in minority lycées, which in numbers overwhelm the Romanian ones, just [now] since the war when the cultural national process has turned in our favor.[171]

With the closing of some classes at the Romanian lycée, an equal number of classes were opened at the minority schools, leading the Braşov lycée staff to wonder rhetorically, what "the interest of the Romanian state in the regions with minority populations" was, "to abolish schools which are sixty-eight years old, like this lycée, so that similar minority schools might double the number of their classes and build new schools, as is the case in Braşov?"[172]

When the Ministry of Education had suggested in 1927 a renewed "cultural offensive" to educate the masses, especially in multilingual regions "where the minorities formed real majorities," a school inspector from

---

lower secondary school) be funded by the state, leaving out of the budget the higher course of secondary study. What Sighet needed more, according to the report, was a trade school and a higher peasants' school, instead of "intellectual" schools attended by foreigners. Ibid.

[170] Ibid.

[171] AA xv/ Varia 2, 1933, n.d. According to the memo, in the previous few years many minority pupils had started to attend the Romanian lycée, at long last proving its superior quality and "the affirmation of Romanian culture in full ascendancy over the culture of . . . the Saxons and Hungarians."

[172] Ibid.

Odorhei County objected. Because his district was so overwhelmingly non-Romanian he felt that it might be better to "leave" the minorities "in the dark." He asserted that "a cultural offensive left to itself and uncontrolled may give results contrary to the interests of the [Romanian] people (*Neamu-lui*)."[173] In this statement, education emerges as a dynamic, political, and possibly dangerous process, that could either benefit the Romanian nation or, if left in the hands of disloyal or ignorant teachers and clerics, harm it. The conditions necessary for a positive outcome to the cultural offensive were bilingual teachers—to teach Romanian, but also to understand Hungarian; statistical knowledge of the ethnic breakdown of the population—Hungarians, Romanians, and Magyarized Romanians; bilingual textbooks; and adult schools "inside of which . . . our Romanian ethnicity should be mirrored." To activists of the cultural offensive its main object was less the minorities themselves than the *priest* seen as "the bearer of Magyar irredentism. He holds the people under the pressure of the faith, out of which he makes a weapon against the state."[174]

The National Minorities on the Defensive

Transylvania's minority populations viewed with suspicion the "cultural offensive," which unfolded mainly through the nationalization of Hungarian and German schools. The Magyars, for whom the transition from ruling nation to subordinate minority was unacceptable, most particularly did not want to resign themselves to the fait accompli of a Romanian state on a territory long Hungarian. In 1919, they were still hoping for a diplomatic settlement that would undo the Romanian national revolution. In the meantime, they retreated to enclaves of cultural autonomy represented by the Hungarian churches and confessional schools.

But Romanians often felt that if Magyar priests (and notables) made no hostile propaganda, rank and file Hungarians would participate in state schools without incidents.[175] Romanian school inspectors objected to the role played by the Hungarian clergy, whom they accused of turning the Transylvanian Magyars against the Romanian state. An inspector from the Odorhei district claimed in 1927 that there was no struggle going on with the minority people per se in the Szekler region, but that there was one "with the *priest,* who is the bearer of Magyar irredentism. He keeps

---

[173] MIC/1927/7/34–38, December 19, 1927.
[174] Ibid.
[175] See, for instance, MIC/1928/5/9, March 28, 1928.

the people under the pressure of the faith, out of which he forges a weapon against the state."[176]

Slightly less feared than the priests, minority teachers also concerned the Romanian authorities, first, for not readily going along with the new state order, refusing to pledge allegiance to the Romanian state in the wait-and-see period which preceded the Treaty of Trianon, and, second, for not learning Romanian quickly enough to become proper educators of the youth of Greater Romania. Hungarian and Saxon teachers at state and confessional schools were still confronting the language competence problem in the mid-twenties. Minority teachers were admitted to the language competence exams only after attending four semesters of Romanian language and literature, geography, history, and civics. Those who had trouble fulfilling the requirement delayed taking the exams or failed them. Once passed, the exams yielded a "nostrification" certificate.[177] Even so, Romanian administrators sometimes hesitated to certify competent minority teachers of Romanian language, even if they had the proper philological training and background. As one official put it, "It would be desirable in the first place that only Romanians become Romanian language teachers, who, besides their qualification, have also a love for this subject in their soul."[178]

Minority teachers wished to have their own teachers' organizations. The Reformed teachers of the Baia Mare diocese and the Roman Catholic teachers from Oradea both asked permission to establish associations but were refused—although Romanian teachers under Hungarian rule had had their own associations.

One official justified the ban by saying that it was still too early in 1924 to allow minority teachers' organizations: "the wound from which they suffer is still too open."[179] The Romanians' own experience with using autonomous cultural institutions to organize a nationalist movement in Hungarian-dominated Transylvania made them weary of extending analogous opportunities to the Magyars. Clearly, Romanians and minorities alike saw culture as a battlefield of national politics.[180]

The Directing Council felt that it had extended full rights to the minorities in the beginning but that their response had been ungrateful and disloyal.

---

[176] MIC/1927/7/34–38, December 19, 1927. The singling out of Hungarian clergy as "the troublemakers" is very similar to the focus on the Ukrainian priests in Bukovina. (See Chapter 2.) The phenomenon may have as much to do with the role of the minority clergy in Ukrainian and Magyar nationalism as with the central part of Romanian clergy in the early Romanian national movement.

[177] MIC/1922/492; MIC/1923/463; MIC/1923/463/53,61,62; MIC/1924/295/255,261, 278,297; and AA IX/ Varia 2, December 18, 1922.

[178] MIC/1923/463/53,61,62.

[179] MIC/1924/213/56,60.

[180] The Romanians' cultural adversaries were by and large Magyars or Magyarized groups—generally Jews, but also some Romanian renegades—and, to a lesser extent, Germans.

This suspicion seems to have continued throughout the interwar period. A year after the Great Union, Onisifor Ghibu wrote a report to Valeriu Branişte, the head of the Education Department. Despite its title—"The First Political Experience Made with the Magyar Minority in Transylvania"—the document deals with *educational* and *cultural* matters rather than directly with politics. The report is worth citing at length to clarify the Romanian stance:

> The Directing Council of Transylvania, in its desire to ensure the free cultural development of the peoples inhabiting the territories which it administers, inaugurated in the educational field a policy which differs totally from that of former Hungarian governments. Thus, not only did it approve the functioning of all Hungarian confessional schools in existence under the old Magyar administration, but it decided also to open a considerable number of state schools on all levels with Magyar as their language of instruction. It did this in the conviction that the State is obligated to care for the education of all its citizens.
>
> But at the same time, the Directing Council has had to notice to its surprise an attitude on the part of the Hungarian confessions, [which is] not only reserved toward this loyal school policy, but also, in some cases, provocatory. The Hungarian confessions wish to show by their entire bearing that they do not want to recognize the new state of affairs of this country, and, through a series of their actions, they seem to want to start a declared cultural war against the State that so generously pledged itself also to support the cultural interests of the Magyar people. The tendency to open Hungarian confessional schools even in towns located in areas with an overwhelming Romanian majority—in towns where the state still maintains state schools with Magyar as the language of instruction, and where there exist besides these Hungarian state schools, also other Magyar confessional schools—is a provocation which the Romanian State cannot regard with indifference. To admit the multiplication of confessional schools in those places where the State, which must belong to all its citizens, makes the greatest efforts to create also by cultural means peaceful relations of civil life is equivalent to the cultivation of that which divides us rather than that which must bring us together.[181]

Concluding that "some Hungarian secondary schools, far from serving the confessional cultural interests of our Hungarian fellow citizens, tend to be nurseries of centrifugal politics," Ghibu recommended that the Hungarians be allowed to open no more confessional schools "until times have mel-

---

[181] Onisifor Ghibu, "Cea dintâi experienţă politică făcută cu minoritatea maghiară din Transilvania," in *Prolegomena*, pp. 759–760.

lowed" and a study of their needs and those of the state will have been made.[182]

Ghibu was not alone in his views. Other observers agreed that the Hungarians had not appreciated the Directing Council's generous policy of establishing Magyar language schools in the communities and cities with larger Magyar populations. Instead, Hungarian priests had threatened "with anathema the Magyars who sent their children to the state primary school."[183] Protesting the establishment of Magyar language state schools with a standardized Romanian curriculum, the Magyar elites urged their co-nationals to send their children only to the Magyar confessional schools, where the Magyar language, customs, and culture would be preserved.[184] The Hungarian churches, Catholic, Reformed, and Unitarian, opened up new confessional schools and taxed their faithful for them. "The minority schools are alive, while our Magyar sections vegetate without pupils," complained one state inspector.[185] In all of Transylvania there seems to have been a resurgence of confessional schools, the Reformed and Unitarian ones doubling in number from 348 to 690 between 1918 and 1920.[186] Resistance to state policies also expressed itself in the continued teaching of Hungarian history and geography and in the refusal of the confessional school priests and teachers to sign the inspection reports because they were not written in Hungarian.[187]

In some cases, confessional schools also enrolled Romanian pupils, or pupils not of the confession sponsoring a particular school.[188] The Ministry of Education forbade such cross-confessional schooling. Orders no. 100088 and 100099-23 decreed that "each pupil must either go to the school belonging to his own religion or to a State school."[189] The problem was that ethnicity was not always clear. As we have seen, Romanians claimed that Hungarian assimilationist policies had denationalized ethnic Romanians in Transylvania. They considered assimilated Romanians, that is, people who declared themselves Hungarians but who had Romanian names or pasts, to be "hidden Romanians." The Reformed and Unitarian churches complained that "many Hungarian parents are compelled to send their children to Roumanian sections of State schools," a situation

[182] Ibid.

[183] AA IX/ Varia 2, December 30, 1922.

[184] MIC/1922/302/69, October 4, 1922.

[185] AA IX/ Varia 3, December 30, 1922.

[186] Cornish, *Religious Minorities*, p. 77. The breakdown was 322 Reformed and 26 Unitarian schools in 1918, and 641 Reformed and 49 Unitarian ones in 1920.

[187] AA IX/ Varia 2, December 18, 1922.

[188] In Bihor County, thirty girls attending Catholic primary schools by virtue of their parents' "irresponsibility" were forced to withdraw, and Romanian authorities warned the sponsoring monasteries that future admission of Romanian pupils would result in the closing of their schools. AA IX/Varia 2, December 18, 1922.

[189] Cornish, *Religious Minorities*, p. 67.

"frequent in the case of people of the Minority denominations who have Roumanian names, and with those of Gypsy origin." The authorities replied that "the Hungarians were not obliged to send their children to the State schools, but only the children of the Roumanians, of a well proven Roumanian origin, but whose names had evidently been Magyrized." They explained that "the Roumanian state considers that it is its right to bring back to their stock those Roumanians who have been alienated by the Hungarians."[190]

The government went so far as to shut down confessional schools, or what it called "counterschools," institutions that, according to the Romanians, were opened by the Reformed church just to challenge the new Romanian order and to give employment to Magyar teachers who had refused to take the loyalty oath to Romania and were therefore out of jobs. When investigating complaints about the closings, a commission of American and British churchmen were told by the Romanian authorities that these schools "were totally wanting in educational material, had no proper buildings, and worked in the priest's room, in kitchens, sheds, etc." Moreover, Hungarian history and geography were taught instead of the state language and Romanian history and geography, and the whole program was carried on in a Hungarian irredentist spirit.[191]

The dependence of the confessional schools on religious authorities based abroad became a particularly touchy point for the government. The Unitarian, Catholic, and Reformed churches of Transylvania's Magyars and Saxons all depended on hierarchies with headquarters outside of Romania, and they came under constant suspicion of irredentism.[192] Added to an already charged situation, the competition between state and confessional minority schools set the tone of distrust that was to dominate the realm of cultural politics in minority matters in Transylvania. This distrust accounted for the Directing Council's seizure of property from the Hungarian Association of Public Education, Emke, in the fall of 1919.[193] Saxons also fell under some suspicion. Their choral society *Liedertafel* was sequestered early on, and they were not allowed to reopen until it was ascertained that the group functioned without German members and capital.[194]

The National Minorities Treaty signed in Paris on December 9, 1919, gave the minorities in Transylvania a new weapon in their defense of cultural rights. But Romanian authorities felt that the minorities abused

---

[190] Ibid., pp. 110–111.

[191] Ibid., pp. 75–77.

[192] QD 41/194–199R, April 4, 1921, and AA IX/ Varia 3.

[193] Emke was a charitable society whose property derived from private foundations and collections and whose goal was to give aid to poor Hungarian students. QD 41/122–125R, March 11, 1920.

[194] MIC/1919/330/8, February 26, 1919.

and misinterpreted the treaty. They argued that Szeklers and Saxons were wrongly opening not only primary schools in their native tongue, but also "all kinds of secondary schools and even universities with subventions from Berlin and Budapest."[195] The Romanian delegates wanted school autonomy to be a strictly local affair, confined to the commune of residence and to primary education. These schools were not to benefit from foreign stipends, nor were regionwide Saxon and Szekler school organizations to be permitted. Moreover, minority schools had to follow the Ministry of Public Instruction's syllabus and regulations.[196]

Significantly, discussions of the irredentist role of the *Magyar* churches do not always specify the particular denomination in question. Most common are general references to "Magyar" churches, priests, confessions, or confessional schools, as if the national identity of these institutions overrode their denominational difference. In a report from the Oradea region in 1927, for example, the inspector writes that "the schools under the shield of the Catholic and Reformed churches are true hotbeds of hostility toward our country."[197] He then makes the connection between the two churches explicit, saying that, "the misunderstanding between the Reformed and Catholic churches, [which was] so great in the past, has today, under the impact of circumstances, been silenced, and the churches are no longer properly speaking confessional, but rather national, Magyar."[198]

Magyar youth organizations met with even more suspicion than the churches. Whether the societies focused on gymnastics, music, culture, stenography, reading, or general "culture," or claimed to foster knowledge of the national literature, the cultivation of national sentiments, or love of country,[199] authorities suspected them of irredentism. Iuliu Valaori and Constantin Kiriţescu, two Ministry of Public Instruction officials, addressed a confidential report to the Ministry of Interior in 1924. The memo depicted many Hungarian cultural and sports societies in Ardeal as in fact "societies with irredentist tendencies."[200] It was the Ministry of Interior's responsibility to certify these organizations. Although the societies seemed in order from an educational point of view, Valaori and Kiriţescu were convinced that they were a front for activities that threatened state security and they suggested banning or restricting them. Even though

---

[195] QD 41/110–113R, January 12, 1920. The president of the Romanian delegation to the Peace Conference complained too that the Saxons were going to study in Germany, where they participated in pan-German student organizations; as a result, they returned to Romania after their university years "natural agents of German imperialism."

[196] Ibid.

[197] MIC/1927/221/236, May 3, 1927.

[198] Ibid.

[199] MIC/1924/401.

[200] MIC/1924/401/1, January 21, 1924.

the Romanian constitution provided for absolute freedom of association, one could get around that by enforcing the Hungarian laws—formerly used to limit the freedom of assembly of Romanian associations—still in force in Transylvania.[201]

Other school officials agreed with Valaori and Kiriţescu. One inspector, Vasile Candrea, recommended in October 1923 that statutes of cultural, musical, and sports societies at the Reformed Rectory in Cluj not be approved. Although the rules seemed in order, he had been informed that "the instruction at the Gymnastics Circle is done according to standards received from Hungary, from Horthy's organization troops, so that in case of need the pupils from the fifth grade and up could also do military service." During an inspection, Candrea had become "convinced that a well-organized struggle was being waged against the National Romanian sentiment."[202] He argued that even school instruction proper went against the Romanian spirit, for some manuals contained irredentist pieces. Although the offending textbooks and maps were sooner or later confiscated, pupils had continued access to these books at home. The importance of the cultural circles and societies was precisely that they—unlike schools—escaped inspection and could thus complete in somewhat organized fashion the irredentist education that the classroom itself had to limit. Since their statutes stipulated different types of members besides the ordinary ones (supporting, founding, honorary, extraordinary), the role of these societies was that much more suspect, insofar as they seemed to be the perfect "front" for outside agitation.[203]

Feeling harassed, non-Romanian elites found indirect ways to counter their opponents and resist Romanian school policies. In one instance, an inspector from the Cluj region complained that in "the new areas, . . . the cities being populated largely by foreigners, it is very hard for us to obtain buildings. The municipalities are not showing us the least good will."[204] Hungarian teachers and priests could also sabotage the patriotic spirit which the schools were attempting to instill in pupils by refusing to celebrate those Romanian national holidays that commemorated the 1918 union or other important landmarks in the history of Greater Romania.[205]

In Transylvania, as in other provinces, opposition to cultural nationalization policies seemed to come less from the mass of the minority populations than from their notables. The Magyar churches were the most important

---

[201] Ibid.

[202] MIC/1924/401/77–79, October 1923, n.d.

[203] Ibid.

[204] The report suggested that the state itself pay for building new schools and dormitories, or that, as a last resort, in Ardeal towns, buildings be expropriated and used in the cultural interests of the Romanian nation. AA IX/ Varia 2, August 6, 1923.

[205] MIC/1924/213/42, n.d.

institutional setting for resistance to Romanization, but authorities also suspected youth, cultural, sports, and song societies and ethnically defined professional unions of irredentist aims.

Intellectuals in Transition

The process of cultural change in Ardeal was problematic to many Romanian intellectuals of that province. As a group, they were closely involved with the program of Romanization, and they stood to reap its benefits. Yet these men, the local vanguard of the national revolution, found that the transition from a persecuted opposition to the Hungarian state to a group affiliated with the new Romanian state provoked an identity crisis. Their crisis reflects in part the centrality of the *Kulturkampf* in the process of unification of the Ardeal, the crucial role of intellectuals in this transformation, and the direct effect of the changes on this particular layer of Romanian society in Transylvania.

After 1918, the Ardeleni became the main power brokers in Transylvania. A formal and social shift began. Hungarian notables were replaced by Romanians or were required to pledge their allegiance to the Romanian state. Meanwhile, however, Hungarian culture persisted, its prestige intact; the perceived inferiority of Romanian culture persisted as well. This inequality may in fact have been exacerbated by the reversal of political authority. Even observers sympathetic to the Romanian cause, like the French diplomats who hoped to benefit from Romania's expansion, were reserved in their evaluations of Romanian cultural policies in Ardeal. One French diplomat wrote that "the Romanian administration, having deprived the Hungarian colony of its leaders and its intellectuals by its regime of expulsions and evacuations, is trying to destroy it [the Hungarian colony] by the measures taken against the schools and the churches," adding that, "the struggle in Transylvania between the Romanian and Hungarian cultures has its main arena in fact in the universities and the schools."[206] The French Legation reported that the recently created Romanian University of Cluj "will evidently have for some time a slightly artificial character in a city where, in spite of everything, what counts from the intellectual point of view is still Hungarian or German."[207] Describing the expropriation of the former Hungarian state schools and of many confessional schools, the report expressed a mixture of approval and disapproval. On the one hand, French diplomats praised the "policy of Romanizing Transylvania by means of the school and the university," which they

---

[206] QD 41/150–152RV, September 12, 1920.
[207] Ibid.

said, "derived from a just and great idea," and which was in accord with France's interest in the support of Latin culture in Central Europe. On the other hand, the same people had reservations about the clumsy manner in which the Romanian version of "Latin culture" was imposed in Transylvania.[208] In spite of their sympathies, the French found the Romanian approach to *Kulturkampf* heavy-handed, and therefore embarrassing: "Expulsions, evacuations, schools closed down, attacks against the churches, all of these measures are destined to Romanize Transylvania," rued the same report.[209]

By contrast, at least one segment of the Romanian intellectuals of Transylvania—the nationalist militants who had put themselves on the line for the achievement of union with Romania during the period of Hungarian rule—felt that post-union, they lacked direction in the struggle against lingering Hungarian hegemony. They tended to find fault with the Romanian state for not being sufficiently involved with the process of nationalization in their province. As members of a formerly, and still, isolated vanguard, these intellectuals looked for unqualified commitment and leadership from the state they had helped bring to power.

One periodical in particular spoke out on this issue repeatedly: Octavian Goga's *Ţara noastră* (Our Country). *Ţara noastră* was outspokenly nationalist and opposed to the National and later, the National-Peasant parties, which it accused of regionalism. Although the magazine later became quite radical, it was well within the mainstream of Transylvanian public opinion in the 1920s. Articles written in the mid-1920s drew attention to Transylvanian Romanian intellectuals' prolonged discomfort in the face of the difficult process of Romanizing their province. In a 1925 article, "Transylvanian intellectuals after the union," Petre Nemoianu conceptualized the position of these intellectuals, himself undoubtedly among them, as deriving from their "colonizing mission." The colonization of which he spoke was a social process more than a territorial resettlement though migration to cities was also mentioned. Nemoianu compared the plight of these intellectuals with the happier fate of the Romanian peasants. They had "voted for the union, danced the *hora,* and then gone home." The intelligentsia, on the other hand, had "to change [its] whole way of life" following the union.[210]

According to Nemoianu, the Romanian intellectuals in Ardeal had formerly been the cadre of the peasantry. They had now become a distinct stratum whose function it was to exercise the sovereignty of the Romanian state and to prepare the middle layer of which they were themselves the

---

[208] Ibid.
[209] Ibid.
[210] *Ţara noastră,* October 18, 1925.

seed. The intellectuals had been transposed to a "new social continent," which entailed moving to the cities and adopting radically different economic, political, and social goals. Whereas the peasantry had been given the vote and had presumably benefited from land reform without having had to change venue, the intellectuals had to undertake a traumatizing move within the province to an unfavorable—urban—"foreign domain" and had to erect a whole new urban social structure: "In the framework of its new mission, our urban population is not waiting for the elaboration of an already existing household . . . but rather for its very creation. For this purpose it disposes of no support except for that of the official elements . . . Aside from its own labors, [our urban population] is in need of the actual collaboration of the state, until such time as it will have become consolidated into a new social configuration."[211] In Nemoianu's view, the state had not yet done everything it could to strengthen this urban Romanian embryo, although this should have been a priority in any nonpartisan Romanian program. He concluded that "the Romanians in the cities stood in a direct relationship to Romanian rule (*stăpânirea*), which this population could uphold if aided, but bring down (*coboară*) if abandoned."[212]

In a 1924 piece entitled "Transylvania's economic emancipation," Nemoianu had complained that the state was not taking an active enough role in protecting "national intellectual capital," which he deemed to be in more need of protection than Romania's financial capital. He explained that this passive attitude had negative implications for future generations of Romanians since, lacking encouragement, they would not embrace any careers other than ones they had traditionally practiced. The state's neutrality, he wrote, also left the door open to an onslaught of foreigners. Finally, the Romanian state itself would suffer, for Romania—based in the Old Kingdom—would subordinate itself to the more industrially advanced Ardeal, the economy of which was still in the hands of minority elements.[213]

Nemoianu's articles proposed active state intervention to support the Romanian urban intellectual and professional element in Transylvania. They reflect Transylvanian intellectuals' frustration with the insufficient presence, not to say absence, of the state, and they signal the self-perceived weakness of the professional, urban, and intellectual layers of Romanian society in Ardeal. Nemoianu is almost rueing the frailty of Romanian civil society (*avant la lettre*) in 1920s Transylvania.

During the same period, a piece appeared in *Ţara noastră* entitled "The Crisis of the legal profession in Ardeal."[214] The article intimates that Transylvania's Romanian lawyers also had an uneasy relationship to the Roma-

[211] Ibid.
[212] Ibid.
[213] Ibid., January 27, 1924.
[214] Ibid., February 3, 1924.

nian state which constituted a virtual identity crisis. Under the Hungarian regime this profession had represented a real calling. At that time, lawyers had been the "vanguard" of the Romanian urban intelligentsia. They had been forced toward this career, on the one hand, by a Hungarian regime that only allowed Romanian intellectuals to practice the free professions, and, on the other hand, by their desire to defend the rights of their co-nationals. Before 1918, they usually resided in small provincial towns, close to their home villages, earning a secure, if not lavish, existence. They were "a sort of village emissary, having the mission of maintaining contact with a foreign world which was hostile . . . , with which there was no mutual understanding," and which they avoided.[215]

After the union many Romanian lawyers moved to the larger cities. The article described them as troubled not only by their antiminority feelings (exacerbated now by their dwelling in the heart of resilient minority enclaves), but also by their loss of economic security. The Romanian regime, whose support they had counted on, was not sufficiently forthcoming. Under such conditions these lawyers felt that though they were still intermediaries to the cities, they no longer knew between whom and whom. The few openings offered by service to the state, as notaries, for example, were steeped in corrupt politics (*politicianism*), making them not worth considering, and there was not enough of such positions to consolidate a social group (*tagmă*), anyway.[216]

Clearly, these Romanian lawyers of Ardeal were confused by the structural transformations of their society. They had fought for these changes, but had not foreseen the practical results of success, least of all the effects of such success on themselves; they had understandably assumed substantial, even limitless, improvement. Since the source of their dissatisfactions before 1918 had been the Hungarian state, they looked to the Romanian state for redress. Disappointment was inevitable because the expectations of this group were so formless and positive, so thoroughly based on the experience of the past under Hungarian rule, and so little geared to the realities of Greater Romania. The Romanian state seemed unable to provide the unqualified support the Transylvanians sought.

The lawyers' case is a striking example of the crisis of the Transylvanian Romanian intelligentsia. As activists they questioned their role under the new regime that they felt they had to represent. In general, they were often repelled by the practices of this regime, and they were particularly disappointed by the neutral stance the state—in their eyes—adopted toward themselves. They believed that the only possible positive resolution to their

---

[215] Ibid. Other lawyers, of noble descent—therefore Hungarian—monopolized the positions allocated by the state as well as most of the commercial and corporate posts in the large cities.

[216] Ibid.

dilemma could have come from a militant state carrying on the nationalist revolutionary project they themselves had begun. They could represent such a Greater Romanian state in Transylvania without feeling that they were betraying their beliefs and traditions. But the practices of the Bucharest-based government did not endow it with revolutionary righteousness. Most objectionable of all was the apparent lack of interventionism of this seemingly faraway state. The Transylvanians perceived themselves as "going it alone" in the difficult project of urbanizing the Romanians and of Romanizing Transylvania. The dilemma of these intellectuals could make them, along with other dissatisfied groups in Transylvania and elsewhere, amenable to the ideological and political solutions offered by a growing fascist mobilization, the first wave of which was the nationalist student movement.

5

The View from Bucharest:
Foreigners and Jews

[Let the teachers] follow and complete the [work of] the soldiers who died
on the battlefield for the unification of the [Romanian] people, in the sense
of awakening the national consciousness in Romanian souls, to foster this
people; [let it] be shown to them that the cultural training of the villager is
a necessity today, when between Romania's frontiers live people who are
more advanced from a cultural point of view. The weapons with which we
must set off to battle are the souls of the teachers.

—Speaker at a teachers' conference
in Urlaţi-Prahova, 1927

The cultural and educational problems of Greater Romania looked
different to observers in the Old Kingdom (or Vechiul Regat)
than to those in the new provinces. The Old Kingdom was not
properly speaking one province but the historical product of two,
that is, the previous principalities of Wallachia and truncated Moldavia
which had united in 1859. Vis-à-vis the three newly acquired territories,
each with separate personalities, the two parts of the Regat shared an
important institutional history. Thus the Regat became a useful concept
in the interwar period. Although the Regat was just one of the component
elements of the unified state, it was the "center" or the "metropolis" in
terms of the 1918 union, and it made a preponderant contribution to the
formation of Greater Romania (much as Serbia during the same period
contributed disproportionately to the unification of Yugoslavia.)[1]

---

[1] Serbia's overwhelming role in creating and maintaining Yugoslavia has recently come
into focus. Some have proposed changing the country's name to "Serboslavia."

Even discounting the important non-Romanian populations in Greater Romania, the encounter of the Regat and the new provinces was shaped both by the new regions' divergent heritages and by the Regat's dowry. The unification, and the land and electoral reforms with which it coincided, had unexpected effects on the social and educational structures of all the newly united territories. The Regat leadership formulated policies to unify the educational systems of the four Romanian provinces which combined traditional patterns of the Old Kingdom with changes brought about by expansion. Ideologically, the Regat adjusted to becoming the core of a larger and more multiethnic state in part by turning to integral nationalism and an anti-Semitism that built on an older anti-Jewish tradition, and that was nourished after 1918 by the insecurities of expansion and of ethnic dilution.

As described in earlier chapters, Romania's territorial expansion required subsequent educational expansion, especially of secondary schools. In a complementary way, Romanians from the new provinces attempted to emerge inter alia by means of schools and other cultural institutions from their previous subordinate status. Thus the "nationalization" of culture— turning German, Hungarian, and Russian schools into Romanian ones, replacing or supplementing the contents of German, Hungarian, and Russian libraries with Romanian books—received a dual impetus. The process of nationalizing Romania's elites, and the cultural institutions that produced them, implied an attempt to introduce rural Romanians into the urban areas of the new Romanian territories, and it brought with it heated struggles. But whereas the educational and cultural infrastructure clearly had to be recast in the new territories, it is not obvious how or if this process affected the educational landscape of the Old Kingdom itself. The Regat had in fact its own version of these struggles in the period under consideration.

The prominent prewar educator Spiru Haret whose career is discussed in Chapter 1, had attempted to modernize Romanian schools and make them more responsive to the particular needs of his country, especially those of the numerous indigent and illiterate peasants who had erstwhile been neglected. In spite of his affiliation with the National Liberal Party, Haret's persistent concern with the peasantry points to an important populist element in his politics, unthinkable in liberals west of the Elbe. After World War I, the National Liberal Party continued Haret's work by unifying the schools in the Romanian sister provinces under the school system he had created. In the interwar period, however, the social question that had preoccupied Haret was submerged. With the national question in the forefront, the peasants became "the people," and, hence, the Romanian nation. The equation of peasant and nation happens to be embedded in the Romanian lexicon: the Romanian word for peasant, *ţăran,* is derived

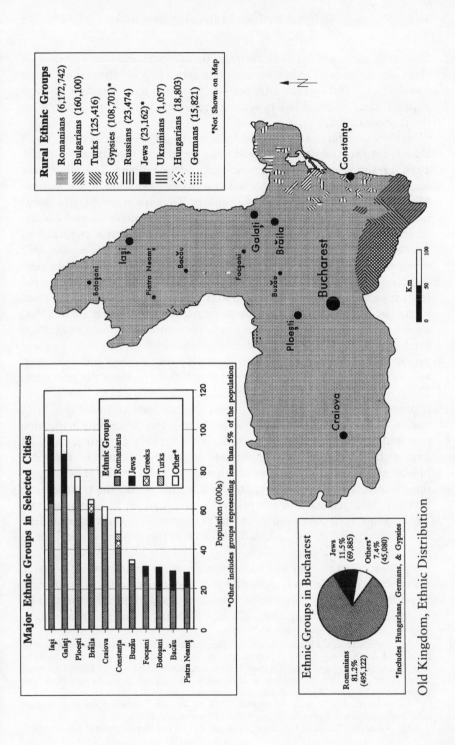

Rural Ethnic Groups

- Romanians (6,172,742)
- Bulgarians (160,100)
- Turks (125,416)
- Gypsies (108,701)*
- Russians (23,474)
- Jews (23,162)*
- Ukrainians (1,057)
- Hungarians (18,803)
- Germans (15,821)

*Not Shown on Map

N

Botoşani
Iaşi
Piatra Neamţ
Bacău
Focşani
Galaţi
Buzău
Brăila
Ploeşti
Bucharest
Constanţa
Craiova

Km
0   50   100

Major Ethnic Groups in Selected Cities

Population (000s)

Iaşi
Galaţi
Ploeşti
Brăila
Craiova
Constanţa
Buzău
Focşani
Botoşani
Bacău
Piatra Neamţ

0   20   40   60   80   100   120

Ethnic Groups
- Romanians
- Jews
- Greeks
- Turks
- Other*

*Other includes groups representing less than 5% of the population

Ethnic Groups in Bucharest

Romanians
81.2%
(495,122)

Jews
11.5%
(69,885)

Others*
7.4%
(45,080)

*Includes Hungarians, Germans, & Gypsies

Old Kingdom, Ethnic Distribution

from *ţară*, the word for both countryside and country or motherland. A close similarity also exists between the term *Român* (Romanian), and *Rumân* (serf). Nationalists after the war exploited these linguistic connections to score political points against those they wished to exclude from the Romanian polity.

Nationalism did not make a sudden appearance in Romania after World War I. Interventionist sentiment during the period of neutrality, 1914–1916, presupposed an existing nationalist public opinion. The subsequent war effort had been widely regarded as a struggle for national unification. Moreover, scholars of turn-of-the-century Romania have already documented the importance of nationalist ideology in defining and linking diverse intellectual movements, and in forming the state's cultural and social policies.[2] In the nineteenth century, there was already a xenophobic nationalism that excluded foreigners, particularly Jews, from many political, economic, social, and cultural activities and rights.[3] Jews were barred from naturalization on the basis of their non-Christianity; as perpetual foreigners they were then kept out of many aspects of Romanian life. But, on the whole, the *role* of nationalism in the effort of national integration in the pre–World War I years differed substantially from that of the postwar period. Before 1916, the state was concerned with its own and Romanian society's stability, the main challenge to which came from the peasantry. The poverty of this class, its lack of enfranchisement, and its illiteracy put it outside the polity. Potentially, then, the peasants constituted a force hostile to the landlords and the state. Fears of such hostility had come true with a vengeance in 1907 when a violent peasant uprising engulfed large parts of the Regat. As discussed in Chapter 1, one of the main objectives of prewar cultural policies had been to diffuse the peasant question, to educate the peasantry, and to integrate it and the populist and socialist intelligentsia into the polity by means of an inclusive national ideology and such populist institutions as cooperatives and village circles.[4] The Jewish question, too, generally came up in this context of rural social and economic problems.

By contrast to this prewar social agenda, the primary task of postwar Romanian nationalism was to fuse the recently unified Romanian provinces by nationalizing their elites, cultural institutions, and urban areas, and by Romanizing or excluding ethnically non-Romanian populations. In part,

[2] See, for instance, Catherine Durandin, "Une image de l'idéologie nationale roumaine: La voie de l'état nation paysan," paper delivered at Table ronde internationale de C. N. R. S., "La Réinvention du paysan par l'état en Europe centrale et balkanique," Paris, December 9–12, 1981; and "Les intellectuels et la paysannerie roumaine de la fin du XIXe siècle aux années 1930," *Revue d'histoire moderne et contemporaine* 26 (1979).

[3] Carol Iancu, *Les Juifs en Roumanie (1866–1919): De l'exclusion à l'émancipation* ([Aix-en-Provence]: Éditions de l'Université de Provence, 1978).

[4] See Durandin, "Image de l'idéologie," esp. pp. 10–12, and "Intellectuels et paysannerie."

the peasant question had been alleviated by the land reform; in part, it was obscured by the pressing need to realize the political unification. Nationalism thus took on political problems instead of social ones, although the political issues that gained primacy in the interwar period did not in themselves lack social content. Most immediately this nationalism focused on the Jews.

The Jewish Presence in the Old Kingdom

While the Romanian majority was the most politically privileged nationality in the Old Kingdom, the Jewish minority was often perceived as more privileged economically, and—in an urbanizing society—socially as well. In old Romania, political, landed, and cultural elites had been Romanian, while the urban and rural middle classes were a mixture of Jews, Romanians, and other nationalities whose Christianity had enabled them to assimilate to a greater degree than the Jews. (See map 6.)

In the Old Kingdom, particularly in Moldavia, the Jews were an important urban presence and a significant segment of the petty commercial and artisanal sector of the economy, although until their emancipation after World War I they were specifically barred from the civil service, teaching, and law. Next to the Romanians, the Jews formed the largest group of the urban population, artisans, and merchants. They were conspicuous by their absence from rural areas and occupations and by their concentration in urban areas and in petty bourgeois occupations in contrast to the Romanians, the overwhelming majority of whom lived in the countryside.[5]

The Jews had lived chiefly in towns, including shtetls and small market towns, since the nineteenth century.[6] In 1859–1860, Jews constituted 3 percent of the Regat population—almost 9 percent in Moldavia and .4 percent in Wallachia. In Moldavia, Jews constituted 47 percent of the population of the capital, Iaşi; 29.7 percent of the district capitals; 26.2 percent of middle-sized towns; and 50 percent of small towns. Jews were only 1.4 percent of Moldavia's rural population. Although only 9,234 Jews lived in Wallachia in 1860, almost two-thirds of these resided in Bucharest, the capital of the recently united principalities. By 1899, the Jewish segment of the population had grown to 4.5 percent—10.5 percent

---

[5] After the war, the Jews were a minority, though often a conspicuous one, in 53 Regat towns. They constituted a majority in 22 other towns, 20 of them in Moldavia. Wilhelm Filderman, "My Life," YV/P 6 Z–I, pp. 474–509.

[6] In 1844, the Jews were forbidden from residing or owning taverns in villages. Even if the law was not strictly enforced, the urban residence pattern of Jews was reinforced. Verax [Radu Rosetti], *La Roumanie et les Juifs* (Bucharest: I. V. Socec, 1903), p. 27.

in Moldavia and 1.8 percent in Wallachia. Jewish inhabitants formed 50.5 percent of the population of Iaşi, 34.5 percent of that of the twelve district capitals in Moldavia, and 39.4 percent of Moldavia's middle-sized towns. In Wallachia, where the total number of Jews had grown significantly—to 68,852—63 percent of them lived in Bucharest and most of the rest in district capitals. After the turn of the century and until World War I, the proportion of Jews decreased slightly, and in 1912 Jews represented 3.3 percent of the Old Kingdom's total population.[7]

The Jewish urban presence increased, to the distress of some Romanians, with the addition of the new territories. Simion Mehedinţi depicted the problem as he saw it in 1923:

> Before the war the area [inhabited by] the Jewish element in Romania looked like this: the black points got closer to each other as you went up the map from Oltenia toward the border with Bukovina; since the Romanian lands have joined the Regat too, the map has darkened even more: Chişinău, Cernăuţi, Satmar, Oradea-Mare, Arad, Timişoara ... lie like large black points on the edges, and if you look at the townlets of Bessarabia, Bukovina, and Maramureş you realize that the flux of Jewish population keeps extending toward the villages too.[8]

With his visualization of "black" Jewish settlements and the "darkening" of Romania's changing map, Mehedinţi, a prominent Romanian geographer and onetime minister of education, described in alarming terms a modern-day *"Jewish invasion,"* the intensity of which, he claimed, reached a climax following the Bolshevik revolutions in Hungary and Russia. *"The Jewish invasion is the greatest event of all the ones that have taken place until now on Romanian soil,"* he wrote. "The Asiatic invasions that historians usually portray uncritically as cataclysms are nothing compared to the great invasion of the nineteenth century."[9] Mehendinţi concluded that Romania was *"the only State on the face of the earth whose towns are for the most part foreign."*[10]

At the beginning of the twentieth century, about three-fourths of the Jewish population lived in the Moldavian part of the Regat, and about 80

[7] Iancu, *Juifs en Roumanie*, pp. 142, 143.
[8] Simion Mehedinţi, "Numerus clausus pentru Români," *Convorbiri literare* 55 (February 1923): 199.
[9] Ibid.
[10] Ibid., p. 200. The author conceded that Poland was in a similar situation. Romanian Jews defended themselves against such assertions, often employing statistics. Wilhelm Filderman, for example, the president of the Union of Romanian Jews, showed that in most of Greater Romania's "foreign"-dominated towns the Jews were themselves a minority, forming less than half the population of 53 of 75 Regat towns, 9 of 12 Bessarabian towns, and 52 of 53 Transylvanian towns. Filderman, "My Life," pp. 474–509.

percent of Jews made their living in the commercial and artisanal economic
sector. In Bucharest, a high concentration of Jews in trade and small
manufacturing coincided with a broader foreign presence. Only 51.5 percent of workers and masters in Bucharest in 1904 were Romanian citizens.
The rest were non-Romanian subjects of which the largest group were the
Jews—17.1 percent. Austro-Hungarian subjects were almost as numerous,
constituting 16.1 percent of all Bucharest artisans; other ethnic groups
completed this variegated community. For the Regat as a whole, Romanians made up 55.4 percent of urban artisans. The remaining 44.6 percent
were foreigners, 21 percent of which were Jewish. Many Jews were also
active as traders, although Romanian merchants were three times as numerous as Jewish ones.[11]

By 1930, Jews constituted 4 percent of Romania's population,[12] but 13.6
percent of the urban population, representing a concentration second only
to ethnic Romanians, who constituted 58.6 percent of the urban population (see table 10). Only 1.6 percent of Romania's rural population was Jewish. The villagers were largely, that is 75.3 percent, ethnic Romanians.[13]

These statistics, and the occupational and geographic distribution of
Jews, were given new meaning by the emancipation of Romania's Jewish
population as a result of the treaties signed with Germany and with the
Allied Powers in 1918 and 1919.[14]

Table 10. The population of the Old Kingdom and Moldavia, by ethnicity, 1930

| | | Old Kingdom | | | | |
		Romanians	Jews	Bulgarians	Turks	Gypsies
Total	8,791,254	7,782,996	252,066	191,125	153,857	137,663
(%)		88.5	2.9	2.2	1.8	1.6
Urban	2,088,594	1,610,254	228,904	31,025	28,441	28,962
(%)		77.1	11.0	1.5	1.4	1.4
		Moldavia				
Total	2,433,596	2,185,632	158,421	—	—	32,194
(%)		89.8	6.5			1.3
Urban	592,127	419,081	136,643	—	—	—
(%)		70.8	23.1			—

Source: Institutul central de statistică, *Recensământul general al populaţiei României din 29 decemvrie 1930,* vol. 2, pp. XXXII–III, XXXVI–VII.

[11] Filderman, "My Life," pp. 242, 243.
[12] ICS, pp. 62, 74.
[13] Dumitru Şandru, *Populaţia rurală a României între cele două războaie mondiale* (Jassy: Editura Academiei R. S. R., 1980), pp. 51, 54.
[14] Iancu, *Juifs en Roumanie,* pp. 271–272.

From the middle of the nineteenth century, Jewish attendance in Romania's public schools fluctuated according to their tolerance in and exclusion from Romanian society, and according to the Jewish community's own traditionalist or assimilationist tendencies. In the interwar period this tension between acceptance and exclusion was exacerbated, for in the changed circumstances the triumph of either tendency seemed imminently possible.

According to the Romanian Jewish historian Elias Schwarzfeld, the golden age of modern Romanian Jewry occurred after 1848 and before Romania's first constitution of 1866.[15] During that time, a modus vivendi existed between the Jewish communities (whose authority over Jews still went largely undisputed) and institutions of local Romanian government, like the police. Certain state institutions helped the community enforce its authority, especially the collection of taxes, which in turn guaranteed the economic survival of Jewish institutions—prayer houses, hospitals, schools, and so on. Although direct taxes were no longer allowed, the *gabela* imposed on kosher meat, poultry, and wine brought an income from which each community could maintain itself.[16] Although the orthodox supported traditional *hadarim,* or religious schools, the Jewish modernizers backed the Israelite-Romanian primary schools, which had government-certified teachers teaching Romanian according to the government's own requirements. Graduates from the latter schools could enroll directly in secondary public schools without further testing.[17] During this period, because of the Israelite-Romanian schools' propitious position, very few Jewish children enrolled in Romanian primary schools.[18]

In those "golden" years, a modern Romanian system of education had not yet appeared. Only in the 1860s, after the union of the Romanian principalities,[19] after the 1864 law on public education which made elementary schooling free and compulsory, and after the inauguration of the constitutional era in 1866,[20] did conditions emerge to bring larger numbers of Jewish children into the public school system. In the 1860s, the government began controlling private schools more carefully,[21] while the advent of the constitution signaled the dissolution of communal privileges and thus the loss of resources necessary to maintain Jewish schools. Meanwhile, however, more public schools were established, which meant public education for larger numbers of children, including Jews.

---

[15] Elias Schwarzfeld, *Chestia şcoalelor israelite şi a progresului israelit în România* (Bucharest: Imprimerie de l'Orient, 1878), p. 6.

[16] Ibid., pp. 6–7.

[17] Ibid., p. 7.

[18] Iancu, *Juifs en Roumanie,* p. 145.

[19] Ion Zamfirescu, ed., *Monografia Liceului "Gh. Lazăr" din Bucureşti, 1860–1935, cu prilejul împlinirii a 75 de ani dela înfiinţarea lui* (Bucharest: Luceafărul, 1935), p. 43.

[20] See Article 23 of the 1866 Constitution, in Iancu, *Juifs en Roumanie,* p. 192.

[21] Zamfirescu, *Monografia,* p. 43.

By specifying that only foreigners of Christian faith could become naturalized Romanian citizens, the 1866 Constitution inaugurated an era of civil limitations for Romanian Jews.[22] Paradoxically, however, exclusion of Jews from schools ended for the first time at this moment. The initial reluctance of Jews to attend state schools soon gave way, and by 1878–1879, 11 percent of the total number of pupils enrolled in urban primary schools were Jewish; in some towns the proportion was as high as 30 to 50 percent. Five years later that had risen to 15 percent— 30 to 75 percent in some towns—since the number of Jewish pupils had almost doubled from 3,805 to 5,969.[23]

Secondary schools saw a similar Jewish "stampede,"[24] and the phenomenon is arguably most significant at this level, certainly in terms of the reaction that it eventually encountered. An interwar Romanian educator, Ion Zamfirescu, has proposed that in Romania the institution of the secondary school reflected the very "structure of bourgeois life":[25] "The same motives, which in the economic sphere lead to protectionist measures or in the political sphere lead to the recognition of all freedoms, in the sphere of school policy lead to the organization of a secondary school closely tied at all times to the interests of the middle classes."[26] Following Zamfirescu, the establishment of new secondary schools in the Regat in the second half of the nineteenth century and the influx of Jewish youth to those schools are developments related to the genesis of the Romanian bourgeoisie. Initially, Zamfirescu argues, urban Jewish merchants participated intensely in this process, as school statistics show. By 1897–1898, the proportion of Jewish youth attending state secondary schools was 11 percent overall. Zamfirescu further implies that the eventual diminution of Jews just before World War I resulted from the advancement of Romania's bourgeoisie.[27]

Detailed ethnic statistics exist for one of Bucharest's best high schools, established in 1859, as the Gymnasium and then Lycée "Gheorghe Lazăr." In 1935, Zamfirescu published an analysis of these statistics in a commemorative monograph about the school. He divides the school's history into three periods: 1859–1890, 1890–1916, and 1916–1934. Jewish enrollments were high in the first period, at an average of 16.5 percent. They dropped in the second period to an average of 7.1 percent, rising again to an average of 20.4 percent of the student body between 1916 and 1934.[28] Leaving the last period aside for the moment, let us look at the pre–World

---

[22] See Iancu, *Juifs en Roumanie,* chap. 2, esp. pp. 63–68.
[23] Ibid., p. 192.
[24] Ibid. The phrase used by Iancu is "une véritable ruée."
[25] Zamfirescu, *Monografia,* pp. 101–102.
[26] Ibid.
[27] Ibid., pp. 145–146, and Iancu, *Juifs en Roumanie,* p. 194.
[28] Zamfirescu, *Monografia,* pp. 148–150.

War I fluctuations. Zamfirescu's periodization highlights the physical move of "Gheorghe Lazăr" from its initial abode in the yard of Old St. George's Church, located in the middle of Jewish and commercial neighborhoods.[29] The school's move in 1889 to the Boulevard Elisabeta in the cultural and political center of Bucharest coincides with its transformation from gymnasium to lycée and, according to Zamfirescu, also with its metamorphosis into a school of the Romanian haut bourgeois and aristocratic elite, which was starting to come into its own. The move from the Jewish and commercial part of town to the capital's gentile institutional center was thus symptomatic of Romania's bourgeois emancipation from Jewish merchant capital. Zamfirescu's analysis is supported by the class and professional profile of the pupils' parents. In the first period, 1859–1890, the largest group of pupils—almost a third of the student body—was composed of sons of medium merchants, of which it is assumed most were Jews.[30]

Although Zamfirescu's periodization is significant from the point of view of the school's history, especially its relocation, it is not entirely germane to the social and ethnic processes for which he tries to account. The Jewish contingent of the student body does not drop sharply in the 1890s either in absolute or in relative terms. In fact, 1897–1898 was the first year since the inception of the school that the Jewish student body reached the figure of one hundred. While there was a slight downward trend in the relative enrollment of Jewish pupils, due mostly to a larger total enrollment, in absolute terms Jews continued their previous levels of attendance. It seems, therefore, unlikely that the school's move had a discouraging effect on Jewish enrollments at "Gheorghe Lazăr." These numbers seem rather to have had their own "natural" limit determined by the size of Bucharest's Jewish bourgeoisie, while the proportion of Romanian pupils could and did reach consistently higher levels of enrollments because of the larger facilities of the new lycée. A definite drop in Jewish enrollments at "Gheorghe Lazăr" came only after the turn of the century: at no time from 1901–1902 until the war years were more than 5.5 percent of all students at "Gheorghe Lazăr" Jewish.[31] Although he records this fact, Zamfirescu denies that the drop in Jewish enrollments at "Lazăr" was motivated by anti-Semitism. According to him, the phenomenon was traceable to the ascendancy of the Romanian bourgeoisie and not to "very pronounced anti-Semitic impulses":

---

[29] For its first year the gymnasium was temporarily housed in the private residence of Boyar Măcescu, but its first permanent location was in the yard of Old St. George's Church. Ibid., pp. 50, 265.

[30] Ibid., pp. 140–141, 145.

[31] Ibid., pp. 148–150.

The Romanian bourgeoisie had started to emerge from the stage in which foreign assistance had been indispensable. . . . The Romanians were seeing themselves in a new country, in full creative activity. It was the fertile epoch in which the doctrine of national feeling was beginning to be woven . . . based on deeper understandings vis-à-vis Romanian sensibilities and potentialities of action. Romania appeared like a fallow field, in which creative actions were expected to be thrust richly and fruitfully. A work of achievements and of Romanian hegemony appeared to the generations like a life credo entrusted to them by the problems of their time.

In the epoch preceding the Great War, "Gheorghe Lazăr" was among the institutions which produced and forcefully sustained this spirit. Of course, in this atmosphere, foreigners could not easily integrate themselves. Around the school a faith had hatched which was instinctively respected by both sides.[32]

Ion Zamfirescu's stress on the national élan of turn-of-the-century Romania and his emphasis on the coming of age of the country's national bourgeoisie in accounting for the reduction in Jewish students at a leading secondary school are very suggestive. But an obvious explanatory element is missing. Zamfirescu overlooks the most direct, and indeed complementary, reason for the drop in Jewish attendance at "Gh. Lazăr." The metaphysical nationalism that the Jews presumably respected by attending in fewer and fewer numbers had concrete administrative and legislative counterparts. Beginning in the 1890s, the Jewish presence in public schools was increasingly left to the discretion of school directors, and Jewish pupils had to pay tuition.

These measures seem to have been a reaction to the ready Jewish embrace of public schools after 1866. According to Elias Schwarzfeld, Jewish public school enrollment was equal to or higher than that of Romanians in relative terms after 1866, especially in the bigger towns where the more cultured and less traditional Jews tended to live. Schwarzfeld, who would have preferred Jews to attend Jewish schools, wrote that, "every year the number of Israelites [in public schools] progresses in a frightening way."[33] He cited the apparently well-known fact that, "in Bucharest, the gymnasium 'Lazăr' and in Iaşi the primary school 'Trei-Ierarhi' and the gymnasia 'Ştefan-cel-Mare' [and] 'Alexandru-cel-Bun' . . . are called Jewish schools." In those schools the number of Jews was apparently often greater than that of gentiles, resulting in some classes having "almost only Israelites."[34] The trend upset those Jews who worried about the dissolution of communal ties.

For their part, Romanian nationalists resented the "invasion of the schools by the Jews," and tried already in the 1880s, before the passage

[32] Ibid., pp. 145–146.
[33] Schwarzfeld, Chestia şcoalelor, p. 24.
[34] Ibid.

of any restrictive legislation, to influence school directors to exclude Jews. The Ministry of Public Instruction itself seemed to concur, sending circulars permitting the rejection of Jewish pupils if schools were overcrowded.[35] The ground having thus been prepared, two school laws passed in 1893—one on vocational education,[36] the other on primary and normal education—incorporated antiforeigner measures aimed at excluding or reducing the number of Jewish pupils. Instrumental in proposing the amendment which contained these restrictions was A. C. Cuza, the father of Romanian anti-Semitism, then a young conservative politician.[37] The "Take Ionescu" law on primary and normal education gave priority in admissions to ethnic Romanians. Foreign children allowed to enroll, if there was room, had to pay tuition. Subsequent modifications of the 1893 law under the ministries of Poni and Haret left this article intact.[38] Secondary and higher-education legislation passed in 1898 under Haret, and all subsequent education laws until World War I, incorporated similar measures.[39] The proportion of Jewish pupils in state secondary schools fell from 11 percent in 1897–1898 to 7.5 percent of the total the next year.[40] A justification for this wave of exclusionary school laws was offered by the ephemeral minister of education Petru Poni, who told parliament in 1896: "Anybody who possesses secondary education in a country is fatefully destined to govern, [and] to control the brakes of that country."[41] The idea that Jews could be in that position while Romania still denied them full political and civil rights of course made no sense.

With education viewed increasingly as a workshop for the forging of a national elite, arguments for using the schools to assimilate Jews lost ground. The childhood experience of Wilhelm Filderman, future leader of the Union of Romanian Jews, is telling. Born in 1882, he was sent by his mother in the late 1880s to a public elementary school, even though a Jewish school was equally close to their home. She clearly thought in assimilationist terms, "that being born in Romania where . . . [her son] would live out . . . [his] life, it was well to know . . . [the country's] people,

---

[35] Iancu, *Juifs en Roumanie,* p. 192.

[36] *L'Indépendance roumaine,* February 8, 1893.

[37] Iancu, *Juifs en Roumanie,* p. 193; I. Ludo, *În jurul unei obsesii* (Bucharest: Editura Adam, 1936), pp. 11–14; Uniunea Evreilor-Pământeni, "Memoriul Evreilor-Pământeni votat de Congresul extraordinar al Uniunei Evreilor-Pământeni dela 3 şi 4 novembre 1913: Legi, regulamente şi măsuri administrative îndreptate împotriva străinilor şi aplicate Evreilor-pământeni," p. 40, YV/P 6 12.

[38] Iancu, *Juifs en Roumanie,* p. 193.

[39] See Uniunea Evreilor-Pământeni, "Memoriul," pp. 40–44, and Iancu, *Juifs en Roumanie,* pp. 194–196.

[40] Iancu, *Juifs en Roumanie,* p. 194.

[41] Quoted in H. Gherner and Beno Wachtel, *Evreii ieşeni în documente şi fapte* (Jassy: n.p., 1939), p. 34.

language, and history."[42] In Filderman's grammar school class there were
only four or five other Jews. In his memoirs he recalls no anti-Semitic
"incidents" or "offenses" either in elementary school or later in high
school.[43]

But by the time Wilhelm's younger cousin, Jacob, was ready to enter
high school some time after 1897, the situation had changed. To enter the
lycée, Jacob had to take an exam, even though he had had a 95 percent
average; he was refused two years in a row by the director who was
authorized to give first priority to Romanians and admit foreigners only
if there were enough available places. Jacob finally tried out for the School
of Commerce. The director here made remarks about the admission exam
classroom "smelling Jewish," but many more Jews were admitted because
there were fewer Romanian candidates. Jewish boys also began to attend
two private Jewish gymnasia, "Cultura" and "Libros," established by
wealthy Jews in the aftermath of the exclusionary legislation. Looking
back at the period after 1898, Filderman observed that "state public schools
were closed to us [Jews], and unimaginable obstacles were placed in the
way of the development of our own school establishments." The Jewish
minority was the only one not to receive any state subsidy; degrees from
Jewish schools were not always recognized, making it necessary for their
graduates to pass expensive state exams to certify their diplomas; and Jews
were not admitted to teaching seminaries, making the training of teachers
for the Jewish community a problem.[44]

An atmosphere of high-pitched nationalism or, as others saw it, an
"enseignement du mépris" for the Jews,[45] was manifested in petty verbal
harassment by anti-Semitic teachers and textbooks and clearly played a
role in alienating Jews from Romanian public schools. But the exclusionary
legislation that began in 1893 and was extended to secondary schools in
1898 should be considered directly responsible for the sharp drop in Jewish
attendance in secondary schools such as the Lycée "Gheorghe Lazăr" at
the turn of the century. The laws must also have given a signal that informal
anti-Semitism was acceptable.

The exclusionary measures legitimized by the emerging nationalist ideology had the practical effect of relieving the "tragic school situation"—the
overcrowded schools and rampant illiteracy that had so struck Spiru Haret
at the beginning of his career.[46] The laws of 1893, 1896, 1898, and 1899,

---

[42] Filderman, "My Life," pp. 1, 5.
[43] Ibid., pp. 5, 8.
[44] Ibid., p. 444.
[45] Iancu, *Juifs en Roumanie*, p. 195.
[46] Durandin, "Image de l'idéologie," p. 12.

drafted with Haret's collaboration or under his ministry and intended to correct these conditions all contained exclusionary clauses.[47]

The secondary literature on Spiru Haret focuses on his educational and social ideas and achievements, especially (as discussed in Chapter 1) his broadening of the school's radius to reach the peasants not just as temporary schoolgoers but as a class with well-defined social and economic needs. Authors concentrating on the social aspect of Haret's work in the context of the 1907 peasant revolt are aware of the nationalism mixed in with Haret's social concerns. Philip Eidelberg, for instance, notes the cooperative movement's "very strong note of nationalism, usually expressed in an attack on the foreign *arendaşi* [leaseholders]." He observes further that "Haret did not declare war on the *arendaşi* as a class, but only on those who were foreign."[48] Although the "foreigners" among the *arendaşi* were not only Jewish, but also, in Wallachia, Bulgarian and Greek, Haret was most adamant about the Jews concentrated in Moldavia, who, he warned, might have an "understanding [with each other] . . . to eliminate the Rumanian *arendaşi.*" According to the ideologues of the popular banks and village cooperatives, Romanian peasants and landlords shared interests opposed to those of the foreign *arendaşi.*[49] Romanian *arendaşi* could in principle redeem their position by buying the land they were leasing, a choice not legally open to "foreigners."

Although little has been written on Haret's stance toward Jews in educational institutions, the laws and regulations passed during Haret's three ministries were all intended to protect and give preferential treatment to ethnic Romanians and thus they encouraged barring Jews from public schools. Such exclusion would have been compatible with Haret's "social nationalism" in the peasant question, his concern with the education of peasants as part of the solution to their economic plight, and with the Liberal Party's interest in building up the national economy by excluding foreigners from land ownership, some forms of trade, and the professions.

After the Great Union of 1918, Romanian peasants and the urban Jews, in different ways, became even more relentlessly the object of nationalist discourse. As the land reform alleviated the most blatant inequalities of rural society, nationalists increasingly depicted residual rural misery as the fruit of "foreign" urban domination. Moreover, politicians began encouraging peasants to aspire to positions in the urban Romanian elite that was to expand in order to achieve dominance throughout the new Romania.

[47] Ibid.
[48] Philip Gabriel Eidelberg, *The Great Romanian Peasant Revolt of 1907: Origins of a Modern Jacquerie* (Leiden: Brill, 1974), pp. 119, 120.
[49] Ibid., pp. 122, 124–125.

Peasants and Jews

The two emancipations, that of the peasantry through land reform and universal male suffrage and that of the Jews by mass naturalization, resulted inter alia in a social transformation of the school population. After the war, schools in the Old Kingdom faced the dual influx of peasants and Jews. The two groups of newcomers met with quite different receptions: whereas many school officials felt the Jewish presence to be illegitimate and unbalancing to the school's social and cultural function of Romanian elite formation, the peasants enjoyed an a priori welcome as a rich national reservoir from which the Romanian elite might replenish its ranks and draw strength to counter the "foreign" Jewish invasion.

Authorities reluctantly dismantled the legal bulwarks against "foreigners" erected before the war. Old habits nevertheless lingered, and discriminatory practices against Jews continued. In 1919, for instance, in Bârlad, gentile and Jewish students had to take gymnasium entrance exams separately, and in Botoşani, Jewish candidates were still considered "foreign" and excluded from schools despite receiving passing grades on admissions exams.[50] But school officials sensed that restrictive "administrative measures" directed at the "new citizens—the Jews" would eventually have to cease, since they were "demanding their rights in the state school."[51] They thought of the impending larger Jewish presence as a necessary evil which they hoped nonetheless to block with the peasantry, Romania's ethnic reservoir.

This type of thinking is evident in the *exposé de motifs* to the draft bill for the reform of secondary education of 1928. Constantin Angelescu described the country's shortage of qualified cadre and his hope for relieving it with the peasantry's help. He wrote that with the two great reforms (electoral and land), the war had "awakened the consciousness of the popular masses and opened up new perspectives and paths to them." Having been called to "public life," the Romanian peasantry could contribute its ethnic essence to the state if it renounced its previous latent life. "Our peasantry, today well-to-do, is longing for culture and civilization. This phenomenon is that much more interesting and gratifying since this peasantry constitutes not only an immense reservoir of energies, but also, at the same time, the purely Romanian element from which the cadre for the national organization of the Romanian state can be drawn up."[52]

[50] AIU/VIII C53, n.d.

[51] See MIC/1918/253A/266–271, November 10, 1918, Dumitru M. Cădere's memorandum to the minister of cults and instruction on "the question of establishing preparatory schools and higher normal seminaries."

[52] Ministerul instrucţiunii, *Proect de lege asupra învăţământului secundar teoretic* (Bucharest: Cartea românească, 1928), p. 4.

As the previous discussion of Haret reveals, the peasants had been under-schooled before the war. Distance and expense tended to discourage rural youth from attending high schools generally located in towns. Simion Mehedinți railed against the policies that had deprived the Romanians of a professional and urban elite—too few accessible schools and scholarships meant that the competitive odds against rural youths were overwhelming:

> Instead of feeling that the towns cannot be Romanized without our seeking the help of the villages; instead of understanding that we cannot have plenty of merchants, industrialists, architects, doctors, magistrates, professors, and everything a modern country needs, unless we mobilize the rural stratum by as thorough an education as possible in school, our politicians were so myopic that they did not even let those children who somehow managed to finish the elementary school grades in the village into towns [for further study]. . . . In addition to economic serfdom, we had therefore condemned our people to eternal cultural serfdom as well.[53]

Mehedinți contended that "by crowding all the secondary schools into towns, Romania's leaders had subjected the entire mass of the Romanian peasantry to *numerus clausus*. The whole rural layer had to pass through the narrow pass of the few dozen scholarships, while the millions who could not squeeze through had to remain outside the sphere of culture."[54]

For Mehedinți, as for many others, "the cultural question" was tied to that of the towns. Had peasants in old Romania been able to pursue a secondary education, he argued, the towns would have become almost entirely Romanian by 1916.[55] Although reviling prewar politicians, Mehedinți's real focus in 1923 was the postwar situation, in which peasants' access to schools was still far from satisfactory. The very title of his article, "Numerus clausus for Romanians," and the reference in the text to a *numerus clausus* supposedly applied to Romanian peasants are clear allusions to the nationalist student slogan launched a year earlier to demand a quota on the number of Jews admitted to the universities—*numerus clausus*. Implicitly, Mehedinți's criticism of policies that restricted educational opportunities for villagers signaled agreement with the nationalist students. To leave no doubt about his position, however, Mehedinți introduced the Jewish theme—the obsession of the students—directly: "Had the Jews been the ones to look after Romanian education until now, had they put all the secondary schools in the cities, and had they forced the children of rural [inhabitants] to pass through the Caudine forks of the

---

[53] Mehedinți, "Numerus clausus pentru Români," p. 202.
[54] Ibid., p. 203.
[55] Ibid.

few dozen scholarships, of course all the indignation would be directed at the Jews."[56] In this view, the Jews and the peasants were pitted against each other, representing bad and good solutions to the problem of national development. Mehedinți called for a *"numerus maximus* [for Romanians] in all the institutions of culture in order to keep for the Kingdom its Romanian character and to guide its destiny according to our ethnic ideal. The great hope is, therefore, in the growth of the Romanian population and of the villagers' culture."[57] Mehedinți appealed to the "new generation" to expiate the sins of its parents and compensate for the myopia of contemporary politicians "by the most energetic and systematic national offensive." The final words of his article, "face to the village!"[58] summarized Mehedinți's implicit agenda of militant Romanization.

"Face to the village" also describes the program of other personalities, school administrators, and members of the Romanian rural elite. Starting from the fact that only nine percent of primary school graduates went on to secondary schools, Dumitru Cădere, a Ministry of Education official, proposed in a 1918 memorandum doubling the number of seminaries, gymnasia, and normal schools.[59] He analyzed the problem from a "social and ethical" point of view, showing that villagers had no local secondary schools and that few of them could afford to send their children to town as boarders, an undesirable situation in any case, since rooming houses were "hotbeds of physical and moral destruction." According to Cădere, the "time had come to give the villager his own secondary school, in the middle of large villages, in an atmosphere that agrees with him, and without endangering the health and soul of the children." He rounded out his "social and ethical" arguments with national ones:

> By the creation of the new Romanian citizens—the Jews—who were until now kept away from the secondary school by measures of an administrative nature, but who will also be claiming their rights in the future inside the state school, the access of village sons to gymnasia and even normal schools is even more endangered; this danger is especially threatening to the towns of Moldavia, where in a few years the majority of the school population in gymnasia and lycées will be of Semitic origin. Nobody can remain impassive in the face of this prospect. The creation of new but still urban gymnasia will not solve the problem; while the creation of such schools in villages, where the Jewish population is so far still rare, will give an opportunity to the Romanian element to penetrate into all categories of schools.[60]

[56] Ibid., pp. 203–204.
[57] Ibid., p. 204.
[58] Ibid.
[59] MIC/1918/253a/266–271, November 10, 1918.
[60] Ibid.

Others portrayed this problem in more emotional ways. In 1922, the director of a lycée in Galaţi, in southern Moldavia, complained that Romanians had been driven to the edge of town by economic factors he left unnamed. He feared that, at this rate, the Romanians would become "extra muros," and he advocated the cultural fortification of Galaţi so that it might become "a bulwark to the waves from without and the waters from within, which wear away at our foundations."[61] The "waves" and the "waters" were "foreigners" and their "crazy ideas." Galaţi would then be *"like a fire on a mountaintop,"* "a true Roman camp of our culture [and] . . . national sentiment."[62] The director went on to suggest that Romanians were becoming *extra muros* in the schools as well. He asked pointedly whether "in the heat of the terrible competition which the co-inhabiting foreign peoples engage us in, are we not alienating from the arena of struggle [persons of] value . . . left to wander away? And for the most part, [are these not] *children from the country,* less polished, superficially less quick, but who have in them the inner strength of our plains?" Against the backdrop of this rhetoric he requested the expansion of the lycée and the establishment of two more gymnasia, one more lycée, and a dormitory for boarders. The letter concluded: "Only with the rural element will we conquer the cities for our Nation."[63]

Such requests and complaints came not only from Moldavia, where Jewish settlement was densest, but also from Wallachia, where the Jewish communities were quite small. A 1923 petition for the opening of a gymnasium in the commune of Zătreni, in Vâlcea County, mentioned the need to develop the peasants' culture as a way to safeguard the political structure of the state against the co-inhabiting national minorities.[64] Obstacles to the cultural development of the peasants included the long distances from villages to the closest town, the noisy and cosmopolitan nature of existing cultural centers, and the high cost of urban living, which caused peasants' resources to end up in "the pockets of speculators, especially foreigners." The petitioners wrote:

> In any commune, it is therefore rare for anyone to be found whose child is in a higher level school. . . . For these reasons, in this region, culture is inaccessible to distinguished elements . . . from the rural population, so that many talent[ed persons] among the people are languishing, condemned to lead an inferior life, while [other] mediocre or even inferior elements manage

---

[61] AA VI/ Varia 17, n.d.

[62] Ibid. The word I translated as "Roman camp" is *castru* from the Latin *castrum,* evoking the Latin origins of the Romanian people.

[63] Ibid.

[64] MIC/1923/476/9–18, March 15, 1923.

to educate themselves because they dispose of sufficient material means, [and] later inundate the professions and administration of the country.

So, the foreigners who have taken over our industry and commerce, and who live in the towns, can cultivate themselves more easily; in this way we will come to the point shortly that the administration will be in their hands, which means on top of economic domination, also cultural and administrative [domination]. The recent student movements are proof that the foreigners have flooded secondary and higher education and that they tend in this way to make out of our political rule a mere shadow. The only solution for remedying and preventing this wrong, that we see, is in moving the cultural centers in the midst of the village population.[65]

Secondary school authorities also worried that an influx of "foreign" pupils and teachers would taint the atmosphere in the schools. Some wanted the cultural "gates" to remain closed as long as Romanian culture was not fully consolidated. This consolidation would eventually enable secondary schools to "bear the desired fruit," but only if the necessary steps were taken to strengthen native culture by "calling on the villages, even forcing them" to participate in the nation's cultural life. It was important that this take place soon, before the mentality of the educators was itself transformed.[66]

In 1924, Minister of Education Constantin Angelescu expressed his own eagerness to replace "those in the annexed territories who hold the entire commerce and entire industry in their hands with Romanian elements." To this end, he advocated an increase in applied schools and the proliferation of boarding secondary schools:

It is no longer permissible today that a secondary school not have a dormitory. Only in this way, will we be able to give children from the country a chance to come to the cities to get schooling . . . And this . . . is of capital importance in the annexed territories. I have requests from all areas, every day, to create new dormitories; many of you come to the Ministry and ask me to create, as quickly as possible, those boarding schools, because there is no place for their [sic] children, in those towns [which are]—permit me [to use] the word—abroad.[67]

The desired solutions differed. But the concern with a "foreign" infestation of the schools and the worry about the schools' urban and "foreign" environments were widespread. Undoubtedly, this alarm was aggravated

[65] Ibid.
[66] AA VI/ Varia 17, n.d. Concretely, it was suggested that urban lycées all add dormitories to enable villagers to send their offspring to secondary schools.
[67] Ministerul instrucţiunii, *Lege,* p. 163.

by the incorporation of the new provinces, whose urban and secondary school populations were at first predominantly non-Romanian. The Old Kingdom appropriated the problem of the foreign elites in the new territories by a renewed emphasis on the "otherness" of native Jews, who since the nineteenth century had constituted a substantial urban and school presence and whose newly gained civil and poltical rights turned them into even more formidable and disliked competitors. It was the Old Kingdom, threatened with the potential ethnic dilution posed by the new territories and by its newly enfranchised Jewish citizens, that was most influential in promoting and indeed glorifying the culture of the Romanian peasantry.

II

STUDENT

NATIONALISM

6

The Universities:
Workshops for a National Elite

Within the boundaries of a unitary state like ours the University, as an emanation of this state, can naturally be nothing other than national. This is the spirit that created it, and to this spirit it must remain forever true.
                                                              —Ion Nistor, 1920

Whereas cultural institutions were generally important in the process of nation building in interwar Romania, the country's universities were particularly significant in the creation of elites. It was here that future educators, bureaucrats, lawyers, engineers, doctors, academics, and journalists of Greater Romania were trained. The universities grew in response to the need for larger numbers of Romanian professionals and functionaries after 1918, but they still could not meet the demand. The larger student bodies at universities and the consequent overcrowding apparently resulted from a spontaneous social response to the opportunities and rhetoric of national expansion.[1]

I purposely excluded higher education from the earlier regional discussion of cultural struggles, for the universities and other post-secondary schools form a separate category from primary and secondary schools. First, there were only four universities in Greater Romania, whereas there were thousands of primary and secondary schools. Second, higher educa-

---

[1] For a discussion of higher education in four European countries, see Konrad H. Jarausch, "Higher Education and Social Change: Some Comparative Perspectives," in Konrad Jarausch, ed., *The Transformation of Higher Learning, 1860–1930: Expansion, Diversification, Social Opening, and Professionalization in England, Germany, Russia, and the United States* (Chicago: University of Chicago Press, 1983). On the development of German universities and the enrollment explosion there mostly in an earlier period, see Jarausch, *Students, Society, and Politics in Imperial Germany: The Rise of Academic Illiberalism* (Princeton, N.J.: Princeton University Press, 1982), esp. chap. 2.

tional institutions attracted a more national clientele than primary and secondary schools, which recruited mostly locally. Third, since university students were of a political—and volatile—age, educational and cultural problems were more directly and rapidly politicized in the universities than in the schools: issues which in lower schools had at least the appearance of pedagogical debates were more nakedly ideological and political in the universities. The universities, moreover, became the locus of a self-consciously generational politics whose protagonists, the students, identified themselves as members of the "new generation," which fought not only for certain concrete goals but also against the older generation and its political style.

Prewar Higher Education in the Old Kingdom

The universities of the Old Kingdom were established in 1860 and 1864 in Iaşi and Bucharest, respectively, soon after the unification of the two principalities. The first Romanian university opened in Iaşi, the former Moldavian capital, just after Moldavia unified with Wallachia.[2] A project for instituting a single national university with branches, or *facultăţi,* in both Iaşi and Bucharest was considered between 1860 and 1864, but this idea died with the inauguration of Bucharest University in July 1864.[3] Thereafter, the two universities remained autonomous.

The founding of the two universities was the culmination of educational developments begun in the sixteenth century when princely academies were first established to teach the sons of the nobility the educated languages of the day—Greek, Latin, and Old Church Slavonic. In both principalities, princely academies came and went, affected by religious conflict and the political fortunes of various rulers.[4] In 1828, a Romanian school to train clerks for Moldavia's civil service opened at the Trei Ierarhi Monastery in Iaşi followed by Academia Mihăileană in 1835.[5] Public service in the

[2] D. Berlescu, "Universitatea din Iaşi de la 1860 pînă la 1918," in *Contribuţii la istoria dezvoltării Universităţii din Iaşi 1860–1960,* vol. 1, Universitatea Al. I. Cuza, Iaşi, Studii (Bucharest, 1960), pp. 101–103; and Marin Popescu-Spineni, *Instituţii de înaltă cultură* (Vălenii-de-Munte: Datina românească, 1932), p. 29.

[3] Berlescu, "Universitatea," p. 121. A *facultate* is a department or school teaching a particular branch of knowledge; but here it also refers to different branch locations of one national university.

[4] Ion Ionaşcu, "Academia domnească şi Colegiul Sf. Sava din Bucureşti," in Ion Ionaşcu, ed., *Istoria Universităţii din Bucureşti,* vol. 1 (Bucharest: Tip. Universităţii din Bucureşti, 1977), p. 3; C. Cihodaru, "Învăţământul în Moldova în sec. XV–XVIII. Şcoala domnească din Iaşi," in *Contribuţii,* vol. 1, pp. 13–15; and Vlad Georgescu, *The Romanians: A History* (Columbus: Ohio State University Press, 1991), p. 112.

[5] Some historians consider Academia Mihăilenă a university-level establishment. Valerian Popovici, "Învăţămîntul în limba naţională pînă la 1860," in *Contribuţii,* vol. 1, pp. 39, 50–55.

Danubian Principalities was soon off limits to those without academic diplomas. Before modern universities opened in the principalities in the 1860s, many sons of gentry went abroad to earn their education.[6]

The two Romanian universities were preceded by the establishment of individual *facultăți* that developed initially as advanced courses within secondary schools. The first institution to anticipate the founding of Iaşi University was the Law School, which opened in 1856, followed by Philosophy a year later. By 1860, Iaşi University had three schools: Law, Letters and Philosophy, and Sciences. It added a Medical School in 1879. In Bucharest, the Law School was organized in 1859, followed by the School of Letters and Philosophy in 1860 and by the School of Sciences in 1864.

The fact that few people had a higher education in mid–nineteenth century Romania was related to the country's backward economy and thus limited positions in the professions and administration. But there may have been boyar resistance to the government's increased emphasis on clerks possessing diplomas.[7] Educated people were more often employed in administration than in the professions; thus, from the beginning of modern higher education in Romania, its main orientation was toward the civil service. Barbu Ştirbei, prince of Wallachia from 1849 to 1856, and an early reformer of secondary and higher education, wrote that his reforms were mainly "geared toward secondary schools and higher education [which was] destined to train special people for the different public departments." By this he meant lawyers most of all.[8] Given this context, it is not surprising that university enrollments were much lower in Iaşi, which had lost the status of political capital with the union of the principalities in 1859, than in Bucharest, which had gained in prestige and bureaucracy by becoming the capital of a much larger state. As elsewhere in Europe, these patterns indicate the firmly entrenched relationship between university training and state employment.[9]

The difference in the size of enrollments between the two universities widened particularly after the turn of the century, reflecting the progressive development of Bucharest as the undisputed cultural and political capital of the United Principalities. Iaşi University opened with 80 students in

[6] R. W. Seton-Watson, *A History of the Roumanians from Roman Times to the Completion of Unity* (Cambridge: Cambridge University Press, 1934), p. 217; Cihodaru, "Invăţămîntul," p. 14; Andrew Janos, "Modernization and Decay in Historical Perspective: The Case of Romania," in *Social Change in Romania, 1860–1940: A Debate on Development in a European Nation*, ed. Kenneth Jowitt (Berkeley: Institute of International Studies, University of California, 1978), p. 80; and Popovici, "Învăţămîntul," pp. 49–50.

[7] Janos, "Modernization," p. 81, and Popovici, "Învăţămîntul," p. 60.

[8] Ionaşcu, "Academia domnească," pp. 99–100.

[9] For comparisons to the Hungarian universities of Budapest and Cluj, see Andrew Janos, *The Politics of Backwardness in Hungary, 1825–1945* (Princeton, N.J.: Princeton University Press, 1982), pp. 42–43, and Stelian Neagoe, *Viaţa universitară clujeană interbelică*, vol. 1 (Cluj: Editura Dacia, 1980), pp. 30–31.

Table 11.   University enrollments in Bucharest and Iaşi, before 1918

	Bucharest	Iaşi	Bucharest as percentage of Iaşi (%)
1864–1865	143	56[a]	255.4
1871–1872	316	160	197.5
1876–1877	398	171	228.1
1888–1889	517	225	229.8
1898–1899	3,109	511	608.4
1905–1906	4,118	495	831.9
1915–1916	4,380	—	—

Sources: D. Berlescu, "Universitatea din Iaşi," p. 183, and Alexandru Balaci and Ion Ionaşcu, eds., *Bucharest University,* p. 43.
   [a] Figure for 1863–1864.

1860–1861, and had an entering class of only 29 in 1865–1866. Its freshman classes fluctuated but never went above 100 before the 1890s. The total number of registered students varied from 56 in 1863–1864 to a high of 652 in 1901–1902, dropping again to between 480 and 555 in the years before World War I.[10] Bucharest University opened with 143 students in 1864–1865. The number of students there continued to rise, surpassing four thousand in the years before the Great War (table 11).

Continuing an earlier pattern, many Romanians swelled the ranks of the educated by studying at universities abroad. For example, between 1895 and 1915, 35.2 percent of Romanian parliamentarians had studied in West European universities. According to Andrew Janos, "up until the end of the nineteenth century, most members of the [Romanian] upper classes received their education in France and other West European countries."[11]

By far the most popular university department in the nineteenth century, probably because it constituted the entry to government positions, was law. The total number of first-year enrollments at Iaşi University between 1860 and 1894 was 2,382 students, of whom 1,034 (or 43.4 percent) entered law, 531 (or 22.3 percent) letters and philosophy, 471 (or 19.8

---

[10] Berlescu, "Universitatea," pp. 182–183, 189–194. Actual attendance at the University of Iaşi was even lower than the enrollment statistics show. Of the 360 students enrolled in law from 1860 to 1870, only 22 had been able to pass all required examinations. For the same period, in letters and philosophy only 3 students of 118 had passed all their exams. In the sciences only 3 students out of 60 passed all required exams. For Iaşi University enrollments, see also Gheorghe Platon, "Universitatea din Iaşi în epoca de constituire a României moderne (1860–1918): I. Condiţiile materiale, legislaţie, structură," in *Istoria Universităţii din Iaşi,* ed. Gheorghe Platon and Vasile Cristian (Jassy: Editura Junimea, 1985), p. 82.

[11] Janos, "Modernization," p. 107.

A. C. Cuza in front of a group of his Iaşi Law School students (1913). Courtesy of Cabinetul de Stampe. Biblioteca Academiei Române, Bucharest

percent) sciences, and 346 (or 14.5 percent) medicine—a department started in 1879.[12] Law continued to be popular later on, too. Between 1898 and 1908, 701 first-year students enrolled in law as opposed to 344 in letters and philosophy, 324 in sciences, and 384 in medicine.[13]

The close relationship between higher education and the civil service in Romania in part explains the small number of Jews in higher education before 1918, since Romania's Jews were not yet emancipated. In the nineteenth century, the Ministry of Education instructed the School of Letters and Philosophy in Bucharest, which trained high school teachers, to turn away Jewish candidates on the grounds that higher education was not only an intellectual but also a moral training, and that teachers had to be "national personalities."[14] In June 1865, the Ministry of Education advised the rejection of a Jewish candidate from admission to the teacher qualifying exams, arguing

[12] Berlescu, "Universitatea," pp. 182, 183.
[13] Ibid., pp. 182, 195. These statistics are somewhat skewed because many law students obtained second degrees in letters and philosophy. Ibid., p. 183.
[14] Popescu-Spineni, *Instituţii*, p. 32.

that . . . the fundamental law of our country excludes from political rights those who are not Christian; . . . that the teacher is bound to the exercise of the most interesting political rights; . . . that the school is intended to impart not only science, but also the education which, for each people, has to be national; . . . [and] that, if the preceding consideration is true of all professions, it is that much more weighty when Philosophy is in question, which is closely related to religion.[15]

Jews were not only barred from degrees leading to teaching positions. Since they could not become civil servants, they had little reason, not to mention opportunity, to study law. According to D. Berlescu, "[With] the . . . state refusing Jews the right to occupy public functions, their presence in the Schools of Sciences, Letters, and Law could only have been an exception." Between 1860 and 1895, about twenty Jews enrolled in these schools at Iaşi University and only three of them completed their studies.[16]

Jews did attend schools of medicine in larger numbers, for medical school prepared them for a profession unrelated to the civil service. The medical degree allowed them to practice without too much interference from the state. By 1893, at the University of Bucharest Medical School Jews formed 34.4 percent of the student body, whereas in Iaşi they constituted 44.9 percent of a smaller total number of medical students.[17]

Among 654 new and continuing students at the University of Iaşi in 1899–1900, there were 101 "foreigners," presumably mostly Jews. Of these, 71 were in the Medical School.[18] The high proportion of Jewish medical students, however, prompted attempts to limit their admission through the imposition of extremely high tuition payments for foreigners.[19]

Student societies also tried to exclude Jews. In 1875, the Iaşi University Students' Club adopted a clause restricting membership to Romanians. A group of revolutionary socialists within the club favored an ethnically open membership. These debates and struggles led the nationalists to defect and found new organizations—Naţionalitatea (Nationality), Solidaritatea (Solidarity), Comitetul naţional studenţesc (the National Student Committee), and Zorile (Dawn); these came under the influence of Nicolae Iorga

---

[15] Quoted in ibid., pp. 32–33.

[16] Berlescu, "Universitatea," p. 191.

[17] Carol Iancu, *Les Juifs en Roumanie (1866–1919): De l'exclusion à l'émancipation* ([Aix-en-Provence]: Éditions de l'Université de Provence, 1978), p. 194.

[18] Berlescu, "Universitatea," p. 192.

[19] The progressively higher fees in the Letters, Law, and Medical schools, respectively, were imposed on the basis of the 1898 Law on Secondary and Higher Education. It stipulated that foreigners' sons could be admitted to institutions of higher learning to the extent that native needs were satisfied first. The state would have to provide a free education only to "the sons of Romanians." Ibid., p. 193, and Iancu, *Juifs en Roumanie*, p. 194.

A. C. Cuza and Nicolae Iorga (1913). Courtesy of Cabinetul de Stampe. Biblioteca Academiei Române, Bucharest

and Alexandru C. Cuza.[20] At least before the end of the century, then, the socialists apparently had the upper hand within the main student club at Iași University. Socialist proposals for disregarding nationality as a criterion for membership in the student societies, however, repeatedly failed to pass. As late as 1913, a student circle at the University of Iași excluded Jews from membership.[21] Moreover, Centrul studențesc universitar Iași (the University Student Center of Iași), founded in 1909 as a branch of the General Society of All Romanian Students, and having exclusive representation of the student body at Iași University beginning in 1910, also promoted "chauvinism, a nationalism often grafted on a ferocious anti-Semitism, as advocated especially by their professor A. C. Cuza." Through manipula-

---

[20] On the early anti-Semitism of Iorga and Cuza, see Leon Volovici, *Nationalist Ideology and Antisemitism: The Case of Romanian Intellectuals in the 1930s* (Oxford: Pergamon, 1991), pp. 18, 22–28, 31–33; William Oldson, *The Historical and Nationalistic Thought of Nicolae Iorga* (Boulder, Colo.: East European Monographs, 1973), pp. 84–88; and Oldson, *A Providential Anti-Semitism: Nationalism and Polity in Nineteenth-Century Romania* (Philadelphia: American Philosophical Society, 1991), pp. 132–137.

[21] Berlescu, "Universitatea," pp. 204–212, and (AIU)/VII/C/42, February 12, 1913. Socialists were in fact responsible for interuniversity contacts between Iași and Bucharest until 1880, when a countrywide student society was established, also under socialist influence.

tion, the Iaşi Center managed to obtain and keep the right of representa-tion.[22]

Unlike the general student societies, the medical students' societies were primarily centers of socialist activity. In Bucharest, socialists led the Society of Medical Students founded in 1875.[23] At the University of Iaşi a similar society established in 1894 was open to students of all ethnic groups. Although such tolerance made sense in view of the large concentration of Jewish students in the medical school, nationalists opposed this liberal membership policy and eventually founded a separate organization called Societatea studenţilor în medicină români (the Romanian medical students' society).[24]

In many ways, higher educational trends in the Old Kingdom before World War I foreshadowed developments that intensified during Romania's expansion after 1918. The pattern of university training geared toward bureaucratic employment, present since the nineteenth century, continued. So did nationalist students' attempts to exclude "foreigners" from university training and student societies. In the Regat, with only minor exceptions, the term "foreigner" had been limited to Jews. After 1918, it also applied to other national minorities, whose presence aggravated earlier anti-Jewish tendencies. In Greater Romania, bureaucratic expansion stimulated both larger enrollments and higher expectations for prestigious jobs and rapid advancement. The growth of the population and its ethnic diversification made postsecondary schools even more of a battleground between non-Romanian and Romanian elites than before the war.

The Universities after 1918: Growth and Crisis

After the Great Union of 1918, the universities adjusted to meet the state's increased needs for elite cadres. The universities of Iaşi and Bucharest were joined in this task by those of Cluj and Cernăuţi, once these were Romanized. The provisional local administrations of Transylvania and Bukovina executed the actual takeovers of the universities, but the Ministry of Education in Bucharest also became involved, and the two Old Kingdom universities had an auxiliary role in supervising the nationalization of the two "new" ones.[25]

[22] Berlescu, "Universitatea," pp. 212–214.
[23] Documente privind istoria României. Războiul pentru independenţă, 1877–1878, vol. 1, pt. 1 (Bucharest: Editura Academiei R. P. R., 1954), pp. 576–581.
[24] Berlescu, "Universitatea," p. 214.
[25] This role seems to be implied in a 1918 address from Constantin Angelescu, Minister of Education, to the two universities of Bucharest and Iaşi, telling them that "their eyes must be turned toward Cluj and Cernăuţi." Cited in Popescu-Spineni, Instituţii, p. 155.

Before the war, the universities of Bucharest, Iaşi, Cluj, and Cernăuţi had had sixteen schools or *facultăţi* among them. Under separate administration, higher schools of veterinary medicine, commerce, engineering, agronomy, and architecture had operated in Bucharest; Cluj had commercial and agricultural academies; and Oradea Mare featured a law school. A total of 8,632 students attended these institutions in 1913–1914.[26] After the war, higher education expanded in several ways. The universities enlarged their schools and staff, and they took over some of the higher schools or academies, turning them into university departments. New institutions of higher education outside the universities were created as well. Bucharest University, the largest in the country, increased its faculty almost ten times, from 166 in 1918–1919 to 1,036 in 1937–1938. It also added a school of veterinary medicine in 1921, and a school of pharmacy in 1923. An institute of physical education was established in Bucharest, and the prewar engineering school expanded into a six-section polytechnic. Iaşi University opened two new schools, agronomy and theology, both located in Chişinău, the capital of Bessarabia. In 1920, as a result of largely local initiative, a new, two-section polytechnic opened in Timişoara, the capital of the Banat, in western Transylvania.[27] In all, if we count the *facultate* as a unit, there were twenty-nine institutions of higher learning in the interwar period, quite an increase over the fourteen in the Old Kingdom before the war. Despite this growth in the base of Romanian higher education, the clientele of these burgeoning institutions grew even faster.[28]

Transylvania

Cluj University (the Royal University of Kolozsvár) founded by the Hungarian government in 1872, was taken over by representatives of the Directing Council on May 12, 1919. It opened its doors under Romanian management in the fall of 1919. The seizure of the university by Transylvania's provisional government that spring had all the drama and suspense of revolutionary expropriations of land, factories, and government buildings, pointing clearly both to the national revolutionary nature of the events in

[26] Constantin Kiriţescu, "Problema 'educaţiei dirijate' în legătură cu suprapopulaţia universitară şi şomajul intelectual," *Arhiva pentru ştiinţa şi reforma socială* 14 (1936): 850–857.
[27] Gheorghe T. Ionescu, "Contribuţii la istoricul Universităţii din Bucureşti după 1918," *Studii* 17 (1964): 1309; Kiriţescu, "Problema 'educaţiei dirijate,' " p. 852; and AA XIII/ Varia 3, [n.d.], 1935. Although the Timişoara Polytechnic was part of postwar expansion, it had already been under debate since 1911.
[28] Kiriţescu, "Problema 'educaţiei dirijate,' " p. 852, and Dimitrie Gusti, *Un an de activitate la Ministerul instrucţiei cultelor şi artelor, 1932–1933* (Bucharest: Tip. Bucovina, 1934), p. 313.

Transylvania and to the political importance of the university as a cultural power center.

The University of Cluj had existed in one form or another since the sixteenth century. In 1581, Stephen Bathory, king of Poland and prince of Transylvania, had founded a Jesuit college in Koloszvár (Cluj) in an effort to stem the tide of religious reform. Albeit with some long interruptions, it functioned as a Jesuit college until 1773. Empress Maria Theresa reopened it as a Piarist institution in 1786, and later Joseph II demoted the university to a *lyceum regium*. The royal lycée had a more liberal spirit than its predecessors, making it possible for more Romanians to attend. Romanians first formed, for a time, a majority of the student body at the lycée in the middle of the nineteenth century.[29]

During the 1848 revolution, the Romanians protesting at Blaj demanded, among other concessions, the opening of a Romanian university in Transylvania. Instead, a German legal academy opened in Sibiu (Hermannstadt) in 1850, followed by a Magyar legal academy in Cluj in 1863. A project for a bilingual German and Romanian university that same year failed to materialize because of conflicts over its location: Romanians wanted it to be in Transylvania's "natural capital," Cluj, whereas the Germans preferred the Saxon capital, Sibiu. After the *Ausgleich* of 1867, a multilingual university was again projected for Cluj. In keeping with the new political realities, Romanians scaled down their demands, calling for parity of the Romanian and Hungarian languages within the future university.[30]

But the modern University of Cluj, which opened in 1872, was a purely Hungarian institution, with only one chair of Romanian language and literature.[31] Only 18 of the 269 students in the first entering class were Romanian. Over the next four decades, Romanians constituted no more than 15 percent of the student body, which was 83 percent Hungarian, an indication of Magyar hegemony in the province: Romanians formed a majority of the population but not of Transylvania's elite.[32] In this incarnation, the University of Cluj offended the national sentiment of Transylvanian Romanians.[33]

From the Romanian standpoint, the wrong of 1872 demanded a radical corrective: the nationalization of Cluj University. Certainly a political act,

---

[29] Onisifor Ghibu, *La a douăzecea aniversare a Universității Daciei Superioare* (Cluj: Institutul de arte grafice Ardealul, 1939), pp. 8–16. See also Neagoe, *Viața,* vol. 1, pp. 6–14.
[30] Ghibu, *La a douăzecea,* p. 17; Sextil Pușcariu, *Memorii* (Bucharest: Editura Minerva, 1978), p. 384; Onisifor Ghibu, *Universitatea românească a Daciei Superioare: Cu prilejul împlinirei a 5 ani de activitate* (Cluj: Tip. Viața, 1924), pp. 6–10; and Neagoe, *Viața,* vol. 1, pp. 16–28.
[31] Miron Constantinescu, ed., *Din Istoria Transilvaniei,* vol. 2 ([Bucharest]: Editura Academiei R. P. R., 1961), p. 403.
[32] Neagoe, *Viața,* vol. 1, pp. 32–33.
[33] For example, Onisifor Ghibu wrote: "The establishment in this form of the University

the measure also constituted a vindication of Romanian culture. Nationalists saw the establishment of a Romanian university in the middle of
Transylvania as a necessity "not only by reasons of national political
prestige, but especially by higher necessities of a biological cultural creative
order." In 1926, Onisifor Ghibu wrote that without the University of
Cluj:

> the entire life of the Ardeal would have a sorry aspect; its presence there is
> . . . a lighthouse, which sends its rays of light up to the farthest distances of
> the Ardeal: to Satu-Mare and to Beiuş, to Lugoj and to Pietroşani, to Sighişoara
> and to Făgăraş, enlivening everywhere with the magic wand of science the
> weak and lost souls, and inspiring at the same time respect from the
> Hungarians and Saxons. Through its scholarly work, which is known [even]
> in foreign scientific circles, Cluj University is a valuable collaborator for the
> progress of world science, and at the same time, a defender of our right over
> the Ardeal, of which we are proving ourselves deserving.[34]

The immediate and total takeover of the university by no means had
universal support, for it seemed both too difficult to accomplish and too
ruthless towards the Magyars. Onisifor Ghibu, secretary general in the
Department of Public Education of Transylvania's Directing Council, however, favored such a solution from the beginning. He persuaded others of
its benefits, and was instrumental in implementing it.[35]

Ghibu's role in Romanizing the University of Cluj was an important
one, and he left ample documentation of the process. Sextil Puşcariu's
word of warning, however, is well taken: "The one who had the most
merits [in the Romanization of the university,] but who would like to
appropriate all of them, was Ghibu."[36] On January 15, 1919, Ghibu wrote a
memo to his superior, Vasile Goldiş, arguing for the forceful and immediate
takeover of the university. The memo cites the French takeover of Stras-

---

in Cluj was nothing but a usurpation of the rights for which the Romanians had fought for
decades, and which in theory had even been granted to them by those in power." Ghibu,
Universitatea, p. 11.

[34] Onisifor Ghibu, Introduction to manuscript of an unfinished study about the University
of Cluj. Arhiva O. Ghibu, and Ghibu, "A cincea universitate a României: Universitatea din
Chişinău," in *Prolegomena la o educaţie românească* (Bucharest: Editura Cultura românească,
1941), pp. 430–431. According to Octavian Ghibu, Onisifor Ghibu's son, his father drafted
the introduction in 1929 or 1930. Octavian Ghibu, personal communication, 1984.

[35] As discussed in Chapter 4, under the Directing Council administration in 1918–1920
in Transylvania, Ghibu was both Secretary General of Education and Director General of
Higher Education. Onisifor Ghibu, "Amintiri în legătură cu fondarea Universităţii româneşti
din Cluj," (I) fragment din *Pe baricadele vieţii*, capit. "Alma Mater Napocensis—1919,"
1956. Ms. transcribed from written text by Octavian Ghibu in 1979. Arhiva O. Ghibu.

[36] Puşcariu, *Memorii*, p. 388.

bourg University the previous November and the Czechoslovak takeover of Bratislava University in December:[37] "In 48 hours' time they [the French] packed up all the German professors, [put them on a] train, and sent them to Germany. The Czechs too proceeded in about the same way with the University of Bratislava: they closed it and it remained closed for a long time, but they no longer allowed it to function as a Magyar university."[38]

Although Goldiş did not immediately accept Ghibu's proposal, the latter nevertheless soon attempted to proceed. The Cluj police prefect first charged with the task was repulsed by the Hungarian rector of the university: "This is a Magyar university, Mr. Prefect," he said. "How do you imagine that we would give you the university? We do not recognize the Alba Iulia agreement. You can do what you want, but we won't allow any Romanian to set foot in here!"[39] The Hungarian administration of the university refused even to register a request to transfer the university to Romanian hands on the grounds that the letter was written in Romanian, not in Magyar, the official language of the university. After this second failure, the prefect preferred not to involve himself with the university expropriation, a task he deemed beyond his power and competence. In addition, Ghibu's new superior, Valeriu Branişte, felt that changes in the university's structure should be implemented gradually. As chairs became vacant, they were to be filled by Romanians; in time, within two or three decades, Romanization would be completed.[40]

Nicolae Iorga also spoke out against the immediate nationalization of the University of Cluj in his newspaper *Neamul Românesc,* recommending instead the creation of a modern, more technical, university in Ardeal that would concentrate on mining, forestry, and commerce, rather than yet another humanist, theoretical Romanian university to rival those of Bucharest and Iaşi. He argued that the minority nationalities deserved the opportunity to receive in their native country an education in their mother tongue; moreover, there were not enough trained people available to staff an

---

[37] Ghibu, *La a douăzecea,* p. 28. For a recent history of the Strasbourg episode, see John E. Craig, *Scholarship and Nation Building: The Universities of Strasbourg and Alsatian Society 1870–1939* (Chicago: University of Chicago Press, 1984), chap. 7 ("From Universität to Université"), esp. pp. 208–211. On Bratislava University, see Owen V. Johnson, *Slovakia 1918–1938: Education and the Making of a Nation* (Boulder, Colo.: East European Monographs, 1985), pp. 219–220.

[38] Onisifor Ghibu, "Amintiri în legătură cu fondarea Universităţii româneşti din Cluj," (II) fragment din "Din amintirile unui pedagog militant," p. 3. Text established in 1968 by Octavian O. Ghibu on the basis of tape recordings. Arhiva O. Ghibu.

[39] Ibid.

[40] Ibid., pp. 3–4. Another account, also by Ghibu, differs slightly. The prefect Vasile Poruţiu requested that the university professors take an oath of allegiance to the Romanian state. The rector responded in a letter dated March 9 that the request had been discussed with members of the university senate and registered with the number 2300/1919. While not specifically refused, Poruţiu's request was ignored. See Ghibu, *La a douăzecea,* pp. 29–30.

entirely Romanian university in Cluj. A third consideration for Iorga was the possibility that a Romanian university in Cluj "would feed a provincial particularism . . . , the most dangerous thing in the realm of the spirit."[41]

As in the case of the secondary schools, and despite other people's gradualist views on the matter of the university's nationalization, Ghibu had no qualms about implementing the most urgent and radical solution. Although some Romanians were concerned about the fate of the two thousand Hungarian students attending Cluj University, Ghibu felt that it was the Romanians who deserved concern: "We are today the cultural invalids of an unequal war that has lasted for one thousand years. The Romanian state cannot worry now about the healthy ones; it must take to heart its own invalids."[42] His resolve hardened during a "field trip" to Cluj in mid-April 1919, at a time when the fate of Ardeal was still being fought militarily.[43] Ghibu noted the nervousness in Romanian circles at the state of military uncertainty. Perhaps more important, a tour of the city's public schools and higher educational institutions, where he found very few Romanian pupils, students, or staff, reminded Ghibu of the ravages of Magyarization in the city and reinforced his determination to reverse them at once. He expressed himself unequivocally: "We would have to be irresponsible to tolerate for years or for decades longer such revolting conditions. At the price of any sacrifice we have to correct history as soon as possible."[44]

The university became the last public institution in Cluj to be nationalized. Valeriu Branişte, Iuliu Maniu, the head of the Directing Council, and the Directing Council as a whole finally approved Ghibu's takeover plan. An ultimatum to the rectorate demanded that the faculty pledge allegiance to the Romanian king and laws. To preempt a possible Magyar counterstrategy based on technicalities, the documents included official Hungarian translations. The response had to come within forty-eight hours, by 10 A.M. on May 12.[45] Ghibu was armed with an authorization to take over

[41] Ghibu, *La a douăzecea*, p. 31. Regionalism may have become a factor in the life of Cluj University after its nationalization. In 1926, a law professor, I. C. Cătuneanu, protested to the rector of the university that Regăţeni (those from the Old Kingdom) were systematically excluded from appointment to the dean's office. He was indignant at the "regionalist mentality" evident there, "seven years after the Union, [at] the highest cultural institution this side of the Carpathians." MIC/1926/436/98, n.d.

[42] Ghibu, *La a douăzecea*, pp. 35–36.

[43] Ibid., pp. 32–33.

[44] Ibid., p. 35.

[45] Ibid., p. 36, Ghibu, "Amintiri" (II), p. 11, and Ghibu, *La a douăzecea*, pp. 40, 42. Without the loyalty pledge, the faculty would still be allowed to teach in a special summer semester, for the benefit of those mobilized during the war, under Directing Council supervision.

the university if loyalty pledges were not forthcoming. The staff of the university were to remain at their functions, under orders of the Romanian military command in Cluj, and Romanian army units stood by ready to assist in any way necessary. What Ghibu most feared was an offer of compromise from the Hungarian professors, which would have delayed a confrontation and postponed the transfer of power. The Magyar answer, however, did not disappoint him. Each of the four schools of the university expressed the faculty's unwillingness to take the oath of loyalty to the Romanian state, clearing the way for the Romanian seizure.[46] The determined Romanian response to the Hungarians' hedging took the latter by surprise. The rector, Stephen Schneller, was apparently prepared for protracted negotiations with the Directing Council, or at least for another chance to discuss the matter with his deans. Had the Magyar university staged an immediate retaliatory work strike, Romanian authority might well have faltered. But no organized resistance occurred.[47]

The official communiqué on the nationalization of the university announced that "following the unwillingness of the professors at the University of Cluj to pledge the official oath, the Romanian Directing Council found itself obliged to dismiss them from service, to take measures for organizing the university, and to appoint new professors to all the chairs of the four schools of the university."[48] By virtue of decree 4090, the Magyar university in Cluj became Romanian as of October 1, 1919. The official inauguration of the university was postponed until February 1–2, 1920, partly for political reasons, partly to allow for proper preparations for the festive event to which roughly three hundred foreign guests, academics, and diplomats were invited.[49]

Because of the political importance of Cluj University, routine festivities there often took on a highly visible and at times "diplomatic" aspect. A decade later, a letter to the Ministry of Education from the Cluj University rector, the distinguished speleologist Emil Racoviță, expressed the opinion that the tenth anniversary of the university's nationalization "should have besides its national face, an international face," in order, among other

---

[46] Ghibu, *La a douăzecea,* pp. 40–45.

[47] See Vasile Pușcaș, "Însemnătatea și semnificația înființării universității românești din Cluj și opinia internațională," *Studia Univ. Babeș-Bolyai, Historia* 25, no. 1 (1980): 42, 47–48; and Ghibu, "Amintiri" (I), p. 7. According to Pușcaș, the rector's name was Ștefan Schuller.

[48] *Gazeta oficială* (October 4-7-11-13); see MIC/1929/531/14.

[49] Constantin Hamangiu, *Codul general al României,* vol. 9–10 (Bucharest: L. Alcalay, n.d.), p. 223. The decree was issued on September 23, 1919. The university opened its doors as a Romanian institution on November 3, 1919. See Pușcaș, "Însemnătatea," pp. 42, 47–62, and Gheorghe Iancu and G. Neamțu, "Contribuții documentare cu privire la organizarea și inaugurarea universității românești din Cluj (1919–1920)," *Studia Univ. Babeș Bolyai, Historia* 30, (1985): 44–46.

things, to combat Magyar propaganda to the effect that "the transfer 'of the famous Cluj University' from under the authority of the civilized Magyar people to that of the uncivilized Romanian people is a great loss for human culture." Racoviţă argued that foreign university guests had to be invited, as they had been for the university's inauguration in 1920. The festivities would prove to foreigners the falseness of Magyar propaganda.[50]

In this spirit, the tenth anniversary of the Romanization of Cluj University, celebrated in October 1930, turned into an extravagant occasion on which the Romanian government spent 1,800,000 *lei*. Foreign guests, the Romanian royal family, the diplomatic corps, and Romanian dignitaries and parliamentarians joined in a celebration one newspaper headline called "The Cluj Apotheosis." Honorary degrees were granted to a number of international personages who were friends of Romania such as the Comte de Saint-Aulaire, former French ambassador to Romania, Emmanuel de Martonne, the Sorbonne geography professor who worked on Romania and who had taught at the University of Cluj in 1921, and R. W. Seton-Watson, the British historian whose efforts on behalf of the Romanian national cause before and during the war were greatly appreciated. Her Majesty Queen Maria was also made doctor honoris causa on this occasion.[51]

Beyond the decrees and festivities, the integration of Cluj University into the Greater Romanian system was a lengthy process rather than an event. The institution's internal organization was initially kept on the grounds that the higher education legislation of the whole country was to be overhauled. Sextil Puşcariu, a Romanian philology professor at the University of Cernăuţi, former dean of the Letters and Philosophy school in Cernăuţi, and a native Transylvanian, was chosen to organize the new Romanian University of Cluj and to be its first rector. He accepted the task, but insisted that he be appointed not by the Directing Council, but rather from within the university. Having taken this principled stand, he was then able to resist pressures originating in the Old Kingdom to allow the universities of Iaşi and Bucharest to take a "more decisive role" in organizing that of Cluj.[52] Puşcariu felt that it would have been pointless to merge Cluj University with its Old Kingdom counterparts under an unsatisfactory set of

[50] MIC/1930/510/6–9, November 21, 1929.

[51] MIC/1930/510/10; Alexandru Kiriţescu, "Apoteoza dela Cluj," *Cuvântul*, October 27, 1930; "Deschiderea solemnă a cursurilor universitare din Cluj," *Cuvântul*, October 23, 1930; Lucian Predescu, *Enciclopedia Cugetarea* (Bucharest: Cugetarea–Georgescu Delafras, 1939–1940), pp. 530, 776; QD 238/10–12, October 22, 1930; and Hugh and Christopher Seton-Watson, *The Making of a New Europe: R. W. Seton-Watson and the Last Years of Austria-Hungary* (London: Methuen, 1981).

[52] Puşcariu, *Memorii*, pp. 358, 361, 390–391, 444, 450–451, 454.

laws.[53] Indeed, full Romanian higher education legislation was extended to Cluj only in 1925.[54]

In July 1919, a commission of twelve distinguished professors from the universities of Iaşi and Bucharest and eight Transylvanians was set up under the guidance of Sextil Puşcariu to hire faculty for the new Romanian University of Cluj.[55] The university commission and the Directing Council together searched for and appointed many new faculty, generally young ones, but also a number of established professors from the Old Kingdom, Romanian scholars working abroad, and foreign scholars—a group of French professors was the most important numerically[56]—to replace the disloyal Hungarian faculty.

One area of the university that escaped immediate Romanization was the Reformed Teacher Training Institute affiliated with the theological school. Romanian authorities closed down the institute once they realized that only some of its students belonged to the Reformed Church. The institute did not follow official regulations regarding the use of Romanian, and, according to Romanian authorities, it "had organized its own university," so that its students might not need to attend the requisite courses at Cluj University.[57]

Vestiges of Magyarization were more persistent among the clerical and technical staff than at the professorial level, since all the faculty of the former Hungarian university had been replaced. The university staff was expected to pass a Romanian language exam, but not all of them had even tried to take it by 1928.[58] The new university administration also worried about Magyar activities outside the official curriculum and thus denied Magyar students the right to form their own student society.[59]

The significance of the Romanian University of Cluj was acknowledged in Transylvania and in Romania as a whole, but also beyond international boundaries, and most poignantly in Hungary, where the Romanization of Cluj University registered as a major loss. To the displeasure of Romanian authorities, Hungary reacted by opening two new universities in Szeged and Debrecen, close to the border with Romania. Dimitrie Călugăreanu, the rector of Cluj University in 1921–1922, declared:

[53] Ibid., pp. 417–418.
[54] Another Transylvanian institution of higher learning, the Legal Academy of Oradea Mare, functioned under the Magyar legislation of 1872 until 1930. MIC/1930/557/4, n.d.
[55] Ibid., pp. 388–389, 397–400.
[56] Ibid., pp. 390–395; QD 41/49, October 4, 1919; and QD 142/16–18, June 20, 1919. See reference to "misiunea profesorilor francezi" in Puşcariu, Memorii, p. 445, and Petre Sergescu, "Les relations franco-roumaines à l'Université de Cluj," Revue de Transylvanie 3, no. 3 (1937): 311–314.
[57] MIC/1922/466/279–281, n.d.
[58] See MIC/1929/570/12–19, December 15, 1928.
[59] MIC/1930/508/62–69, April 2, 1930.

The creation of the two new Magyar universities on our frontier, is intended for the formation of cultural and political converts, seeking to further maintain the Hungarians' cultural domination in these parts. In these universities the students are granted extraordinary favors, which shows that these university centers do not aim at the propagation of culture, being rather centers for the preservation of Magyar chauvinism.[60]

The University of Szeged elicited particular resentment because it took the old name of the "Royal University of Cluj, continuing to grant diplomas as if it still functioned in Cluj."[61] Both new Hungarian universities attracted Transylvanian Magyars, in part by offering a purportedly lenient academic regimen. Romanian authorities claimed that when these Transylvanian students returned home for the holidays, they brought with them "tens of thousands of brochures and manifestoes which they distributed everywhere," and that "they were celebrated in all of Transylvania as Magyar heroes."[62]

Romanian authorities therefore wanted to stop the traffic of Magyar students and diplomas across Transylvania's borders. When the Hungarian government stopped recognizing Romanian and Czechoslovak university degrees, Romanian officials welcomed the excuse to cease to recognize diplomas from Hungarian universities.[63] More directly, the Ministry of Education simply denied Romania's Magyars the right to travel to Hungary for their studies. The youths could sometimes circumvent these restrictions by requesting to travel to Germany and Austria.[64]

Bukovina

In keeping with Bukovina's history of accommodation and gradualism developed under Austrian rule, the Romanian takeover of Cernăuţi (Czernowitz) University had a milder quality than the seizure of Cluj University.

Czernowitz University had been established in 1875 exactly one hundred years after Bukovina had been taken by Austria from the Moldavian Principality. R. W. Seton-Watson called the founding of the university "the chief event in the quiet annals of Bukovina under the Dual System."[65] To the disappointment of many Romanians from the province, the Franz Joseph University had opened as an "österreichische Universität deutschen

[60] MIC/1922/466/172–173, March 13, 1922.
[61] Ibid.
[62] Ibid.
[63] Ibid., and MIC/1922/466/176–177, n.d.
[64] MIC/1922/460/336, n.d.
[65] Seton-Watson, *History of the Roumanians,* pp. 558–559.

Geistes." Whereas the Austrians saw it as their easternmost "outpost of German culture on the Pruth,"[66] some Romanians perceived it as a deeply hostile institution having "the mission of fully denationalizing" Bukovina.[67] In trying to convince the government in Vienna to fund a university in Czernowitz, Constantin Tomaszczuk (Tomaşciuc), a delegate in Bukovina's parliament, argued that it had been a mistake to allow the universities in Cracow and Lemberg to be Polonized in 1870–1871 and that the monarchy was well advised to attempt to recover ground by expanding culturally to the east. A German university in Czernowitz, he declared, could be "an intellectual fortress, which will secure the unity and the integrity of the monarchy much better than bastions lined with cannons." It was, moreover, to be a "German cultural fortress to the east of the Polish-Magyar fortresses in Lvov and Cluj."[68]

Rudolf Wagner, a German author and former literature student at the University of Czernowitz from 1930 to 1932, vigorously disputes the view that the Franz Joseph University had a Germanizing mission. He cites the involvement of Constantin Tomaszczuk, "a gifted Romanian liberal" politician from Bukovina, dedicated to a supranational Austria, in the founding of the university, as well as the support of Romanian aristocrats, led by Baron Gheorghe Hurmuzaki in Bukovina's Landtag. Tomaszczuk, had received his doctorate in law from the University of Lemberg in 1864, before the Polonization of the university. He was of Ukrainian and Romanian parentage, but his ethnic loyalties seem to have been primarily Romanian. A successful Bukovinian and Austrian politician, he was eventually rewarded for his efforts toward the founding of Czernowitz University by being appointed its first rector. Wagner depicts the Franz Joseph University as a sensitive and sensible compromise solution to competing local ethnic and cultural interests. He argues that a Romanian university in Czernowitz in the 1870s would have been opposed by the non-Romanians who, taken together, were a majority of the population. A Ukrainian university there would have faced similar opposition from all non-Ukrainians.[69]

Nevertheless, the imperial charter for the university read, "As the German, so the Romanian and the Slav gladly quenches his thirst and draws strength from the fountain of German science; this in greater measure will offer him the means to retain and nurture his individuality; but it will also be an inducement to work and strive together toward the happiness and glory of our beloved fatherland, Austria."[70] Professor Wildauer's inaugura-

[66] Ibid., p. 559, and Rudolph Wagner, Vom Moldauwappen zum Doppeladler: Ausgewählte Beiträge zur Geschichte der Bukowina (Augsburg: Hofmann-Verlag, 1991), p. 271.
[67] Ion Nistor, Istoria Bucovinei (Bucharest: Humanitas, 1991), p. 242.
[68] Wagner, Vom Moldauwappen, p. 280, and Nistor, Istoria, p. 212.
[69] Nistor, Istoria, p. 212, and Wagner, Vom Moldauwappen, pp. 275–276, 290–291, 301, 563.
[70] Cited in Popescu-Spineni, Instituţii, pp. 175–176, 178.

tion speech conveyed the same message: "Let us build a university in Czernowitz and place it like a spiritual lighthouse in the middle of all the people to shine on them equal light, to illuminate them with the same Enlightenment, and to satisfy all of them through the consciousness of [our shared] community."[71] In his own inauguration speech, Constantin Tomaszczuk also echoed this direction toward an institution at once supranational and German:

German science has a claim to universality. And because German education has a universal importance, non-German sons of Bukovina also strive for this German university. . . .

Beware to the nation which has to be afraid of the influence of foreign cultures. This nation is signing its own death certificate. . . . We are not only Poles, Germans, [and] Romanians, we are in the first place human beings, with roots in the same soil out of which we draw our common strength, and by this I mean our Austria. And the university in Czernowitz is an authentic Austrian concept.[72]

The Romanians in Bukovina had first expressed an interest in a local university in 1848, when they demanded the upgrading of the local Theological Institute into a *facultate*, and the creation of two others—law and philosophy—so that Romanian youths would not have to travel to Lemberg, Graz, Prague, or Vienna for higher education.[73] The Franz Joseph University, however, was not inaugurated until October 4, 1875. According to Romanian historians, its Austrian founders intended it to rival the Romanian university of Iaşi, established during the previous decade and struggling in the 1870s through a period of crisis and reductions. Through the university in Czernowitz, Austria could exert an influence in Moldavia and Bessarabia and much of the Balkans by attracting students to the Austrian-German institution. And indeed once the university opened, local youth traveled abroad for studies far less.[74]

At its inauguration, the University of Czernowitz's main section was the Theology School, transformed from the Theological Institute founded in

[71] Franz Hieronymus Riedl, "Die Universität Czernowitz, 1875–1920: Ein Blick auf ihr Wesen und Ihre Entwicklung Beziehungen zu Ost- und Mitteldeutschland," *Mitteldeutsche Vorträge* 2 (1971): 10.

[72] Wagner, *Vom Moldauwappen*, p. 282. Today some graduates of the pre-1918 University of Czernowitz still consider it to have had both a "deutschsprachiger Character" and a "Character als Nationalitätenuniversität," the two not necessarily seen as contradictory. See ibid., pp. 299–300.

[73] Ion Nistor, *Originea şi Dezvoltarea Universității din Cernăuți*, Biblioteca Astrei Basarabene Nr. 4 (Chişinău: Tip. Eparhială Cartea românească, 1927), p. 3, and Wagner, *Vom Moldauwappen*, p. 274.

[74] Berlescu, "Universitatea," p. 137; Nistor, *Originea*, p. 4; and Nistor, *Istoria*, p. 229.

1827. As projected, students came from all over southeastern Europe; thus the university influenced more broadly the Eastern European Orthodox world. Theoretical courses were taught in German, but practical theology, catechism, and homiletics were in Romanian and Ukrainian. In addition to theology there were two other *fakultäten,* law and political economy, and philosophy, philology, and natural sciences. For secular subjects the teaching language of the university was generally German.[75] A chair of Romanian language was soon added in the philosophy school, and, in 1911, a chair of Southeast European history with special emphasis on Romanian history. Ukrainian chairs were also introduced, and Ukrainian professors taught and "habillitated" at the university. Czernowitz University was the first "western" university with chairs in East European and Southeast European History.[76] Such offerings and the patriotic student societies Arboroasa and Bucovina contributed to the maintenance of an important kernel of Romanian culture.

In spite of these attempts at multiculturalism, advanced for their time perhaps, Czernowitz University remained a German institution, for it was German culture and science that had the recognized claim to universality. Between 1875 and 1918, 87 of the 127 professors on the faculty were German, 20 Romanian, 12 Jewish, 5 Ruthenian, 2 Slovenian, and 1 Czech.[77] These figures and the rural character of the Romanian and Ukrainian populations meant that the university was more welcoming to Germans and urban Germanized Jews than to Romanians and Ukrainians. In 1875, the university opened with 208 students, of which 82 were "Germans" (that is, 31 ethnic Germans and 51 Jews), 53 Romanians, 42 Ukrainians, and 28 Poles.[78] In 1900, 218 of the 392 students at the university were German (including Jews), 89 Romanian, 35 Ukrainian, and 41 Polish. No Germans or Jews attended the Theological Faculty, which was oriented to Orthodox Theology and which attracted ethnic Romanians and Ukrainians, Orthodox and Uniate students from Hungary, Romania, and Bosnia and Herzegovina. On the other hand, the Law Faculty was more German than the university as a whole, with 62.6 percent of the 306 students being

[75] Nistor, *Istoria,* p. 5; Wagner, *Vom Moldauwappen,* p. 282; and Emanuel Turczynski, "The National Movement in the Greek Orthodox Church in the Habsburg Monarchy," *Austrian History Yearbook* 3, pt. 3 (1967): 127.

[76] Nistor, *Originea,* pp. 5–6; Popescu-Spineni, *Instituţii,* pp. 175, 181; Ann Sirka, *The Nationality Question in Austrian Education: The Case of Ukrainians in Galicia, 1867–1914* (Frankfurt am Main: Peter D. Lang, 1980), pp. 142–143; Wagner, *Vom Moldauwappen,* pp. 276, 282, 293, 285; and Nistor, *Istoria,* pp. 229–230, 242.

[77] Erich Prokopowitch, *Gründung, Entwicklung und Ende der Franz-Josephs-Universität in Czernowitz (Bukowina-Buchenland)* (Clausthal-Zellerfeld: Piepersche Buchdruckerei und Verlanganstalt, 1955), p. 38.

[78] Riedl, "Die Universität Czernowitz," p. 19.

German and only 14.7 percent Romanian and 9.5 percent Ukrainian.[79] In 1913–1914, the university had 1198 students, 458 of whom were German (of these 57 ethnic Germans and 401 Jews), 310 Romanian, 303 Ukrainian, and 86 Polish.[80]

After the union of Bukovina with Romania in January 1919, the Romanian administration headed by Ion Nistor, the new rector of the university, decided to Romanize all the departments. While the department of theology had quite a number of Romanians, given its Orthodox orientation, all but three of the faculty of the other two secular departments of the university, law and letters and philosophy, were Austrians who did not know Romanian. The non-Romanians were thus invited to learn the land's new official language, failing which they would have to leave. Only four Austrian professors consented to these conditions and remained on the faculty. The others were replaced by new Romanian cadre.[81] Decree 4091 of September 23, 1919, formally transformed the German university of Cernăuți into a Romanian one. A year later, on October 24, 1920, the Romanian University of Cernăuți was inaugurated in the presence of the royal family and other dignitaries and academics. Romanian professors were appointed to new chairs established to extend the offerings related to the study of Romanian culture. Full higher education legislation extended to the University of Cernăuți on June 13, 1925.[82]

Bessarabia

Although one method of integrating the new territories was to promote Romanian universities, one of Romania's newly acquired provinces remained without one. Unlike Bukovina and Transylvania, Bessarabia had no existing foreign university to be appropriated by the new government. This lack may have made it both more difficult and less urgent to establish a university. Indeed, the insistence on the immediate transformation of existing universities in Cluj and Cernăuți into Romanian institutions, compared with the lack of urgency shown in bringing a full-service university to Chișinău, suggests that the major emphasis in university Romanization in Greater Romania was the replacement of foreign elites, rather than the

[79] Akademische Senate, *Die K. K. Franz-Josephs-Universität in Czernowitz im Ersten Vierteljahrhundert ihres Bestandes: Festschrift* (Czernowitz: Bukowinaer Vereinsdruckerei, 1900), pp. 161 ff. After World War I, Marcel Gillard wrote that the Jews of Bukovina constituted "a prosperous, active, upper class supported by the numerous intellectual elements who were trained before the war at the German university of Cernăuți." Marcel Gillard, *La Roumanie nouvelle* (Paris: Alcon, 1922), p. 68.

[80] Riedl, "Die Universität Czernowitz," pp. 19.

[81] Nistor, *Istoria*, pp. 410–411.

[82] Hamangiu, *Codul*, vol. 9–10, pp. 223; Popescu-Spineni, *Instituții*, pp. 186–187; Nistor, *Originea*, p. 6; and MIC/1930/557/4, n.d.

creation of Romanian elites. If we are to take the fortress metaphors seriously, and these were used by all sides when articulating the need for creating universities, it seems that where university "fortresses" existed, they had to be overpowered and neutralized, but where they did not, the need to erect them was less pressing.

A full-scale Greater Romanian university, costly to build and equip, never came about in Bessarabia, although from 1917 on some local business groups and residents demanded it. The Central Union of the Syndicates of Home Owners from all Bessarabian Cities repeatedly called for a university in Chişinău. After a theology school opened in Chişinău in 1926 as a branch of Iaşi University, the union wrote to the prime minister:

> The establishment in the city of Chişinău of the Theological School, and the echo produced by it in the bosom of local society which has from the beginning given to this school such an eminently prepared public, has once again underscored the thirst for learning in general, and in particular the tendency toward higher education which exists in Bessarabia.
>
> Not only that: the initiative and unifying activity of Chişinău in this sacred cause [of unification] have proven that our city is a true cultural center of the province, and that it is maintaining the role that belonged to it in the past.[83]

The letter stressed the advantages of a local university that would eliminate the need for Bessarabian youth to travel outside the province for their studies:

> This tradition of love and respect for culture, which has been a lasting one in local society, creates a fruitful atmosphere for the young pupils. The modesty and industrious tranquility of life in Chişinău give our city the privileges of a quiet university center.
>
> It is known and even recognized by everyone that the crowding of youth thirsty for education in the large, noisy centers, with their high cost of living, the distance of the young people from their families, the housing shortage, and the wanton allurements often cannot be in anyway balanced by the opportunities offered by the teaching of scientific celebrities.[84]

Referring to the example of German provincial universities, and to the benefits of "true culture," the authors ended with a direct appeal for a university in Chişinău: "Thus, the establishment in Chişinău of a university is of capital importance and shared benefit. We consider it our duty to bring our conviction to the Government's attention, and we ask that the

---

[83] MIC/1930/558/77–78, December 28, 1929.
[84] Ibid.

Government resolve this question favorably as soon as possible, since the number of Bessarabians from all layers of society, thirsty for higher studies, is growing every day."[85] Another appeal for a university in Chişinău came from the local Chamber of Commerce and Industry, which also alluded to numerous other petitions "from multiple Bessarabian institutions" which had pleaded the same cause. The chamber argued for a university in Chişinău on the grounds of the large number of Bessarabian students attending higher educational institutions throughout the country. This already large number, which in itself would have been sufficient to justify a local Bessarabian university, would grow even bigger if a university functioned locally, reducing the costs of higher education for local youths.[86]

Arguments for a university in Chişinău also came from nationalists outside of Bessarabia, and authorities in Bucharest occasionally implied promises to establish such an institution.[87] Onisifor Ghibu favored a fifth Romanian university in Chişinău since it could play the important cultural role of drawing Russianized Romanians back into a Latin and Romanian fold. It could, of course, also discharge a political function: "Bessarabia is the defensive wall of Romanianism before the invasion of Slavism," he said. "We cannot fortify this wall with bayonets alone; we must strengthen it by means of souls steeled through higher education. . . . We have to have our General Headquarters just near the Dniester, so that by its constant presence in the midst of those to be supported, it might strengthen their morale, it might be able to observe the enemy from closer up, and it might make victory more certain."[88]

While a full-fledged university did not materialize in Bessarabia in the interwar period, two schools affiliated with Iaşi University did open there. These schools of agriculture and theology suggested the province's identity as, on the one hand, prominently rural and, on the other hand, the embattled Orthodox neighbor of the recently established atheist Soviet state. Bessarabian intellectuals had been deeply affected by Russian culture, and were, as a group, stereotyped as leftists during the interwar period. An Orthodox theology school in Chişinău could, in principle, exert a Romanian and religious influence that might diminish the effects of Russian culture and Soviet ideology. The Theology School was established in Chişinău in 1926 at the initiative of Bessarabian clergy,[89] apparently spurred by the "vacancy" provided by the fall of the Russian Empire and the

[85] Ibid.

[86] MIC/1930/558/26, January 17, 1930.

[87] Ghibu, "A cincea universitate a României," in *Prolegomena*, pp. 426–427.

[88] Ibid., p. 428.

[89] Onisifor Ghibu, "Basarabiei nu-i este de ajuns o Facultate de Teologie," in *Prolegomena*, p. 436.

concomitant decline of the Eastern Orthodox center immediately to the east.[90]

The Iaşi University School of Agricultural Sciences opened in Chişinău in 1932–1933. The agricultural section of the Iaşi University School of Sciences had grown beyond the capacity of its facilities. Especially in the years of economic crisis just prior to 1932, it lacked teaching staff, classrooms, laboratories, practice farms, and subventions. Under the circumstances, a Bessarabian project to move the agricultural higher education to Chişinău was as attractive as it seemed appropriate:

> The most fitting solution was to transfer [higher agricultural education] from Iaşi to Chişinău, endowing it handsomely. The fact that Bessarabia is the province with the most pronounced agricultural character, and the fact that the intellectual youth of Bessarabia have the greatest inclination for agricultural studies, were indications that if at issue is the question of endowing Bessarabia and Chişinău with higher education, this should be done in the form of agricultural education.[91]

The idea of a higher agricultural institute in Chişinău had been around since 1914, when Bessarabia was still part of the Russian Empire. The fifteenth anniversary of Bessarabia's union with Romania provided yet another occasion for a proposal from Bessarabian leaders for such an institution. Iaşi University approved the proposal to move the agricultural section of its School of Sciences (changing the section's status to that of a full-fledged department) to Chişinău on the grounds of the precarious situation of the section in Iaşi and of the great advantages offered by Chişinău: adequate space, 2,000 hectares of practice farmland, an endowment, and the possibility of hiring additional faculty. In actuality, the transfer of higher agricultural education from Iaşi to Chişinău was rougher than expected, for the government initially withheld some of the promised funding, and even after this obstacle was overcome, monies for hiring additional faculty were delayed.[92]

---

[90] Ibid., pp. 442–443. According to Onisifor Ghibu, Romanian public opinion opposed the establishment of a theology school in Chişinău, the association ASTRA (The Transylvanian Association for the Literature and Culture of the Romanian People) and the newspaper *România nouă*, which he edited, being the exceptions. See Onisifor Ghibu, *Ardealul în Basarabia: O Pagină de istorie contimporană* (Cluj: Institutul de arte grafice Ardealul, 1928), p. 135.

[91] *Anuarul Universităţii Mihăilene din Iaşi, 1930–1935* (Jassy: Editura Universităţii Mihăilene, 1936), pp. 12, 67.

[92] Ibid., pp. 67–69.

New Elite or Intellectual Proletariat?

Romanian higher education expanded in physical facilities and in the number of institutions in the interwar period, as we have seen. But this growth in facilities was less dramatic than that at the primary and secondary levels. The most telling measure of the expansion of higher education lies in the growing number of university students. The student population rose from 8,632 in 1913–1914 to 22,379 in 1924–1925, to 31,154 in 1928–1929, and to 37,314 in 1929–1930.[93] Almost two-thirds of the students were concentrated in Bucharest, and predominantly in the university. The number of students enrolled at the University of Bucharest rose from 4,380 in 1915–1916 to 6,272 in 1918–1919, and to 22,902 in 1929–1930. Their numbers then fell slightly, owing presumably to the economic crisis, to 18,070 in 1931–1932, and to 15,636 in 1932–1933.[94] In 1931–1932, 23,091 students enrolled at various Bucharest institutions.[95] Of the provincial universities, Iaşi was the largest in the interwar period, with 5,891 students in 1931–1932, or 16.3 percent of the total student population.[96] In the same year, Cluj had over 3,000 students,[97] and Cernăuţi had 2,708 students, or 7.9 percent and 7.5 percent, respectively, of the total student population.[98]

In terms of disciplines, the trends established in the prewar period continued, with the highest concentration of students pursuing law. In 1928–1929, of 31,154 students, 38 percent were in law, 26 percent were in letters and philosophy, 16 percent were in sciences, 7 percent were in veterinary medicine, 5 percent were in theology, 4 percent were in pharmacy, and 1 percent were in medicine. In 1931–1932, law was again the most popular department, attracting 38.9 percent of the university population.[99] Law was the preferred discipline of the new elite partly

[93] Ibid., pp. 853–854, and Iosif I. Gabrea, "Statistică şi politica şcolară," *Buletinul oficial al Ministerului instrucţiunii, cultelor şi artelor*, ser. 2, no. I (April 1932), p. 28. Gusti quotes 36,112 students in 1931–32, a figure that does not include about 900 medical and pharmacy students at the University of Cluj. See Gusti, *Un an*, p. 299. Kiriţescu thinks that the postwar statistics represent an overestimation of about 15 percent, owing to persons studying for dual degrees. See Kiriţescu, "Problema 'educaţiei dirijate,'" pp. 855–856. But as already noted, such double counting also occurred before the war. The figures for 1928–1929 cited in Gabrea refer only to students enrolled in regular university departments, excluding those in the commercial and agricultural academies, the polytechnic, and the architecture and physical education institutes.

[94] Gusti, *Un an*, pt. 1, tabloul nr. 2; and Ionescu, "Contribuţii la istoricul Universităţii," p. 1312.

[95] Gusti, *Un an*, pt. 1, tabloul nr. 2.

[96] Ibid.

[97] The figure minus the approximately 900 medical and pharmacy students is 2,844. See ibid.

[98] Ibid.

[99] See Gabrea, "Statistică," p. 28, and Gusti, *Un an*, pt. 1, tabloul nr. 2.

because "the state in its eagerness for new functionaries made law the only profession for which one could prepare without full-time university attendance."[100] From 1921–1922 until 1931–1932 the higher educational system produced 17,779 graduates, of which 43 percent received law degrees, 29 percent degrees in letters and philosophy, 16 percent degrees in the sciences, 7 percent degrees in pharmacy, and 5 percent degrees in theology.[101] The successful completion of a degree varied with the field of study and perhaps with the conditions within the department, including the faculty-to-student ratio. In law schools this ratio was 1 : 121, in theology 1 : 55, in letters and philosophy 1 : 34, and in pharmacy 1 : 32.[102] Only 10 percent of the matriculated students completed their studies. Law students did worse than the average, only 8 percent of them completing their studies successfully, while 28 percent of students in letters and philosophy graduated.[103] The faculty-to-student ratio at Iaşi University worsened considerably from 1860 on, and especially after World War I: it was 1 : 6 in 1860, 1 : 8 in 1897, 1 : 18 in 1921, and 1 : 38 in 1932.[104]

Rising enrollments after the first world war quickly outstripped the facilities of Iaşi University. According to Valeriu Dobrinescu, "The University became completely inadequate to the number of students. Thus, for example, the law school had only three auditoriums which could accommodate 300 of the 1800 [law] students. The 548 students in letters had only three classrooms, while the department of agricultural sciences having only several small rooms, [before it moved to Chişinău], used part of the University's corridors." Hot, overcrowded classrooms sometimes made students faint. In the medical school, where the number of students had quadrupled by 1924, no new faculty appointments were made and no new laboratories were opened. In the winter, fuel shortages sometimes made it necessary to cancel classes or to underheat university buildings to the point where students had to wear overcoats. Student dormitories and

---

[100] Katherine Verdery, *Transylvanian Villagers: Three Generations of Political, Economic, and Ethnic Change* (Berkeley: University of California Press, 1983), p. 292. If we look at higher education in general, not just the universities, for the year 1931–1932, law was followed by the sciences with 15.3 percent, letters and philosophy with 13.3 percent, commercial academies with 10.3 percent, theology with 5.5 percent, medicine with 4.9 percent, polytechnics with 3.5 percent, agricultural academies with 1.7 percent, veterinary medicine with 1.2 percent, architecture with 0.7 percent, and physical education with 0.6 percent. See Gusti, *Un an*, pt. 1, tabloul nr. 2.

[101] Gusti, *Un an*, p. 315. These figures are somewhat suspect as they seem to exclude graduates in medicine and veterinary medicine.

[102] Ibid., pp. 312–313, 318.

[103] Ibid., p. 313. For 1928–1929, only 8.2 percent of the enrolled students graduated with first degrees or received doctorates. See Gabrea, "Statistică," pp. 28–29.

[104] Valeriu Florin Dobrinescu, "Studenţimea ieşeană în viaţa social-politică a României contemporane (1918–1947)" (Ph.D. diss., Universitatea Al. I. Cuza, Iaşi, Facultatea de istorie-filozofie, 1975), p. 12.

cafeterias were similarly underfunded and inadequate, as were scholarships for needy youths.[105]

These trends and conditions suggest that the dynamism of Greater Romania's higher educational development was not altogether positive. Sudden, fast-paced growth in enrollments was accompanied by overcrowding, dismal faculty-student ratios (particularly bad in the most popular departments), insufficient classroom and laboratory space, uncertain employment prospects, and, consequently, an unsettled and flustered student body and a low rate of degree completion.

It is against this background of a rapidly growing but cramped, demoralized, and dissatisfied student body that the ethnic factor came into play. Although ethnic Romanians were represented in the student body at 79.9 percent, beyond their proportion in the general population (which was 71.9 percent according to the 1930 census), many observers felt that Romanians remained the underprivileged ones. The educator Iosif Gabrea noted that of 1,256 pharmacy students enrolled in 1928–1929 "in the whole country only 426 were Romanians, and 830 [were] of other nationalities" (table 12). He asked rhetorically, "Might these numbers not mean something?"[106] Furthermore, the number of Romanians in the universities did not correspond with the number of Romanian children 5–18 years of age receiving primary or secondary schooling. Only .8 percent of Romanian children in primary and secondary schools went on to receive a higher education. Although low, this proportion was higher than that of all other ethnic groups, except the Jews. Jewish students in higher educational institutions constituted 3.6 percent of the number of Jewish children 5–18 years of age receiving lower schooling. Romanians, however, also had a higher proportion of unschooled children than most minority ethnic groups. Only Russians were worse off. Jews were the most highly schooled group, few Jewish children remaining totally outside the school system. They were followed by Germans, Hungarians, Bulgarians, Romanians, and Russians, in that order.[107]

More detailed ethnic statistics, although not by discipline, exist for one particular year during this period. In 1928–1929, 30,228 students participated in higher education. Of these, 24,144 were Romanians, 4,295 Jews, 624 Hungarians, 433 Germans, 253 Russians, and 219 Bulgarians (table 13).[108]

Whereas gentile minorities tended to concentrate in the universities of their native province: Magyars in Cluj, Germans in Cernăuţi and in Cluj,

---

[105] Dobrinescu, "Studenţimea ieşeană," pp. 3–4, 10–15, 31–32.

[106] Gabrea, "Statistică," p. 28.

[107] Ibid., p. 32. See also *Enciclopedia României,* vol. 1 (Bucharest: Imprimeria naţională, 1938), p. 480.

[108] It is likely that, since no separate heading exists for Ukrainians, they are included in one category with Russians.

and Ukrainians in Cernăuți, Jewish students were a significant presence in all four universities. Bucharest, where the student body was very diversified, was an important exception. In Greater Romania, higher education was highly concentrated in the capital, and Bucharest attracted many students from the provinces, including youth of non-Romanian ethnic backgrounds.[109]

Minority students were roughly 20 percent of the student body, but they were statistically more significant in Romania's two new universities. George Alexianu, a law professor and dean at the University of Cernăuți, considered the situation there "serious" because Romanians were outnumbered by minorities. He connected this ethnic imbalance to the social problem of rural poverty. The university administration tried to address

Table 12. Profile of university departments, by ethnicity, 1921–1933

	Romanians (%)	Jews (%)	Others (%)
All departments	77.1	16.4	6.5
Law	77.0	16.5	6.5
Letters	81.5	11.2	7.3
Science	81.3	11.8	6.9
Medicine	67.9	26.8	5.3
Theology	96.3	—	3.7
Pharmacy	40.0	51.1	8.9
Veterinary Medicine	80.0	—	20.0

Source: Calculated from *Enciclopedia României,* vol. 1 (1938), p. 480.

Table 13. Profile of university student body, by ethnicity, 1928–1929

	Number of students	Percentage of total
Romanians	24,144	79.9
Jews	4,295	14.2
Hungarians	624	2.1
Germans	433	1.4
Russians	253	0.8
Bulgarians	219	0.7
Others	260	0.9
	30,228	100.0

Source: Iosif I. Gabrea, "Statistica și politica școlară," p. 32.

[109] Gusti, *Un an,* p. 325. Magyar students began attending the University of Bucharest in 1922; by 1927, there were 70 or 80 Magyars there. "Interpelația d-lui Iosif Sandor rostită în ședința senatului din 5 aprilie 1927, în chestia înființării unei catedre de limba și literatura maghiară la Universitatea din București," *Glasul minorităților* 5 (May 1927): 171.

this by aiding underprivileged Romanian rural students as best it could given very limited resources.[110]

Zvi Yavetz, an Israeli scholar who grew up in Cernăuți during the interwar years, recollects the sense of the university as the stage for ethnic conflict:

> At the end of the first world war, Rumanian youth was full of hope. Rumania had doubled its area and population. There were plenty of openings in government bureaucracy and an academic degree could easily open doors. This is how the unversity turned into the main agency of social mobility, and Rumanian students practically stormed the doors of nearly all faculties, not just the schools of law and medicine where academic requirements were high and minority students formed the majority. Any academic degree could guarantee some government job and would satisfy most Rumanian students, who came from primitive villages, were poor, and hoped to be absorbed into the growing cities. However, the number of places in the student dormitories was limited, rents were high, and government scholarships few. Jewish students, however, came from urban areas, lived at home with their parents, and even if they were not rich, appeared as such in comparison to Rumanian students. Any antisemitic propaganda thus fell on fertile ground.[111]

Similarly, the rector of Cluj University, Florian Ștefănescu-Goangă, commented on the "exceptional situation" at his university, claiming that in 1933, Magyars, Saxons, and Jews constituted "50 percent of the student body, with a tendency to outnumber the Romanian element which came from the countryside and lacked the rich resources of the minorities."[112] Closer inspection, however, reveals that this claim is not quite true. In 1932–1933, when Ștefănescu-Goangă made his assessment, ethnic minorities made up not 50 but just under 40 percent of the student body at Cluj University. Romanians were even more numerous relative to the minorities in the years preceding and following 1932–1933. For example, in 1928–1929, they constituted 70.4 percent, and in 1931–1932, 61.6 percent, of the total student body at Cluj University. In 1933–1934, 64.1 percent of the registered students were ethnic Romanians.[113] It is nevertheless important to

---

[110] Gusti, *Un an*, pp. 1309–1310. Cernăuți University appealed to members of the Interuniversity Council, asking other, richer universities to help Bukovina's Romanian students, sons of teachers, priests, and petty clerks, most of them poor.

[111] Zvi Yavetz, "An Eyewitness Note: Reflections on the Rumanian Iron Guard," *Journal of Contemporary History* 26 (1991): 599.

[112] Minutes of the Consiliul interuniversitar meeting of October 10, 1933, in Gusti, *Un an*, p. 1310.

[113] Calculated from Neagoe, *Viața*, vol 1, p. 225; vol. 2, pp. 48, 74; and "Statistica generală," *Anuarul Universității Regele Ferdinand I Cluj pe anul școlar 1931/32* (Cluj: Institut de arte grafice Ardealul, 1932), pp. 64–65.

Table 14.　Growth of general and university-student populations,
between 1914 and 1930

	1914	1930	Increase %
General population	7,771,341	18,057,028	252.2
Student population	8,632	37,314	432.3
Percentage of students in general population	0.1	0.2	200.0

Source: Constantin Kirițescu, "Problema 'educației dirijate,' " pp. 853–854, and Institutul central de statistică, *Anuarul statistic al României, 1937 și 1938*, p. 41.

note that such claims were made and believed, since perceptions, rather than actual reality, influenced people's ideology and actions.

An Intellectual Proletariat?

The dramatic growth in the university student body, the conditions of overcrowding due to scarce resources and to inadequate growth in faculty and facilities of all kinds, and the persistence of ethnic minorities in the universities informed the protracted debate in interwar Romania over the purported excess of university graduates, the ethnic make-up of Romania's intellectual elite, and the unfair competition Romanian students and graduates might face from "foreigners." The number of university students did in fact rise out of proportion to the general population growth (table 14).

Although in absolute terms the ratio of students to the general population was not extremely high in Romania, some scholars consider Romania's educational growth at the turn of the century and after World War I a "cultural revolution," and find the expansion in *higher* education particularly revolutionary.[114] On the subject of Romanian development at the turn of the century, Andrew Janos writes:

> Ironically from a political point of view, the adverse consequences of economic stagnation were aggravated by the relative success of cultural policies, above all the rapid development of a nation-wide system of public education. . . . After World War I, the population of the new, enlarged country was on the whole more literate and educated, yet efforts to improve the educational system were redoubled in an attempt to raise the general level of literacy up

[114] Janos, "Modernization," pp. 107, 108.

to the level of the more literate national minorities, and thus in time to assimilate them. As a result, the number of schoolchildren increased from three-quarters of a million in the Old Kingdom to 3.9 million, a fivefold increase (compared to a 250 percent increase in the population of the country.)[115]

While the general population more than doubled in the period between 1914 and 1930, the university student population more than quadrupled. Where there had been one university student for every 830 inhabitants in 1914, there was one for every 484 inhabitants in 1939. The growth in university population almost kept up with the growth in the number of schoolchildren, which, according to Janos, increased fivefold. One would normally expect the highest levels of education to grow much less rapidly than the lower. In short, the pattern of educational development that Romania experienced in the interwar period was intense and potentially destabilizing.

University professors and educational administrators heatedly debated the need to limit the number of students in universities. At a university professors' conference in 1929, one speaker argued that the universities were overpopulated, that intellectual careers were becoming proletarianized, and that the universities were no longer able to absorb the great influx of students.[116] Constantin Kirițescu, who held several important posts at the Ministry of Education during the interwar period, believed that "the intellectual market was saturated." He claimed that "those who had diplomas could only with difficulty find for themselves positions as public employees, in private enterprises, or in the free professions." Kirițescu warned that "intellectual unemployment promised to be one of the most worrisome aspects of the general economic unemployment."[117] In his end-of-term report to the University Senate, the renowned speologist Emil Racoviță, rector of Cluj University in 1929–1930, apologized for leaving among the "great unsolved problems" that of "the amazingly rapid consolidation of a large intellectual proletariat":

The youth from the countryside has been driven into higher education, and now mobs have invaded a University unprepared to receive and to train them. Without appropriate buildings, staff, and materials the Romanian University cannot educate and train 35,000 students, graduates of high schools that are

---

[115] Ibid., p. 98.
[116] "Congresul profesorilor universitari la Cluj," *Transilvania,* Organul Societății culturale Astra 60 (September 1929): 717.
[117] Kirițescu, "Problema 'educației dirijate,'" p. 848.

very weak for the same reasons. The University, as it is endowed, cannot mold this youth into a class of intellectuals that are useful to society and themselves.

. . . At the same time, the villages have been ravished of their most intelligent and progressive elements in order to subject their bodies to urban physiological mysery, their minds to an imperfect training, and their souls to the pessimist urges of a life full of suffering. And the multiplication of "diplomas" does not balance out the serious troubles that excessive competition can provoke in the recruitment and future of the free professions.[118]

Dimitrie Gusti, a well-known sociologist and the National Peasant minister of education for 1932–1933, felt that when he took office the crisis of education extended to the highest levels, the university having "become a diploma factory for professors without chairs, for lawyers without trials, for doctors without patients, for theologians without parishes." Gusti himself favored more selectivity in secondary schools, so as to limit access to the university and allow it to "become a true institution for the molding of the national spiritual elite."[119]

It was not so much that Romania had more students or more universities than other European countries;[120] the issue was that these numbers were set against "the persistent condition of backwardness" in which the career that made most sense was a bureacratic one.[121] Indeed, as we have seen, the most solicited branch of higher education was law, both before and after World War I. Some observers believed that the prevalence of Romanian students in law did not correspond to the country's social life and needs.[122] Noting that 38 percent of Romanian students went to law schools, Iosif Gabrea proposed in 1932:

Since 87.1 percent of this country's citizens live from agriculture, let us imagine that in time, alongside every university, an agricultural section or academy had been organized in which these 38 percent of university youth would have got higher agricultural training! And that then they had gone to villages in order to serve permanently as advisors—on a scientific basis—to agriculture! [Had this happened] it is certain that it would not have been said, as it is

---

[118] Cited in Neagoe, *Viaţa,* vol. 1, p. 186.

[119] Gusti, *Un an,* pp. ix, 316.

[120] In a senate speech in 1927, Onisifor Ghibu said that "Romania was almost the last country in Europe with regard to the number of universities relative to its population," mentioning that in England there was a university for every 2 million inhabitants, in Germany a university for every 2.5 million, in Italy a university for every 1.5 million, in Hungary four universities for 5 million, while Romania had only four universities for 17 million inhabitants. See Ghibu, "Basarabiei nu-i este de ajuns o Facultate de Teologie," in *Prolegomena,* p. 441.

[121] Janos, "Modernization," p. 107.

[122] Gabrea, "Statistica," p. 29.

today, that "there are too many students!" and maybe . . . the economy of the State would be different too.[123]

In fact, the structure of higher education, though perhaps not well-suited to Romania's "real" needs, was adapted to the existing structure of Romania's economy and society in the interwar period. In the 1920s and 1930s, Romanian industrialization was quite limited in scope, taking off, if at all, in capital-intensive sectors. At the same time, given the postwar land reform, many peasants resisted proletarianization; in the countryside the level of consumption increased, while agriculture remained basically small-scale. These economic trends meant that there was some upward mobility; poor peasants were becoming somewhat better off and buying more land. The wealthier peasants advanced socially by sending their sons to the city to receive a university education and become "gentlemen," that is, bureaucrats.[124] Conservative trends in Romanian society reflected the resistance of agriculture and industry to modernization, the scarcity of native capital, and the reluctance of Romanians to venture into industrial and business professions. The dynamic trends in Romanian society came from the political and social project of nation and elite building through which the state attempted to lead and complete the national revolution begun during the postwar territorial expansion.

The discussions in academic circles over the unwise and uncontrolled expansion of the ranks of the educated contained real concerns, as well as elements of emotionalism and alarm. Some participants in this ongoing debate sometimes confused the issues by focusing attention on an exaggerated number of non-Romanian students and depicting it as an underlying reason for the insufficient educational resources. When picked up and reflected in the rhetoric of radical nationalist student circles, this debate over an "intellectual proletariat," scarce resources for higher education, and the possibility of reducing university enrollments was transformed into an insistent and strident demand for the "*numerus clausus*," a limit to the number of minority, especially Jewish, students admitted to Romanian universities.

[123] Ibid., p. 30.
[124] Verdery, *Transylvanian Villagers*, pp. 292–297.

7

The Generation of 1922: From Student Movement to Iron Guard

In these times, the madness of the world is reflected more obviously than anywhere else in the University. For the minds of fair-minded people say that this is where the devil has planted much of the filth with which he wants to undermine the beauty of life given [us] by the good God. And whence one expects light to spread, the darkness of many lies and passions flows forth.
—Priest Ilie L. Imbrescu, 1940

The Legionary movement was a movement of the new generation; its cadres were students and intellectuals who had recently left the universities.
—Horia Sima, Head of the Iron Guard since 1938

In an article published on December 10, 1934, on the twelfth anniversary of the start of the nationalist student movement, Ion Moța, a veteran of that movement and by 1934 a prominent Iron Guard ideologue, referred to "our nationalism" as "[the nationalism] of a previous generation of students who gave [us] December 10, 1922—celebrated today—and [the nationalism] of the generation of students and youth of today."[1] By defining "our nationalism" in this way, from the position of fascist leadership which he held in 1934, Moța indicated the direct link between the mature Iron Guard of the 1930s and the nationalist student movement that congealed in 1922. The right-wing student movement had also spawned Liga Apărării Național Creștine (LANC, or the League of National Christian Defence) in 1923 and the ephemeral groupings Fascia Națională (The National Fascio) and Acțiunea Românească (Romanian Action). Although moderate democratic and left-wing intellectuals were certainly part of Romania's political and cultural scene, by the

---

[1] Ion I. Moța, "Sensul naționalismului nostru," *Cuvântul studențesc*, December 10, 1934, reprinted in Ion I. Moța, *Cranii de lemn: Articole* (Munich: Ediția Monumentul MM, Colecția Omul Nou, 1970), p. 165.

mid-1930s the radical nationalists took center stage and came to stand for the "new generation" as a whole.[2] Radical nationalists were so widely recognized as principal spokesmen of the young generation that when the student movement was mentioned in the interwar period, the reference was generally to the extreme nationalist branch of that movement, which after 1922 dominated other political currents.[3]

The ideological and political beginnings of Romanian fascism can thus be traced to the student movement of the early 1920s. Radical nationalist protest erupted on university campuses, where students were particularly dissatisfied with the overcrowding and competition for insufficient resources described in the previous chapter. In the course of a few years campus nationalists reduced these complex problems to a general complaint against the large number of minority students with whom they had to compete in higher education and with whom they soon would have to compete also for jobs in the elite sectors of state and private employment. Attacks against the minority students were aimed particularly at the Jews; in fact, the term "minority" was usually a codeword for one particular ethnic group, the Jews. The fact that Jewish students formed the largest national minority in the general university population legitimated for many ethnic Romanians the most frequent nationalist demand for limiting their number. Although focused primarily on university issues, the nationalist student movement was also a backlash against the socialist activism that had surged immediately after the war. Nationalists connected this red wave with possible Bolshevik Russian (and, briefly, Bolshevik Hungarian) designs on Romania's newly acquired territories. Complicating the matter were the large number of Ukrainian Jewish refugees coming to Bessarabia during the Russian civil war and the sizable Jewish student body (especially those from Bessarabia) at the universities of Iaşi, Cernăuţi, and Cluj.

The nationalist student movement gained national attention not only because of its considerable dimensions and violence, but also because it reflected in a raw and exaggerated way many of the main concerns of mainstream nationalists and of the ethnic Romanian population at large. Chief among these shared interests was the desire to fashion a truly Roma-

---

[2] On the "new generation," see Z. Ornea, *Tradiţionalism şi modernitate în deceniul al treilea* (Bucharest: Editura Eminescu, 1980), pp. 454–464; George Călinescu, "Noua generaţie. Momentul 1933," in *Istoria literaturii române de la origini pînă în prezent*, 2d ed. (Bucharest: Editura Minerva, 1982), pp. 947–971; and Irina Livezeanu, "Excerpts from a Troubled Book: An Episode in Romanian Literature," *Cross Currents: A Yearbook of Central European Culture* 3 (1984): 298.

[3] In doing the research for this book, I had an experience that confirmed the hegemony of the extreme nationalists in the interwar student movements. On several occasions I conducted interviews with aging contemporaries of interwar youth movements or with historians who were well acquainted with the period of my study. When I explained neutrally that I was studying Romania's interwar student movements, the most common first reaction of my interviewees was to say that those youth movements were nationalist and anti-Semitic.

nian elite with which to replace still powerful minorities in the new territories and the need to Romanize the "foreign" cities. Nationalists of all stamps were distinctly uncomfortable with the cultural and urban minority enclaves.

The differences between the generations, however, are equally important: the young directed their intransigence not only at the "foreign" enclaves but also at the "soft," compromising, and often corrupt older generation of politicians. They condemned the constitution of 1923 for "selling out" Romania to the Great Powers by complying with the Minorities Protection Treaty of 1919 and guaranteeing the civil and political rights of the country's national minorities. The mainstream National Liberal Party, meanwhile, during whose administration the constitution had been passed, though agreeing that the Great Powers were meddling in Romania's internal affairs, understood the international treaties to be a condition for the very existence of Greater Romania. Two prime ministers—Ion Brătianu and Arthur Văitoianu—resigned in succession rather than sign the Minorities Protection Treaty,[4] but it was finally sealed by Alexandru Vaida-Voevod, another nationalist politician, and both Brătianu and Văitoianu remained fixtures of mainstream Romanian politics. Even the radical nationalist League of National Christian Defense (LANC) practiced an older, more conservative form of extreme nationalism than that increasingly demanded by the "Generation of 1922." The latter's split from LANC in 1927, when the students "graduated" and formed the Legion of the Archangel Michael, came in part over Cuza's insistence on using traditional parliamentary means to carry on the nationalist program. Such tactics were unacceptable to the youths under Corneliu Zelea Codreanu's leadership.[5]

University politics provides an ideal locus for studying the convergence and divergence between mainstream and extreme nationalism and between the older and younger generations of Romanian nationalists. Here we can best observe how the goals of the Romanian state and conservative elites, trying to achieve equilibrium in a still loosely integrated state, and those of the young generation, attempting to assure its place in the new state, dovetailed in such a way as to foster the beginnings of an important fascist movement.

---

[4] Carol Iancu, *L'Émancipation des juifs de Roumanie (1912–1919)* (Montpellier: Centre de recherche et d'études juives et hébraïques, 1992), pp. 285–298.

[5] Gheorghe T. Pop, *Caracterul antinaţional şi antipopular al activităţii Partidului Naţional Creştin* (Cluj: Editura Dacia, 1978), pp. 58–64, and Aron Petric, "Cu privire la periodizarea fascismului în România," in *Împotriva fascismului* (Bucharest: Editura Politică, 1971), p. 45. In his memoirs, Codreanu criticizes Cuza for not being an efficient leader, for not coordinating parliamentary and extra-parliamentary actions, for backing certain traditional parties, and for expelling leading LANC members without due process. See Corneliu Zelea Codreanu, *Pentru legionari (1936)*, vol. 1, 6th ed. (N.p.: Editura Legiunea Arhanghelului Mihail, 1979), pp. 263, 283–291.

The strictly political and organizational turning points in the life of the Romanian fascist movement have been recorded in some of the standard treatments of the Iron Guard,[6] but little attempt has been made to understand in a precise way the fit between the fascist movement and mainstream Romanian politics, society, and sociopolitical thought, nor the identification of the post-World War I young generation predominantly with radical nationalist, and increasingly fascist, ideas. Without exhaustively studying the Romanian fascist phenomenon,[7] I locate fascism within the nation-building agenda, focusing on the appeal of fascism to Romania's young generations and the legitimacy this ideology received from the older ones.

The Ascendance of the Left

Like other countries of interwar Europe where the radical right gained political primacy after a spectacular if short-lived moment of left-wing prominence, Romania too experienced a wave of revolutionary militance at the end of World War I. Much of the Romanian orthodox Marxist literature on the interwar period claimed (predictably) that nationalist right-wing forces were far outweighed by "democratic" moderate or left-wing forces. The influence of the right was uniformly minimized by Romanian communist historiography.[8] The credibility of much of the literature that predominated until 1989 is certainly not beyond suspicion, and the following discussion of Romania's brief "red years" is not intended to confirm that, ungenuine, Marxist perspective on Romania's interwar history. But the evidence suggests that in the first few years after the war—and never after that—the left did make a show of force in strikes and street demonstrations that shook the fragile foundations of the newly enlarged Romanian state.

[6] Eugen Weber, "Romania," in *The European Right,* ed. Hans Rogger and Eugen Weber (Berkeley: University of California Press, 1965); Mihai Fătu and Ion Spălăţelu, *Garda de fier: Organizaţie teroristă de tip fascist* (Bucharest: Editura politică, 1971); Francis L. Carsten, *The Rise of Fascism* (Berkeley: University of California Press, 1971), pp. 181–193; and Zev Barbu, "Rumania," in *Fascism in Europe,* ed. Stuart J. Woolf (London: Methuen, 1981).

[7] This study has been done recently by Armin Heinen, in his thoroughly documented *Die Legion "Erzengel Michael" in Rumänien: Soziale Bewegung und politische Organisation* (Munich: R. Oldenburg Verlag, 1986).

[8] See, for example, Maria Totu et al., *Din istoria studenţimii române: Presa studenţească (1851–1978)* (Bucharest: Universitatea din Bucureşti, Facultatea de istorie-filosofie, 1979), p. 3; Florea Dragne and Constantin Petculescu, *Frontul Studenţesc Democrat: Pagini din lupta antifascistă a studenţimii române* (Bucharest: Editura politică, 1977), p. 5; Stelian Neagoe, *Triumful raţiunii împotriva violenţei (Viaţa universitară ieşană interbelică)* (Jassy: Editura Junimea, 1977), p. 437; and *Viaţa universitară clujeană interbelică (Triumful raţiunii împotriva violenţei),* vol. 2 (Cluj: Editura Dacia, 1980), pp. 143, 178.

Politically, this strength showed in the negotiations mainstream parties arranged with leftist spokesmen. In 1918, General Averescu and Constantin Argetoianu of the People's League contacted socialist leaders to discuss possible collaboration in a future government.[9] The left's insurgency in Romania was perceived against the background of, and in fact connected to, revolutionary developments in neighboring states from which Romania had gained the territories of Bessarabia and Transylvania.[10] Communist victories in Russia and Hungary gave rise to an identification between Bolshevism and threats to Greater Romania's territorial integrity. In the case of Bessarabia these perceptions were well justified. As Lucien Karchmar has written:

> For the next three years [after 1917], the Communists in Bessarabia functioned primarily as a resistance organization, whose principal purpose was to assist in the reconquest of the province by the Red Army. For that reason, the party was able to attract support from many who normally would have shied away from its policies and even gained a strong following among the Ukrainian and Russian peasantry. But for the same reason, it found support only among those who resented Romanian rule, that is, among the Slavs and the Jews, and virtually cut itself off from any possibility of recruiting among the Moldavians.[11]

Fear of Bolshevism swept the country at different levels of society. Although Romanian troops maintained military discipline as the Russian soldiers turned from war to desertion and revolution, Bolshevik and "maximalist" propaganda was somewhat effective among the lower classes, prompting King Ferdinand to promise extensive land and electoral reforms in April 1917 during the infectious first stages of the Russian revolution.[12]

The specter of Bolshevism haunted Romanian authorities in the form of social unrest and of possible territorial losses. French diplomatic and military sources generally confirm the impression of a Bolshevik threat in

[9] Constantin-Titel Petrescu, *Socialismul în România 1835–6 septembrie 1940* ([Bucharest]: Biblioteca socialistă, [194–]), p. 314.

[10] On the influence of the Revolution of 1917 on Romania's left, see Keith Hitchins, "The Russian Revolution and the Rumanian Socialist Movement, 1917–1918," *Slavic Review* 27 (June 1968): 268–289.

[11] Lucien Karchmar, "Communism in Romania, 1918–1921," in *The Effects of World War I: The Class War after the Great War; The Rise of Communist Parties in East Central Europe, 1918–1921*, ed. Ivo Banac (Boulder, Colo.: East European Monographs, 1983), p. 154.

[12] See [Aleksandr Nikolaevitch] Winogradsky, *La guerre sur le front oriental* (Paris: Charles-Lavauzelle, 1926), p. 316; Nicolae Iorga, *Histoire des roumains et de la romanité orientale*, vol. 10: *Les Réalisateurs de l'unité nationale* (Bucharest: L'Académie roumaine, 1945), p. 543; and Hitchins, "Russian Revolution," pp. 275–276, 284–285.

Romania,[13] especially in the new provinces adjacent to the Soviet and Hungarian states, both in terms of possible armed hostility from the neighboring states and in terms of Soviet-inspired domestic radicalism.[14] Outside agitation is almost always an assumption in these reports, but local conditions in the aftermath of the war were themselves propitious to left-wing organizing. For example, a French report on the social question in Romania from the spring of 1921 mentioned communist organizing efforts in a Transylvanian mining region near Petroşani, but linked them to the nonpayment of salaries. The report also commented on the serious situation in Bessarabia, where local communist organizations were joined by agents from across the Dniester. All the Jewish organizations in Bessarabia, including the Bund, were reported to be in a block with the Communist Party and in close contact with Russia.[15]

In 1918 and 1919, Romanian diplomats in Paris tried to impress upon the French government the dangers of famine and shortages in Transylvania by stressing the associated problem of Bolshevik intrigues. Christian Rakovsky, the Bulgarian-born Romanian socialist who had spent several years in Russia, was accused of attempting to provoke Bolshevik disturbances in that province.[16] French military sources also reported that Rakovsky headed up the Bessarabian section of a "League for the Liberation of Peoples" created at the Moscow Ministry of Foreign Affairs. (They may have meant Rakovsky's post as secretary of the Federation of Balkan Socialist parties).[17] Rakovsky held a number of important positions in Soviet Ukraine from 1919 to 1923,[18] and the Soviet state certainly had an interest in recapturing Bessarabia. Rakovsky's views on Bessarabia had changed considerably since 1912, when, as a Romanian social democrat, he had inveighed against Russian imperialism in Bessarabia. After the Russian revolution of 1917 his main concern became "the spread of the revolution through the Balkans into Europe."[19] Romanian authorities werealarmed about the communist organizations they found in Bessarabia,

[13] Some French military reports, however, disclaim the existence of any true Bolshevik danger in Romania. For instance, in a telegram in 1919, General Berthelot flatly denied that uprisings or strikes were a problem in Romania in the first months of 1919: "*Situation ici très calme. Bolcheviquisme néant.*" QD 6 27/67, February 23, 1919.

[14] V 7N 1459/3; V 7N 1458/1,2; QD 55/3-4RV, 5R; QD 10 27/165, February 1, 1920; QD 29/47RV, 48, August 29, 1924. For the German perspective on the postwar situation, see Hitchins, "Russian Revolution," n. 64.

[15] QD 55/156–160, May 28, 1921.

[16] QD 41/30RV, 31, December 5, 1918, and QD 3 27/63, January 7, 1919.

[17] V 7N 3043, January 1920, and Francis Conte, *Christian Rakovski (1873–1941): A Political Biography* (Boulder, Colo.: East European Monographs, 1989), p. 102.

[18] See Gus Fagan, Introduction to Christian Rakovsky, *Selected Writings on Opposition in the USSR, 1923–1930* (London: Allison and Busby, 1980), pp. 22–23.

[19] Fagan, Introduction, p. 31; Michael Shafir, " 'Romania's Marx' and the National Question: Constantin Dobrogeanu-Gherea," *History of Political Thought* 5 (Summer 1984); and Victor Frunză, *Istoria Partidului Comunist Român*, vol. 1 (Arhus: Nord, 1984), pp. 31–32.

which, they believed, were made up mostly of Russian Jews.[20] Fear of Bolshevism also spread into Transylvania. During the Văitoianu government in the fall of 1919, state-sponsored anti-Bolshevik propaganda called for a fight to the end against "the red beasts." Government posters claimed that only Jews were Bolsheviks. A series of photographs of Hungarian Bolsheviks from the recently evicted Bela Kun regime bore captions of mostly Jewish names and identified the subjects as deserters from the Romanian army.[21]

The domestic labor and social militance of Romania's lower classes after several years of war and deprivation was of serious concern to the authorities. In the aftermath of the war and German occupation, peasant and working-class living standards had fallen. The government, faced with competing demands from different strata of the population, favored the civil servants, granting them salary increases. This measure resulted in price increases that affected the lower classes most heavily. The war had also caused massive dislocation and the militarization of labor in many enterprises. These conditions produced a wave of working-class militance in 1918–1921, manifested in work stoppages, strikes, and demonstrations.[22] In December 1918, groups of workers in Bucharest participated in socialist-led demonstrations in support of a printers' strike.[23] Close to the royal palace, protesters proclaimed "a social republic" and were fired on. According to the conservative nationalist historian and politician Nicolae Iorga, "Romanian blood reddened the unspeakably dusty streets of a totally savage capital." About one hundred demonstrators died and over two hundred were wounded in this incident.[24]

Commenting on this situation, Nicolae Iorga claimed that it "was all that was needed to produce a series of revolutionary phenomena, to which the governments that succeeded each other did not pay the necessary

[20] QD 22 27/250R, December 15, 1920.

[21] AIU/viii/C 53.

[22] Institutul de studii istorice şi social-politice de pe lîngă C. C. al P. C. R., *Documente din istoria mişcării muncitoreşti din România, 1916–1921* (Bucharest: Editura politică, 1966); Iorga, *Réalisateurs*, p. 543; Mircea Muşat and Ion Ardeleanu, *Political Life in Romania, 1918–1921* (Bucharest: Editura Academiei R. S. R., 1982), pp. 25–26, 248–249; Karchmar, "Communism in Romania," pp. 140–141; and Şerban Voinea, "Memorii," in *Şerban Voinea 1894–1969: Contribution à l'histoire de la social-démocratie roumaine,* ed. Paul H. Stahl, Sociétés européennes 6 (Paris: n.p., 1990), pp. 23–24, 28–29.

[23] Ioan Scurtu, *Viaţa politică din România 1918–1944* (Bucharest: Editura Albatros, 1982), pp. 72–73; Institutul de studii istorice şi social-politice de pe lîngă C. C. al P. C. R., *File din istoria U. T. C.,* 2d ed. (Bucharest: Editura politică, 1980), pp. 64–65.

[24] Iorga, *Réalisateurs,* p. 543; Scurtu, *Viaţa politică,* pp. 72–73; and QD 2/27/62, January 1, 1919. The Quai d'Orsay document, based on an English source, reports a conflict in Bucharest on December 6, 1918, during a Bolshevik demonstration; according to this report the troops reestablished order, some people were killed, and the leaders were arrested. Iorga mistakenly dates the incident to December 1919, a year later than it took place. See also Voinea, "Memorii," p. 23.

attention." The "phenomena," or "movements," as Iorga also called them, "in which it was difficult to distinguish between the socialism that was emerging and the penetration of communism, turned up in Bucharest and elsewhere, during the entire course of the year after the return [of the government] from Moldavia," where it had taken refuge from December 1916 until November 1918. Strikes affected the railroads, the postal service, power stations, the direction of government monopolies, the army and navy, and public tramways in many cities and industrial centers, and they involved workers ranging from civil servants to street sweepers.[25] Perhaps the most dangerous moment for the stability of Romania came in November 1918 after the withdrawal from Bucharest of the German occupation army,[26] but agitation continued into the next decade. This lower-class militance culminated in a general strike in October 1920. The Averescu government, which had come to power the previous March, put down the strike and severely repressed the left's political organizations.[27] According to Iorga, there began under Averescu a struggle between "red" and "yellow" workers, the latter having the backing of the police.[28]

In the early postwar period, however, the struggle against Bolshevism encompassed not only the state's direct repression of labor unrest, but also cultural propaganda projects that were propelled by local initiative but appealed to the state for support. These projects surfaced more frequently in industrial regions, where socialist and labor activity was concentrated. Local notables initiated "cultural hearths" that had a decidedly nationalist agenda, and they published and distributed anti-Bolshevik brochures to artisans, workers, and peasants in order to combat socialism. A priest and school committee president from the commune of Cornu, Prahova County, for instance, petitioned for the opening of a cultural hearth to combat local socialist activity:

> Since the seed of Bolshevism began to take root in our Community, as the majority of the inhabitants are workers at the petroleum enterprises from Câmpina, together with all the enlightened people of the village, we began an action against this seed.
>
> The planters of this seed, having taken note of our activity and being afraid that this seed might disappear from the village, established a subsection of the socialist party.
>
> They hold regular meetings and from time to time a more stuck-up comrade from Câmpina comes to make their heads spin. . . .

[25] Iorga, Réalisateurs, p. 543.

[26] Ghiță Ionescu, Communism in Rumania, 1944–1962 (London: Oxford University Press, 1964), p. 11, and Hitchins, "Russian Revolution," pp. 288–289.

[27] Voinea, "Memorii," pp. 28–29; Petrescu, Socialismul, pp. 349–358; File, p. 80; and Mușat and Ardeleanu, Political Life, pp. 189, 248.

[28] Iorga, Réalisateurs, p. 545; and Ionescu, Communism in Rumania, pp. 14–15.

They set up a library with poisonous books which they distribute to the citizens.

As a measure against them we rented a house in the center of the *village,* where we will lay the groundwork for a society of the village's enlightened people.

We do not have a library in the village, since the war destroyed everything; [and] there is no one else for us to appeal to; therefore we plead with your Highness, to be so kind as to approve our laying the foundations of a *"Cultural Hearth,"* with the aid of which we will be sure that we will paralyze the action of the comrades and we will save 800 families from perishing.[29]

Another priest from the parish of Comarnic, near Câmpina, asked for books from Casa şcoalelor for a cultural hearth, also in the spirit of countering Bolshevik propaganda, "to show our villagers the dangerous consequences of the feverish and criminal propaganda of the *Tovs* [comrades, from the Russian *Tovarishchi*] from the Third International, who aim to imprint in our society the anarchic character of the Adventist-Bolshevik utopia. We thought up this kind of measure of social prophylaxis because otherwise, finding ourselves very close to Câmpina, their center, the contamination of our parish could be accomplished very easily."[30] In response to another local initiative, Casa şcoalelor sponsored the free distribution of a brochure entitled "The Eradication of Bolshevism" to craftsmen, workers, and peasants. The author, Costică Porumbescu, stated: "Seeing the Bolshevist danger— propounded and safeguarded by the Revolutionary-Socialist party—which threatens us [more] day by day, we have decided to issue several thousand brochures with a national character, with the goal of repressing the Bolshevist movement."[31]

A general left-wing upsurge, albeit short-lived and ultimately easily contained, was compounded in the public mind by the influx of thousands of Ukrainian Jewish refugees to Bessarabia from across Romania's eastern border. This transient population alarmed Romanian authorities. An estimated 22,000 to 60,000 persons had entered Bessarabia by the end of 1921.[32] The Romanian government at one point believed that there were

---

[29] CS/1920/7/106, April 21, 1920. This initiative was praised, the request was approved, and books were sent.

[30] CS/1920/7/124, May [n.d.], 1920.

[31] CS/1920/6/274–276, n.d.

[32] Dumitru Şandru, *Populaţia rurală a României între cele două războaie mondiale* (Jassy: Editura Academiei R. S. R., 1980), p. 84; CA/RM 133/2, October 22, 1921; "Les Israélites de Roumanie," *Paix et droit,* October 1921; AIU VIII/C56. See also Wilhelm Filderman, "My Life," Ms., YV/P 6-2 1, pp. 115, 118. He estimates that in 1921 there were 35,000 refugees in Bessarabia, of which 6,000 were in Chişinău. Filderman also writes that "the accusation of Bolshevism, of Communist propaganda, thrown at the heads of the refugees was a pretext to justify the internment camps [planned by Romanian authorities but never implemented]."

100,000 refugees involved, and the Bessarabian historian Ştefan Ciobanu told Nicolae Iorga in a conversation about Bessarabia on May 15, 1922, that "the number of refugees, up to one million, does us much harm."[33] The right-wing daily *Universul* took up the question of the Jewish refugees as late as 1925, arguing that the Soviet Union had encouraged the Jews to stage a mass exodus. Communists, anarchists, criminals, and vagabonds had come to Bessarabia in order to create a pro-Soviet climate and to denationalize the province.[34] Some of Romania's more liberal press, not to be confused with that of the National Liberals, mocked the fear that these Jews would Russify newly annexed Bessarabia. In an article of October 27, 1921, Emil Fagure ridiculed the idea of moving the refugees from Bessarabia to less peripheral Romanian provinces: "The motive? Lest the Ukrainian Jews Russify Bessarabia. Well, I visited with these refugees, [and] I did not hear one Russian word, they all speak the jargon: Yiddish." Their real motives for fleeing Russia, he claimed, could be read on their frightened faces: pogroms and the excesses of the Soviet regime.[35]

In their suspicion, Romanian authorities and *Universul* were echoing the anti-Semitism of the White armies from whose pogroms the Jews had fled. Initially at least, the Jews, mostly artisans and tradesmen, were hurt by the economic policies of War Communism, and put their hopes in the anti-Bolshevik Volunteer Army, but after bitter experience they learned to prefer the Red Army, which engaged less in anti-Semitic violence.[36] These subtleties were lost on alarmed Romanian officials. They attempted to resolve the problem, in part with the cooperation of Jewish organizations, by setting up refugee camps, evacuating the refugees to nationally less fragile regions—ones that unfortunately also had smaller Jewish communities to welcome the fugitives—and pressing for the Jews' migration to other destinations, including repatriation.[37] Although most were bound for the

---

[33] Nicolae Iorga, *Memorii,* vol. 3 (Bucharest: Editura Naţionala S. Ciornei, n.d.), p. 305. These inflated figures indicate the alarm with which the desperate aliens were perceived. Jewish agencies claimed that the Jews were running from the Bolshevik revolution, that is, from pogroms, shortages, antibourgeois policies, and the Red Army draft—the most immediate effects of the revolution on them. Romanian authorities and right-wing public opinion, however, suspected the refugees of communism, and felt that they contributed to Bessarabia's Russian aspect. "Les Refugiés d'Ukraine en Roumanie," *Paix et droit,* November 1921; AIU/VIII/B/77, May 16 and November 10, 1921; Lucien Wolf archive, YIVO, 4/113/15491–99, May 8, 1921; and *Westminster Gazette,* May 26, 1919.

[34] "Chestia 'refugiaţilor' evrei-ruşi din Basarabia," *Universul,* May 17, 1925.

[35] *Adevărul,* October 27, 1921.

[36] See Peter Kenez, *The Defeat of the Whites: Civil War in South Russia, 1919–1920* (Berkeley: University of California Press, 1977), pp. 166–177. According to French diplomatic sources, the fugitives were almost all lower-class Jews, scared of pogroms. QD 55/119–120, February 2, 1921.

[37] Filderman, "My Life," pp. 118, 125; *Curierul israelit,* October 9, 1921; AIU/VIII/C/56, October [n.d.], 1921, and November 11, 1921; AIU/VIII/B/77, November 10, 1921; and CA/RM/133/3, December 11, 1924.

United States or Palestine, a small number wished to settle in Romania. But it seems that Romanian authorities worried less about the refugees' permanent settlement in the area than about the problem of a large number of transient Jews adding to the cultural and ethnic heterogeneity of Bessarabia.[38]

In addition, Romanian and international Jewish organizations working to resolve the refugee problem became associated in the public mind with the Bolshevik menace. A French report from 1921 on the social question in Romania reflects this perspective:

It seems established ... that these Jewish organizations in Bessarabia have support from outside. In Bessarabia has been formed an American committee for aid to the Jews, whose funds come from the Jewish *Alliance Universelle* with its headquarters in London. Recently naturalized Americans, most often in uniform, armed with legal passports, are crisscrossing the country distributing relief funds and brochures, [and] at the same time facilitating for the Israelites who wish to emigrate the means to do so. It is possible that among them there may be some who have been really delegated by the foreign associations for the pursuit of philanthropic ends. But it is likely that under this cover militant communists are hiding who have found the means to act this way surely and without danger. In any case, it should be noted that the American committee is regarded with the greatest suspicion by the Romanian authorities.[39]

The same report suggested that nearby Iași in Old Kingdom Moldavia, where the university was dominated by Jewish students, was also an important center of communist propaganda.[40] In the summer of 1922, the Ministry of the Interior established an Underinspectorate of General Security in Iași, justifying it on the grounds that "the elements of disorder from Bessarabia, in their majority Jews and refugees from Russia, are pursuing their subversive activities among the youth of the schools of Iași, among the international population of the port town of Galați, and generally in the towns and market towns inhabited by Jews."[41] According to this report, the danger of leftist subversion was spreading from the Jewish refugees in Bessarabia to the youth of Iași.

In postwar Romania, particularly in the northeast in Bessarabia and Moldavia, an area that was closest to communist Russia and had a higher population of Jews than other provinces, an identification emerged between

[38] MIC/1921/273/11–12, May 30, 1921, and AIU/VIII/B/77, November 10, 1921.
[39] QD 55/156–160, May 28, 1921.
[40] Ibid.
[41] *Monitorul oficial*, August 11, 1922, cited in *Paix et droit*, October 1922.

Jewishness and Bolshevism.[42] Anti-Semitism and anticommunism became signposts for the extremist version of the national ideology.

Codreanu and the Student Movement

The ideology of Corneliu Zelea Codreanu, the student who became the "*Căpitan*" of the Legion of the Archangel Michael (Iron Guard), was shaped by the widely assumed equation between Jew and Bolshevik and by a reaction to what might be called Romania's "red years." In *Pentru legionari* (1936), the book that was to the Iron Guard leader what *Mein Kampf* was to Hitler, Codreanu described his impressions of Iaşi just at the end of the war: "Every three or four days on the streets of Iaşi there were huge communist demonstrations. Those 10–15,000 starved workers, maneuvered by the Judaic criminal hand from Moscow, paraded the streets while singing the Internationale, yelling: 'Down with the King!' 'Down with the army!' and carrying placards on which one could read 'Long live the communist revolution!' 'Long Live Soviet Russia!' "[43] One reason not to discount Codreanu's impressions is that they read like an amplified version of the concerns of many Romanians in the political mainstream for the country's social, political, and territorial security. In 1936, Codreanu claimed that he had been frightened by the revolutionary phenomena he observed after the war and that the authorities had not responded to the leftist and Jewish danger vigorously enough. Impressed by the possibility of a Bolshevik invasion, in 1917, at the age of eighteen, he had called a secret meeting of high school friends to plan for that eventuality:

> I called these young comrades together to discuss a grave problem though our life was but budding. What are we going to do if the Bolsheviks invade us? My opinion, with which the others were in accord, was this: if the Bolshevik army crosses the Dniester, then the Pruth, reaching our region, we shall not submit, but will take refuge in the woods armed; we will organize there a center of Romanian action and resistance, and by skillful action shake up the enemy; we will maintain a spirit of non-submission, and keep alive a spark of hope amidst the Romanian masses in villages and towns. We all took an oath in the middle of the ancient forest. This forest was a corner of that

[42] On the legionary movement's identification of Jews with communism, see Leon Volovici, *Nationalist Ideology and Anti-Semitism: The Case of Romanian Intellectuals in the 1930s* (Oxford: Pergamon, 1991), p. 64.

[43] Corneliu Zelea Codreanu, *For My Legionaries (The Iron Guard)* (Reedy, W. Va.: Liberty Bell Publications, 1990), p. 9. The first edition of *Pentru legionari* was published in Sibiu by Editura Totul pentru ţară in 1936. It was later translated into several foreign languages, including French, English, and German, and has appeared in numerous editions in Romania and elsewhere.

famous woods of Tigheciu on whose paths, throughout Moldavia's history, many an enemy found death.[44]

These adolescent plans were never realized. When the war ended, Codreanu became a law student at the University of Iași. On coming to the city in September 1919, he was impressed by the ascendancy of the left not only in the workers' milieux, but also at the university. That Iași was in fact briefly a hotbed of leftism at the end of the war resulted from several factors: the proximity to the locus of a successful socialist revolution, the large number of refugees from Russia's civil war, and the fact that Iași, as Romania's makeshift capital during the German occupation in 1916–1918, became a teeming refuge of government, enterprises, labor unions, and socialist organizations. These efforts increased as the war drew to a close. Iași socialists endeavored to make the city a regional propaganda center able to coordinate actions and supply other Moldavian towns and villages with brochures, membership cards, speakers, electoral expertise, and legal and financial aid. A Moldavian-wide regional conference of labor unions and socialist organizations held in Iași on September 27 and 28, 1919, proved the success of the efforts of Iași socialists: At two previous conferences in the last year "about 20 anemic circles from all of Moldavia" had been represented, while "today [Moldavia's] capital alone counts over 20 numerically strong organizations," reported a socialist who attended. He continued, "A year ago the delegates were barely trying to find a way to revive fragments of the prewar movement. At this new conference the spokesmen of Moldavia's workers have set the agenda for intensifying propaganda among unorganized masses and for strengthening the existing organizations." The author also noted positively the city's youth, commenting that "Iași, a cultural town [full] of high school and college students who are becoming 'infected' with socialism and are spreading it to all the towns, could become Moldavia's cultural hotbed."[45]

Codreanu's reaction to the "redness" of Iași was, we learn from his later Guardist associates, one of "great disappointment":

Instead of finding university youth mobilized against Communism, youth thinking and feeling like himself, he finds a mass of individuals the great majority of which had already slipped toward the left.

Marxist theories were in vogue, propagated by the professors themselves from their lecterns. The intellectuals had already forgotten the hundreds of thousands of soldiers fallen on the field of honor, and were fraternizing with

[44] Ibid., p. 3.
[45] See doc. 108, "Conferința regională a organizațiilor sindicale și socialiste din Moldova ținută la Iași în zilele de 27 și 28 septembrie 1919," in Institutul de studii istorice, *Documente din istoria mișcării muncitorești*, pp. 247, 249–250. See also docs. 36 and 71.

the mortal enemy of the Romanian people. For these perverted intellectuals, Marxist doctrine represented the last word of science and progress. Whoever spoke of Fatherland, Church, and King, was derided, [and] considered anachronistic and retrograde.[46]

After the war, the student body encompassed both a democratic and a nationalist camp, but the left or democratic group was initially stronger.[47] Moța, a nationalist student leader at Cluj University who became very close to Codreanu, wrote that in 1920–1921 "a large part of the students . . . were involved in Marxist-Communist politics."[48] Most student societies were led by communists.[49]

Mirroring the fears of Romanian authorities about Jewish refugees from Bessarabia, Codreanu saw himself and the few nationalists on campus as "overwhelmed by the immense mass of Jewish students . . . from Bessarabia, all communist agents and propagandists."[50] In 1921, the moderate student newspaper *Viața studențească* (Student life) estimated that 4,500 Bessarabian students were attending the four Romanian universities. Three-quarters of these were in Iași.[51] The Bessarabians were thus an important presence in themselves, in addition to which they were mostly leftists. In an article in *Viața universitară*, the weekly of the leftist Union of Independent Students, Professor Grigore T. Popa of Bucharest University described the tensions between the Bessarabians and the nationalists:

> You should not find it strange that the first cohorts of students arrived from Bessarabia were welcomed with hatred and brutality by the Iași "*nationalists.*" The masterfully manipulated atmosphere made the Bessarabian into *a foreigner.* . . . The pure language [of the Moldavian dialect], the deliberate Moldavian gestures, the kindness of spirit characteristic of the idealistic Bessarabians could not serve as a basis for brotherhood . . . because socialism was an issue. All the Bessarabians were socialists, that is striving for social justice and for the progress of man in the eyes of humans. . . . [F]or this reason our [nationalists'] eyes regarded those of the broad words and the Russian caps . . . with hostility.[52]

[46] Horia Sima, *Histoire du mouvement légionnaire* (Rio de Janeiro: Editora Dacia, [1972]), p. 18.
[47] In interwar Romania, "democratic" tended to be a codeword for socialist-leaning.
[48] Moța, *Cranii*, p. 187.
[49] Sima, *Histoire*, p. 18.
[50] Codreanu, *For My Legionaries*, p. 8.
[51] "Studențimea basarabeană," *Viața studențească*, June 16–30, 1921, p. 3. Totu, *Din istoria studențimii*, p. 11, identifies this periodical as having "a bourgeois-democratic character."
[52] Grigore T. Popa, "Pentru studenții basarabeni," *Viața universitară*, September 20, 1925.

Still *Viaţa studenţească* noted the irony of the Bessarabians being regarded as "Bolsheviks" or "ultra-revolutionaries" in the Romanian context, although Russian revolutionaries had considered them reactionaries, and Bessarabia Russia's "Vendée," a reference to one of France's most royalist regions during the French revolution. Moderates, meanwhile, viewed the Bessarabian students as constitutionalists who sought in Romania the civil rights that tsarist Russia had previously denied them.[53]

The reason for the large number of Bessarabians at Iaşi University was that Ministry of Education authorities and some faculty members favored a generous admissions policy towards Bessarabian students, indicating the universities' "national duty to open wide the gates to the youth of Bessarabia which longed for Romanian culture." If they were not admitted, the argument went, these students would end up at Russian universities.[54] For geographic reasons, Iaşi University received the largest influx of Bessarabian students. The university's administration appealed to the Ministry of Education for funds to accommodate the newcomers. In his 1918 appeal for financial help, the rector claimed that the eight hundred new arrivals from Bessarabia (as well as Transylvania) did not simply constitute a local problem: after one hundred years of separation from their brothers in Moldavia, they were part of "a great national question which concerned the Romanian State."[55] The university could only afford to feed twenty five of the eight hundred, and the rector feared that without ministerial aid, "the Bessarabian students would be forced to leave for universities in Ukraine, where it is said that the State has made great sacrifices to be able to attract them." In response to these requests, the Romanian state initially subsidized dormitories and cafeterias for students from Bessarabia (as well as for the smaller contingents of students from Bukovina, Ardeal, and Macedonia).[56]

This effort to open wide the universities and make them financially affordable to the youth of the new territories, however, incurred the animosity of Old Kingdom youth who were receiving no extraordinary treatment.[57] Ethnic and political considerations enhanced the animus toward the Bessarabians. Of the 4,062 Bessarabian students enrolled at Iaşi University from 1918 until 1930, only 1,306, or one-third, were ethnic Romanians. The 1,794 Jews represented 44.2 percent of the Bessarabian students, Russians made up 11.3 percent, Bulgarians 4.5 percent, and Ukrainians

---

[53] "Studenţimea basarabeană," *Viaţa studenţească*, June 16–30, 1921.
[54] MIC/1918/193/11, August 22, 1918; and MIC/1918/193/15, August 6, 1918.
[55] MIC/1918/188/3, August 24, 1918.
[56] Ibid. Socialists from Bessarabia also argued that their "Romanian consciousness stopped them from seeking light outside of the Romanian land." Cited in Marin C. Stănescu, *Depun mărturie în faţa istoriei: Timotei Marin militant şi publicist comunist (1897–1937)* (Jassy: Editura Junimea, 1977), p. 16.
[57] MIC/1918/188/2, September 6, 1918.

4 percent. Smaller numbers of other Bessarabian nationalities were also represented in the Iaşi student body.[58] The University of Iaşi had an unusually large number of students from the newly annexed territories. Of the 4,656 students registered at the university in 1921–1922, over half were from Bessarabia, Bukovina, and Transylvania.[59]

As a group, the Bessarabian students, as we have seen, started out largely under leftist influence. Within the Bessarabian student organization in Iaşi a struggle for power ended in the triumph of a socialist leadership at the end of 1919.[60] Bessarabian communists had been reluctant to consider themselves part of the Romanian movement, lest that signify acceptance of Romania's annexation of the province. In 1920, however, they shifted tactics and opened up branch headquarters in Iaşi and Cernăuţi.[61] In 1921, Ministry of War officials discovered a "Bolshevik nest" in Iaşi, and warned the Ministry of Education of the anti-Romanian activities of Bessarabian students: meetings and posters agitating against police interference with political activities on campus.[62]

In 1921, with the approval and financial support of the Ministry of Education, the Bessarabians organized themselves formally into a "Circle of Bessarabian Students."[63] The Ministry sent the circle's president a note supporting the formation of organizations of Romanian students from the new territories, "in view of the beautiful and difficult role that [the students from the new territories] will have in the organization of Greater Romania."[64]

While the Ministry and university administrations wanted to help the Bessarabians outgrow their regional identity through the circle, as well as by other means,[65] the Bessarabian student society may have worked in the

---

[58] Calculated from Onisifor Ghibu, "Basarabia în statistica Universităţii din Iaşi," Extras din Arhiva pentru Ştiinţa şi Reforma Socială, vol. 10 (Bucharest: Monitorul oficial, Impr. naţională, 1932), p. 22.

[59] Arhiva Universităţii Alexandru Ioan Cuza, 2/1922/539–540, cited in Stănescu, Depun mărturie, p. 14.

[60] Stănescu, Depun mărturie, p. 15.

[61] Ibid., and Karchmar, "Communism in Romania," p. 155.

[62] MIC/1921/273/3,5,6. Posters signed by the Executive Committee of the Bessarabian University Student Circle in Iaşi called for a three-day protest strike for March 28–30, apparently in response to the arrest of communist student leaders. The Ministry of War wanted a thorough check on the certificates and personal papers of Bessarabian students, presumably in order to find and expel dangerous or illegitimate ones. See Stănescu, Depun mărturie, pp. 22–24, and MIC/1921/273/3–6, April 12, 1921.

[63] MIC/1921/263/13, March 29, 1921, and MIC/1921/263/17,18, n.d.

[64] MIC/1921/263/14, n.d.

[65] MIC/1922/479/13, March 31, 1922. Traian Bratu, the rector of the University of Iaşi, suggested sending Bessarabian students to spend the summer with peasant families, to put them "in contact with the mass of Romanian peasants, [who are] the most advanced in cultural things, possessed by the most powerful national sentiments, and [have] the healthiest political sense."

opposite direction, towards maintaining a regional separatism that was reinforced by prevalently leftist leanings. Differences of opinion certainly existed within the group, but the right was at first unable to assert itself successfully. An article in *Scânteia* of June 1923 talked about the failed "attempt of a small grouplet of students to impart to our Circle an anti-Semitic coloring."[66] The anti-Semitic Bessarabian students deplored their leftist colleagues as fellow travelers of the disaster in Russia from which, one wrote, "we and the Christian people of Bessarabia turn our heads in horror." According to this anti-Bolshevik group, the leftists "who spoke in the name of the Bessarabians were a tiny minority."[67] Minority or not, the leftists remained in charge until 1922.

Perhaps because the university seemed so hopelessly leftist in the early postwar years, Codreanu's first organized political experience came in a short-lived nationalist workers' organization called Garda Conştiinţei Naţionale (The Guard of the National Conscience).[68] The Guard was created in Iaşi in the summer of 1919. Its counter-socialist strike-breaking activity peaked in the spring of 1920. The labor-repressive measures of the Averescu government soon thereafter seem to have eliminated the Guard's raison d'être.[69]

In 1920–1921, Codreanu turned his attention to student politics, and at first faced an uphill struggle. In Iaşi as in Bucharest, relations between ethnic groups and different political camps were cordial, and political discussion had not been radicalized to the point where one viewpoint was hegemonic and all other ones illegitimate. In Iaşi, according to Horia Sima, there were no more than about forty nationalist students, as opposed to "the great majority of the others, dominated by the Communist organizations." But even if communists were not as strong as Guardist memoirs record, pluralism may have been enough to upset Codreanu and his associates.[70] Codreanu writes about this period of his political activity in his memoirs:

The advancement of these anti-Romanian ideas supported by a compact mass of professors and students, and encouraged by all enemies of unified Romania,

[66] *Scânteia*, June 7, 1923. (This periodical is not to be confused with the Romanian Communist Party organ of the same name.) *Scânteia* (The Spark), was subtitled "Organ pentru apărarea intereselor intelectualilor" (Organ for the defense of intellectuals' interests). It was published in Iaşi from February to October 1923, edited by Timotei Marin, a Communist Bessarabian student. See Stănescu, *Depun mărturie*, p. 51. Totu, *Din istoria studenţimii române*, p. 11, reports that the paper appeared May to October 1923.

[67] *Cuvântul Iaşului* 1, no. 6. (*Cuvântul Iaşului* began to appear in 1923.)

[68] The Romanian word *conştiinţă* has the dual meaning of consciousness and conscience.

[69] Codreanu, *Pentru legionari*, pp. 18–30; Fătu and Spălăţelu, *Garda de fier*, p. 35; Pop, *Caracterul antinaţional*, pp. 42–43; and Sima, *Histoire*, pp. 19–20.

[70] Sima, *Histoire*, p. 21; Codreanu, *Pentru Legionari*, pp. 15–16, and I. Reichman-Şomuz, "Înainte şi după începerea agitaţiilor studenţeşti din România," *Toladot* 4 (July 1975): 11–14.

Nae Ionescu (*right*) next to General Cantacuzino-Grănicerul, leader of
the Iron Guard front *Totul pentra țară* (All for the fatherland), February
1937, at the station in Bucharest waiting for the funerary train of Moța
and Marin, two legionnaires who died fighting for Franco in the Spanish
Civil War. From the "Lotta e Trionfo" album. Courtesy of Cabinetul de
Stampe. Biblioteca Academiei Române, Bucharest

found among the student body no Romanian resistance. A few of us who were still trying to man the barricades, were surrounded by an atmosphere of scorn and enmity. On the streets or in the halls of the university, colleagues holding other opinions, those with "freedom of conscience," and who preach every other kind of freedom, spat behind us as we passed and became increasingly aggressive. Thousands of students in meeting after meeting in which Bolshevism was propagated, attacked Army, Justice, Church, [and] Crown.[71]

Unable to rally massive support for the cause of nationalism, Codreanu resorted to lonely, heroic actions. Occasionally accompanied by a few others, he interfered with the autumnal return to classes (because he was outraged at the skipping of the traditional religious ceremony); he interfered with the production of Jewish plays; he vandalized Jewish and democratic publication offices; and he scuffled with liberal Jewish newspaper editors whom he held responsible for favoring the enemies of the nation.[72] With a few followers, Codreanu captured and burned the Russian-style caps of Bessarabian students, which he felt they wore "ostentatiously, to indicate their Bolshevist nuance."[73] The official student society repudiated these actions. In May 1921, Codreanu's behavior was still no more than a nuisance that the university's main student organization felt sure it could contain with the help of the administration. A 1921 student letter to the rector attempted to enlist his help in stopping Codreanu:

> His behavior has found imitators, and now Mr. Codreanu has about ten or fifteen lackeys, who distinguish themselves by the noise they make at student gatherings, but none of whom is as impulsive as Mr. Codreanu.
> Mr. Codreanu is the one who provoked all the scandals and misunderstandings in our student life, estranging the students from the Regat from those from Bessarabia, [and] by his insults forcing them to leave our gatherings every time that they came to meetings.
> In view of all these things, Mr. Rector, we ask that you give the most severe sanctions for the purification of student life.[74]

In response to student entreaties, to a complaint from a journalist assaulted by Codreanu, and on the basis of Codreanu's overall record of disruptive actions, the University of Iaşi expelled him on June 2, 1921.[75] But this

---

[71] Codreanu, *For My Legionaries*, p. 9.
[72] Ibid., pp. 26–39; MIC/1921/176/6, May 30, 1921; MIC/1921/176/7, May 31, 1921; MIC/1921/8–9, June 2, 1921; and Neagoe, *Triumful*, pp. 93–101.
[73] Codreanu, *For My Legionaries*, p. 38.
[74] MIC/1921/176/7, May 31, 1921.
[75] MIC/1921/176/8–9, June 2, 1921, and Neagoe, *Triumful*, pp. 100–101.

decision had no practical effect, since Codreanu received the full support of the Law School where he was enrolled within Iaşi University, and where the dean was the renowned anti-Semitic leader A. C. Cuza. Codreanu also indirectly received the support of the minister of instruction, Constantin Angelescu, who hesitated to enforce the Iaşi University Senate's decision to expel Codreanu. In a memo of November 1922 to the Ministry of Education, Traian Bratu, the rector of Iaşi University, wrote that the ministry had "left the solution [to the problem of Codreanu's expulsion and Cuza's opposition to it] up to the University. In fact Professor Cuza has thus attained his goal: the former student Zellea-Codreanu [sic], despite the whole punishment of his expulsion which was determined legally in June 1921, continued as a student until June 1922, has passed all his exams, and now he is pursuing his studies in Germany, most probably as a graduate of our Law School."[76]

During his last year at the Iaşi Law School, Codreanu asserted himself decisively as a nationalist student leader. Capitalizing on the notoriety created by his expulsion and by his reinstatement within the Law School, he was elected president of the Law Students' Association.[77] He used this position to introduce a weekly study group on various aspects of the "kike question in the light of science."[78] This series attracted many students from the Law School and even from other departments. Since the Law School was, in any case, the best-attended branch of the university, Codreanu's position there was strategic. The extracurricular seminars he organized did not occur in a vacuum. They built on the anti-Semitic courses of A. C. Cuza, who taught political economy and whose lectures were very popular.[79] The official university-wide student society, which was initially dominated by the left, began to lose influence to the Codreanu-led organization. On May 21, 1922, Codreanu founded Asociaţia Studenţilor Creştini (the Association of Christian Students), which seems to have replaced the General Association of Iaşi Students.[80] By virtue of its name, the former excluded Jews and also many leftists, isolating both groups, and reducing communist influence among Iaşi University students.[81]

There was nothing new about Cuza's anti-Semitic theories, which he had developed at the turn of the century and on the basis of which he had

---

[76] MIC/1921/176/1, June 19, 1921; MIC/1921/176/3–5, June 11, 1921; MIC/1921/176/10–14, June 8, 1921; Sima, *Histoire*, p. 21; MIC/1922/476/59, January 29, 1922; for quotation, see MIC/1922/476/30, November 15, 1922.

[77] Neagoe, *Triumful*, p. 110.

[78] Codreanu, *Pentru legionari*, p. 48.

[79] Sima, *Histoire*, p. 24; and Codreanu, *Pentru legionari*, pp. 49–50.

[80] Neagoe, *Triumful*, p. 113. See also Codreanu, *Pentru legionari*, p. 60. The date he gives is May 20. At the same time, Codreanu and his disciples dissolved the General Association of Iaşi Students, an adversary, leftist organization.

[81] Sima, *Histoire*, p. 21.

founded the National Democratic Party in association with the historian Nicolae Iorga in 1910.[82] Codreanu initially embraced this anti-Semitic tradition wholesale, especially as it was conveyed to him by A. C. Cuza. Yet, at first, right after the war, both Codreanu and his mentor Cuza stood on the fringes of university politics.[83] The reactualization of these theories, with difficulty at first, as the credo behind the students' mass protests and the motto of the new generation was made possible by the repression of the left-wing upsurge, the constitutional debate preceding the passage of the 1923 constitution, and the broader legitimacy offered indirectly by the policies of nation building introduced by mainstream politicians.

The Generation of 1922 and the League of National Christian Defense

The massive outbreak of nationalist student protest in late 1922 coincided with the parliamentary debates on the Liberal-drafted constitution and preceded the organization of LANC, Liga Apărării Național Creștine, (the League of National Christian Defense) under the leadership of A. C. Cuza. These three events are closely related.

In January 1922, A. C. Cuza, Nicolae Iorga's former political associate in the National Democratic Party, and Nicolae Paulescu, a professor of physiology at the Bucharest Medical School, had founded Uniunea Național Creștină (the National Christian Union). The union opposed the St. Germain Treaty's minority protection clauses, whose inclusion in the Romanian constitution was then being debated,[84] and its aim was to resolve

[82] On pre–World War I Romanian anti-Semitism and on Cuza's and Iorga's collaboration, see William Oldson, *The Historical and Nationalistic Thought of Nicolae Iorga* (Boulder, Colo.: East European Monographs, 1973), pp. 84–88; William Oldson, *A Providential Anti-Semitism: Nationalism and Polity in Nineteenth-Century Romania* (Philadelphia: American Philosophical Society, [1991]), esp. pp. 132–138; Radu Ioanid, *The Sword of the Archangel* (Boulder, Colo.: East European Monographs, 1990), pp. 28–35; Volovici, *Nationalist Ideology*, pp. 18–41; and Petre Țurlea, *Nicolae Iorga în viața politică a României* (Bucharest: Editura Enciclopedică, 1991), pp. 64–69.

[83] Although I have focused this discussion on Iași because that was Codreanu's point of origin, in Bucharest the first few postwar years were also infertile ground for radical nationalism in the university. See Reichman-Șomuz, "Înainte și după," pp. 11–14.

[84] The National Democratic party had factionalized at the beginning of World War I. While Cuza adhered to a unionist federation of parties opposing the Liberal government for its hesitation to join the conflict immediately, Iorga backed the government in the face of crisis. At about the same time, the two men also diverged on the Jewish question, Iorga becoming much more moderate in his views, even promising to change the anti-Semitic clauses of the National Democratic Party's statutes to permit Jews to join. See Țurlea, *Nicolae Iorga*, pp. 96–99, and "Lettre de Bucarest: Les Élections roumaines et les Juifs," *Paix et droit*, March 1922, p. 4. On Iorga's interwar views, see Volovici, *Nationalist Ideology*, pp. 32–35. A *Paix et droit* correspondent referred to Iorga as "the historian, yesterday an anti-Semite, but today returned to better sentiments." *Paix et droit*, February 1922, p. 7. See also QD 29/6, May 20, 1924.

the Jewish question. Its most immediate agenda was to vote quickly on the constitution before "foreign agitation" mobilized to make it a clear document of Jewish emancipation.[85] The union's demands were to keep Article 7 of the old constitution, thus negating the Jewish emancipation; expel the Jews who had come to Romania since 1914; apply the *numerus clausus* in schools, universities, trade, industry, and the liberal professions; exclude Jews from teaching in state institutions; exclude Jews from the army and make them pay an additional tax instead; disallow Jewish candidates from running for office on any general lists; and establish Jewish electoral curias.[86]

Apărarea națională (National Defense), the union's newspaper which started to appear in April of that year, was read avidly by Codreanu's crowd at Iași university. But Cuza and the nationalist student movement did not connect formally in a political organization until March 4, 1923, when LANC was formed.[87] LANC was constituted after the turning point in student politics in December 1922, and after the nationalist student movement had clearly become a force to be reckoned with; LANC was then very much a product of the student movement.

Until the end of 1922, Cuza and the nationalist students had hoped that they could force the university to exclude, or at least limit, the number of Jewish students, thus turning the university into an embryonic example of the wider program of the National Christian Union. The union greatly expanded its activities during the troubled winter of 1922–1923, hoping to use student militance to move the government to implement some of the exclusionary nationalist demands of both groups. When that hope failed to materialize, Codreanu convinced his followers that they needed to form a real political organization, no longer restricted to the universities, but having all the goals of the student movement and more. This organization would mobilize mass support for the students' program. Public opinion would then force Parliament to ratify the *numerus clausus* program, limiting the number of Jewish students in universities. Cuza became the formal head of LANC, and the students were its vanguard.[88]

Cuza saw his role as one of giving "theoretical guidance to the movement." He asserted that the league was anti-Semitic because the "Kikes" had disrupted the principle of nationality by living in the midst of other peoples, because they were the enemies of Christianity, and because,

[85] *Apărarea națională*, April 1, 1922; Pop, *Caracterul antinațional*, p. 43; and M. Schweig, *Arme ruginite: Conferință* (Bucharest: Institut de arte grafice Eminescu, 1923), p. 6.

[86] "Roumanie: Le programme de l'Union Nationale Chrétiènne," *Paix et droit*, February 1923, p. 11. While postwar legislation had already emancipated most of Romania's Jews, about 30 percent were still without rights. See "En Roumanie: La Constitution roumaine et la question juive," *Paix et droit*, February 1922, pp. 5–6.

[87] Codreanu, *Pentru legionari*, p. 51; and Sima, *Histoire*, p. 25.

[88] Sima, *Histoire*, p. 25.

through their excessive numbers in Romania, they had taken hold of the cities, destroyed the native middle class, and were endeavoring to become the leadership class "as one can see from their large-scale invasion of the universities." Thus, LANC had "set as its first objective *the elimination of the Kikes* from all branches of activity, especially the universities." Cuza, a law professor, equivocated on the legal grounds for his position. Claiming that he recognized Romania's existing laws which guaranteed equal rights to Jewish citizens, he said that the Romanian state had been "violated" by the St. Germain Treaty and therefore had the right to revise those laws.[89]

The formative experience of the nationalist student movement, and, by extension, of the fascist movement into which the former developed, took place in 1922. Mass protests erupted on all Romanian campuses. Students demanded the exclusion of Jewish students from universities or at least limits to Jewish enrollment in accord with their proportion in the general population. As elsewhere in Central and Eastern Europe such demands became known as "numerus clausus." The nationalist students were concerned not only with the ethnic balance of the universities, but with that of society at large. Since the universities produced the leadership stratum,[90] these were their most immediate target.

Anti-Semitic incidents perpetrated mostly by youth had intensified in the summer and fall of 1922. The abuse was first directed at theaters producing Jewish plays in Moldavia. In his memoirs Codreanu depicted the struggle over Romania's theaters:

> The summer of 1922 did not pass peacefully. On the stages of Romanian national theaters or communal ones in Moldavian towns, Jewish plays began to be performed in Yiddish by the "Kanapof" troupe. Our youth considered this a threat, for it saw a beginning of the alienation of this institution, meant to be for the national and moral education of the Romanian people. Expropriated in commerce, industry, in the richness of the Romanian soil and subsoil, in the press, we will see ourselves one day expropriated also from the stages of our national theaters. The theater, together with the school and the church, can elevate a decayed nation to the consciousness of its rights and historical mission. It can prepare and motivate a nation to liberating struggle. From now even this redoubt shall be taken away from us.[91]

In Codreanu's view, the high school and college students took it upon themselves to intervene because their elders were inexcusably absent from

---

[89] Alexandru C. Cuza, *Mişcările studenţeşti şi cauzele lor* (Declaraţia făcută înaintea comisiunei de anchetă) (Bucharest, 1925), pp. 9–11.

[90] Sima, *Histoire*, pp. 21–23; and "Situaţia la Cernăuţi," *Cuvântul studenţesc*, May 30, 1923. The nationalist students in Cernăuţi said that they wanted "numerus proportionalis" not only in the university, but in all branches of social activity.

[91] Codreanu, *For My Legionaries*, p. 49.

the nation's observation post. In the fall, anti-Jewish demonstrations broke out in connection with the national and local celebrations in honor of King Ferdinand's coronation as the monarch of Greater Romania. The troublemakers were mostly high school and university students, occasionally encouraged by teachers and school administrators. These activities were serious enough to prompt a reaction from the minister of public instruction.[92]

Soon the universities also became centers of anti-Semitic disturbances. By November 1922, campus demonstrations were occurring frequently.[93] At the beginning of December the right-wing student movement became an uncontrollable threat to peace and order. This first great outburst of nationalist student protest has been called by its veterans a "spontaneous explosion" and a "spasm of the sick nation." At the time Codreanu had already graduated and was continuing his law education in Germany.[94] He was particularly hopeful about the spontaneous character of the disturbances:

> I was still in Jena, when one day I was surprised by the news that the entire Romanian student body from all universities arose to battle. This collective demonstration of the Romanian youth, unsuspected by anybody, was a volcanic eruption rising from the nation's depths. . . . The entire Romanian student body rose to its feet as in a time of great peril. . . . A great collective electrifying moment, with no preparation beforehand, without any pro and con discussions, without any committee decisions, without those in Cluj even knowing those in Iaşi, Cernăuţi or Bucharest. A great moment of collective enlightment [sic] like the lightening in the middle of a dark night, in which the entire youth of the country recognized its own destiny in life as well as that of its people.[95]

Ion Moţa also emphasized the instinctiveness of the movement:

> Not we, this or that particular student gave birth to the "movement." It was born spontaneously from the soul of the mass of students, superimposed on

---

[92] CA/RM 38, n.d.; Codreanu, *Pentru legionari*, pp. 67–69; "Lettre de Bucarest: Troubles antisemites," and "Une Circulaire du ministre de l'instruction publique," *Paix et droit*, November 1922, pp. 6–8.

[93] MIC/1922/479/57, November 6, 1922. The Minister of education was worried enough to ask the rector of Iaşi University to carry out an investigation and report to him on the anti-Semitic student demonstrations. See also Neagoe, *Triumful*, p. 171; and Zsombor de Szasz, *The Minorities in Roumanian Transylvania* (London: Richards Press, 1927), p. 336.

[94] Sima, *Histoire*, p. 22; Codreanu, *Pentru legionari*, p. 77; Moţa, *Cranii*, pp. 230–231; and Neagoe, *Triumful*, pp. 119, 178.

[95] Codreanu, *For My Legionaries*, p. 54.

the soul of the nation. Without any kind of preliminary organization or premeditation. And the proof that it did not start from a few isolated spirits, who might have been sick or degenerate, is the fact that with lightning speed, it was recognized by the entire body of university youth—with insignificant exceptions—as being the mirror of their own spiritual process. Those who criticize this past, therefore, do nothing but protest against an organic social phenomenon of a suffering nation: they criticize a spasm, they criticize a generation, which precisely out of healthy feeling and thought, did not deign to break itself away from the body of the nation, but received its pulsations of life and for life.[96]

The wave of student disturbances, surprisingly, did not begin in Cuza's Iaşi, where the ground had been well prepared, but in the Transylvanian capital of Cluj.[97] The immediate incident that sparked off the nationwide protests took place at the Cluj Medical School. Ethnic Romanian students demanded that their Jewish colleagues provide their own Jewish cadavers for dissection.[98] This demand quickly came to symbolize the sense of social and national wrong that pervaded the ethnic Romanian student body. Evoking the atmosphere of Cluj in 1922, Ion Moţa later wrote:

Misery, dampness, a housing shortage, overcrowded dormitories for the Romanians. Carefree leisure, terrible increase, lack of worries for the foreigners who had become defiant. On street corners one heard that that year, in the first year of medical school, there were four times as many Kikes as Romanians. . . . And, as if we had not had enough with the mud, the cold, the lack of shelter, and all the rest of the material and especially moral miseries of these worries in our clean Romanian souls, one day there came to strangle us the news of the suicide of a female student, obviously a Romanian, a woman from Oltenia, [in the Old Kingdom], brought to the University of Cluj by her love for the Ardeal. . . . She had neither a scholarship, nor a place in the dorm, nor relatives. For she had left a note that she was taking her own life, no longer able to endure that misery. When we climbed the Feleac with the funeral convoy (the whole university was at the funeral), above our heads triumphed all the frightening ghosts of our nightmares. They had beaten us again, and more cruelly.

---

[96] Moţa, *Cranii*, p. 231.
[97] Neagoe, *Triumful*, pp. 178–179. In his later monograph, *Viaţa universitară Clujeană interbelică*, which deals with the University of Cluj in detail, Neagoe does not analyze the situation in Cluj student circles on the eve of the disturbances. He writes laconically, "Unfortunately, the peacefulness of student life was to be disturbed during this school year. Cluj University was not spared—just as the Universities of Prague, Budapest, Vienna, Berlin, and the others in our country [were not spared]—the sterile anti-Semitic movements of the year 1922–1923." Vol. 1, p. 207.
[98] Szasz, *Minorities*, p. 290.

Only a few days passed and, after new and unheeded complaints met [by the administration] with irony, the tremor of the first news shook us all: the medical students broke the chain that was choking us, they chased the Kike students out of the dissection room.[99]

On December 10, 1922, student delegates from all four Romanian campuses gathered in Bucharest to formulate a unified list of demands, which they pressed by declaring a general university strike.[100] The list publicized in the press began with the decision not to abandon the goal of a *numerus clausus* which the students were convinced "served the higher interests of the fatherland." The nationalists insisted on Jewish medical students providing their own Jewish cadavers; they called for severe sanctions against the Jewish press that had insulted the Orthodox religion and the Romanian state. They also called for the expulsion of Jews who had come to Romania's annexed provinces after August 1914; in no case were these latecomers to be granted naturalization. In the future, the students asked, foreign Jews should be kept from entering Romania, and Jews should be forbidden from changing their names.[101]

The Jewish question was not equally important on the different campuses, and it required concerted ideological work to make it the unifying element of the nationwide student movement. Although there was a large urban Jewish population and a tradition of anti-Semitism in Romania's northeast (in Moldavia, where Cuza and Codreanu were based, and in Bessarabia and Bukovina), the number of Jews was smaller, and political anti-Semitism less important in the other provinces.[102] In 1923, Codreanu was frustrated by the "materialism" of the student leadership in Bucharest and Cluj. Rather than making the Jewish problem the central point of their program, these activists resisted Codreanu's leadership and buried the *numerus clausus* demand among claims for improved dormitories, laboratories, cafeterias, and other measures to improve university conditions. With the government likely to give in on all the demands except the solution to the Jewish question, Codreanu worried that the student movement might be coopted. Codreanu's close associates from Iaşi traveled to Bucharest and Cluj to teach their colleagues the gravity of the Jewish question.[103] Where anti-Semitic traditions were more superficial, then, promises of economic security in a fully nationalized society apparently appealed more to the students than anti-Semitism itself.[104]

[99] Moţa, *Cranii,* pp. 228–229.
[100] Codreanu, *Pentru legionari,* p. 79.
[101] "Les désordres juifs en Roumanie," *Paix et droit,* February 1923.
[102] Eugen Weber, "The Men of the Archangel," *Journal of Contemporary History* 1, no. 1 (1966): 115–116.
[103] Codreanu, *Pentru legionari,* pp. 113–117.
[104] Lucreţiu Pătrăşcanu, *Sub trei dictaturi* (Bucharest: Forum, 1944), pp. 203–206.

Under Codreanu's leadership and Cuza's mentorship, students' tactics alternated between their own strikes and lock-outs of the Jewish students from classes and exams through intimidation and violence. The universities attempted to keep their institutions operating as normally as possible; when normalcy was not an option, they closed down until the spirits were calmer. The entire school year of 1922–1923 was declared lost for educational purposes. But in Iaşi, at least, the university administration backed down and later agreed to recognize student attendance for 1922–1923 if they passed exams.[105]

Henceforth during the interwar period, nationalist students celebrated the date of December 10, often violently, as a symbol of the generation of 1922's continued struggle for its original goals. The National Peasant newspaper *România* dubbed the yearly celebration of December 10 "the holiday of broken windows," because of the vandalisms perpetrated regularly in Jewish neighborhoods on these occasions.[106] The *numerus clausus* remained at the core of the demands, but, since the constitution and naturalization were no longer live issues after 1923, the list reflected the changed situation. Among other demands, students now asked for language exams to test the competence of the "foreigners" in Romanian, and they pressed for the state's encouragement of the native element in Romanian culture and for ethnic Romanian predominance in all branches of public activity.[107] December 10—and thus the whole project of Romanizing Romania's education, economy, towns, and politics—was recognized, despite its violence and illegality, as an official holiday when Octavian Goga was minister of the interior in 1926.[108]

Although they did not resolutely repress the student movement, the administrations of Romania's universities also did not clearly concede to nationalist demands. The student movement and Cuza therefore took the struggle into the political arena by transforming the National Christian Union into the League of National Christian Defense (LANC) in March 1923. They thus escalated the struggle for the *numerus clausus* in the universities and against Jewish rights in Romanian society at large at the very moment when the Romanian parliament was debating the new constitution, which was to consecrate the Jewish emancipation imposed by the Allied powers at the Paris Peace Conference.[109] The automatic and

---

[105] Neagoe, *Triumful,* pp. 180, 210–212, 249, 255. Pamfil Şeicaru claimed that the government was to be blamed for repressing the students. "Numerus Clausus," *Hiena,* February 14–21, 1923, p. 2.

[106] Cited in "Roumanie: Nouveaux désordres," *Paix et droit,* December 1926, p. 6.

[107] For a list of student demands submitted in February 1926 see "Roumanie: les désordres dans les Universités," *Paix et droit,* March 1926, pp. 10–11.

[108] Dragne and Petculescu, *Frontul studenţesc democrat,* p. 16.

[109] Carol Iancu, "L'Émancipation des Juifs de Roumanie devant la Conférence de Paix de Paris (1919)," *Shvut* 16 (1993): esp. p. 278.

complete naturalization of all the Jews of Greater Romania was a condition of the St. Germain Treaty, signed grudgingly by Romania's leaders in 1919. In this context, the nationalist student paper *Cuvântul studenţesc* (Student Word) was calling for a Romanian, not a Jewish, constitution.[110] The League of National Christian Defense, formed right around the time the Liberals presented the project to Parliament,[111] also protested "with special vehemence" against the civil and political rights the constitution was to grant Romanian Jews. As a historian of the 1923 constitution has written, "LANC incited particularly the students, which took to hooliganic anti-Semitic acts in the cities of Bucharest, Iaşi, Cluj, Oradea, etc. Memoranda of protest against the naturalization of the Jews, according to the provisions of the peace treaties, came to the address of the Parliament and of the Prime Minister from the district organizations of LANC."[112]

"New Wine" and the "National Idea on the March": Mainstream Views of the New Generation

The new Romanian constitution was voted in the two houses of the Romanian parliament on March 26 and 27, 1923. It included the Jewish emancipation provisions imposed by the Allied Powers in Paris. Despite this immediate setback, the more general goals of the generation of 1922— namely of mobilizing support for an integral nationalist, anti-Semitic, and anti-democratic program—in time gained acceptance. Mainstream public opinion proved quite supportive of the new generation as Codreanu's nationalists had succeeded in defining it. This support is embodied by the widespread perception of the student struggle as justified and righteous because of the "overwhelming" and unfair proportion of Jews in higher education and the urban professions. Even persons opposed to the violent form of the student struggle nevertheless could sympathize with its motivations and program and thus accorded it legitimacy. The rights of free expression of the incendiary student movement, which the government occasionally tried to control and censor, were often defended by mainstream patriots.[113] Although such positions may be construed as libertarian and not specifically based on political sympathy, the repeated acquittal of

[110] "Les Désordres antijuifs en Roumanie," *Paix et droit,* February 1923, p. 5.

[111] Eufrosina Popescu, *Din istoria politică a României: Constituţia din 1923* (Bucharest: Editura politică, 1983), p. 129; Nicholas M. Nagy-Talavera, *The Green Shirts and the Others: A History of Fascism in Hungary and Rumania* (Stanford, Calif.: Hoover Institution Press, 1970), p. 261.

[112] Popescu, *Din istoria,* p. 129. See also p. 191.

[113] The Peasant Party, for example, a center-left party with democratic and populist appeal, protested the suppression of student newspapers, gatherings, and demonstrations in the spring of 1923. Reported in *Cuvântul nostru,* February 18, 1923.

nationalist political criminals in jury trials is further proof of public support of the students' radical nationalist goals.

Moreover, encouragement for the student movement often came from mainstream nationalists who were highly respected players in Romania's academic world. One need not refer merely to the fervid anti-Semitic radicals, Cuza, Şumuleanu, Găvănescul, and Paulescu, or to the sophisticated philosopher Nae Ionescu, recognized in the 1930s as the mentor of the new generation. Although radical proto-totalitarians like Ionescu had an important impact,[114] moderate support for the students from less dazzling and less openly political personalities is probably more significant for gauging the movement's general acceptance in the 1920s. Professors like Petru Bogdan, Florian Ştefănescu-Goangă, Sextil Puşcariu, Nicolae Şerban, Dimitrie Onciul, and Simion Mândrescu, among other scientists, social scientists, and humanists, who countenanced the students were pillars of the Romanian academy.

That is not say that the support for extreme nationalism was unanimous. Far from it. Many public personalities and academics were outraged by the exclusionary demands of the student movement and fought against them, at least in the early 1920s. An informal survey (*anchetă*) in the magazine *Hiena* in 1923 reported the responses of nine intellectuals on the topic of the *numerus clausus* soon after the agitation had reached its peak in late 1922. Only two of the respondents—Wilhelm Filderman and Aureliu Weiss—were Jewish, but all of them concluded roundly that the students' demand for limiting the entry of Jews in the universities and the professions was inadmissible, although they manifested varying degrees of sympathy for the students' miserable material conditions that most respondents felt were behind their demands.[115]

Among those surveyed by Pamfil Şeicaru in *Hiena* was Professor Nicolae Iorga, who had earlier been a mentor to nationalist students, but who became very outspoken against the radicalized postwar student movement. In the spring of 1923, Iorga resigned his chair at the University of Bucharest in protest against the students' demand for *numerus clausus*. Indeed, his struggle with the nationalist youth and the Iron Guard continued to the end of his life—in November 1940, Iorga died at the hands of Iron Guardists during their brief stint in power. Professor Cantacuzino, who held the chair of international law at the Bucharest Law School, resigned along with Iorga. Professor Constantin Bacaloglu of the Iaşi University Medical School rebuffed the students' demand that he expel Jewish students as impinging on his clinic's autonomy. C. I. Parhon, the dean of the Iaşi

---

[114] See Ileana Vrancea, *Confruntări în critica deceniilor IV–VII (E. Lovinescu şi posteritatea lui critică)* (Bucharest: Editura Cartea românească, 1975), pp. 114–123; and Livezeanu, "Excerpts," pp. 298–299.

[115] "O anchetă în lumea intelectualilor: 'Numerus Clausus' " *Hiena*, February 14–21, 1923.

Medical School also opposed the Cuzist students. Traian Bratu, a long-time rector of Iaşi University, led the losing fight against A. C. Cuza's attempt to make the Iaşi Law School a rebel stronghold of anti-Semitism; he opposed the exclusionary goals of the student movement, as did many others in the Iaşi University administration. Like Iorga, Bratu incurred the wrath of the extremists, and in 1937, lost his left ear in an attack by militant nationalist youths who had intended to assassinate him. On at least three occasions, the Iaşi University Senate and Council accused Cuza of being the moral author of the student movements. In the spring of 1927, thirty-six professors from the University of Iaşi addressed a protest to the Ministry of Public Instruction. They deplored the lack of measures taken to reestablish the rule of law and noted the difficulty of maintaining scholarly excellence under those conditions.[116]

In the main, however, support for the student movement (sometimes explicit, but more often implicit, that is, in the shape of shared assumptions) was substantial, some thought overwhelming, in academic circles as elsewhere, and it became ever more so as the first postwar decade drew to an end. Petru Bogdan, a chemist at the University of Iaşi who later held important administrative positions, was opposed to the *numerus clausus* agitation. But he lent it legitimacy by commenting on the small number of ethnic Romanian students, especially in the schools of law, medicine, and pharmacy, and by recommending a kind of affirmative action program for the Romanian majority:

> As a Romanian I realize . . . that all efforts and sacrifices must be made so that the Romanian element be represented in this higher stratum in proportion to its number and its importance in the state . . . This problem was marvelously understood by Mr. S. Mehedinţi, who created the rural secondary schools. Unfortunately he was not understood, nor followed. If the rural schools had been nurtured we would now have a much larger number of Romanian students. . . . But naturally, the state must make sacrifices, organizing primary, secondary, and higher education in order to arrive at this result. This might be the formula and program of national activity which we might all embrace, both we and the students.[117]

---

[116] Cuza, *Mişcările studenţesti*, pp. 3–6; "Les Universités et les étudiants juifs," *Paix et Droit*, March 1923, pp. 5–6; "Roumanie: Un appel à l'union," *Paix et droit*, March 1924, p. 9; "Roumanie: Les désordres dans les universités," *Paix et droit*, March 1926, pp. 10–11; "Le Mémoire des professeurs de Jassy," *Paix et droit*, May 1927, pp. 10–11; and Emilian Bold, "Universitatea dim Iaşi în epoca contemporană (1918–1985): Implicarea în viaţa politică," in Gheorghe Platon and Vasile Cristian, eds., *Istoria Universităţii din Iaşi* (Jassy: Editura Junimea, 1985), p. 196.

[117] Cited in Neagoe, *Triumful*, p. 214.

In 1923, Nicolae Şerban, a professor of French literature at Iaşi University, intimated that the grievances of the student movement were justified, citing the "overwhelming" proportion of Jews in several educational institutions, while Florian Ştefănescu-Goangă, professor of psychology at the University of Cluj, expressed his indignation at the high proportion of Jews in some lycées and university departments.[118]

In March 1923, the linguist Sextil Puşcariu, professor of philology and former rector of Cluj University, declared in the Cluj newspaper *Conştiinţa românească* (Romanian Consciousness/Conscience) that the student movement was "a healthy and spontaneous reaction of the national preservation instinct"; he applauded the 15,000 youths grouped together in one cause, without trace of regionalism, and manifesting a cohesion rare for Romania.[119] Speaking at a conference to the Circle of Bukovinian Students, Puşcariu said that the *numerus clausus* was of interest to all those who wished the country well, explaining what the two Latin words meant in Romania: "In our country [which we] gained with so many sacrifices, we no longer have air to breathe; the invasion of the foreign element stifles us, chokes us."[120]

The *Cuvântul nostru* obituary for Dimitrie Onciul, dean of the School of Letters in Bucharest and president of the Romanian Academy, praised the scholar's ardent support for the student movement. He had told the students, "You are like *turburelul*, like the new wine which is fermenting, and your enthusiasm is natural. You are fermenting great ideals, of which we approve, and we will approve you even more if need be."[121]

Even those who acknowledged that the university issues were complex, at times perceived the student movement as a natural and healthy, if simplistic, reaction. Simion Mândrescu, a German literature professor, explained that at the root of the movement was the students' legitimate worry for the country's cultural future: "If we did not have [Romanian pupils] with whom to populate the lycées preparatory for the universities, then it is self-evident that we could not have [Romanian students] with whom to populate the universities [and] the newly created higher schools, and [that] it was necessary for the minorities with a happier past than ours to populate them, and it was necessary for *a single minority* [i.e., the Jews] to constitute the population of the [University of] Iaşi."[122]

[118] Note from the Bucharest daily *Universul* reproduced in *Cuvântul nostru*, February 18, 1923.
[119] *Cuvântul nostru*, March 25, 1923.
[120] Ibid.
[121] Ibid. "*Tulburelul*" (col. *turburelul*) is the idiomatic expression for wine so new that it is still in fermentation and thick with unsettled sediment, thus murky, or "*tulbure*." Onciul was probably also punning on the word *tulburări*, disturbances, often used to describe violent student demonstrations in the Romanian press. The student movement also received support from the National Union of Former Fighters, a veterans' organization.
[122] Ibid., May 6, 1923.

In a 1927 interview with *Cuvântul studenţesc* (The Student Word), the Cluj law professor Ioan Cătuneanu, a well-known anti-Semite, said that the *numerus clausus* was a just demand given the enormity of the "kike question." He argued further that the *numerus clausus* had not been invoked against Christian minorities because they were adapting themselves in a natural way and were expected in time to identify with the interests of the Romanian state. For Cătuneanu, who agreed with Codreanu that only a radical ethnic solution to the Jewish question was acceptable, the material amelioration of the students' lot was clearly not the point.[123]

Reflecting on such statements and the lack of an articulate opposition to the nationalist students, one journalist wrote in the Liberal organ *Viitorul* (The Future) on May 5, 1923, that it was useless to try to hide the fact "that the majority of those in charge of instructing our public opinion, whether unconsciously or for lack of [good] judgment, are abstaining from disapproving of the troublemakers. A national sentiment, possibly a legitimate one, but a blind or blinded one, makes them sympathize with the students in the spirit of vengeance for the economic competition [posed] by the Jews."[124] A few years later, the *Viaţa românească* (Romanian Life) journalist Mihail Sevastos, expressed his outrage at the anti-Semitic activity he perceived as a constant in Romania's public life, especially in the universities:

> There has been no pogrom in Romania; but stores, printing presses, publishing houses, [and] synagogues have been devastated. The Jews have been beaten in the streets [and] in public places, and thrown off the trains. They have been shot at with revolvers. The struggle has taken place mainly in the universities where Romanian students have expelled their Israelite colleagues by sheer strength. . . . Call these things what you will. . . . We for one find them monstrous. Here it is precisely the students that play the role that the dregs of society used to have in Russia, while our intellectual world is sitting with its arms crossed, since it is terrorized by the press of the sects and of the agents provocateurs.[125]

One of the nationalist students' most eloquent and prestigious supporters was the Transylvanian poet Octavian Goga. Until his death in 1938, Goga was Romania's greatest living poet. His political career spanned, in the course of less than two decades, the National Party of Transylvania, Averescu's People's Party, the National Agrarian Party, and the National Christian Party. As a politician, Goga is best remembered for ruling together with

[123] *Cuvântul studenţesc,* December 10, 1927.
[124] Cited in "Lettre de Bucarest," *Paix et droit,* May 1923, p. 8.
[125] Cited in "Le gouvernement et les juifs," *Paix et droit,* February 1927, p. 10.

A. C. Cuza in the forty-four-day-long "Goga-Cuza government," from December 1937 to February 1938, but he served also as minister of the interior in 1920–1921 and 1926–1927. According to Paul Shapiro, it was only after 1932 that Goga "turned increasingly toward extreme nationalism and anti-Semitism, toward the 'immovable' Professor Cuza." It is interesting, therefore, to look at Goga's views of the student movement in the 1920s, when, as a ranking member of the People's Party, he was well within the range of mainstream nationalism.[126]

Beginning in 1922, Goga directed and frequently contributed to the Cluj magazine *Ţara noastră* (Our Country). In 1927, a volume appeared under the title *Mustul care fierbe* (Simmering Must).[127] It was a collection of essays from *Ţara noastră,* and it opened with a warm dedication to the new generation:

> These are pages torn from the daily agitation, fragments of the spiritual dissipation exacted by the problems of our existence. They [can] all be reduced to a fundamental life principle, to the national idea—the mystery of this people's [the Romanians'] procreation and its only formula for tomorrow. Today, when everything is still in [the process of] becoming, when our disjointed society is [like] fermenting must, only this credo can keep us on our feet.
>
> It is proof of the health of the people that the new intellectual generation professes this dogma [of the national idea] and starts down its course with these slogans. This is a guarantee that out of the present ferment our organic truths will come out victorious, and that the scum will sink to the bottom.
>
> With hope for the great renewal, I dedicate my book to the young generation.[128]

Goga's gift of his "young wine" book to the young generation indicated the extent to which he shared their obsessions, notably the danger of losing Romanian culture, art, literature, and the press to an invading—implicitly or explicitly—Jewish intellect, and the already acknowledged loss of Romania's cities to the same foreign spirit. He praised the students, who had

---

[126] Paul A. Shapiro, "Prelude to Dictatorship in Romania: The National Christian Party in Power, December 1937–February 1938," *Canadian-American Slavic Studies* 8 (Spring 1974): 46–49. Others place Goga's politics within a moderate range until even later. Vasile Curticăpeanu dates Goga's turn toward "the forces of domestic and international reaction" to 1936–38. See his "L'Action d'Octavian Goga pour l'unité politique roumaine," *Revue roumaine d'histoire* 9, no. 1 (1970): 106.

[127] Octavian Goga, *Mustul care fierbe* (Bucharest: Imprimeria Statului, [1927]). "*Must*" is the sweet juice of pressed grapes before it has started to ferment to produce wine. There is a subtle distinction between *tulburel,* mentioned by Onciul, and *must,* but this is reduced by Goga's usage in the title which blends the two terms.

[128] Goga, *Mustul,* p. 7.

instinctually "noticed a threat, and put themselves in its way: I do not see you as narrow spirits refractory to ideas of progress, but rather as an ingenuous expression of a whole people. Ten thousand boys sprung from the people, representing all social classes, . . . cannot amount to a case of collective madness. That you may also have incorrect slogans is possible, but your inspiration is from the normal course of our past, you are the national idea on the march, the new halting place for tomorrow."[129]

Goga's point was that a people's "literary and artistic patrimony" was its supreme asset, and thus admitted no pluralism. Ostensibly more politically liberal than Cuza, Codreanu, and their followers, Goga still defended his nation's "prerogatives of blood" and deplored "any inopportune infiltration" into Romanian culture:[130]

> If in political life, we, who have a conception of tolerant civilization, will never contest the rights guaranteed by our international treaties, if on behalf of all the ethnic minorities we stand by absolute civic equality, [yet] we do want to maintain our spiritual unity safe from dissolving promiscuities. This is why we stand by the gate of our ancient heritage in a watchful posture, and we want to mark well our intellectual boundaries on this patch of land, fully conscious that the day when we tolerated spiritual invasions, our struggle would be irremediably lost.[131]

Like the spokesmen of student nationalism, Goga also talked about an actual foreign invasion, clearly an allusion to the Jewish inhabitants of Romania's new territories:

> We give the impression that we are a sick body, and on sick bodies, you know very well, parasites usually appear. Look around you, as in some new California, from all the parts of the globe fortune-seekers are descending upon this blessed land, with which they share nothing but its exploitation. From all sides, our frontiers are invaded by guests with scrutinizing glances, who sow corruption and execration, making grow the dubious froth of cities, and awakening a trail of awkward discouragement in the pure soul of our peasants. This wave of foreignism grows ceaselessly, like a column of conquerors.[132]

Curiously, despite his strong stand on the Romanian people's exclusive rights to its culture and cities, Goga denied all accusations of anti-Semitism. His response, in a 1924 article, is interesting because it demonstrates the

---

[129] "Ideia Naţională: Conferinţă în faţa studenţilor universitari din Cluj," in ibid., pp. 38–39.
[130] Ibid., p. 37.
[131] Ibid., pp. 37–38.
[132] Ibid., pp. 29–30.

ways in which someone who emphatically did not consider himself an anti-Semite per se nevertheless harbored a nationalism that was nothing if not vigorous sponsorship of the new generation's radical anti-Semitism. Goga defined the central dogma of *Ţara noastră* as the attempt to bring about an indissoluble Romanian unity by means of a "national faith" consisting of "the idea of our racial cohesion [and] the precise sentiment of ethnic difference which . . . has affirmed itself everywhere as the most powerful state-constitutive element. In this religion, upon which depends the very existence—or the political fall—of Românism in the present period, . . . we have decided to proselytize fanatically."[133]

Ţara noastră was, then, a militant organ of the "national faith" through which Goga had first asked for a Romanian press led by a national spirit *"in this epoch of united Romania's fragile adolescence."* This leadership could not be left to the Jews, even assimilated ones, whom Goga liked to unmask by calling them by their original Jewish names rather than by their Romanian-sounding pennames. Second, *Ţara noastră* had demonstrated the "danger of international cliches slipped into art and literature through the intermediary of hurried guests," clearly an allusion to leftist "foreigners," that is, Jews. Third, Goga and his magazine had focused on the strangers who had invaded the country in exorbitant numbers, changing its demography and disturbing its economy; hence the demand that the Jews who were not Romanian citizens according to the peace treaty be forced to leave. Covering more anti-Semitic stereotypes, Goga also railed against foreign investors in Transylvania, banking middlemen, and politicians who were prisoners of high finance. Finally, Goga acknowledged his defense of the Romanian student movement, aimed at the exclusion of Jews and demanded protection for *"our future intellectual generation."* In spite of these anti-Jewish demands and commonplaces, Goga concluded with an explicit denial of any anti-Semitism: "Anti-Semitism as a doctrine, with its well-defined concept, with its well-known ideology prescriptive of the Jews' political, social, and economic relations in a state's life according to special norms, the militant Christian attitude in opposition to Judaism's tendencies of universal expansion, did not see the light in even two lines of this publication. Everything was limited to this . . . the defense of the national idea and the removal of the main obstacles lying in its way."[134]

The influence of Goga's support for the extreme nationalist stance of the new generation was enhanced by his towering literary prestige and popularity. Yet one might still question the significance of one man's jyopinions, even if he was Romania's poet laureate. The evidence for broad public approval for the student movement, however, also includes a fairly

---

[133] "Răspuns unor provocări," *Ţara noastră,* May 4, 1924.
[134] Ibid.

long list of judicial acquittals for crimes committed by fanatical young nationalists, members or sympathizers of Cuza's League of National Christian Defense, and, after 1927, of Codreanu's Legion of the Archangel Michael, later known as the Iron Guard. The acquittals sent a signal to radical nationalists that their ideology was widely respected and their violent deeds tolerated, even admired. Foreign observers noted the destructive message conveyed by the establishment's judicial leniency toward these young criminals. In a 1925 "Memorandum on the Anti-Semitic Movement in Roumania," Lucien Wolf documented the widespread anti-Semitic propaganda and the consequent suffering visited on Romanian Jews: "In several towns there have been demonstrations, followed by destruction of property. . . . Jewish travellers on the railways are assaulted and forced to leave the trains; Jews are driven out of cafes and theatres, and are set upon in the streets; Jewish schoolchildren are attacked in schools and students in the Universities, and Synagogues have been desecrated. The culprits are never punished. Last year some students conspired to murder several Jews. They were arrested and confessed their intention, but were nevertheless acquitted."[135]

The student plot Lucien Wolf referred to was a conspiracy to assassinate Jewish rabbis, bankers, and journalists and Romanian politicians who in the plotters' eyes had sold out, for instance, by supporting the Jews' naturalization. It had been Ion Moța's idea for keeping alive student resistance after a discouraging stalemate in the *numerus clausus* agitation. The terrorist conspiracy was hatched and discovered in 1923. In prison, on the eve of the conspirators' trial, Moța assassinated the young man who had betrayed the plot. Moța remained in prison, but the others, including Codreanu, were acquitted on March 29, 1924. The verdict was based ultimately on a technicality, but the atmosphere created around the trial was undoubtedly important to the outcome.[136] Horia Sima describes the pressure created by student supporters who had gathered in Bucharest from all four Romanian universities in late March 1924:

The thousands of students concentrated in Bucharest maintained the capital in a continual effervescence, and succeeded in winning public opinion to their cause.

[135] The Joint Foreign Committee of the Board of Deputies of British Jews and the Anglo-Jewish Association, *The Jewish Minority in Roumania: Correspondence with the Roumanian Government respecting the Grievances of the Jews. Presented to the Board of Deputies of British Jews and the Council of the Anglo-Jewish Association, June 1927*, 2d ed. (London: Joint Foreign Committee of the Board of Deputies of British Jews and the Anglo-Jewish Association, 1928), p. 5.

[136] Codreanu, *Pentru legionari*, pp. 168–174, 187–192, and Sima, *Histoire*, pp. 28–32.

Corneliu Zelea Codreanu surrounded by Ilie Gârneață, Radu Mironovici, Ion Moța, Tudose Popescu, and Corneliu Georgescu, the student conspirators imprisoned at Văcărești (March 1924). From the "Lotta e Trionfo" album. Courtesy of Cabinetul de Stampe. Biblioteca Academiei Române, Bucharest

The day of the trial the Court was guarded by powerful cordons of gendarmes, themselves encircled by tens of thousands of men, who intoned patriotic songs and demanded the acquittal of the students.

The trial took place in an atmosphere that managed to disconcert governmental circles. The roles had been reversed: it was no longer a question of trying the students, but rather the ruling class. THE ACCUSED STUDENTS HAD BECOME THE ACCUSERS OF THE GOVERNMENT, THE TRUSTEES OF THE NATIONAL CONSCIENCE. Public opinion had identified the true culprits in the ranks of the government.

The pressure of public opinion annulled the apparatus of intimidation of the Government, as well as the influence of the press controlled by the Jews. The jury gave an acquittal verdict, to the applause of the whole audience.[137]

---

[137] Sima, *Histoire,* pp. 31–32.

In the wake of large student demonstrations six months later, Ion Moța, not just a plotter but an assassin, was acquitted as well. Moța's defense was based on the argument that the betrayal of the nationalists actually deserved punishment. The jury evidently agreed.[138]

On October 25, 1924, emboldened by these verdicts, Codreanu assassinated the Iași police prefect C. G. Manciu, a hated and feared adversary of the student movement, who had used harsh means, including torture, toward its repression. Codreanu also wounded two other police officers.[139] A special edition of the Iași student newspaper *Cuvântul Iașului* (the Iași Word) published the following text signed by the Association of Christian Students:

> *Romanians!* He who for over a year has mocked and beaten everything Romanian for *Judas's silver* has received his punishment. The gesture of our colleague Corneliu Zelea Codreanu *is ours, all of ours.* By defending his own honor, he has defended the honor of all students. The students and the nation in gratitude cry out to him with one voice: Long live Corneliu Zelea Codreanu![140]

Although the crime and the arrest had both occurred in Iași, the case was to be tried in Focșani, where the government had more control. The town, located on the Moldavian-Wallachian border, had a substantial Jewish population, about six hundred families among roughly thirty thousand inhabitants.[141] Codreanu, who was transferred to a Focșani prison, estimated Focșani to be a hostile location, "the strongest Liberal citadel in the country," and "the only place in the country where the national movement had not caught on."[142] The local population, however, soon went over to Codreanu's side. As support shifted, Jewish shops were vandalized and troops were sent in from Bucharest to reestablish order.[143] It became likely that the charged atmosphere in Focșani on the eve of the trial would influence the jury toward a favorable verdict for the assassin. On March 17, 1925, just after the trial started, it was adjourned, and the

---

[138] Codreanu, *Pentru legionari*, p. 212.

[139] Fătu and Spălățelu, *Garda de fier*, p. 52; Codreanu, *Pentru legionari*, pp. 203–235; Sima, *Histoire*, pp. 35–37; and "Lettre de Bucarest: L'assassinat du Préfet de Jassy," *Paix et droit*, November 1924, p. 9. The *Paix et droit* correspondent wrote that "this assassination was generally foreseen and expected" after the acquittal of the plotters against Jewish notables and Romanian ministers the previous spring.

[140] *Cuvântul Iașului*, vol. 2, special ed., October 27, 1924. The article went on to argue that Manciu's violence toward the students and the impossibility of bringing him to justice legally justified Codreanu's deed.

[141] "En Roumanie: Apologie d'un assassinat. Excès de Focshani," *Paix et droit*, April 1925, pp. 3–4, and *Enciclopedia României*, vol. 2 (Bucharest: Imprimeria națională, 1938), p. 623.

[142] Codreanu, *Pentru legionari*, p. 240.

[143] Ibid., and *Paix et droit*, March 1925, p. 10.

proceedings moved to less prejudicial surroundings. Protest riots broke out, described by local officials as twenty-four hours of terror.[144] Dinu Dumbravă, a reporter for two left-of-center newspapers, wrote: "The traveler arriving during the night by train has the clear feeling that he has entered a town devastated by an enemy army, or that an insane revolution has struck the town of Focşani."[145] The damages were apparently inflicted by about 100 students and another 200–300 vagabonds, but the ground had been prepared by anti-Semitic propaganda in the local schools.[146]

Nationalist spirit ran high in Focşani; even after the riots, despite orders for the confiscation of inflammatory leaflets, a local bookstore window exhibited a portrait of Codreanu "mounted and framed in a place of honor" alongside a special edition of the nationalist student newspaper *Cuvântul studenţesc*, which "was point-blank inciting to crime in the name of the Romanian people, stating that the 'entire student body was in solidarity with Manciu's punishment.' "[147] A local resident referred to the Focşani riots and to Codreanu's trial, which was to reconvene in May, in menacing metaphors: "What was done after Codreanu's [adjourned] trial was only a rehearsal, a lesson to be remembered. It was only the betrothal; the wedding will be in May! All the Jews must be hanged, hanged or chased with rocks!"[148]

According to Dumbravă's investigation of the Focşani riot, the police had not intervened very effectively, apparently because they had orders not to.[149] In fact, these orders are curious. The Liberals had acknowledged their earlier slackness in dealing with the student militants and the need to get serious in punishing them.[150] Liberal politicians who wanted to move the trial to a calmer, less prejudicial location where an indictment might actually be brought against Codreanu had strangely ordered the police to close their eyes to his symphatizers' rioting in frustration at the trial's adjournment. The paralysis of the forces of law and order may indicate not simple complicity, but rather the public-opinion victory of the radical nationalist camp. It is likely that the Liberal government, having lost its

[144] Dinu Dumbravă, *Fără ură! Pregătirea şi dezlănţuirea evenimentelor din Focşani în zilele de 17 şi 18 martie 1925. Cercetări. Documente. Mărturisiri*, Anchetă întreprinsă după evenimente ca trimes special al ziarelor *Dimineaţa* şi *Adevărul* (Bucharest: Editura Adevărul, [1925?]), p. 6, and "En Roumanie," pp. 3–4.

[145] Dumbravă, *Fără ură*, p. 7.

[146] Ibid., p. 6. Choir teachers, for example, had taught the anti-Semitic "Students' Hymn" to their pupils.

[147] Ibid., p. 8.

[148] Ibid., p. 22. Codreanu's real wedding was also scheduled to take place in Focşani in the summer of 1925. Codreanu, *Pentru legionari*, pp. 251, 255–256.

[149] Dumbravă, *Fără ură*, p. 6; see also "En Roumanie: Apologie," pp. 3–4.

[150] The Liberal leader Brătianu said that there had been a time when "we hesitated" with regard to the young nationalists, who had seemed more ridiculous than dangerous. "Roumanie: Désordres universitaires," *Paix et droit*, December 1924, p. 11.

confidence in its ability to control potential social violence and obtain a guilty verdict against Codreanu in Focşani, decided to adjourn and move the trial to a less charged location. Yet the Liberals may have wanted to avoid the armed suppression of the aroused pro-Codreanu nationalist crowds in order to preserve their own nationalist credentials.

Turnu Severin was chosen to host the reconvened trial. This town, and indeed the whole surrounding region, had a relatively small Jewish population, numbering about 500 persons (or 180 families, two-thirds of them Sephardic) among 25,000 inhabitants.[151] The town had had no experience of violent anti-Semitic agitation, although certainly there were some anti-Semites—a few young merchants and commercial clerks, "naturally a group of students," and some teachers. The Liberal-affiliated weekly also gave vent to occasional anti-Semitic attacks. The anti-Semitic movement had not, however, taken root among the population at large. The county police prefect and the local Liberal Party chief promised to collaborate to maintain order before and during the trial, and local authorities had "guaranteed" the government the accused's condemnation. The initial confident prognosis for Codreanu's indictment at Turnu Severin notwithstanding, radical nationalists mobilized public opinion successfully here as well, and created an atmosphere sympathetic to the accused.[152]

In his memoir of the Turnu Severin trial, Sabetay Sabetay, a former resident of Turnu Severin, describes the change in the mood of the town and the jury's consequent acquittal verdict.[153] The following account is based on Sabetay's recollections. The mood swing in Turnu Severin owed a great deal to the pilgrimage of hundreds—and later thousands—of Codreanu supporters, especially students. Under their influence, local anti-Semitic merchants put Codreanu's portrait in their windows. Daily meetings, involving ever larger groups of the local population, were organized by Codreanu supporters under different pretexts. The town thus turned into a "general headquarters of anti-Semitism."[154] Local Jews did not ultimately suffer much violence thanks only to increased patrols and to defensive measures. The Jewish community felt more and more in a state of siege: Jews kept their outings to a minimum; Jewish shops kept their shutters lowered, and they closed earlier than usual in the evenings; in synagogues prayers were whispered; in Jewish homes and synagogues lights were kept dim. The tension rose as the trial approached. "Everything seemed to forecast a pogrom."[155] On the eve of the trial, the whole town was wearing

---

[151] Sabetay S. Sabetay, "Procesul Codreanu la Turnu Severin," *Toladot* 4 (March 1975): 17–18.
[152] Ibid., and Sima, *Histoire*, p. 38.
[153] Sabetay, "Procesul."
[154] Ibid., p. 20.
[155] Ibid., p. 19.

national colors, people sported swastikas, and walls were covered with incendiary manifestoes. Postcards with Codreanu in national folk costume had been sent by the thousands to the provinces, and the route he was supposed to travel to the courtroom was covered with flowers.[156]

The trial itself lasted six days. It took place in the theater in the very center of town. The local weekly, *Tribuna,* appeared daily and occasionally twice a day to cover the event. On the day when the sentencing was to take place, Jewish merchants agreed to keep their shops closed to avoid devastation. The Romanian Bar Association had resolved not to let members represent Manciu's widow.[157] According to Sabetay, "This decision made quite an impression not only in Turnu Severin, but in the whole country. It was undoubtedly a warning, and an indication for the jury members."[158]

Codreanu had considerable support nationwide by the time of the trial. Some of the wide-circulation newspapers like the Bucharest right-wing daily *Universul* campaigned in his favor. Although the prosecution did manage to get its own lawyer, the prejudicial mood in which the trial was judged cannot be doubted. Corneliu Zelea Codreanu himself had the last word for the defense on May 26—and it was not contrite. Seeming to expect admiration for his nationalism of the deed, he said, "Gentlemen of the jury. Everything we have fought for was out of faith and love for our country and the Romanian people. We assume the obligation to fight to the end. This is my last word."[159] The prosecutor's demeanor and statement to the jury is also telling: "With a tear of regret in his eye," Titu Constantinescu asked the jury for a condemnation, arguing that no one had the right to take justice into his own hands. But he qualified his plea by mentioning the extenuating circumstances of the crime. He explained that, "Anarchy had penetrated the university because of the large number of foreigners," adding, "like everyone, I say also: Romania for the Romanians first of all."[160] The acquittal by the jury, all of whom wore swastikas on their lapels, came as no surprise. The defendant was carried triumphantly out of the courthouse covered with flowers, and he made a hero's entrance back in Iaşi. In Turnu Severin the flag was raised atop public buildings as was the custom on official holidays. Large demonstrations in Iaşi, Bucharest, and other cities greeted Codreanu's triumph. Police were out in force around the country to protect Jewish neighborhoods from the celebrations.[161]

---

[156] "Lettre de Bucarest," *Paix et droit,* June 1925.
[157] Sabetay, "Procesul," p. 19.
[158] Ibid.
[159] Codreanu, *For My Legionaries,* p. 178.
[160] "Lettre de Bucarest," p. 6. See also Fătu and Spălăţelu, *Garda de fier,* pp. 52–53.
[161] "Lettre de Bucarest," p. 6, and "Roumanie: L'agitation antijuive," *Paix et droit,* June 1925, p. 7. According to Sabetay, the jury members wore Codreanu's insignia hidden on the reverse of their lapels all through the trial, but brought them out after the sentence was given. See Sabetay, "Procesul," p. 20.

Until very recently, Romanian historians working within an orthodox and rather wooden Marxist model to explain the rise of Romanian fascism had generally argued that in Romania bourgeois politicians were the accomplices of fascist criminals and, conversely, that the nationalism and anti-Semitism of the fascists were instigated by the capitalist class in collusion with bourgeois governments to divert the lower classes from developing class consciousness.[162] In a 1980 study, to give but one of many examples from the literature, Gheorghe Zaharia and Mihai Fătu stress first of all the *imported* nature of extreme right-wing ideologies in Romania, but acknowledge that some "internal factors also created the climate favorable to the germination, appearance, and evolution of fascist organizations.... Among these factors, in a prominent position is situated the effort of the bourgeoisie's leaders to obstruct the revolutionary movement of the proletariat and other working masses in Romania [in their struggle against] exploitation and domination, and for democratic rights and freedoms."[163] Such arguments were meant to account for the great influence of radical nationalists on Romania's mainstream political life and for such phenomena as the leniency of the police and judicial system in the face of fascist crimes.[164] At first glance the Manciu assassination trial seems to be a case in point. But under more careful scrutiny the "bourgeois complicity" argument at best only describes the effect of the Liberals' insufficient intransigence in this case, and not the mechanics or possible motivations of Liberal strategy.

In a report to the French Ministry of Foreign Affairs on May 31, 1925, the French minister to Bucharest wrote that the Brătianu government had tried to subject Codreanu to a fair trial but that public opinion, especially among Romania's intellectuals, had resulted in the acquittal verdict.[165] The French diplomat seems exactly right. Clearly, had the government wanted to acquit Codreanu, it would not have bothered to move the trial to Turnu Severin. The Liberals were unhappy at having lost control of the trial proceedings in Focşani. It certainly appears that they wanted to try to convict Codreanu, and therefore moved the trial from Focşani where an acquittal seemed imminent, to Turnu Severin where they hoped

[162] See Pătrăşcanu, *Sub trei dictaturi*; Fătu and Spălăţelu, *Garda de fier*; and Ioan Scurtu, *Viaţa politică*. When Pătrăşcanu wrote his book in 1944, the Marxist interpretation was still fresh, and he was among the first to look empirically—and critically—at the Romanian right, against which the tide was just beginning to turn.

[163] Gheorghe Zaharia and Mihai Fătu, "Romania," in Institutul de studii istorice şi social-politice de pe lîngă C. C. al P. C. R., *Regimurile fasciste şi totalitare din Europa*, vol. 2 (n.p.: Editura militară, 1980), p. 248. One even finds this type of "fascism as diversion from the true class struggle" explanation in the writings of Romanian scholars publishing more recently in the West. See Ioanid, *Sword of the Archangel*.

[164] See, for example, Fătu and Spălăţelu, *Garda de fier*, pp. 52–53.

[165] QD 26/207–208, May 31, 1925.

for a neutral atmosphere and a conviction. The leniency of the police under the guidance of higher authorities in Focşani during the riots in March, and the subsequent weak plea of the prosecution, are more likely to have resulted from intense public pressure in favor of radical nationalism than from voluntary Liberal complicity. Without risking political suicide, the Liberals could not take a totally intransigent stance against Codreanu, for he had successfully defined himself as a towering nationalist spokesman. In short, rather than the Liberals using the radicals as a diversion, they were more likely themselves manipulated.

This explanation accounts for the nationalist political capital that Codreanu and the organizations to which he belonged—the League of National Christian Defense, and later the Legion of the Archangel Michael and the Iron Guard—were able to deploy in their recruitment efforts and in gaining broader societal support for crimes committed "in the name of the nation."[166] It also accounts for the kid-glove treatment nationalist students received from mainstream nationalists and institutions even when their *numerus clausus* agitation reached criminal proportions.[167] The violent repression of the Iron Guard in the 1930s, including the murder of Codreanu in November 1938, was the other side of that coin. Since Romanian civil society and its justice system were unable to marginalize the radical nationalists, the only way for the mainstream political establishment to secure itself against their threat was by raw force.

Toward a World Based on Faith

Having expanded his political capital in the heroic actions and the judicial trials of the early and mid-1920s, Codreanu went on to consolidate his organizational base. He and a small group of followers split away from LANC and founded the League of the Archangel Michael in 1927. In the 1930s, Codreanu began reaching beyond the young generation, into the very heart of the Romanian nation, the peasantry.

[166] Besides the instances analyzed here, fascist criminals were repeatedly acquitted in Romania: Neculai Totu for the murder of David Fallik in 1926; Gheorghe Beza after the attempted assassination of the Liberal undersecretary of state in 1930; the legionnaires involved in the Borşa arson in 1930; Emil Siancu for the assassination of Mauriciu Tischler in 1933. Even after the assassination of the Liberal prime minister I. G. Duca in 1933, the moral authors were acquitted, and only the actual assassins were condemned. See Fătu and Spălăţelu, *Garda de fier*, pp. 66–68, 98, 104–105.

[167] See "Le pogrome roumain," *Paix et droit*, December 1927, pp. 1–2, in which an anti-Semitic student congress that took place in Oradea in December 1927 is described.

In May 1927, Codreanu's young comrades asked him to return promptly from Grenoble where he was studying for an advanced law degree. The emergency request came because of internecine fighting within the older generation of LANC activists. As undisputed leader of the young generation of nationalists, Codreanu had been in charge of national organizing for LANC since 1923. Returning from abroad in 1927, he purportedly attempted to minimize the damage to the nationalist movement by protecting the younger generation from the factional disputes affecting their elders. Codreanu gathered together the most loyal young activists and on June 24 founded the Legion of the Archangel Michael (LAM).[168]

From the beginning, Codreanu was proud to say, the legion lacked money and a program, thus defying both materialism and political conventions.

> We differed fundamentally from all the other political organizations, the Cuzists included. All of these believed that the country was dying because of lack of good programs; consequently they put together a perfectly jelled program with which they started out to assemble supporters. . . . *This country is dying of lack of men, not of lack of programs;* at least this is our opinion. That, in other words, it is not programs that we must have but *men, new men.* For such as people are today, *formed by politicians* and *infected by the Judaic influence,* they will compromise the most brilliant political programs.[169]

Instead of programs, the legionnaires had "God in their souls inspiring them with the indomitable power of faith." Codreanu described the early legion as characterized by a fierce belief in God, unflinching confidence in its mission, love of the members for one another, and singing of songs.[170]

Despite the "soft" connotations of this portrait, Codreanu devoted much energy to creating a strong organizational framework, the unit of which was the *cuib,* or nest, consisting of three to thirteen men "under the command of a single person." The female version of the nest was the *cetăţuie,* or fortress. *Frăţii de cruce* (brotherhoods of the cross) were cells for youth up to nineteen years of age, and *frăţiori de cruce* (little brotherhoods of the cross) organized youths under fourteen. The nest-based organizational structure gave the few, isolated individuals who started the legion a chance to recruit others. The initiator of each nest became its leader. As in other fascist movements, leadership in the legion was supposed to emerge organically. In time, a hierarchical network of cells arose, organized by village, county, region, and province.[171] In January 1929, after a

---

[168] Codreanu, *Pentru legionari,* pp. 266–297.
[169] Codreanu, *For My Legionaries,* pp. 219–220.
[170] Ibid., pp. 298–299, 302–303.
[171] *Cărticica şefului de cuib* (n.p., n.d.), p. 5; and Codreanu, *Pentru legionari,* pp. 336–337, 340.

Legionnaires at a work camp for making bricks, Ungheni (1924–1925). From the "Lotta e Trionfo" album. Courtesy of Cabinetul de Stampe. Biblioteca Academiei Române, Bucharest

national meeting of nest leaders, Codreanu concluded that his system was working, that the organization was spreading, indeed that the movement was "*growing especially in the ranks of youth.*"[172] The first couple of years of the legion had gone to building the organization, instilling the legionnaire spirit, starting a regular publication, *Pământul strămoşesc* (The Ancestral Land), and finding a solid subscription base for it. Building projects performed in work camps and long marches constituted another side of the legion.[173] The rigorous work and marches were occasions to get to know the ancestral land, build esprit de corps, and train the legionnaires in martial discipline. In 1929, Codreanu decided to deepen the movement by "going to the people," taking the legion to agitate in rural areas. By his own account, his first public rally in the town of Târgu Bereşti, "a Kikes' wasps' nest" in Covurlui County, lasted only five minutes; Codreanu and two other legionnaires made short speeches. The high point of the event was the horseback tour of the villages surrounding the market town. Codreanu borrowed a horse and rode through the area accompanied by followers

[172] Codreanu, *Pentru legionari,* pp. 350–351.
[173] Sima, *Histoire,* pp. 79–81.

on foot. In each place he spoke briefly to the crowd gathered around the church.

> The people all came, men, women, and children. I spoke few words to them and I did not present any political program. "Let us all unite, men and women, to cut out for ourselves and our people a different fate. The hour of resurrection and of the Romanians' salvation is at hand. He who has faith, who struggles and suffers, he will be recompensed and blessed by this people. New times are knocking at our doors! A world with a dry and sterile soul is dying, another is being born, one that belongs to those whose soul is full of faith. In this new world everyone will have a place, not according to schooling, intelligence, or knowledge, but according, in the first place, to faith and character."[174]

As Codreanu went from place to place in Covurlui County, he gathered other riders on horseback around him. Eventually they improvised a uniform by adding turkey feathers to their hats. As word spread about the feather-hatted group, villagers all around the area anticipated their arrival with great excitement. By the end of the day, over three thousand people marched back into Târgu Bereşti, concluding the legion's first propaganda tour.[175]

That winter (1929–1930) the legionnaires undertook other such circuits in forlorn parts of Transylvania and Bessarabia. Appearing not to discuss programs, they were full of promises of salvation for the Romanians' souls after centuries of injustice. They were gratified by the peasants' warm reception and by the lack of politicization of the simple people in these peripheral areas. They found no "political parties, nor conflict, nor clashes of interests, nor 'blind disunity,' nor fratricidal struggles, but rather *unity and harmony*." The politically undifferentiated fabric of rural society, corresponded to LAM's own monolithic vision of an ethnically homogenous Romanian nation unfragmented by a variety of perspectives and allegiances. In Cahul, in western Bessarabia, the largest such rally brought together three hundred legionnaires with twenty thousand peasants. The villagers heard Codreanu promise that the legion would not forget them "in their slavery to the Kikes," that they would once again become masters of their country, and that in the present struggle the peasantry need only have faith to be rewarded with justice and glory.[176]

---

[174] Codreanu, *Pentru legionari*, pp. 365–366.

[175] Ibid., pp. 366–367. For another description of the legion's activity in the countryside, see Nagy-Talavera, *The Green Shirts and the Others*, pp. 246–247. The author recalls his impressions of Codreanu during a 1937 propaganda tour in the Transylvanian mountains.

[176] Codreanu, *Pentru legionari*, pp. 368–375. On the legion's strength in particularly poor and ill-connected rural areas, see Eugen Weber, "The Men of the Archangel," *Journal of Contemporary History* 1, no. 1 (1966): 110–117.

The success in Cahul made Codreanu dream of a heroic march through all of Bessarabia. As a way of confronting the authorities' opposition to such an enterprise, Codreanu and his associates decided to form a new organization in the spring of 1930 "for combatting Kike communism." The Iron Guard was to include the Legion of the Archangel Michael, as well as other youth groups, regardless of party affiliation. The intention of enrolling all of Romania's youth into a broad movement with a nationalist anticommunist credo was not fully realized, and LAM alone officially became part of the proposed Iron Guard. The name of the Iron Guard, however, stuck, becoming the preferred appelative for Codreanu's organization.[177]

In 1930, anti-Semitic disturbances took place in Maramureş, Bukovina, and Bessarabia. According to Armin Heinen, the heightened anti-Semitic tensions in northern Romania at that time were reason to fear "the very [outbreak of] pogroms."[178] Unlike the earlier anti-Semitic "troubles" that surfaced mainly in university centers and at student congresses in Bucharest, Iaşi, Cluj, and Oradea, the disturbances this time broke out mostly in little-known rural areas around market towns and villages, Borşa, Balancea, Putna, Vama, Târgu Bereşti, and Bălţi, to mention some, often where LAM activists had already prepared the ground in earlier propaganda tours. The turbulence involved thousands of peasants incited by LANC or LAM agitators.[179]

One of the most striking such episodes occurred in Borşa, the largest rural commune in Maramureş, with a population of twelve thousand, of which four thousand were Jews. As elsewhere in Maramureş, the Jews occupied the center of town, their houses lining the main street. A reporter for the newspaper *Cuvântul*, Gheorghe Vornicu, remarked: "In Borşa, as you get off the train at the station and up to the village Şesul-Poenei toward Prislop, for a distance of about 10 kilometers, you see only Jews to the right and the left of the road."[180] Whereas some wealthy Jews owned wooded estates in Maramureş, others worked as lumberjacks alongside Romanian peasants.[181]

In the summer of 1930, a fire had consumed all but a few houses for about one kilometer along the main street. One hundred twenty eight houses and 67 annexes were destroyed, but no lives were lost. In addition to the Jewish households, four Romanian and four German ones had also

---

[177] Codreanu, *Pentru legionari*, p. 377, and Sima, *Histoire*, pp. 85–86.

[178] Heinen, *Die Legion "Erzengel Michael,"* p. 200.

[179] "En Roumanie: La propagande de haine," *Paix et droit*, February 1930, and "En Roumanie: L'élection de Couza—Troubles antijuifs," *Paix et droit*, May 1930.

[180] Gheorghe Vornicu, "O anchetă în Maramureş: Borşa şi necazurile ei," *Cuvântul*, August 6, 1930. According to "En Roumanie: Une vague de pogromes," *Paix et droit*, September 1930, p. 3, Borşa had 15,000 inhabitants, the majority of whom were Jews.

[181] Eugen Relgis, "Întoarcerea . . . ," *Adam* 3, no. 48 (1931): 8.

burned down. The fire had apparently started in the daytime. Romanian peasants told Vornicu that they would not have been so crazy as to commit arson "in broad daylight. Even if there'd been a madman among us, he would have had enough sense to do it at night."[182] One government investigation of the events in Borşa had concluded that the fire had been the result of fate, and a second that its cause was mysterious.[183]

According to a *Paix et droit* article, in May 1930 about one thousand peasants armed with bludgeons and axes rioted against the town's Jews, set fire to the Jewish neighborhood, and forced the Borşa Jews to flee into the nearby forest. Another article published four months later by the same paper dates the arson to July 18.[184] Both sources agree that the instigator of the riot had been the "Cuzist"[185] student agitator Dănilă. He had first come to the area in March, sent by the anti-Jewish association The Cult of the Fatherland, and his associates were priests, teachers, and students. Dănilă had held cultural conferences with anti-Semitic messages. He had returned to Borşa at the beginning of May and had led aggressions aimed at chasing the Jews away from the area. He had incited the peasants to throw the Jews in the River Tisza; some Jews were also forcefully baptized in another river. The agitators called for setting fire to the Jewish quarter as the only way to rid the town of Jews. The two hundred-year-old Borşa Jewish community became alarmed and called on the local authorities for protection. Dănilă courted the poverty-stricken peasants by saying that the Jews could stay only if they cancelled the debts of the Christians, gave up their land, and promised no longer to employ Christian servants.[186]

The affair was shrouded in mystical ritual reminiscent of Codreanu's style on his rural propaganda tours. Church bells were rung to gather the rioters who circled the church in procession seven times; religious oaths—like the ones legionnaires took upon joining LAM—were taken "between Dănilă's hands." In that high-strung political season, when even intellectuals were expecting King Carol to return from exile and rescue Romania from an imperfect democracy, Dănilă actually claimed to be Carol, returned to save the Christian population from the Jewish

---

[182] Vornicu, "Borşa şi necazurile ei." One Jewish source indicates that 140 houses were burned, of which about 10 belonged to gentiles, the rest to Jews. See "En Roumanie: Une vague de pogromes," p. 3. Another Jewish source mentions 167 houses burned in Borşa. See AIU/II/B/18, April 18, 1931.

[183] "En Roumanie: Une vague de pogromes," p. 4.

[184] "En Roumanie: L'élection de Couza—Troubles antijuifs," *Paix et droit*, May 1930; and "En Roumanie: Une vague de pogromes," *Paix et droit*, September 1930, p. 4.

[185] Despite the 1927 split between Codreanu and Cuza, the term "Cuzist" continued to be generally employed to describe aggressive anti-Semites of all kinds.

[186] "En Roumanie: L'élection de Couza," and "En Roumanie: Une vague de pogromes," p. 4.

Victorious legionnaires marching in Bucharest before the statue of Carol I, opposite the royal palace, September 6, 1940, when the Iron Guard came to power in coalition with General Antonescu. From the "Lotta e Trionfo" album. Courtesy of Cabinetul de Stampe. Biblioteca Academiei Române, Bucharest

yoke.[187] Or so the rumor went. A peasant told Vornicu: "Sir, among us it is said that Dănilă was no other than our emperor Carol the new, dressed like any gentleman, and who before going to Bucharest went through the country to see what's what, and so came among us too."[188]

In the third report in his investigative series on the Maramureş disturbances, Vornicu said that Dănilă had come "to Borşa with an authorization allowing him to hold a cultural conference, as [was done] in other villages, at the school. But while Dănilă was holding the conference, the Jews attacked the school, broke the windows, and ruined the door and the walls."[189] Although the authorities intervened to keep the peace then, the Christians of Borşa wished to hold a rally with priests and flags to celebrate a national holiday a few days later. In response to Jewish pleas, the authorities forbade the rally. But then the peasants "who were without work" asked the priests to hold a week-long service, which they began. The authorities tried to get the peasants to leave the churches, and they appeased them materially by sending five railroad carloads of corn. Of these, two were supposed to be distributed to the Jews, which raised tensions once again.[190]

The Borşa episode is portrayed somewhat differently in Codreanu's *Pentru legionari*. According to Codreanu, two priests and a peasant from Maramureş had come to see him in Iaşi at the beginning of June 1930, their mission being to implore him and the students to help their congregations, which were in desperate economic straits. The delegates' memoranda to government officials had remained unanswered. Codreanu responded by sending four legionnaires to Borşa to recruit the peasants into LAM and reassure them that they were not alone. Local peasants then enrolled by the thousands in the Iron Guard.[191] Codreanu's dating of the visit of the Maramureş delegation to June 1930 is consistent with the second of the *Paix et droit* articles, which dates the Borşa arson to July 18, 1930. The first *Paix et droit* account to mention arson in Borşa, however, not only dated the fires to May, but appeared in the May issue of the paper, indicating perhaps that several incidents took place in mounting succession. Another article recounting the trial of the participants in the Borşa events confirms that disorders and intimidations began in early May and culminated in mid-July. On July 16, when the Jewish neighborhood burned down, the gendarmes found in Borşa "four students who were from out-

---

[187] A certain I. Dănilă was a close associate of Codreanu's. Heinen, *Die Legion "Erzengel Michael,"* p. 204; "En Roumanie: L'élection de Couza,"and "En Roumanie: Une vague de pogromes," pp. 3–4.

[188] Gheorghe Vornicu, "Semne rele prin satele maramureşene," *Cuvântul*, August 26, 1930.

[189] Gheorghe Vornicu, "O anchetă în Maramureş: Cum s'a ajuns la mişcările din Borşa," *Cuvântul*, August 7, 1930.

[190] Ibid.

[191] Codreanu, *Pentru legionari,* pp. 379–380.

pof-town and, contrary to police regulations, unannounced to the authorities."[192]

In Satu-Mare on November 17, in an atmosphere suggesting a state of siege, eighty-three people, of which eighteen were Jews accused of "provoking disorders," were tried. Chief among the gentiles on trial were Dănilă and the priests Andrei Berindei and Ion Dumitrescu. A prestigious team of anti-Semitic lawyers that included Ion Moţa, Corneliu Zelea Codreanu, and law professor Ion Cătuneanu defended them. The trial ended with a five thousand *lei* fine for Dănilă and otherwise a general acquittal, described by some newspapers as "diplomatic," for both "arsonists and victims."[193]

Although Codreanu acknowledged that a destructive fire had been set in Borşa, he charged the evil Jews themselves with ultimate responsibility. The Jews, he argued, felt threatened by the legion's successful organizing effort and acted desperately: "The Jews realized the peril of a Romanian renaissance and they began to provoke. Seeing that their system was not succeeding, they then took an infernal recourse. They [themselves] set fire to Borşa, blaming the Romanians for this. The Kike newspapers began right away to scream, demanding energetic measures against the Romanians who wanted to stage pogroms." The Jews accused and chased with stones the two priests who were caught by the authorities and thrown in jail. The four legionnaires and some of the peasants were also arrested.[194]

After his initial fairly successful attempts at mobilizing the masses, Codreanu increasingly led the Iron Guard into electoral politics. The turning point came in 1930. The economic crisis had created desperate conditions for the peasants, and they were therefore receptive to apocalyptic solutions. Politically, too, the moment was ripe for dramatic change. The National Peasantists had been elected two years earlier by a landslide on the basis of a reform program but they had, of course, failed to deliver on many of their promises in that short time. The peasants were disappointed, as were many young intellectuals of oppositional bent. In a first step on a steep ideological incline, many from the noncommunist antibourgeois opposition were whipped into a monarchist frenzy around King Carol's return from exile. Increasingly, ethnic Romanian intellectuals

[192] "En Roumanie," *Paix et droit,* December 1930, p. 4.
[193] Ibid.
[194] Codreanu, *For My Legionaries,* p. 279. As always, this quotation from Codreanu is from the copyrighted English translation. But here the translator does not fully convey the tone of the original Romanian text. For the original text, see Codreanu, *Pentru legionari,* p. 380. Codreanu used the word *"Jidani,"* a more faithful translation of which would be "Kikes," not "Jews," which in Romanian is *evrei.*

discarded traditional party politics as old-fashioned and corrupt, and they opted instead for utopian, populist, and even revolutionary solutions.[195] Codreanu's messianic politics progressed on parallel tracks. In the middle and late 1930s, the Iron Guard and LANC won significant electoral victories, and the hearts and minds of much of Romania's intellectual elite followed the lead of the *Căpitan*.

[195] Irina Livezeanu, "A Jew from the Danube: *Cuvântul,* the Rise of the Right, and Mihail Sebastian," *Shvut* 16 (1993): 306–310.

Conclusion

Post-1918 Romania included four regions that had long been separated from one another. However one evaluates the partitions historically imposed by the Eastern European empires on the Romanian lands, they had abiding effects on the demography, cultural and linguistic orientation, and social composition of the different provinces and provincial elites newly joined in Greater Romania. The union of 1918 brought into being a deeply fragmented polity, and the startling effects of centuries of political separation presented great challenges to the newly enlarged state and to the sense of national identity of its population. The brittle, sectional nature of the unified state came as something of a surprise to Romanian nationalists, for little in prewar, irredentist nationalism had prepared them for the multinational and regionalized nature of their country.

In this book, I have attempted to relate the ethnic nationalist ideology, increasingly dominant in Romania after the unification of 1918, to the concrete processes of nation building that the Romanian government sponsored and to which nongovernmental social groups and local elites gave an independent and somewhat unpredictable dynamic. Far from being the last act of the Romanian national pageant, the annexation by the Regat in 1918 of long-lost Romanian territories can be viewed as a curtain rising on the Greater Romanian drama whose plot revolved around the enlarged country's social, political, and cultural integration. The main characters in this "play" were the Romanian elites from the old and new territories, Romania's "new generation" that identified regionally far less than its elders and itself aspired to become the country's uncontested, pure, ethnic elite, and the old elites of the new territories, who were generally not ethnically Romanian but Russian, Hungarian, German, and Jewish.

In Russian Bessarabia, Austrian Bukovina, and Hungarian Transylvania before 1918, Romanians had been for the most part the lower-class rural population. Sparsely represented among the educated elites, they had had only a modest impact on the urban and high-cultural spheres of social life.

Indeed, the Romanians' stamp on the urban landscape of the new provinces was even smaller than their actual numbers. Several factors accounted for the Romanians' lack of proper urban and cultural visibility. Urban Romanians in the new provinces fell essentially into three categories: First, there were Romanians who had considerable status—doctors, priests, entrepreneurs, teachers, professors, lawyers, and journalists—but who functioned mainly within the Romanian community, and were thus "ghettoized." To paraphrase a 1924 article about Transylvania's Romanian lawyers, such professionals had considered themselves the prewar emmissaries of the Romanian villages to the alien urban world, which they viewed as hostile to the Romanians.[1] If Romanian lawyers had had such a mediating role, though always on behalf of the Romanian community, most Romanian teachers, journalists, and Orthodox or Uniate priests had had even less contact with the larger, non-Romanian community. They had functioned as "professional Romanians" within the confines of their own community.

Second, a larger number of lower-class urban Romanians worked in menial jobs, as servants and unskilled laborers. Their lack of status and their unease in the urban setting served to perpetuate their self-image as peasants despite their urban residence. They retained primary, more positive ties in their village of origin. That the Romanians' "peasantness" or their lower-class status in urban Bukovina, Bessarabia, and Transylvania was merely historical accident is beyond doubt. Such ethnic stratification occurs in most multiethnic societies. In Old Kingdom cities ethnic job segregation typically put Hungarian women in servants' and nannies' positions, for example, while many Jews performed as roofers, ironsmiths, and other manual laborers. Nevertheless, ethnic Romanians' inferior social status in the newly annexed regions was a painful transitional reality in the immediate postwar period.[2]

Last, there were Romanians who had assimilated to the non-Romanian urban languages and cultures of the Romanian diaspora, thereby prospering and rising socially in the Hungarian, Austrian, and Russian systems. Their success had come at the cost of their original ethnic identity. Denationalized Romanian elites, as we have seen, continued to be something of a problem in the interwar period. The low profile of the urban Romanian communities in the new areas was further aggravated by the foreign culture of the major cultural institutions—schools, universities, media, theaters, and such—that Greater Romania inherited.

Romania's oversized bureaucratic state, in alliance with the nationalist intelligentsia of which it was the largest employer, tried to compensate for

---

[1] "Criza avocaturii în Ardeal," *Ţara noastră,* February 3, 1924.
[2] See University College, London, Mocatta Library, Moses Gaster Archive, "Memoirs," p. 59. I am grateful to Victor Eskenasy for emphasizing this point and for this reference.

the thinness of ethnic Romanian, urban civil society with active, interventionist, cultural policies. They aimed to recast the country's educational infrastructure by empowering the Romanians at the expense of previously privileged non-Romanians, expanding the country's ethnic Romanian elites, ousting non-Romanian elites, and Romanizing the enlarged country's cultural institutions and towns. The promotion of Romanians at the expense of non-Romanians made sense from the Romanian point of view. It is necessary to remember, however, that Romanian governments were not free to pursue this project openly, since the Minorities Protection Treaty, passed against considerable Romanian opposition, had been the condition for Romania's postwar expansion. Thus no *numerus clausus* legislation was officially implemented in Romania until the Goga-Cuza government in 1938.[3]

Among the most important instruments of national integration and mobilization was literate Romanian culture provided in a nationalistically charged way by schools and other institutions. In the interwar period they were widely viewed as the most effective weapon in the arsenal of national *Kulturkampf*. Representatives of the state and independent nationalists tended to agree about the importance of the schools to the nation's security and consolidation. The speaker at a cultural circle conference held in 1921 expressed this perspective clearly: "In school everyone gets accustomed to feel the same way, think the same way, [and] have the same sentiments of race, kin (*neam*), and blood, because a nation maintains itself through the school first, and only second through [force of] arms. The school is called upon to shape the unitary national consciousness and to strengthen the nation."[4] In this spirit, massive educational expansion was justified by reference to the "awakening" of the peasants, a process equivalent to the strengthening of the nation. Romanian peasants were called to public life, to leave behind their previous "latent" life, and to contribute their ethnic essence to the state. The schools' function was to train them for their public—national—role. Even more than primary and secondary schools, which were enlisted to shape and homogenize the nation, institutions of higher learning had the direct mission of creating a national elite; the universities were quickly politicized and became sites of national conflict.

In schools, universities, and other cultural settings Romanization took various forms, depending in part on the local ethnic, regional, and social context. Among these manifestations were the affirmative ones of expanding the educational network at all levels so it could teach and train more Romanians, favoring Romanian teachers and pupils, building

[3] Paul A. Shapiro, "Prelude to Dictatorship in Romania: The National Christian Party in Power, December 1937–February 1938," *Canadian-American Slavic Studies* 8 (Spring 1974): 51–52 and 71–72.

[4] CS/1921/330/47–48.

dormitories to enable Romanian peasant youth to attend urban secondary schools while living in ethnically protected environments, and moving secondary schools to rural settings. Negative measures—from the non-Romanians' point of view—included retraining non-Romanian speakers and discouraging the use of other languages for purposes of instruction, preventing non-Romanian schools and clubs from developing freely, and attempting to keep minority students from attending Romanian universities in too large a proportion. Such pro-Romanian nation-building policies were devastating to non-Romanian elites, including many assimilated Jews whose ancestors had lived in the area for generations and who wished to be identified primarily as Romanians.

The "new generation" took a critical view of the somewhat haphazard process of elite replacement pursued by local notables and Bucharest functionaries. Their objections arose not from any principled disagreement with this direction; on the contrary, they felt the policies carried out in a muted fashion by conservative politicians, local administrators, and Bucharest-based ministries were not fast-paced and resolute enough. During the 1920s, ethnic Romanian youth attending higher educational institutions in Greater Romania increasingly subscribed to a militant nationalist ideology. Romania's "new generation," as this group of young nationalists came to be known, represented the embryo of the heretofore largely missing category of an urban ethnic Romanian civil society, and, as such, formed a valuable link between the state and rural society. As a cohort they were an emerging national elite—most of them were recently transplanted to the urban universities from the countryside—and they held pan-Romanian, antiregionalist views. They saw themselves and were recognized by society at large as the vanguard of the nation. The British historian C. A. Macartney commented in 1937 on the attraction of right-wing extremist parties to Romania's young generation and on this youth's pan-Romanianism:

> The[se] . . . groups, which between them command the allegiance of most of the Roumanian youth, are all "Fascist." . . . They are all intensely nationalist, and . . . not one of them seems to make . . . any distinction between one brand of Roumanian and another. . . . Among the intellectuals of Roumania, the true line of cleavage is not regional, but one between the new generation and the old. The young men, all over the country, are struggling to form a new Roumania, more national, more united than the old.[5]

Ethnic Romanian nationalist students satisfied a number of important requirements that had emerged with the accelerated state- and nation-

[5] Carlile A. Macartney, *Hungary and Her Successors: The Treaty of Trianon and Its Consequences, 1919–1937* (London: Oxford University Press, 1965), p. 283. The book's first edition came out in 1937.

building process. Youthful radical nationalists became the most committed freelance nation builders. Although they were stringent critics of the establishment and of the more moderate nationalist forces associated with it, the "new generation" was in fact the state's ally in the labor of nationalization.

Meanwhile, mainstream and right-of-center public opinion looked to the young generation for national salvation, much the way that it idealized the Romanian peasantry. In fact, the two embodiments of the nation—the peasantry and youth—were linked in the writings of right-wing ideologues. Nichifor Crainic, an influential right-wing literary and political figure, editor of the Orthodoxist journal *Gândirea* (Thought), and professor of theology at the Chişinău and Bucharest Theology Schools,[6] tried to account for Romanian youth's choice of a religious, monarchist, and nationalist ideology:

> If we were to look for an explanation of this truly wonderful fact of the spontaneous and autonomous orientation of our youth, to me at least it would seem easy to find: In their great majority, our students, and especially those who set the tone . . . of collective life, are country kids. They are sons of peasants or, when they are townsfolk, they are peasants' grandsons. Through their soul, in spite of all the temptations of high culture and urban civilization, gushes forth the moral health of our people. This mysterious patrimony is today the support for their entire collective life. It is not hard to discover through a summary analysis the peasant character of this patrimony.[7]

One theme of this book has been the process of fusing the previously separate territories of the Greater Romanian state. Another, closely related, theme has been the nature of the nationalist ideology that both aided the national integration project and was itself transformed and strengthened in the process. In looking at Romanian nationalist ideology in the interwar period, I have approached it in its immediate political and cultural context, while working with a broad definition of ideology. I have attempted to understand the concrete conditions of a highly generalized form of ethnic nationalism as it developed in newly unified Greater Romania. The style, codes, and outcomes of nationalist discourse—are expressed—in the correspondence of minor, often anonymous figures who discuss scarce cultural resources and ambitious nationalization plans, in the exchanges between

---

[6] See Keith Hitchins, "*Gîndirea*: Nationalism in a Spiritual Guise," in *Social Change in Romania, 1860–1940: A Debate on Development in a European Nation,* ed. Kenneth Jowitt (Berkeley: Institute of International Studies, 1978), pp. 148–156, and Lucian Predescu, *Enciclopedia Cugetarea* (Bucharest: Editura Cugetarea–Georgescu Delafras, [1939–1940]), p. 231.

[7] Nichifor Crainic, "Tineretul şi creştinismul," in *Puncte cardinale în haos,* 2d ed. (Bucharest: Editura Cugetarea, n.d.), pp. 20–21.

provincial officials, school teachers, and ministerial functionaries, and in the parliamentary and courtroom speeches defending nationalist rabblerousers and assassins. These diverse sources reveal the perceptions and pressures that drove centralizing bureaucrats, provincial elites, and rebellious youth to new forms of ideology.

Romanian ideology was transformed in the post–World War I period in response to the demographic, cultural, and social realities accompanying the Great Union. Most nationalists shared a desire for a unified, homogeneous Romanian state encompassing all and only ethnic Romanians. This nationalist dream, however, ran afoul of the multiethnic, multiregional, and multicultural realities of Greater Romania. The Romanian, Bucharest-based state held political and coercive power, but in the newly annexed provinces it lacked strength in the civil society represented by the urban milieu and culture. Urban elites and cultural institutions that were remnants of previous political and social structures initially exceeded the reach of the Romanian state, and were therefore inimical to it. At the same time they blocked the way of aspiring young ethnic Romanians emerging from village environments. Given the ethnic disposition of Greater Romania's urban elites, nation builders chose an ideological "definition" of the Romanian nation as fundamentally rural. The towns and their inhabitants were therefore alien and suspect. Thus, the peasantist definition of the nation, along with the mobilization of rural layers of the population and the attempt to minimize the cultural impact and activities of non-Romanians, seemed logical solutions to the problem of alien urban society and culture.

Romanian statemakers focused on education as the primary means to expand ethnic Romanian elites, since they felt that together with the sons and daughters of Romanian peasants they could roundly conquer the towns and cultural strongholds. For the peasant, schools of all levels were the road to full nationhood and, thereby, to a higher social status, to a bureaucratic white-collar job, and to a higher living standard and more personal power. By advancing into the urban world of high culture previously dominated by foreigners, the Romanian peasant could bring Greater Romania closer to the nation-state ideal. Romanians, especially those of the new generation, regarded the conquest of the urban areas and the acquisition of elite positions as a national mission. So much the better if such victories were also in their self-interest.

Romanians' attitudes toward their national minorities differed according to various factors, including degree of urbanization. The Ukrainians and Szeklers, for example, were predominantly rural, and they were therefore considered more assimilable to the Romanian "peasant nation" than the more urban Magyars, Germans, and Jews. The latter, in addition to being the most urban ethnic group, were also a religion apart; they were thus considered least assimilable of all, although among certain urban, educated,

Old Kingdom Jews assimilation to Romanian culture was widespread. The postwar Jewish emancipation had brought a legal solution to the much belabored "Jewish question," but many nationalists felt the imposed emancipation itself a problem and considered illegitimate the civil and political rights that the Jews received. Nor was Jewish desire to blend in with Romanian society welcomed by Romanian intellectuals concerned with maintaining the purity of their culture. Octavian Goga, publicist, patriot, politician, and poet laureate, as we have seen, offers a case in point. Nichifor Crainic shared Goga's sentiments. In an essay entitled "The Autochthonous Spirit," in which he urged Romanians to recapture the feeling of being the masters of their own country, Crainic argued in favor of the anti-Semitic movement, distinguishing carefully between Jews and Romania's other ethnic minorities:

> The point of view of Judaism in our country is the uprooting of our people (*neamului*) from their own country. In this respect a clear distinction is necessary between Christian minorities and the Jews. In our ethnic body, the minorities are localized islands, sometimes with centrifugal tendencies, but with very few tendencies of internal expansion. The Jews, however, represent the force of general infiltration, and a multiple assault toward our subjugation.[8]

Romanian nationalists hoped that foreign urban elites, of which the Jews were an important symbol, could be displaced by the influx of educated Romanian peasants bringing to bear their ancestral culture. Unlike peasant foreigners, who could conceivably be assimilated into such a culture, foreign urban elements, who were carriers of previously reigning high cultures, could not, in this view, be accepted by the Romanian nation. The early and essential urbanism of the Jews and their identification with previous regimes and urban elites made them least acceptable of all—despite the fact that politically they were less threatening than the Hungarian, Ukrainian, and German minorities, which stood to become active irredentas. The centrality of anti-Semitism as an element in interwar Romanian nationalism had to do with the "economy" of the Jew as a symbol of everything non-Romanian. The Jews were proportionally more urban than the Romanians, and, for that matter, than any other co-inhabiting ethnic group. Furthermore, the assimilated Jews in the new territories were associated with the political and cultural dominion of the foreign powers from which those lands had been retrieved, at a time when the Romanian nation was being projected as a peasant, Christian Orthodox nation, and when the

---

[8] Nichifor Crainic, "Spiritul autohton," in his *Ortodoxie şi etnocraţie* (Bucharest: Editura Cugetarea, [1936]), pp. 183–184.

power of Greater Romania was asserting itself against that of the failed multinational empires.

The extreme nationalist ideology of the young generation had a fundamental legitimacy in interwar Romania precisely because it was so well suited to the goal of most mainstream politicians: to build a nation of "true" Romanians. The radicals of the new generation and their more moderate, more conservative elders shared also the idea of using the state for the Romanian nation, not for a society of equal citizens, and a commitment to creating an ethnic Romanian elite large enough to administer the expanded state and pure enough to do it the Romanian way. In addition they shared an idiom, which, though to establishment nationalists was sometimes a demagogic shortcut in election campaigns, to Codreanu's followers was true credo. For all of these reasons the nationalist establishment neither suppressed nor marginalized the radical nationalists.

Radical nationalism also derived support from groups disaffected with state policies and the political abuses associated with the Bucharest political establishment. The radicals thus profited both from their de facto alliance with the state and from their principled opposition to it. Transylvanian nationalist politicians and intellectuals are examples of Romanian patriots whose militant patriotism was not easily satisfied by the policies of the state based in Bucharest. The regionalist sensibilities of some older-generation Transylvanians were offended by rapid centralization measures, and these dissenters who considered themselves nationalist purists reacted intolerantly to the corrupt practices they felt stemmed principally from the Old Kingdom. Thus, the "extremely unlikely electoral non-aggression pact" of 1937 between Iuliu Maniu's National Peasant Party and Codreanu's Iron Guard was perhaps not so unlikely an accord as it at first appears, for the two groups shared a deep opposition to the Liberal Party's power and corruption.[9]

The Transylvanian intellectuals grouped around Octavian Goga's magazine, *Țara noastră,* were aggrieved patriots as well. As discussed in the concluding section of Chapter 4, their malaise stemmed from the insufficient intervention of the state in the task of Romanizing their province. Like the National Peasants' electoral alliance with the Iron Guard, Goga's political metamorphosis and his eventual association with Cuza may have been almost predictable in light of the grievances aired in the 1920s in the magazine he edited, and given his early support for the nationalist student movement.

[9] Shapiro, "Prelude to Dictatorship," p. 56. See also Stephen Fischer-Galati, "Fascism in Romania," in *Native Fascism in the Successor States, 1918–1945,* ed. Peter Sugar (Santa Barbara, Calif.: ABC Clio, 1971), p. 116.

Nation Building, Nationalism, and Fascism

In the winter of 1923–1924, several Romanian officials and clerics corresponded about a rumor that teachers and priests, in Transylvania especially, were propagating fascism. The Metropolitan of the Orthodox Church in Bucharest responded to an inquiry from the Ministry of Education, which in its turn had been querried by the Ministry of War. The Primate asked to be given some concrete examples, but also expressed his puzzlement about fascism:

> Some speak well of it, others show it to be an anarchic organization. The former say that fascism works for the salvation of the Romanian organism against corrupt and corrupting foreignism; thus [according to them] . . . [fascism] would defend the interests of our people (*neamului*). The others say that . . . [fascism] is an organ of destruction of order and legality in our state, and that it uses revolutionary means; thus [according to them it would be] an organization harmful to our people.[10]

Without declaring himself for fascism, the Metropolitan explained that if fascism were indeed a legal form of defense of the Romanian people, the church would have little reason to be against it.[11] By formulating this naive question about the good or evil of fascism in Romania, this document expresses essential features of the fascist paradox in the Romanian context. It suggests first that although Codreanu's League of the Archangel Michael was not formally founded until 1927, an extreme nationalist movement that some labeled fascist was already making itself felt in the first half of the 1920s. Although the nomenclature evidently derived from Mussolini's victorious movement, il Duce's revisionist standpoint would not have made him a good model for Romanian nationalists. Italian fascism was also problematic for Romanian nationalists because it initially lacked the anti-Semitic component so central in the Romanians' mission.[12] Mussolini's fascism-in-power may have suggested the name and given Romanian radical nationalists inspiration, then, but the phenomenon itself was home-

[10] MIC/1924/211/51–54, December 18, 1923, and February 25, 1924.
[11] MIC/1924/211/53, February 25, 1924.
[12] Until 1929, according to Jerzy Borejsza, fascist Italy "was only a passive example." See his "Italian Fascism and East-Central Europe: Problems of Typology and Links," in *Dictatorships in East-Central Europe, 1918–1939: Anthologies,* ed. Janusz Żarnowski (Wrocław: Zakład Narodowy im. Ossolińskich Wydawnictwo Polskiej Akademii Nauk, 1983), p. 157; and Borejsza, "Italian Fascism and East-Central Europe, 1922–1943," in *Poland at the 14th International Congress of Historical Sciences in San Francisco: Studies in Comparative History* (Wrocław: Zakład Narodowy im. Ossolińskich Wydawnictwo Polskiej Akademii Nauk, 1975), p. 278. On the influence of Italian fascism in Romania, see Theodor Armon, "Fascismul Italian și Garda de Fier," *Toladot* 1 (January–March 1972): 13–16.

grown. Significantly, Romanian fascism was already identified as such in the early 1920s, a half-decade before any active Italian fascist efforts in Eastern Europe, and a full decade before Hitler's rise to power and the Nazi regime's aggressive policies in the area.

I do not wish to imply that external circumstances had *no* effect on the rise of Romanian fascism. Indeed, Romania's experience in the interwar decades was anything but unique; all of East Central Europe was subject to important common trends and pressures in the 1920s and 1930s. A marked shift in politics to the right of the political spectrum was characteristic of the whole area. The democratic system envisaged by the Western diplomats at Versailles as resting on the newly minted nation-states of East Central Europe faltered in part over the very notion of nation and over how the newly constituted states established their sovereignty in practice, beyond their formal definition in the treaties giving them international recognition. Finally, the whole region's fall from democratic grace clearly relates in some respects to political and economic forces beyond the individual national frontiers of these relatively small, powerless, and mostly new countries.

We cannot ignore several "great-power" factors that played an important part in the rise of authoritarianism and fascism in East Central Europe. Even though some states, including Romania, were net winners of the postwar settlement, the new "Versailles-system" borders, the Allies' role in imposing them, and the obligation to protect national minorities within those frontiers generated resentments in the successor states. In the losing countries, the animus focused, as one would expect, on territorial, population, and resource losses. Even among the winners, however, there was hostility toward the Versailles arrangements. In Romania, and in Poland as well, hostility focused on the Minority Protection treaties, the symbols of Western powers' interference in the nation's internal affairs. Furthermore, the relative isolationism of the North Atlantic democratic states negatively affected East European economic development, both by encouraging autarkic economic strategies and by leaving the way open for eventual German penetration.

Another factor bearing on the drift to the right in interwar Eastern Europe was the establishment of the Soviet state and its real and potential challenge to the new, fragile, smaller, states to its west. These states had been conceived at least partly by the powers at Versailles as a *cordon sanitaire* against communist expansion. Within the East European states, fear of the Soviet threat and example led to the repression of the left, and, equally, of liberals and of national minorities—Jews and Ukrainians—who were considered pro-Bolshevik. The Bolshevik revolution in Russia led the Hungarian establishment to perceive the short-lived native Bolshevik experiment in 1919 as a more potent threat than it probably was. The white terror backlash to the Kun regime also took on antiliberal and anti-Semitic overtones. The equation between liberalism and communism became one of the ideological signposts of the radical right everywhere in interwar Eastern Europe. In Hungary, as elsewhere, the Jews were to form the third term of the nationalist equation (despite the *modus vivendi* that Hungarian society had worked out with its Jews in the nineteenth century). The ideological dynamic set in motion soon after the end of World War I pushed the national minorities toward Marxist parties of internationalist orientation, or toward a nationalist separatism of their own, since mainstream political parties shared in integral nationalist assumptions and were thus unwilling to accept minorities.

"External" factors thus did play a role in the fate of interwar democracies in East Central Europe. These factors, however, do not suffiently account for the strong appeal of the radical right that existed even quite early in the interwar period. Domestic issues were at least as important as international ones in promoting the shift to authoritarian politics and particularly in spawning native fascist movements in Eastern Europe. I concur with a previous generation of scholars that on their very own the East European states were able to and did produce the conditions for fascist movements, and even the movements themselves: "What the existence of fascism in Italy and Germany did was to make the emergence of the movements . . . in the Successor States easier but it did not create them."[13]

I have argued against an older interpretation of fascism that sees it as deriving from the Marxist class struggle. In this view, a desperate capitalist class diverted the burgeoning proletarian movement by means of the false radicalism of fascism. A collusion between fascists and establishment politicians did exist in the interwar period, I submit, but it was based on the politics of nation building. The evidence I have presented suggests that both mainstream and radical nationalists found integral nationalism an appropriate ideological and political solution to the problems of integrating the disparate pieces of the Greater Romanian state. Based on the Romanian case, I would argue more generally that in Eastern Europe the domestic causes of right-wing nationalist and fascist tendencies were grounded in the post–World War I national revolutions—upheavals that resulted in rapid nation building, a restructuring of elites according to new ethnic criteria, and a perceived need to wholly redefine the nation according to these new criteria.

This ideology had important antecedents in Romania's own intellectual nationalism of the previous century and in the strands of fin-de-siècle European thought that anticipated and legitimated the full-blown fascist synthesis of the 1920s. As Zeev Sternhell has written of the broad European intellectual

[13] Peter Sugar, Conclusion to Sugar, ed., *Native Fascism in the Successor States*, p. 156.

background to fascism in Germany, France, Italy, Spain, Switzerland, Belgium, and Eastern Europe (where he draws particular attention to Romania): "Given the number of men writing on the subject [of the revolt against liberal democracy, individualism, and bourgeois society], one may wonder if their prolific output does not account in some measure for the inattentive reception accorded to Hitler; the author of *Mein Kampf* had nothing to say which had not already been said, and not by men of the lunatic fringe, but rather by the ranking intellectuals of the day."[14] One could pursue a parallel analysis of Codreanu and his precursors. And yet the actual fascist synthesis came only in the wake of the Great War. The war, the Russian Revolution, and the Versailles Treaty and its Eastern European variants redrew Europe's map and affected its social organization in so many complex ways that the new order soon faced a multifaceted crisis to which right-wing radicalism seemed to provide a fresh solution. As Romania's case demonstrates, this crisis was no less for the states emerging victorious and enlarged out of the war's debacle.

In Romania as elsewhere, the young generation was largely responsible for the popularization of right-wing radicalism. As Sternhell has written, "This movement [fascism] which saw itself as one of new men was undoubtedly one of young men."[15] It has been well documented that considerable numbers of youths in Eastern Europe were drawn to the ideological and political examples of Mussolini's Italy and Hitler's Germany and to the movements on which the two were based. These movements appeared to successfully defy pluralist democratic European traditions that seemed exhausted and stodgy to some even before the war. But it was for pressing postwar domestic reasons that these "new" radical fascist ideas and movements, made famous first by Mussolini's rise to power, were appealing. For Romania at least, the strong indigenous determination of fascist movements has been widely recognized—except in the communist-period Romanian historiography. I would agree with Geoff Eley, who has typed the two most important East European fascist movements, the Iron Guard and Hungary's Arrow Cross, as "indigenous movements that have strong similarities of ideology, sociology, and style but that originated independently of Italian or German sponsorship."[16] To restate what is hopefully by now self-evident,

---

[14] Zeev Sternhell, "Fascist Ideology," in *Fascism: A Reader's Guide,* ed. Walter Laqueur (Berkeley: University of California Press, 1976), p. 324.

[15] Ibid., p. 342. See also, e.g., Andrzej Micewski, "Polish Youth in the Thirties," *Journal of Contemporary History* 4 (1969): 155–168; George L. Mosse, "Introduction: The Genesis of Fascism," *Journal of Contemporary History* 1, no. 1 (1966): 17–19; and Szymon Rudnicki, "From 'Numerus Clausus' to 'Numerus Nullus,'" in *From "Shtetl" to Socialism: Studies from POLIN,* ed. Antony Polonsky (London: Littman Library of Jewish Civilization, 1993), pp. 359–381.

[16] Geoff Eley, "What Produces Fascism: Preindustrial Traditions or a Crisis of a Capitalist State?" *Politics and Society* 12, no. 2 (1983): 55.

the ascent of radical nationalism in interwar Eastern Europe was overdetermined. It was influenced by international economic and political circumstances. It also drew on older European and indigenous intellectual traditions that facilitated its broad acceptance. And it was, as well, rooted in the crisis-ridden environment of interwar national politics. Nevertheless, in the Romanian case, the immediate domestic determinants stand out from the foregoing account of nation building and cultural politics. Radical nationalist, fascist slogans played off mainstream nationalist nation-building policies and goals. Without the Great Union and the national mobilization that it engendered, a crisis of national identity may not have been felt, certainly not one of the proportions I have documented. The need to Romanize Romania's multiethnic elites would have been moot; fin-de-siècle antirationalist thinking in its autochthonous populist Orthodoxist mode might have made ripples without becoming hegemonic among the "new generation"; and external pressures from the growing Nazi power might have had diplomatic and military effects without inspiring the active, popular emulation of Romania's youth.

Greater Romania and Civil Society

In the wake of the 1989 revolutions in East Central Europe, and to a lesser extent in the period preceding them, the concept of "civil society" has received much attention. Before that fateful year, observers noted the existence of civil society in the network of voluntary dissident organizations not under the control of the state in Poland, Hungary, and Czechoslovakia, organizations seen as harbingers of a market-based, parliamentary Western-style democracy. Prime examples of such groups were the independent labor union Solidarity and the Catholic church in Poland. Others included private enterprises in Hungary and Charter 77 in Czechoslovakia. Although, the post-1968 Czechoslovak state was as repressive as those to the east and south, it could not prevent a small but resilient group of independent thinkers from creating a social and ideological realm independent of the state, a locus of opposition whose sphere they continually attempted to expand by "living in truth." In the Balkans, communist regimes had, in general, better succeeded in preventing the emergence of independent social activity.

Few independently organized groups existed in the Balkans, perhaps fewer in Romania than elsewhere except Albania. Although all of the post-Communist democracies are struggling with economic, political, and cultural hardships, Romanian society seems less equipped than most to embark on the necessary changes. Indeed, many analysts are inclined to view the National Salvation Front regime as a superficially renovated incarnation of its pre-1989 predecessor. This book is hardly the place for an analysis of post-Ceauşescu Romania, but it may offer a useful perspective on, among other things, the longer-term historical traditions that burden contemporary Romanians and obstruct their path to a vital civil society.

It is of course natural for contemporary Romanians, both young and old, to represent the interwar years as a golden age of sorts. And compared with the communist years it in fact was, in many ways. Those born after World War II have projected their fondest hopes onto the precommunist past, while the older generation actually remembers an abundance of agricultural and consumer goods as well as a number of important rights and freedoms: people then could travel as far as their financial means allowed them; rather than one party there were several; a richly varied and free press thrived; writers published their works without censorship; and elections in which candidates from opposing parties ran against one another were the norm. Together these aspects seem to suggest that before its Sovietization Romania had a vigorous civil society—the object of many current debates and aspirations.

The question nevertheless remains, how salient were these features, and did other elements of a less promising nature affect the health of Romania's civil society? A fair evaluation of the interwar period would have to address the sometimes dysfunctional forms of parliamentarism practiced in Romania. What is probably worse than this "disease" was the "cure" offered by an important set of oppositionist intellectuals. Rather than applying themselves to perfecting the party system, many called its very legitimacy into question, demanding the dismantling of a structure that they deemed superficially imitative of the dying and corrupt West. Pointing to the bold experiments of fascism in Italy and communism in the Soviet Union, Nae Ionescu, the widely acknowledged mentor of Romania's "new generation," called for monarchism, a revolution from above, and even a one-party state in his country. His new generation disciples listened and followed. Some of the best and brightest of these rode the crest of the anti-democratic wave (and have been content ever since to leave their one-time radical nationalism unremarked). The eminent philosopher Emil Cioran was an enthusiast for Hitler in 1934 and was rewarded in 1941 with a diplomatic post to Paris by the legionnaire government of Horia Sima. His appointment was confirmed by the government of General Antonescu. The historian of religions Mircea Eliade's career followed a similar path, with official appointments to London, Lisbon, and Madrid beginning in 1940.[17]

---

[17] See Emil Cioran, "Impresii din München: Hitler în conştiinţa germană," *Vremea,* July 15, 1934; Mihail Sebastian, "Jurnal," Ms. November 19, 1937, December 7, 1937, January 2, 1941, and February 12, 1941; and Mac Linscott Ricketts, *Mircea Eliade: The Romanian Roots, 1907–1945,* vol. 2 (Boulder, Colo.: East European Monographs, 1988), p. 922 and chap. 22, "Nationalism and the Primacy of the Spiritual."

In the 1930s, Nae Ionescu and his disciples were not as repulsed by communism as they were by Western-style democracy and political pluralism. Ionescu's preferred political solution was based on the ideal of a purely Romanian state in accord with the ethnicity of the majority. In his view, "Romanian" had particular, unique meanings: the Romanians belonged necessarily to the Eastern Orthodox faith, and their destiny was determined by their peasant ancestry. To stress the organic links binding ethnic Romanians together, Ionescu increasingly, after 1930, used the spelling *Rumân* instead of the standard *Român* for "Romanian" in his newspaper columns in *Cuvântul,* the independent opposition newspaper he directed and which turned decisively toward the Iron Guard in the 1930s. In its 1930s usage, *Rumân,* a medieval term for enserfed peasant, suggested that those who had not shared the ancestral experience of the Romanian peasant could not be part of the Romanian political community.[18] Thus through his arguments and semantics Ionescu evoked the ideal Romanian state: peasantist, ethnically pure, Eastern Orthodox, and economically self-sufficient.

One danger to interwar Romania's autonomous civil society came from the articulation of such antipluralist ideologies. Another threat was represented by the policies of unification themselves, namely those aimed at nationalizing and homogenizing so diversely constituted a country. The remaking of the Greater Romanian multinational state in the unitary image of the nation-state, hailed by indigenous Romanian patriots and implicitly sanctioned by Wilsonian ideals of self-determination, had its own logic of undoing previous civil social traditions. Although it may have made national sense for the Romanian state to attempt to replace non-Romanian elites from the new territories with more trustworthy, ethnically Romanian ones, that very process inevitably eliminated from the Romanian body politic a great store of "civil" experience. These elites and their knowledge and traditions, rather than being assimilated into the emerging Greater Romanian society, were largely excluded. The non-Romanians of the new territories were disproportionately elites and disproportionately urban; an important group of non-Romanians purged by interwar populist nationalism were thus the older, more experienced bourgeoisie.

The etymology of "civil" in civil society is relevant here. Latin *civitas* gives us (the modern) "city" and, from the same root, *civis* (the equal, fraternal, and free individual) "citizen": precisely the cosmopolitan concepts Romania confronted in its non-Romanian Romanian inhabitants. While reluctantly allowing their formal citizenship, the state and its radical nationalist opponents joined in attempting to try to demote these "foreigners" to non-elite status, in order to replace them with educated ethnic

---

[18] For the original meaning of *Rumân* see Daniel Chirot, *Social Change in a Peripheral Society: The Formation of a Balkan Colony* (New York: Academic Press, 1976), p. 51.

Romanians of peasant stock who mostly lacked a previous urban—civil—tradition. At the same time, nationalist Romanian intellectuals in accord with Nae Ionescu questioned the very relevance of the "civil" experience to Romania's situation. In its profound reconfiguring of its elites in the interwar period, Greater Romania dealt a blow to the civil society that some Romanians now seek to reconstruct. While it is true that the ultimate blow was that delivered by the communists, the interwar nationalist transformation was also antithetical to the pluralist project.

A Note on Sources

This study is based on a range of archives, periodicals, and other published sources. The documents from the Romanian Ministry of Education archive at the State Archives in Bucharest were the most important source for Part I. This archive included correspondence between teachers, administrators, and the ministry; petitions from parents; inspection reports; as well as reports and correspondence concerning Romania's universities and college students. The Casa Şcoalelor archive, also housed at the State Archives in Bucharest, was useful for documenting the early years of interwar cultural work, since this institution supplied educational materials to needy or new cultural institutions. The papers of the Liberal Minister of Education, Constantin Angelescu, which are part of the Manuscripts Collection at the Academy Library in Bucharest, supplemented the State Archives materials. The Angelescu Archive contained inspection reports and discussions of various educational matters.

Ministry of Education publications on the educational legislation of the interwar period, and the published volumes of Constantin Angelescu, Dimitrie Gusti, P. P. Negulescu, and Simion Mehedinţi, all ministers of education in the interwar period, were particularly useful for Chapter 1.

Documents from the Onisifor Ghibu archive, and Ghibu's voluminous memoirs, private journal, articles, and books were a substantial source for Transylvanian, Bessarabian, and educational developments throughout this study.

French reports from the Minstère des Affaires Étrangères (Archives Diplomatiques, Paris, Quai d'Orsay, Série Z, Roumanie), and the Ministère de la Guerre (Direction de l'Armée de Terre, Vincennes) offered another perspective on Romanian developments, a particularly useful one given the long-standing cultural ties between France and Romania, and French interest in Greater Romania as a way to increase French influence in East Central Europe.

Jewish archival sources were helpful in documenting different aspects of Jewish life in Romania and of Romanian anti-Semitism. I consulted the

Lucien Wolf papers at the YIVO Institute for Jewish Research in New York; the Wilhelm Filderman memoirs (and other documents) at Yad Vashem, documents on the Romanian Jewish community at the Central Archives for the History of the Jewish People—both in Jerusalem; and the publications and archives of the Alliance Israélite Universelle in Paris.

The bibliography is divided into sections on archives, reference works, published primary sources, memoirs and diaries, periodicals, articles and papers, and books and theses. Certain sources are difficult to classify. Some memoirs, for example, appeared as articles in scholarly journals, while others are part of archival collections. Some histories were written by political personalities and are polemical or memoiristic in nature. In cases of such overlap, I decided somewhat arbitrarily on placement, without listing sources twice. I did, however, compile a comprehensive list of the periodicals used and also listed the more important article titles separately.

Bibliography

Archival Collections

Alliance israélite universelle, Paris, Archives Roumanie (AIU)
Arhiva Onisifor Ghibu
Arhivele statului, Bucureşti, Fond Casa şcoalelor (CS)
Arhivele statului, Bucureşti, Fond Ministerul instrucţiunii şi cultelor (MIC)
Biblioteca Academiei Române (formerly Biblioteca Academiei R. S. R.), Bucureşti,
   Colecţia de manuscrise, Arhiva Constantin Angelescu (AA)
Central Archives for the History of the Jewish People, Jerusalem (CA)
Ministère de la guerre, Direction de l'armée de terre, Vincennes (V)
Ministère des affaires étrangères, Archives diplomatiques, Paris, Quai d'Orsay,
   Série Z, Roumanie (QD)
Yad Vashem Archives, Jerusalem (YV)
Y. I. V. O. Institute for Jewish Research, New York, Archives (YIVO)

Reference Works

Enciclopedia României. 4 vols. Bucharest: Imprimeria naţională, 1938–1943.
Institutul central de statistică. *Anuarul statistic al României, 1937 şi 1938.* Bucha-
   rest: M. O., Imprimeria naţională, 1939. (ICS)
——. *Recensământul General al Populaţiei României din 29 Decemvrie 1930.*
   Bucharest: M.O., Imprimeria naţională, 1938.
Kubijovyč, Volodymyr, ed. *Ukraine: A Concise Encyclopaedia,* vol. 1. Toronto:
   University of Toronto Press, 1963.
Predescu, Lucian. *Enciclopedia Cugetarea.* Bucharest: Editura Cugetarea-
   Georgescu Delafras, [1939–1940].

Published Primary Sources

Anuarul Universităţii Mihăilene din Iaşi, 1930–1935. Jassy: Editura Universităţii
   Mihăilene, 1936.

Anuarul Universității Regele Ferdinand I Cluj pe anul școlar 1931/32. Cluj: Institut de arte grafice Ardealul, 1932.

Ardeleanu, Ion, et al., eds. *1918 la Români: Desăvîrșirea unității național-statale a poporului român. Documente externe 1879–1916.* Bucharest: Editura științifică și enciclopedică, 1983–1986.

"Bukovina." In Great Britain, Foreign Office. Historical Section. *Peace Handbooks.* Vol. 19. London: HMSO, 1920.

Bureau der K. K. Statistischen Zentralkommission. *Statistik der Unterrichtsanstalten in den im Reichsrate vertretenen Königreichen und Ländern für das Jahr 1909/1910.* Vienna: K. K. Hof- und Staatsdruckerei, 1913.

Cărticica șefului de cuib. 6th ed. N.p., 1940.

Cuza, Alexandru C. *Mișcările studențești și cauzele lor.* (Declarația făcută înaintea comisiunei de anchetă.) Bucharest, 1925.

Documente privind istoria României. Războiul pentru independență, 1877–1878, vol. 1. Bucharest: Editura Academiei, 1954.

Dumbravă, Dinu. *Fără ură! Pregătirea și dezlănțuirea evenimentelor din Focșani în zilele de 17 și 18 martie 1925. Cercetări. Documente. Mărturisiri.* Anchetă întreprinsă după evenimente ca trimes special al ziarelor *Dimineața* și *Adevărul.* Bucharest: Editura Adevărul, [1925?].

Ghibu, Onisifor. *Pentru o pedagogie românească: Antologie de scrieri pedagogice.* Bucharest: Editura didactică și pedagogică, 1977.

———. *Prolegomena la o educație românească.* Bucharest: Editura Cultura românească, 1941.

Goga, Octavian. *Mustul care fierbe.* Bucharest: Imprimeria Statului, [1927].

Institutul de studii istorice și social-politice de pe lîngă C. C. al P. C. R., *Documente din istoria mișcării muncitorești din România, 1916–1921.* Bucharest: Editura politică, 1966.

Joint Foreign Committee of the Board of Deputies of British Jews and the Anglo-Jewish Association. *The Jewish Minority in Roumania: Correspondence with the Roumanian Government respecting the Grievances of the Jews.* 2d ed. Presented to the Board of Deputies of British Jews and the Council of the Anglo-Jewish Association, June 1927. London: Joint Foreign Committee of the Board of Deputies of British Jews and the Anglo-Jewish Association, 1928.

———. *The Jewish Minority in Romania: Further Correspondence with the Roumanian Government respecting the Grievances of the Jews.* Presented to the Board of Deputies of British Jews and the Council of the Anglo-Jewish Association, April 1928. London: The Joint Foreign Committee of the Board of Deputies of British Jews and the Anglo-Jewish Association, 1928.

K. K. Statistischen Zentralkommission, *Bewegung der Bevölkerung der im Reichsrate Vertretenen Königreiche und Länder im Jahre 1910.* Vienna: K. K. Hof- und Staatsdruckerei, 1912.

Moța, Ion I. *Cranii de lemn: Articole.* Munich: Ediția Monumentul MM, Colecția Omul Nou, 1970.

Președinția Consiliului de Miniștri. *Pe Marginea prăpastiei: 21–23 Ianuarie 1941.* Bucharest: Monitorul oficial și Imprimeriile statului, 1942.

"Texts of the Ukraine 'Peace.' " In *The Inquiry Handbooks.* Vol. 19. 1918. Reprint. Wilmington, Del.: Scholarly Resources, [1974].

Troinitskii, Nikolai Aleksandrovich, ed. "Prilozhenie k obshchemu svodu dannykh pervoi vseobshchei perepisi naseleniia 1897g. Po imperii, Kartogrammy i diagrammy." *Pervaia vseobshchaia perepis' naseleniia rossiskoi imperii 1897 g.* Vol. 3. St. Petersburg: Izdatel'stvo Tsentral'nago statisticheskago komiteta Ministerstva vnutrennikh diel. 1905.

Memoirs and Diaries

Codreanu, Corneliu Zelea. *For My Legionaries: The Iron Guard.* Translation of *Pentru legionari.* Reedy, W.Va.: Liberty Bell Publications, 1990.

——. *Pentru legionari.* 1936. Vol. 1. 6th ed. N.p.: Editura Legiunea Arhanghelului Mihail, 1979.

Filderman, Wilhelm. "My Life." Ms. Yad Vashem Archives, Jerusalem.

Gaster, Moses. "Memoirs," Ms. Moses Gaster Archive. Mocatta Library. University College, London.

Ghibu, Onisifor. "Amintiri în legătură cu fondarea Universității românești din Cluj," (I) fragment din *Pe baricadele vieții,* capit. "Alma Mater Napocensis— 1919." Ms. 1956. Transcribed from written text by Octavian Ghibu in 1979. Arhiva O. Ghibu.

——. "Amintiri în legătură cu fondarea Universității românești din Cluj," (II) fragment din "Din amintirile unui pedagog militant." (Text established in 1968 by Octavian O. Ghibu on the basis of tape recordings.) Arhiva O. Ghibu.

——. "În vîltoarea revoluției rusești: Însemnări zilnice ale unui ardelean, martor ocular— și mai mult decît atît—al revoluției rusești în anii 1917–1918, începînd cu ziua de 12 martie și pînă în ziua de 6 august 1917. Ms. Arhiva O. Ghibu.

——. *Pe baricadele vieții: Anii mei de învățătură.* Cluj-Napoca: Editura Dacia, 1981.

——. *Pe baricadele vieții IV: În Basarabia revoluționară (1917–1918) Amintiri.* Ms. Arhiva O. Ghibu.

Iorga, Nicolae. *Memorii.* Bucharest: Editura Naționala S. Ciornei, 1939.

Nistor, Ion I., ed. *Amintiri răzlețe din timpul Unirii.* Czernowitz: Institutul Glasul Bucovinei, 1938.

Pușcariu, Sextil. *Memorii.* Bucharest: Editura Minerva, 1978.

Reichman-Șomuz, I. "Înainte și după începerea agitațiilor studențești din România." *Toladot,* July 1975.

Sabetay, S. Sabetay. "Procesul Codreanu la Turnu Severin." *Toladot,* March 1975.

Sebastian, Mihail. "Jurnal." Ms. Boulogne, France.

Voinea, Șerban. "Memorii." In *Șerban Voinea 1894–1969: Contribution à l'histoire de la social-démocratie roumaine,* edited by Paul H. Stahl. Societés européennes 6. Paris, 1990.

Yavetz, Zvi. "An Eyewitness Note: Reflections on the Rumanian Iron Guard." *Journal of Contemporary History* 26 (1991).

Legislation

Board of Education. *Draft of Act concerning Private Teaching.* Bucharest: Editura Cartea românească, 1927.

Hamangiu, Constantin. *Codul General al României: Legi uzuale*. Vols. 9–10. Bucharest: Alcalay, 1919–1922.

Ministerul instrucţiunii. *Lege pentru învăţământul primar al statului şi învăţământul normal-primar*. Bucharest: Editura Cartea românească, 1925.

———. *Proect de lege asupra învăţământului secundar teoretic*. Bucharest: Editura Cartea românească, 1928.

Periodicals

Adam
Adevărul
Anuar pedagogic
Apărarea naţională
Arhiva pentru ştiinţa şi reforma socială
Armenian Review
Austrian History Yearbook
Buletinul oficial al Ministerului instrucţiunii, cultelor şi artelor
Canadian-American Slavic Studies
Canadian Review of Studies in Nationalism
Convorbiri literare
Cross Currents: A Yearbook of Central European Culture
Curierul Israelit
Cuvântul
Cuvântul Iaşului
Cuvântul nostru
Cuvântul studenţesc
Dialectical Anthropology
Glasul minorităţilor
Hiena
History of Political Thought
Ideea Europeană
L'Indépendance Roumaine
Îndreptarea
Jewish Social Studies
Journal des débats
Journal of Contemporary History
Lupta
Monitorul oficial
Nationalities Papers
Paix et droit
Patria
Politics and Society
Revue de Transylvanie
Revue d'histoire moderne et contemporaine
Revue Roumaine d'histoire
România mare
Romanian Jewish Studies

Scânteia: Organ pentru apărarea intereselor intelectualilor
Şcoala şi Vieaţa: Revista Asociaţiei generale a învăţătorilor din România
Shvut: Jewish Problems in Eastern Europe
Slavic Review
Soviet Studies
Studia Universitatis Babes-Bolyai, Historia
Studii: Revista de istorie
Ţara noastră
Toladot
Transilvania: Organul Societăţii culturale Astra
Universul
Viaţa studenţească
Viaţa universitară
Vremea

Articles and Papers

Adamescu, Gheorghe. "Biografia lui Spiru Haret." In Spiru C. Haret, *Operele,* vol. 1. Bucharest: Editura Cartea românească, [1912?]

Angelescu, Constantin. "Treizeci de ani dela moartea lui Spiru Haret." In *Comemorarea lui Spiru Haret de către Academia de ştiinţe, din România în şedinţa din 19 ianuarie 1943.* Publicaţiile Academiei de ştiinţe din România, 3d ser., Memorii şi monografii, no. 1.

Armon, Theodor. "Fascismul Italian şi Garda de Fier." *Toladot,* January–March 1972; 13–16.

Băncilă Vasile. "Învăţământul secundar (Consideraţii generale.)" In *Un an de activitate la Ministerul instrucţiei cultelor şi artelor, 1932–1933,* edited by Dimitrie Gusti. Bucharest: Tip. Bucovina, 1934.

Barbu, Zev. "Rumania." In *Fascism in Europe,* edited by S. J. Woolf. London: Methuen, 1981.

Beck, Erich. "Das Buchenlanddeutschtum in Zahlen." In *Buchenland: Hundertfünfzig Jahre Deutschtum in der Bukovina,* edited by Franz Lang. Munich: Verlag des Südostdeutschen Kulturwerks, 1961.

Berlescu, D. "Universitatea din Iaşi de la 1860 pînă la 1918." In *Contribuţii la istoria dezvoltării Universităţii din Iaşi 1860–1960,* vol. 1. Universitatea Al. I. Cuza, Iaşi, Studii. Bucharest, 1960.

Bihl, Wolfdieter. "Die Ruthenen." In *Die Habsburgermonarchie 1848–1918,* edited by Adam Wandruszka and Peter Urbanitsch, vol. 3. Vienna: Verlag der Österreichischen Akademie der Wissenschaften, 1980.

Bocu, Sever. "Semănători de idei." *România mare,* September 21, 1917.

Boga, L. T. "Populaţia (Etnografie şi statistică)." In *Basarabia: Monografie,* edited by Ştefan Ciobanu. Chişinău: Imprimeria statului, 1925.

Bogza, Geo. "Basarabia." *Vremea,* July 15, 1934.

Boilă, Romul. "Consiliul Dirigent." In *Transilvania, Banatul, Crişana, Maramureşul, 1918–1928,* vol. 1. Bucharest: Cultura naţională, 1929.

Borejsza, Jerzy. "Italian Fascism and East-Central Europe. Problems of Typology and Links." In *Dictatorships in East-Central Europe, 1918–1939: Anthologies,* edited by Janusz Żarnowski. Wrocław: Zakład Narodowy im. Ossolińskich Wydawnictwo Polskiej Akademii Nauk, 1983.

——. "Italian Fascism and East-Central Europe, 1922–1943." *Poland at the 14th International Congress of Historical Sciences in San Francisco: Studies in Comparative History.* Wrocław: Zakład Narodowy im. Ossolińskich Wydawnictwo Polskiej Akademii Nauk, 1975.

Brandmarker, Berthold. "David Fallik." In *Geschichte der Juden in der Bukowina,* edited by Hugo Gold, vol. 2. Tel Aviv: Olamenu, 1962.

Brandsch, Heinz. *Pedagogi Români contemporani.* Biblioteca învăţătorilor, no. 8. Cluj: Editura revistei Satul şi Şcoala, 1937.

Castellan, Georges. "The Germans of Rumania." *Journal of Contemporary History* 6 (1971).

Cihodaru, C. "Învăţământul în Moldova în sec. XV–XVIII. Şcoala domnească din Iaşi." In *Contribuţii la istoria dezvoltării Universităţii din Iaşi, 1860–1960,* vol. 1.

Ciobanu, Ştefan. *Oraşele.* In *Basarabia: Monografie,* edited by Ştefan Ciobanu. Chişinău: Imprimeria Statului, 1925.

Cioran, Emil. "Impresii din München: Hitler în conştiinţa germană." *Vremea,* July 15, 1934.

Ciuciura, Theodore. "Romanian Views on Bessarabia and Bukovina: A Ukrainian Perspective." *Nationalities Papers* 13 (Spring 1985).

"Criza avocaturii în Ardeal." *Ţara noastră,* February 3, 1924.

Curticăpeanu, Vasile. "L'Action d'Octavian Goga pour l'unité politique roumaine." *Revue Roumaine d'histoire* 9, no. 1 (1970).

Dima, Nicholas. "Bucovina, Romania, and the Ukraine." In *The Tragic Plight of a Border Area: Bassarabia and Bucovina,* edited by Maria Manoliu-Manea. Los Angeles: Humboldt State University Press, 1983.

Durandin, Catherine. "Une image de l'idéologie nationale roumaine: La voie de l'état nation paysan." Paper delivered at Table ronde internationale de C. N. R. S.: La Réinvention du paysan par l'état en Europe centrale et balkanique. Paris, December 9–12, 1981.

——. "Les intellectuels et la paysannerie roumaine de la fin du XIX-è siècle aux années 1930." *Revue d'histoire moderne et contemporaine* 26 (1979).

Eley, Geoff. "Nationalism and Social History." *Social History* 6 (January 1981).

——. "What Produces Fascism: Preindustrial Traditions or a Crisis of a Capitalist State?" *Politics and Society* 12 (1983).

Fagan, Gus. Introduction to Christian Rakovsky, *Selected Writings on Opposition in the USSR, 1923–30.* London: Allison and Busby, 1980.

Fischer-Galati, Stephen. "Fascism in Romania." In *Native Fascism in the Successor States, 1918–1945,* edited by Peter Sugar. Santa Barbara, Calif.: ABC Clio, 1971.

——. "Romanian Nationalism." In *Nationalism in Eastern Europe,* edited by Peter Sugar and Ivo Lederer. Seattle: University of Washington Press, 1969.

Gabrea, Iosif I. "Statistică şi politica şcolară." *Buletinul oficial al Ministerului instrucţiunii, cultelor şi artelor,* 2d ser., no. 1 (April 1932).

Galea, Aurel. "Consiliul Dirigent: Organizarea, atribuţiile şi cauzele desfiinţării sale." *Studii: Revista de istorie* 26 (1973).

George, Alexandru. "Studiu Introductiv." In Eugen Lovinescu, *Opere,* edited by Maria Simionescu and Alexandru George, vol. 1. Bucharest: Minerva, 1982.

Georgescu, Titu, and Ion Ilincioiu. "Intelectualitatea şi răscoala ţăranilor." In *Marea răscoală a ţăranilor din 1907,* edited by Andrei Oţetea and Ion Popescu-Puţuri. Bucharest: Editura Academiei R. S. R., 1967.

Ghibu, Onisifor. "Basarabia în statistica Universităţii din Iaşi" (Extras din *Arhiva pentru ştiinţa şi reforma socială* 10). Bucharest: M. O., Imprimeria naţională, 1932.

———. "Naţionalizarea învăţământului românesc în Bucovina." *I Anuar pedagogic (1913),* Sibiu, 1912 [sic].

———. "Şcoala românească în anul 1912." *I Anuar pedagogic (1913).* Sibiu, 1912 [sic].

Ghidionescu, Vladimir. "Spiru Haret: Resumatul unei conferinţe ţinută la Cluj în Decembrie 1932." *Cuget clar* 6 (January–February 1933).

Goga, Octavian. "Ideia naţională: Conferinţă ţinută în faţa studenţilor universitari din Cluj." In *Mustul care fierbe.* Bucharest: Imprimeria statului, [1927].

———. "Răspuns unor provocări." *Ţara noastră,* May 4, 1924.

Hitchins, Keith. "Die Rumänen." In *Die Habsburgermonarchie, 1848–1918,* edited by Adam Wandruszka and Peter Urbanitsch. Vienna: Verlag der Österreichischen Akademie der Wissenschaften, 1980.

———. "*Gîndirea:* Nationalism in a Spiritual Guise." In *Social Change in Romania, 1860–1940: A Debate on Development in a European Nation,* edited by Kenneth Jowitt. Berkeley: Institute of International Studies, University of California, 1978.

———. "The Russian Revolution and the Rumanian Socialist Movement, 1917–1918," *Slavic Review* 27 (June 1968).

Iacobescu, Teodor. "Celui mai bun învăţător, închinare!" *Şcoala şi vieaţa: Revista Asociaţiei generale a învăţătorilor din România* 10, nos. 1–3. Omagiu lui D. V. Ţoni. (September–November 1939).

Iancu, Carol. "L'Émancipation des Juifs de Roumanie devant la Conférence de Paix de Paris (1919)." *Shvut: Jewish Problems in Eastern Europe* 16 (1993).

Iancu, Gheorghe, and Gelu Neamţu. "Contribuţii documentare cu privire la organizarea şi inaugurarea universităţii româneşti din Cluj (1919–1920)." *Studia Universitatis Babeş Bolyai, Historia* 30 (1985).

Ionaşcu, Ion. "Academia domnească şi Colegiul Sf. Sava din Bucureşti." In *Istoria Universităţii din Bucureşti.* Edited by Ion Ionaşcu, vol. 1. Bucharest: Tip. Universităţii din Bucureşti, 1977.

Ionescu, Gheorghe T. "Contribuţii la istoricul Universităţii din Bucureşti după 1918." *Studii: Revista de istorie* 17 (1964).

Janos, Andrew C. "Modernization and Decay in Historical Perspective: The Case of Romania." In *Social Change in Romania, 1860–1940: A Debate on Development in a European Nation,* edited by Kenneth Jowitt. Berkeley: Institute of International Studies, University of California, 1978.

Karchmar, Lucien. "Communism in Romania, 1918–1921." In *The Effects of World War I: The Class War after the Great War; The Rise of Communist Parties in East Central Europe, 1918–1921,* edited by Ivo Banac. Boulder, Colo.: East European Monographs, 1983.

Kiriţescu, Constantin. "Haret, pedagog şi reformator şcolar." In *Comemorarea lui Spiru Haret de către Academia de ştiinţe din România în şedinţa din 19 ianuarie 1943.* Publicaţiile Academiei de ştiinţe din România, 3d ser., Memorii şi monografii, no. 1.

———. "Problema 'educaţiei dirijate' în legătură cu suprapopulaţia universitară şi şomajul intelectual." *Arhiva pentru ştiinţa şi reforma socială* 14 (1936).

Kristof, Ladis K. D. "Russian Colonialism and Bessarabia: A Confrontation of Cultures." *Nationalities Papers* 2 (Autumn 1974).

Lavi, Theodor. "Activitatea Parlamentară a lui Michael Landau." *Toladot*, May 1977.

Livezeanu, Irina. "Excerpts from a Troubled Book: An Episode in Romanian Literature." *Cross Currents: A Yearbook of Central European Culture* 3 (1984).

——. "A Jew from the Danube: *Cuvântul*, the Rise of the Right, and Mihail Sebastian." *Shvut: Jewish Problems in Eastern Europe* 16 (1993).

——. "Moldavia, 1917–1990: Nationalism and Internationalism Then and Now." *Armenian Review* 43 (Summer–Autumn 1990).

——. "Urbanization in a Low Key and Linguistic Change in Soviet Moldavia." Part 1. *Soviet Studies* 33 (July 1981).

McArthur, Marilyn. "The Saxon Germans: Political Fate of an Ethnic Identity." *Dialectical Anthropology* 1, no. 4 (September 1976).

Manuilă, Sabin. "Aspects démographiques de la Transylvanie." *La Transylvanie.* (1938).

Marian, Liviu. "Cultura şi şcoala." In *Basarabia: Monografie,* edited by Ştefan Ciobanu. Chişinău: Imprimeria statului, 1925.

Martonne, Emmanuel de. "En Bessarabie." *Journal des débats,* July 19, 1919.

Mehedinţi, Simion. "Numerus clausus." *Ideea europeană,* August 17, 1919.

——. "Numerus clausus pentru români." *Convorbiri literare* 55 (February 1923).

Micewski, Andrzej. "Polish Youth in the Thirties." *Journal of Contempory History* 4 (1969).

Michelson, Paul E. "Romania." In *Nationalism in the Balkans: An Annotated Bibliography,* edited by Gale Stokes. New York: Garland, 1984.

——. "Unity and Continuity in Romanian History." *Canadian Review of Studies in Nationalism* 8 (1981).

Mosse, George L. "Introduction: The Genesis of Fascism." *Journal of Contemporary History* 1 (1966).

Moţa, Ion. "Sensul naţionalismului nostru." In *Cranii de lemn: Articole.* Munich: Ediţia Monumentul MM. 1970. Colecţia Omul Nou.

Natanson, Ephraim. "Romanian Governments and the Legal Status of Jews between the Two World Wars." *Romanian Jewish Studies* 1 (Spring 1987).

Nemoianu, Petre. "Emanciparea economică a Ardealului." *Ţara noastră,* January 27, 1924.

——. "Intelectualii ardeleni după unire." *Ţara noastră,* October 18, 1925.

Oţetea, Andrei. "Istoriografia răscoalei." In *Marea răscoală a ţăranilor din 1907,* edited by Andrei Oţetea and Ion Popescu-Puţuri. Bucharest: Editura Academiei R. S. R., 1967.

Petric, Aron. "Cu privire la periodizarea fascismului în România." In *Împotriva fascismului: Sesiunea ştiinţifică privind analiza critică şi demascarea fascismului în România. Bucureşti, 4–5 martie 1971.* Bucharest: Editura politică, 1971.

Plamenatz, John. "Two Types of Nationalism." In *Nationalism: The Nature and Evolution of an Idea,* edited by Eugene Kamenka. London: Edward Arnold, 1976.

Popa, Grigore T. "Pentru studenţii basarabeni." *Viaţa universitară,* September 20, 1925.

Popa, Mircea, and Gheorghe Şora. "Studiu introductiv." In Vasile Goldiş, *Scrieri social-politice şi literare,* edited by Mircea Popa and Gheorghe Şora. N.p.: Editura Facla, 1976.

Popa, Vasile. "Aspecte din activitatea lui Onisifor Ghibu la Consiliul Dirigent." *Studia Universitatis Babeş-Bolyai, Historia* 31, no. 1 (1986).

Popovici, Valerian. "Învăţămîntul în limba naţională pînă la 1860." In *Contribuţii la istoria dezvoltării Universităţii din Iaşi, 1860–1960,* vol. 1. Universitatea Al. I. Cuza, Iaşi, Studii. Bucharest, 1960.

Puşcaş, Vasile. "Însemnătatea şi semnificaţia înfiinţării universităţii româneşti din Cluj şi opinia internaţională." *Studia Universitalis Babeş-Bolyai, Historia.* 25, no. 1 (1980).

Relgis, Eugen. "Întoarcerea. . . ." *Adam* 3, no. 48 (1931).

Riedl, Franz Hieronymus. "Die Universität Czernowitz, 1875–1920: Ein Blick auf ihr Wesen und Ihre Entwicklung Beziehungen zu Ost- und Mitteldeutschland." *Mitteldeutsche Vorträge* 2 (1971).

Rogers, Kenneth. "Moldavian, Romanian, and the Question of a National Language." In *The Tragic Plight of a Border Area: Bassarabia and Bucovina,* edited by Maria Manoliu-Manea. Los Angeles: Humboldt State University Press, 1983.

Rudnicki, Szymon. "From 'Numerous clausus' to 'Numerus Nullus.'" In *From "Shtetl" to Socialism: Studies from POLIN,* edited by Antony Polonsky. London: Littman Library of Jewish Civilization, 1993.

Shafir, Michael. "'Romania's Marx' and the National Question: Constantin Dobrogeanu-Gherea." *History of Political Thought* 5 (Summer 1984).

Shapiro, Paul A. "Prelude to Dictatorship in Romania: The National Christian Party in Power, December 1937–February 1938." *Canadian-American Slavic Studies* 8 (Spring 1974).

———. "Romania's Past as Challenge for the Future: A Developmental Approach to Interwar Politics." In *Romania in the 1980s,* edited by Daniel N. Nelson. Boulder, Colo.: Westview, 1981.

Silviu, George. "Tragedia învăţământului secundar." *Lupta* 22 (October 1927).

Starr, Joshua. "Jewish Citizenship in Rumania." *Jewish Social Studies* 3 (January 1941).

Sternberg, Hermann. "Zur Geschichte der Juden in Czernowitz." In *Geschichte der Juden in der Bukowina,* edited by Hugo Gold, vol. 2. Tel Aviv: Olamenu, 1962.

Sternhell, Zeev. "Fascist Ideology." In *Fascism: A Reader's Guide,* edited by Walter Laqueur. Berkeley: University of California Press, 1978.

"Studenţimea basarabeană." *Viaţa studenţească,* June 16–30, 1921.

Sugar, Peter. Conclusion to *Native Fascism in the Successor States, 1918–1945,* edited by Peter Sugar. Santa Barbara, Calif.: ABC Clio, 1971.

Szporluk, Roman. "War by Other Means." *Slavic Review* 44 (Spring 1985).

Taşcă, Gheorghe. "Haret ca economist social." In *Comemorarea lui Spiru Haret de către Academia de Ştiinţe din România în şedinţa din 19 ianuarie 1943.* Publicaţiile Academiei de ştiinţe din România. 3d ser. Memorii şi monografii, no. 1.

Tomescu, D. "Administraţia în Ardeal, după desfiinţarea Consiliului Dirigent." In *Transilvania, Banatul, Crişana, Maramureşul,* vol. 1. Bucharest: Cultura naţională, 1929.

Turczynski, Emanuel. "The National Movement in the Greek Orthodox Church in the Habsburg Monarchy." *Austrian History Yearbook* 3, pt. 3 (1967).

Vago, Bęla. "The Destruction of the Jews of Transylvania." In *Hungarian Jewish Studies,* edited by Randolph L. Braham, vol. 1. New York: World Federation of Hungarian Jews, 1966.

———. "Fascism in Eastern Europe." In *Fascism: A Reader's Guide,* edited by Walter Laqueur. Berkeley: University of California Press, 1976.

Vornicu, Gheorghe, "O Anchetă în Maramureş: Borşa şi necazurile ei." *Cuvântul,* August 6, 1930.

——. "O Anchetă în Maramureş: Cum s'a ajuns la mişcările din Borşa." *Cuvântul,* August 7, 1930.

——. "Semne rele prin satele maramureşene." *Cuvântul,* August 26, 1930.

Weber, Eugen. "The Men of the Archangel." *Journal of Contemporary History* 1, no. 1 (1966).

——. "Romania." In *The European Right: A Historical Profile,* edited by Hans Rogger and Eugen Weber. Berkeley: University of California Press, 1965.

Zaharia, Gheorghe, and Mihai Fătu. "Romania." In *Regimurile fasciste şi totalitare din Europa,* edited by Ion Popescu-Puţuri et al., vol. 2. Institutul de studii istorice şi social-politice de pe lîngă C. C. al P. C. R. Bucharest: Editura militară, 1980.

Books and Theses

Akademische Senate, *Die K. K. Franz-Josephs-Universität in Czernowitz im Ersten Vierteljahrhundert ihres Bestandes: Festschrift.* Czernowitz: Bukowinaer Vereins-druckerei, 1900.

Anderson, Benedict. *Imagined Communities: Reflections on the Origin and Spread of Nationalism.* London: Verso, 1983.

Angelescu, Constantin. *Activité du Ministère de l'instruction, 1922–1926.* Bucharest: Editura Cartea românească, 1928.

——. *Evoluţia învăţământului primar şi secundar în ultimii 20 de ani.* Bucharest: Imprimeriile Curentul, n.d.

Balaci, Alexandru, and Ion Ionaşcu, eds. *Bucharest University, 1864–1964.* Bucharest: Graphic Arts Printing Works, 1964.

Bălan, Ion Dodu. *Octavian Goga.* Bucharest: Editura Minerva, 1971.

Bâldescu, Emil. *Spiru Haret în ştiinţă, filozofie, politică, pedagogie, îvăţămînt.* Bucharest: Editura didactică şi pedagogică, 1972.

Berindei, Dan. *Epoca Unirii.* Bucharest: Editura Academiei R. S. R., 1979.

Biblioteca centrală pedagogică. *Onisifor Ghibu: 100 de ani de la naştere.* Bucharest, 1984.

Bloom, William. *Personal Identity, National Identity, and International Relations.* Cambridge: Cambridge University Press, 1993.

Bodea, Cornelia, and Virgil Cândea. *Transylvania in the History of the Romanians.* Boulder, Colo.: East European Monographs, 1982.

Bogdan-Duică, Gheorghe. *Românii şi ovreii.* Bucharest: Institutul de arte grafice Tip. românească, 1913.

Bratu, Traian. *Politica naţională faţă de minorităţi: Note şi observaţiuni.* [Bucharest]: Cultura naţională, [1923].

Brysiakin, S. K. *Kul'tura Bessarabii, 1918–1940.* Chişinău: Shtiintsa, 1978.

Cadzow, John F., Andrew Ludanyi, and Louis Elteto, eds. *Transylvania: The Roots of Ethnic Conflict.* Kent, Ohio: Kent State University Press, 1983.

Călinescu, George. *Istoria literaturii române de la origini pînă la prezent.* 2d ed. Bucharest: Editura Minerva, 1982.

Carsten, Francis L. *The Rise of Fascism.* Berkeley: University of California Press, 1971.

Chirot, Daniel. *Social Change in a Peripheral Society: The Creation of a Balkan Colony*. New York: Academic Press, 1976.

Cienciala, Anna, and Titus Komarnicki. *From Versailles to Locarno: Keys to Polish Foreign Policy, 1919–1925*. Lawrence: University Press of Kansas, 1984.

Ciobanu, Ştefan. *Cultura românească în Basarabia sub stăpânirea rusă*. Chişinău: Asociaţiei [sic] uniunea culturală bisericească, 1923.

———, ed. *Basarabia: Monografie*. Chişinău: Imprimeria statului, 1925.

Clark, Charles Upson. *Bessarabia: Russia and Roumania on the Black Sea*. New York: Dodd, Mead, 1927.

Constantinescu, Miron, ed. *Din istoria Transilvaniei*. Vol. 2. [Bucharest]: Editura Academiei R. S. R., 1961.

Conte, Francis. *Christian Rakovski (1873–1941): A Political Biography*. Translated by A. P. M. Bradley. Boulder, Colo.: East European Monographs, 1989.

Cornish, Louis C., and the Anglo-American Commission of 1924. *The Religious Minorities in Transylvania*. Boston: Beacon, Press, 1925.

Craig, John E. *Scholarship and Nation Building: The Universities of Strasbourg and Alsatian Society, 1870–1939*. Chicago: University of Chicago Press, 1984.

Crainic, Nichifor. *Ortodoxie şi etnocraţie*. Bucharest: Editura Cugetarea, [1936].

———. *Puncte cardinale în haos*, 2d ed. Bucharest: Editura Cugetarea, n.d.

Deutsch, Karl. *Nationalism and Social Communication*. Cambridge, Mass.: MIT Press, 1953.

Dobrinescu, Valeriu Florin. "Studenţimea ieşeană în viaţa social-politică a României contemporane (1918–1947)." Ph. D. diss., Facultatea de istorie-filozofie, Universitatea Al. I. Cuza, Iaşi, 1975.

Dobrogeanu-Gherea, Constantin. *Neoiobăgia*. 2d ed. Bucharest: Viaţa românească, n.d.

Dragne, Florea, and Constantin Petculescu. *Frontul Studenţesc Democrat: Pagini din lupta antifascistă a studenţimii române*. Bucharest: Editura politică, 1977.

Eidelberg, Philip Gabriel. *The Great Romanian Peasant Revolt of 1907: Origins of a Modern Jacquerie*. Leiden: Brill, 1974.

Fătu, Mihai, and Ion Spălăţelu. *Garda de fier: Organizaţie teroristă de tip fascist*. Bucharest: Editura politică, 1971.

Filipescu, C., and Eugeniu N. Giurgea. *Consideraţiuni generale, agricole, economice şi statistice*. Chişinău: Institutul de arte grafice România nouă, 1919.

Forter, Norman L., and Demeter B. Rostovsky. *The Roumanian Handbook*. London: Simpkin Marshall, 1931.

Frunză, Victor. *Istoria Partidului Comunist Român*. Vol. 1. Arhus: Nord, 1984.

Gabrea, Iosif I. *Şcoala românească: Structura şi politica ei 1921–1932*. Bucharest: Tip. Bucovina, n.d.

Gellner, Ernest. *Nations and Nationalism*. Ithaca: Cornell University Press, 1983.

———. *Thought and Change*. Chicago: University of Chicago Press, 1965.

Georgescu, Vlad. *Istoria ideilor politice româneşti*. Munich: Ion Dumitru Verlag, 1987.

———. *The Romanians: A History*. Columbus: Ohio State University Press, 1991.

Gerschenkron, Alexander. *Economic Backwardness in Historical Perspective*. Cambridge, Mass.: Belknap Press, 1962.

Gherner, H., and Beno Wachtel. *Evreii ieşeni în documente şi fapte*. Jassy, 1939.

Ghibu, Onisifor. *Ardealul în Basarabia—O Pagină de istorie contimporană*. Cluj: Institutul de arte grafice Ardealul, 1928.

——. *Călătorind prin Basarabia: Impresiile unui român ardelean.* Chişinău: Tip. Eparhială, 1923.

——. *La a douăzecea aniversare a Universităţii Daciei Superioare.* Cluj: Institutul de arte grafice Ardealul, 1939.

——. *Nu din partea aceea.* Bucharest: Editura Eminescu, 1985.

——. *Pentru o pedagogie românească: Antologie de scrieri pedagogice.* Bucharest: Editura didactică şi pedagogică, 1977.

——. *Puncte cardinale pentru o concepţie românească a educaţiei.* Sibiu: Institutul de arte grafice Dacia Traiană, 1944.

——. *Universitatea românească a Daciei Superioare: Cu prilejul împlinirei a 5 ani de activitate.* Cluj: Tip. Viaţa, 1924.

——. *Viaţa şi organizaţia bisericească şi şcolară în Transilvania şi Ungaria.* Bucharest: Institutul de arte grafice N. Stroilă, 1915.

Gillard, Marcel. *La Roumanie nouvelle.* Paris: Alcon, 1922.

Giurgea, Eugeniu N. *Din Trecutul şi Prezentul Basarabiei.* Bucharest: Institutul de arte grafice Bucovina–I. E. Torouţiu, 1928.

Greenfeld, Liah. *Nationalism: Five Roads to Modernity.* Cambridge, Mass.: Harvard University Press, 1992.

Gusti, Dimitrie, ed. *Un an de activitate la Ministerul instrucţiei cultelor şi artelor, 1932–1933.* Bucharest: Tip. Bucovina, 1934.

Heinen, Armin. *Die Legion "Erzengel Michael" in Rumänien: Soziale Bewegung und politische Organisation.* Munich: Oldenburg Verlag, 1986.

Hitchins, Keith. *Orthodoxy and Nationality: Andreiu Şaguna and the Rumanians of Transylvania, 1846–1873.* Cambridge, Mass.: Harvard University Press, 1977.

——. *The Rumanian National Movement in Transylvania, 1780–1849.* Cambridge, Mass.: Harvard University Press, 1969.

——. *Studies on Romanian National Consciousness.* Rome: Nagard Publishers, 1983.

Hobsbawm, Eric J. *The Age of Capital, 1848–1875.* New York: New American Library, 1979.

Iancu, Carol. *L'Émancipation des juifs de Roumanie (1912–1919).* Montpellier: Centre de recherche et d'études juives et hébraïques, 1992.

——. *Les Juifs en Roumanie (1866–1919): De l'exclusion a l'émancipation.* [Aix-en-Provence]: Éditions de l'Université de Provence, 1978.

Iancu, Gheorghe. *Contribuţia Consiliului Dirigent la consolidarea statului naţional unitar român (1918–1920).* Cluj: Dacia, 1985.

Illyés, Elemér. *National Minorities in Romania: Change in Transylvania.* Boulder, Colo.: East European Monographs, 1982.

Institutul de studii istorice şi social-politice de pe lîngă C. C. al P. C. R. *File din istoria U. T. C.* 2d ed. Bucharest: Editura politică, 1980.

Ioanid, Radu. *The Sword of the Archangel.* Boulder, Colo.: East European Monographs, 1990.

Ionescu, Ghiţă. *Communism in Rumania, 1944–1962.* London: Oxford University Press, 1964.

Iorga, Nicolae. *Histoire des roumains de Bucovine à partir de l'annexion autrichienne, 1775–1914.* Jassy: Impr. de l'État, 1917.

——. *Histoire des roumains et de la romanité orientale.* Vol. 10, *Les Réalisateurs de l'unité nationale.* Bucharest: L'Académie roumaine, 1945.

Ivănescu, George. *Istoria limbii române.* Jassy: Editura Junimea, 1980.

Janos, Andrew. *The Politics of Backwardness in Hungary, 1825–1945.* Princeton, N.J.: Princeton University Press, 1982.

Jarausch, Konrad H. *Students, Society, and Politics in Imperial Germany: The Rise of Academic Illiberalism.* Princeton, N.J.: Princeton University Press, 1982.

——, ed. *The Transformation of Higher Learning, 1860–1930: Expansion, Diversification, Social Opening, and Professionalization in England, Germany, Russia, and the United States.* Chicago: University of Chicago Press, 1983.

Jászi, Oscar. *The Dissolution of the Habsburg Monarchy.* Chicago: University of Chicago Press, 1961.

Jelavich, Barbara. *History of the Balkans: Twentieth Century.* Vol. 2. Cambridge: Cambridge University Press, 1983.

Jewsbury, George. *The Russian Annexation of Bessarabia, 1774–1828: A Study of Imperial Expansion.* Boulder, Colo.: East European Monographs, 1976.

Johnson, Owen V. *Slovakia, 1918–1938: Education and the Making of a Nation.* Boulder, Colo.: East Euorpean Monographs, 1985.

Kaba, John. *Politico-Economic Review of Basarabia.* N.p., 1919.

Kann, Robert A. *A History of the Habsburg Empire, 1526–1918.* Berkeley: University of California Press, 1974.

——, and Zdenek V. David. *The Peoples of the Eastern Habsburg Lands, 1526–1918.* Seattle: University of Washington Press, 1984.

Kenez, Peter. *The Defeat of the Whites: Civil War in South Russia, 1919–1920.* Berkeley: University of California Press, 1977.

Lacea, Constantin. *La Bucovine.* Paris: Dubois et Bauer, 1919.

Ludo, I. *În jurul unei obsesii.* Bucharest: Editura Adam, 1936.

McCagg, William O., Jr. *A History of Habsburg Jews, 1670–1918.* Bloomington: Indiana University Press, 1989.

Macartney, Carlile A. *Hungary and Her Successors: The Treaty of Trianon and Its Consequences.* London: Oxford University Press, 1937.

——, and Alan W. Palmer. *Independent Eastern Europe.* London: Macmillan–St. Martin's, 1962.

Manoliu-Manea, Maria, ed. *The Tragic Plight of a Border Area: Bassarabia and Bucovina.* Los Angeles: Humboldt State University Press, 1983.

Martonne, Emmanuel de. *What I Have Seen in Bessarabia.* Paris: Impr. des arts et des sports, 1919.

Mehedinți, Simion. *What Is Transylvania?* Miami Beach, Fla.: Romanian Historical Studies, 1986.

Mendelsohn, Ezra. *The Jews of East Central Europe between the World Wars.* Bloomington: Indiana University Press, 1983.

Michelson, Paul. *Conflict and Crisis: Romanian Political Development, 1861–1871.* New York: Garland, 1987.

Micu, Dumitru. *Gîndirea și gîndirismul.* Bucharest: Editura Minerva, 1975.

Ministerul învățământului. *Istoria învățămîntului din România.* Bucharest: Editura didactică și pedagogică, 1971.

Morariu, Aurel. *Bucovina, 1774–1914.* Bucharest: P. Suru, [1914?].

Mușat, Mircea, and Ion Ardeleanu. *De la statul geto-dac la statul român unitar.* Bucharest: Editura științifică și enciclopedică, 1983.

——. *From Ancient Dacia to Modern Romania.* Bucharest: Editura științifică și enciclopedică, 1985.

——. *Political Life in Romania, 1918–1921.* Bucharest: Editura Academiei R. S. R., 1982.

Nagy-Talavera, Nicholas M. *The Green Shirts and the Others: A History of Fascism in Hungary and Rumania.* Stanford, Calif.: Hoover Institution Press, 1970.

Neagoe, Stelian. *Triumful rațiunii împotriva violenței (Viața universitară ieșană interbelică).* Jassy: Editura Junimea, 1977.

——. *Viața universitară clujeană interbelică (Triumful rațiunii împotriva violenței).* Cluj: Editura Dacia, 1980.

Negulescu, Petre P. *Reforma învățământului.* 2d ed. Bucharest: Editura Casei școalelor, 1927.

Nistor, Ion. *Bessarabia and Bukowina.* Rumanian Academy Rumanian Studies, no. 3. Bucharest: [Monitorul Oficial și Imprimeriile Statului imprimeria națională], 1939.

——. *Istoria Basarabiei.* 3d edition. Cernowitz: Glasul Bucovinei, 1923.

——. *Istoria Bucovinei.* Bucharest: Humanitas, 1991.

——. *Originea și dezvoltarea Universității din Cerňauți,* Biblioteca Astrei Basarabene Nr. 4. Chișinău: Tip. Eparhială Cartea românească, 1927.

——. *Problema ucraineană în lumina istoriei.* Czernowitz: Institutul de arte grafice și Editura Glasul Bucovinei, 1934.

——. *Românii și rutenii în Bucovina: Studiu istoric și statistic.* Bucharest: Edițiunea Academiei Române, Librăriile Socec, 1915.

——. *The Union of Bucovina with Rumania.* Bucharest: Éditions Bucovina–I. E. Torouțiu, 1940.

Nowosiwsky, Iwan M. *Bukovinian Ukrainians: A Historical Background and Their Self-Determination in 1918,* translated by Walter Dushhyck. New York: Association of Bukovinian Ukrainians, 1970.

Oldson, William. *The Historical and Nationalistic Thought of Nicolae Iorga.* Boulder, Colo.: East European Monographs, 1973.

——. *A Providential Anti-Semitism: Nationalism and Polity in Nineteenth-Century Romania.* Philadelphia: American Philosophical Society, 1991.

Ornea, Z. *Tradiționalism și modernitate în deceniul al treilea.* Bucharest: Editura Eminescu, 1980.

Oțetea, Andrei, ed. *The History of the Romanian People.* New York: Twayne [1974].

——, and Ion Popescu-Puțuri, eds. *Marea răscoală a țăranilor din 1907.* Bucharest: Editura Academiei R. S. R., 1967.

Paikert, G. C. *The Danube Swabians.* The Hague: Martinus Nijhoff, 1967.

Pascu, Ștefan. *The Making of the Romanian Unitary National State: 1918.* Bucharest: Editura Academiei R. S. R., 1989.

Pătrășcanu, Lucrețiu. *Sub trei dictaturi.* Bucharest: Forum, 1945.

Pelivan, Ion. *Bessarabia under the Russian Rule.* Paris: Impr. J. Charpentier, 1920.

——. *The Union of Bessarabia with Her Mother-Country Roumania.* Paris: Impr. des arts et des sports, 1919.

Petrescu, Constantin-Titel. *Socialismul în România 1835—6 septembrie 1940.* [Bucharest]: Biblioteca socialistă, [194–].

Platon, Gheorghe, and Vasile Cristian, eds. *Istoria Universității din Iași.* Jassy: Editura Junimea, 1985.

Pop, Gheorghe T. *Caracterul antinațional și antipopular al activității Partidului Național Creștin.* Cluj: Editura Dacia, 1978.

Popa-Lisseanu, Gheorghe. *Sicules et Roumains: Un procès de dénationalisation.* Bucharest: Socec, 1933.

Popeangă, Vasile. *Aradul, centru politic al luptei naţionale din perioada dualismului (1867–1918)*. Timişoara: Editura Facla, 1978.

Popescu, Eufrosina. *Din istoria politică a României: Constituţia din 1923*. Bucharest: Editura politică, 1983.

Popescu-Puţuri, Ion, and Augustin Deac. *Unirea Transilvaniei cu România: 1 decembrie 1918*. Bucharest: Editura politică, 1970.

Popescu-Spineni, Marin. *Instituţii de înaltă cultură*. Vălenii-de-Munte: Datina românească, 1932.

Popovici, Andrei. *The Political Status of Bessarabia*. Washington, D.C.: School of Foreign Service, Georgetown University, 1931.

Prokopowitch, Erich. *Gründung, Entwicklung und Ende der Franz-Josephs-Universität in Czernowitz (Bukowina-Buchenland)*. Clausthal-Zellerfeld: Ed. Piepersche Buchdruckerei und Verlaganstalt, 1955.

Reshetar, John S., Jr. *The Ukrainian Revolution, 1917–1920: A Study in Nationalism*. Princeton, N.J.: Princeton University Press, 1982.

Rezzori, Gregor von. *Memoirs of an Anti-Semite: A Novel in Five Stories*. New York: Viking, 1981.

Ricketts, Mac Linscott. *Mircea Eliade: The Romanian Roots, 1907–1945*. Boulder, Colo.: East European Monographs, 1988.

Roberts, Henry L. *Rumania: Political Problems of an Agrarian State*. New Haven, Conn.: Yale University Press, 1951.

Rothschild, Joseph. *East Central Europe between the Two World Wars*. Seattle: University of Washington Press, 1977.

Roumanian University of Cluj, Study and Research Center for Transylvania. *Transylvania*. Paris: Boivin, 1946.

Rusu, Ion I. *Românii şi secuii*. Bucharest: Editura ştiinţifică, 1990.

Şandru, Dumitru. *Populaţia rurală a României între cele două războaie mondiale*. Jassy: Editura Academiei R. S. R., 1980.

Schwarzfeld, Elias. *Chestia şcoalelor israelite şi a progresului israelit în România*. Bucharest: Imprimerie de l'Orient, 1878.

Schweig, M. *Arme Ruginite: Conferinţă*. Bucharest: Institut de arte grafice Eminescu, 1923.

Scurtu, Ioan. *Viaţa politică din România 1918–1944*. Bucharest: Editura Albatros, 1982.

Sebastian, Mihail. *De două mii de ani*. Roman. 2d ed. Bucharest: Fundaţia regală pentru literatură şi artă, 1946.

Şeicaru, Pamfil. *Istoria Partidelor Naţional, Ţărănist şi Naţional Ţărănist*. Vol. 1. Madrid: Editura Carpaţii, 1963.

Seton-Watson, Hugh, and Christopher Seton-Watson. *The Making of a New Europe: R. W. Seton-Watson and the Last Years of Austria-Hungary*. London: Methuen, 1981.

Seton-Watson, R. W. *A History of the Roumanians from Roman Times to the Completion of Unity*. Cambridge: Cambridge University Press, 1934.

——. *Racial Problems in Hungary*. New York: Howard Fertig, 1972. Reprint of the 1908 edition.

Shafir, Michael. *Romania: Politics, Economics, and Society*. Boulder, Colo.: Lynne Rienner, 1985.

Sima, Horia. *Histoire du mouvement légionnaire*. Rio de Janeiro: Editora Dacia, 1972.

Sirka, Ann. *The Nationality Question in Austrian Education: The Case of Ukrainians in Galicia, 1867–1914.* Frankfurt: Peter D. Lang, 1980.

Smith, Anthony D. *The Ethnic Origins of Nations.* Oxford: Blackwell, 1986.

———. *Nationalism in the Twentieth Century.* New York: New York University Press, 1979.

Spector, Sherman D. *Rumania at the Peace Conference: A Study of the Diplomacy of Ioan I. C. Brătianu.* New York: Bookman, 1962.

Stănescu, Marin C. *Depun mărturie în faţa istoriei: Timotei Marin militant şi publicist comunist (1897–1937).* Jassy: Editura Junimea, 1977.

Subtelny, Orest. *Ukraine: A History.* Toronto: University of Toronto Press, 1988.

Szasz, Zsombor de. *The Minorities in Roumanian Transylvania.* London: Richards Press, 1927.

Taylor, Alan J. P. *The Habsburg Monarchy, 1908–1918: A History of the Austrian Empire and Austria-Hungary.* New York: Harper and Row, 1965.

Torouţiu, Ilie E. *Românii şi clasa intelectuală din Bucovina: Notiţe statistice.* Czernowitz: Editura societăţii academice Junimea, 1911.

Totu, Maria, et al. *Din istoria studenţimii române: Presa studenţească (1851–1978).* Bucharest: Unversitatea din Bucureşti, Facultatea de istorie-filosofie, 1979.

Ţurlea, Petre. *Nicolae Iorga în viaţa politică a României.* Bucharest: Editura enciclopedică, 1991.

Vedinaş, Traian. *Onisifor Ghibu educator şi memorialist.* Cluj: Dacia, 1983.

Verax [Radu Rosetti]. *La Roumanie et les juifs.* Bucharest: Socec, 1903.

Verdery, Katherine. *National Ideology under Socialism: Identity and Cultural Politics in Ceauşescu's Romania.* Berkeley: University of California Press, 1991.

———. *Transylvanian Villagers: Three Centuries of Political, Economic, and Ethnic Change.* Berkeley: University of California Press, 1983.

Vitenco, A. *Situation éthnographique en Bucovine.* N.p., n.d.

Volovici, Leon. *Nationalist Ideology and Antisemitism: The Case of Romanian Intellectuals in the 1930s.* Oxford: Pergamon Press, 1991.

Vrancea, Ileana. *Confruntări în critica deceniilor IV–VII (E. Lovinescu şi posteritatea lui critică).* Bucharest: Editura Cartea românească, 1975.

Wagner, Rudolf. *Vom Moldauwappen zum Doppeladler: Ausgewählte Beiträge zur Geschichte der Bukowina.* Augsburg: Hofmann-Verlag, 1991.

Weber, Eugen. *Peasants into Frenchmen: The Modernization of Rural France, 1870–1914.* Stanford, Calif.: Stanford University Press, 1977.

Wheeler-Bennett, John W. *Brest-Litovsk: The Forgotten Peace, March 1918.* New York: Norton, 1971.

Winogradsky, [Aleksandr Nikolaevitch]. *La Guerre sur le front oriental.* Paris: Charles-Lavauzelle, 1926.

Wohl, Robert. *The Generation of 1914.* Cambridge, Mass.: Harvard University Press, 1979.

Xenopol, Alexandru D. *Istoria Românilor din Dacia Traiană.* 3d ed. Vol. 9. Bucharest: Editura Cartea românească, 1925.

Zamfirescu, Ion, ed. *Monografia Liceului "Gh. Lazăr" din Bucureşti, 1860–1935, cu prilejul împlinirii a 75 de ani dela înfiinţarea lui.* Bucharest: Luceafărul, 1935.

Index

Academia Mihăileană, 212
Acţiunea Românească (student organization), 245
Albania, 309
Alexander I, tsar of Russia, 93, 94n11
Alexianu, George, 238
Alliance Israélite Universelle, 86, 152, 255
Allied Powers, 22, 56, 130, 195, 271, 272, 306
Anderson, Benedict, 17
Andrei, Petre, 125n148
Angelescu, Constantin, 29, 34–48 passim, 124, 166n136, 203, 207, 218n25, 264; and baccalaureate exam, 79; and language, 117
Anti-Semitism, 15, 16; in Bessarabia, 120–127, 261; Codreanu and, 256, 258, 263–272 passim, 283–287, 289, 292, 295; in education, 70–78, 123, 198, 200–202, 261, (baccalaureate crisis) 79–87; political, 56, 251, 266–272, 307 (see also Nationalism); protested, 276; rise of, 12–13; Russian, 254–255. See also Jews
Antonescu, General Ion, 310
Antonescu, Lupu, 165
Apărarea naţională (newspaper), 266
Ardeal. See Transylvania
Ardealul (weekly), 120n129
Argetoianu, Constantin, 249
Arion (song collection), 144
Armenians, 56; schools, 116
Arrow Cross (Hungarian fascist movement), 308
Asociaţia Studenţilor Creştini (student organization), 264

Assimilation, 139, 179; of Jews, 136, 153, 196, 200, 300, 303
Ausgleich (1867), 143, 153, 220. See also Habsburg Empire
Austria, 16, 46, 64, 138, 229. See also Bukovina
Austro-Hungarian Empire. See Habsburg Empire (Dual Monarchy)
Autonomy, cultural (Hungarian), 176
Autonomy, regional: in education, 42–43; eliminated, 23; provisional/ transitional, 132, 134. See also Bessarabia; Regionalism; Transylvania
Averescu, General, and Averescan government, 23, 39, 40, 45, 161, 162, 249, 261, 276; dissolves Directing Council, 134; and labor unrest, 252, 261

Bacaloglu, Constantin, 273,
Baccalaureate crisis. See Education
Bacşiş, 84
Bălan, Metropolitan Nicolae, 47, 48
Balkan War, Second, 8
Banat region, 4, 22, 132, 136, 160, 174
Băncilă, Vasile, 40
Baptist schools, 116
Bathory, Stephen, 220
Berindei, Andrei, 295
Berlescu, D., 216
Bessarabia, 59, 64, 89–127, 229; autonomy of, 23, 93–94, 97, 109, 123; education/literacy in, 42, 43, 46, 52, 94–97, 99, 100–122, 158, (student politics) 259–264, (university) 219, 231–234, 259–260; Jewish influx, 123, 246, 253–255, 258, 270,

331